Janua

To dearest Louise,

ENJOY— in
good health

use Cit

Sharon. Ausbacher

ArtScroll Series®

Rabbi Nosson Scherman / Rabbi Meir Zlotowitz
General Editors

Mirrors

Published by

Mesorah Publications, ltd

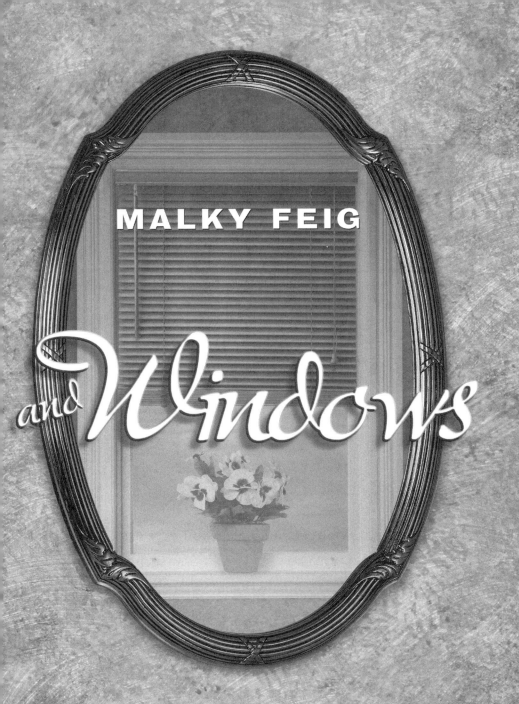

MALKY FEIG

and *Windows*

Stories and reflections from life's experiences

FIRST EDITION
First Impression … December 2005
Second Impression … December 2005

Published and Distributed by
MESORAH PUBLICATIONS, LTD.
4401 Second Avenue / Brooklyn, N.Y 11232

Distributed in Europe by
LEHMANNS
Unit E, Viking Business Park
Rolling Mill Road
Jarow, Tyne & Wear, NE32 3DP
England

Distributed in Australia and New Zealand by
GOLDS WORLDS OF JUDAICA
3-13 William Street
Balaclava, Melbourne 3183
Victoria, Australia

Distributed in Israel by
SIFRIATI / A. GITLER — BOOKS
6 Hayarkon Street
Bnei Brak 51127

Distributed in South Africa by
KOLLEL BOOKSHOP
Shop 8A Norwood Hypermarket
Norwood 2196, Johannesburg, South Africa

ARTSCROLL SERIES®
MIRRORS AND WINDOWS
© *Copyright 2005, by* MESORAH PUBLICATIONS, Ltd.
4401 Second Avenue / Brooklyn, N.Y. 11232 / (718) 921-9000 / www.artscroll.com

---

Typography by CompuScribe at ArtScroll Studios, Ltd.

Printed in the United States of America by Noble Book Press Corp.
Bound by Sefercraft, Quality Bookbinders, Ltd., Brooklyn N.Y. 11232

Dedication

Dearest Babi,
You foresaw this book
way before its conception,
way before
I ever entertained the thought.
I was only 9 or 10
When you read my composition,
Squeezed my hand
approvingly.
"You'll write a book yet one day."
I laughed,
amused at the prospect.
"No," you said,
conviction sparkling
in your blue eyes.
"I mean it,
you'll see.
You're going to write a book one day,
and I'll be the first to buy it."
Dearest Babi,
Here it is,
the book you prophesied.
You can't buy it,
but I see your essence
mirrored in its pages.
And if there are windows on High,
I hope you are looking down,
And smiling.

Acknowledgments

I've formulated these acknowledgments in my mind many times over the past few months, or perhaps the past few years. As I've let a devoted neighbor navigate me through a frustrating tangle on the computer, as I've marveled in silent admiration at a friend's skill for understanding the unspoken, or at my boss's sensitivity unaffected by the harsh pressures of getting a paper out, I'd indulge in the fancy of imagining these special individuals stepping up for honorable mention in the acknowledgments section of my book.

And then, marching in close succession behind them, I'd envision the myriad people who have, in some way or another, helped shape my life. All those individuals who have added color and dimension to my perspective, who have opened windows to new horizons and have held mirrors to the most curious aspects of my own inner landscape.

Indeed, I wish I could take this opportunity to mention each and every one of my siblings, my treasured childhood friends, my teachers who taught me from the first grade on, my aunts and cousins who shared so much of themselves with me. You may be too many to enumerate, but not too many to hold very dear. Thank you for creating the childhood that became the fertile ground for all my dreams and aspirations.

To my parents who have brought me into this world, introduced me to every concept I know, and have been there ever since I can remember. For all the days and nights, the tears and prayers, for all the frustrations and aggravations along the way. For the big and little gifts, the spur-of-the-moment poems, the *kugels* and cakes and cards.

But most of all, for the words, the words of encouragement and empathy, understanding, inspiration and praise. If anyone has taught me the value of words in life, it is you.

To my dearest in-laws, dedicated parents, who have created a new definition of in-laws with your sensitivity and acceptance. Thank you for understanding so deeply, for loving and overlooking, for giving our children the best grandparents in the world.

For the constant care packages, too many and too variant to list, the warm phone calls, the enthusiastic feedback. My gratitude knows no bounds; I cherish our relationship.

To Zeidy and Babi, living examples of perseverance and dedication. For everything you've instilled and continue to embody; for your care and concern all the time. For showering each of us with love and attention and taking pride in everything we do. May you be *zoche* to continue reaping much *nachas* from all of us.

To my dearest sisters, pieces of myself, who have been there for me through thick and thin. No words will ever do justice to what you mean to me.

And to my sisters-in-law, each of whom have impacted my life in a different way. Thanks for being there, for helping and sharing, and for bearing with me when I was too busy writing to reciprocate.

To my closest friends, my oxygen, who have stopped in the middle of their busy schedules to listen to a paragraph, to share an ending, to analyze the effectiveness of a phrase. The fact that this book is coming to fruition is testimony to your unwavering support and dedication.

To Rabbi Pinchus Lipschutz, the editor of the Yated, and his wife Chany. I am forever grateful for the gift of your trust when I was only starting out. It is to you that I owe the success of the column, the germ that eventually gave birth to this book.

To Mrs. C.B. Weinfeld who initially introduced me to the Yated, and who invented the name that stuck: Malky Feig.

And to the entire staff at the Yated office whom I've had the privilege of getting to know. Your incredible patience and understanding have gotten me through some of the toughest deadlines. If stress is the truest judge of character, then working with you, I have encountered greatness.

To Rabbi Nosson Scherman who honored me with the proposal of publishing my articles, and to the professional staff at ArtScroll who have imprinted my work with their seal of excellence.

To my editor, Mrs. Judi Dick, whose warmth and perception made me feel like I was working with a friend. The craft of an editor is to polish, yet preserve. You did a masterful job of both. Mrs. Faygie Weinbaum, proofreader par excellence. To Sara Rivka Spira who corrected the manuscript and to Esty Lebovits for the beautiful layout and pagination — they enhance my words immensely. And most of all to Eli Kroen whose marvelous cover design precisely portrays the image I sought to convey.

To the many, many readers who have taken the time to share their thoughts and feelings, to comment, to connect, to express their appreciation. Though I have never met you, you are a dynamic part of my life. I am touched by your sensitivity, your warmth and insight, and most of all, by your ability to act on inspiration. My sincerest thanks; I treasure each and every bit of your correspondence.

To my husband, my lifelong anchor, and my children, my first and foremost fan club (the only fans who barely even read English!). For your understanding and forbearance, support and enthusiasm. For sharing my time and attention with the computer, bearing with deadline pressures, and taking pride in my writing.

And if not for anything else, for serving as my truest mirrors and windows, giving me a glimpse into your worlds and reflecting back everything I have ever prayed for.

And finally, to He Who has given me the ideas and the inspiration, the time and the talent, the wherewithal, the wisdom and the words. If there is anyone for whom Heavenly assistance is a palpable reality, it is a writer. And if this book inspires any growth, then I am only returning what is His; *ten Lo mishe'Lo, she'atah v'shelcha she'Lo.*

Preface

For nearly the first score of my life, I was a student, planted at a desk behind an open book, my eyes eagerly pinned on the teacher. In those old classrooms with the big windows at the back, I learned to read, to master the skills of writing and reasoning, to memorize multiplication tables and *dikduk* charts. As the seasons rolled by, I discovered the joys of *Chumash* and *Nach*, the excitement of grasping *Rashi* and *Ramban*, of finding the lessons of life within those timeless words.

And then I graduated.

I tasted the thrill of teaching, barely touched the joy of imparting wisdom, before the sweetness of the experience was over. Marriage closed the curtain on everything I had known and opened to a brand-new era. I was off to foreign shores.

The excitement of that unexplored territory held a myriad unknowns: the secrets of hanging laundry and experimenting with

5-percent cheese, the tribulations of facing Israeli bureaucracy and deciphering modern-Hebrew slang.

At times I felt as if I had lost my footing. Where had the inspiration gone? The lessons I had lapped up so eagerly throughout my formative years seemed so remote. The open line between *HaKadosh Baruch Hu* and myself forged by my connection with His word seemed to falter. Where was the penetrating insight, the startling clarity, the shafts of light that had spurred me on to greater heights?

Slowly, it dawned on me. Those shafts of light were still there; my looking glass had simply turned inside out. Instead of finding the lessons of life within those timeless words, I had to find those timeless words within the lessons of life.

If I only looked for them, the interior design of my days abounded with mirrors and windows, swatches of life that shed light and meaning on my destiny. Tingling with the joy of my discovery, I began to detect those mirrors and windows wherever I went.

Sometimes it was a passing comment, sometimes a brush with disappointment, or a nip of justified annoyance. Always, I discovered, if I allowed those first impulsive reactions to dissipate, if I let the colors of mundane events fade, I found that opaque reality gave way to tinted panes. If I only put my eye to the glass, I would awaken to a deeper dimension, to the joy of revelation, to the stark, but exhilarating, encounter with self.

Refreshed and excited, I began to internally sketch my experiences, to stand in front of those panes and catch the panorama of subtle shades before the inspiration waned. And so, dear readers, here, in brushstrokes of prose and poetry, are my crude portraits the way I have seen them through my personal *Mirrors and Windows.*

Table of Contents

Expectations

Beeting Around the Bush

I know I'm kicking in a little late, but I've come to the conclusion. Men and women were made differently. Period.

The inspiration hit as I walked through the door at 10 to 3 one recent afternoon to the sound of deafening silence. I don't have to detail the racket that usually takes place at that hour; lively music, toys clattering, healthy bickering, and the whining repetition of some unanswered question punctuating the tumult.

So I was kind of suspicious when I turned the key in the door to find the father of the household calmly concluding some kind of business with the phone company against the backdrop of utter stillness. There was an unnatural quality about the serenity, something that didn't quite sit right with me.

"Where is everyone?" I asked, as I kicked off my shoes and opened the refrigerator. My eyes perused the shelves absentmindedly, searching for something to take out for supper. There are certain things women do on automatic pilot, even as they're waiting in suspense to hear where their family disappeared.

Men, as I started out saying, are decidedly different.Their automatic pilot function seems to operate in another zone, on different frequency.

"Everyone? The boys are in *cheder* and Chany's out studying with a friend."

That much I knew. I also knew what he was thinking. Or at least I thought I knew what he was thinking. How come she always finds it so hard to make phone calls in the afternoon?

"Where are the little ones?"

Oh, that.

"They're sleeping."

"Sleeping?!"

It was all I could do to echo his reply in a mixture of amusement and disbelief. For a flicker of a moment, I entertained the notion that he was kidding. The angelic silence, though, along with his deadpan demeanor quickly dispelled the thought. A peek into the bedroom lent the final confirmation.

Three little cherubs, alternately clasping dolls and bottles, were sprawled on their blankets, sweet dreams kissing their eyelids. The lights were out and the shades tightly drawn. It could have been 3 o'clock in the morning.

I groaned. In my mind's eye, I saw my plans for the evening evaporate into thin air. It was at that moment, before I broke the wonderful quiet to usher in the storm, that the thought struck me.

Practicality comes in many forms. It's long-term benefits against immediate advantages. And the male version of pragmatism usually opts for the simpler solution to the dual challenge of handling cranky children and urgent chores. Just heed nature's calling and let tired kids sleep. I wonder why Mother never thought of it.

Probably the same reason she never thought it was a good idea to let children play with water, or to give them cookies at 11 o'clock at night. Female rigidity, or whatever you want to call it.

There's no denying it; men have a creative flair when it comes to the pragmatic details of running a home. It isn't limited to babysitting either. Just ask a man to do your fruit order, and you'll see what I mean.

Plum tomatoes instead of cherry tomatoes. Okay. That figures. Plums and cherries were never *that* different. Green bananas. A little sunlight should do the trick. Better than brown bananas. Where are the eggplants? I guess they didn't have — hey, what are *these* doing here?

These are a dozen or so grimy-looking beets. You mentally check your list again. There was nothing that could remotely have been mistaken for beets. You're sure of it. You poke the bag, just to be certain. One, two, three, fourteen beets! Why, it isn't even close to *Pesach*.

You try to sound grateful — no, thrilled. This is the first fruit order; you don't want to blow it. Then, by the way, gently, you ask about the beets. Women have an art of their own.

He looks enthusiastic, not in the least bit put out.

"You know how cheap they were? Exactly half of the eggplants."

"You mean they *had* eggplants?"

"Sure they had eggplants. But can you imagine, I got fourteen beets for the price of two eggplants!"

Fourteen beets!

Never mind that you don't have a single beet eater in the vicinity, or that you've offered to make eggplant parmesan for your sister-in-law's anniversary party. That's irrelevant. The incredible thing is that you've struck a bargain. Fourteen beets for the price of two eggplants!

I've tried it, so I know. It can be somewhat, well, trying. But I guess it's things like these that make life interesting, that add spice and humor to the humdrum rote of unpacking orders and making supper. And we'll certainly have *chrein* to last a year.

Unless anyone knows another recipe that calls for fourteen, slightly aging, beets. I'd definitely be grateful. And until then, I'm grateful for the droll lesson.

Bargains are wonderful, and so are beets, but if you don't need them, they're useless, even costly. If you're trying to make eggplant parmesan, then fourteen, even *forty*, beets, won't get you anywhere. You need those eggplants. Yup, even if they cost twice as much, you've got to buy the eggplants.

We've gotten so used to hunting for bargains that they've become the order of the day. We search for discounts on our time and on our money and on our energy. We look for permanent-press clothing, disposable lenses, frost-free freezers, 10-minute soups, foil pans, precut pastry squares.

Not that there's anything wrong with all of that, per se. No one is going to be indicted for using paper goods, or buying supper, or getting away with ironing. In fact, sometimes these shortcuts are the price tag attached to the eternal values we are trying to acquire. What we've got to ascertain is that convenience and comfort aren't the criteria in and of themselves. There is one yardstick we've got to single-mindedly abide by: What do I really want to buy?

We all know the answer in the back of our minds. Ask any serious Jew to outline his goals in life. Slim chance he'll tell you he's aspiring for a nice car, shiny floors, or a big house. In fact, you'll probably get an answer that sounds like a line right out of every Jewish mother's entreaties at *licht bentching* (candle lighting).

The problem is that many of us live our days the way most husbands keep house; with very little eye out for the total picture. We tackle each chore as a self-contained challenge, not bothering to project past the temporary gratification born of hasty solutions. We keep our long-term goals tucked away in some sentimental safe, as shiny and intact and as far away from everyday use as the day we've been old enough to formulate them.

We've got to take those goals out, and draw up a shopping list for life. As people and parents, educators and professionals, manufacturers and salespeople, we've got to constantly place that list in front of us and remind ourselves what we are ultimately haggling for in this busy marketplace.

Sure, we can get to the wedding half an hour earlier, if we didn't take the time to *bentch* with each child. We can save on taxes by fiddling under the table a little; we can replace the kitchen floor if we left some of our tuition bills outstanding. We can make our institution more exclusive by weeding out some weaker students, we can become sophisticated trendsetters by selling apparel just a trifle inconsistent with the sensitivities of *tzeniyus*.

Yes we can, but what are we trying to buy, eggplants or beets?

Bargains can be tempting; they offer us the fleeting luxury of gained time and comfort, pleasure, prestige and money.

And more often than not, they leave us with a bunch of beets. Which, at worst, shrivel and rot; and at best, make for a lot of *chrein*.

Either way, it's a bitter proposition.

Golden Rings

*L*ately, I've been noticing, the chicken soup has been turning yellow. Without my noticing the subtle dynamics, and without any conscious effort on my part, the simmering liquid in the pot has been taking on a golden hue.

But you probably don't know what soup I'm referring to. And

that the chicken soup turning yellow has become a metaphor in my life ever since that amusing Friday-morning phone call some eleven years ago.

Today she is an experienced mother of seven, an accomplished housewife who probably puts up her family-size pot of chicken soup with an infant in one arm, while admiring a toddler's Lego creation through her side view.

On that Friday morning back then though, she had not an inkling of how to make chicken soup and had religiously consulted her recipe book for some sage advice. After researching the difference between peeling, snipping, trimming, cleaning, and skimming, and armed with a supply of vegetables from the corner produce-market, she set about her task with the earnestness of a sailor embarking on his first voyage.

About a half an hour into her culinary adventure, I heard my phone ring. The voice on the other end was tentative and more than a little worried.

"How's it going?" I queried enthusiastically. Her response was somber.

"To tell you the truth, I'm not sure. I thought I followed all the instructions carefully. I just checked the book again. But there's no mention of it anywhere."

"No mention of what?" I asked.

I tried to use my imagination. What could go awry with a simple chicken soup? I couldn't think of a single instruction whose omission or imperfect execution could sentence a chicken soup to doom.

Besides of course, "I mean, you filled up the pot with water, and you put in chicken?" I checked, trying not to sound like I thought any of these steps were too elementary to forget. You never knew with an amateur cook.

"Yes, of course," she was quick to allay my fears. Now that we were on safe territory (I mean, if she had chicken cooking in water, there had to be some sort of soup), I questioned her about the nature of the problem.

"What's the matter with the soup?" I probed carefully.

"I don't know," she blurted out in consternation, "It's not turning yellow!"

I stifled a chuckle.

"When is it supposed to turn yellow?" she continued miserably. "I'm standing here watching the pot for the past 20 minutes and nothing's happening!"

I smiled, picturing the unhappy scenario, an anxious *balabusta* standing vigil over her chicken soup, willing it with all her might to become yellow.

"Malky," I said gently, "how about the *kugel*?"

"What about the *kugel*?" Now she was frantic.

"Did you make it yet?"

"I had no idea the *kugel* had to be made before the chicken soup. My mother always does it afterward." She was almost crying.

"Malky, leave the soup. Start making the *kugel*."

"You mean you're giving up on my soup. It's hopeless. I knew I must have missed something. Right from the start it just never looked like my mother's chicken soup."

"You didn't miss anything, Malky. It's just not there. Some things simply are not the stuff of recipe books. Once you've followed the directions, you just have to leave the pot simmering on a low flame."

"And it just turns yellow? By itself?"

She was incredulous. Relieved.

"Exactly."

I searched my mind for a guideline, some definitive, tangible measurement I could quote that would make me sound like an expert, the way I fumble when someone insists on knowing exactly how much salt goes into the vegetable salad. But the best I could do was to repeat her magical words.

"It just turns yellow. By itself."

Like I said, she's been making soup for over a decade now, but her broth has become somewhat of a lesson to me. When I find myself worrying sometimes about the myriad of different concerns that fill my days — when I am consumed by anxiety over problems that aren't disappearing, by funds that aren't appearing, by relationships that aren't improving, by earnest attempts that don't seem to be reaping results; when I work myself into a frenzy that I haven't yet gotten it right, that my Hebrew still sounds far from native, and that my knack for shopping just doesn't seem to be getting gotten (Aren't you supposed to "get the knack of it" after a while?) — I remember to put the lid on and find something else to do.

Of course you've got to make sure there's water and the chicken inside. And that the flame's on. Those are the basic attempts at *hishtadlus*. Initially you've got to try and give it your best. Sometimes it means cutting and trimming. Sometimes it's consulting someone with years of expertise for a tip or two. Sometimes it simply entails trusting your taste buds to tell you what could still enhance the flavor. But after you've given it your all and you have a flame of heartfelt *tefillah* burning for the success of whatever it is you've just attempted to create — leave your efforts be.

As much as we would love a promise, a time frame, some practical, doable step in the recipe that will ensure the absolute infallibility of our venture, we have to come to terms with the fact that some results are just a lot more subtle than others. It takes a long time on the flame for the chicken soup to resemble your mother's.

Sometimes we just have to relinquish that desperate human need to feel in charge and in control, and let the *Ribono Shel Olam* do the cooking. There are some things you just can't force to happen, you can't will to happen, some things that just won't happen quicker no matter how much and how frantically you stir them.

Yet they happen. Sooner or later in the scheme of things you uncover the pot and you watch in wonder as golden circles swirl around a perfectly yellow tantalizing chicken soup.

The golden rings may be a peaceful infant who's passed a few colicky months, or it may be that reassuring feeling of having achieved experience in a certain field. They may come in the form of an older child offering sweetly to help, or the pleasure of seeing two siblings, who have in the past caused volcanic eruptions, working on a project together.

Everyone knows what the chicken soup means in his own lexicon. At different stages in life the soup varies, as do the hues and shades that we hope to achieve, but one rule is universal to all chicken soup, anywhere in the world. If your soup's not turning yellow the way you think it should be, take my advice. Go make the *kugel*.

Sand Art

The ocean used to represent serenity to me. I'd envision teal blue waves with white crests slowly lapping at the soft sand beneath a vast umbrella of azure sky. I'd hear the reassuring sound of the surf, as the incoming tide rolled up on shore and then receded back into the ocean.

I'd almost feel my bare soles squishing the warm sand, and then let my whole body relax, as the mild, foamy water gently licked my feet. The clean smell of salty spray in my nostrils, and the far off sound of a sailboat whirring in the distance lent the final calming effect.

That was before I visited the beach.

My perception, since then, has altered. If I had to use a single adjective to encapsulate my summer experiences at the seashore, I'm not sure what word I'd choose. It most certainly *wouldn't* be anything faintly reminiscent of calm. Frantic, hectic, messy, strenuous, noisy, would all be likely candidates. Tiring, disorienting, colorful, would be close competitors. Probably the most vivid one-worder would be the Hebrew *"balagan."*

Perhaps midsummer is an unfair time to test the waters. With scores of buses spewing out throngs of laughing, shouting, chatting vacationers, it's a little difficult to hear the whisper of the waves. With the smell of suntan lotion and super snacks and sweat, heavy in the air, it's a trifle hard to discern the intoxicating scent of the ocean spray.

Instead of having your eyes squint at the horizon and contemplate the vastness of pale blue expanse, your view is bombarded by people; scampering in the sand, sprawling in the sun, bobbing with the waves. But let's assume all that's extraneous to the sea. The explosion of people teeming on shore is an inevitable result of the fact that the beach is free, available entertainment to a bunch of over-eager adults and children.

The noise and the clutter, however, are not the only factor that have punctured my myth of the sea as the epitome of tranquility and peacefulness. It's the thought of those same idyllic descriptions that beckon so romantically on paper, that make me yawn before I even pack my bags to go to the beach.

It's the prospect of all that warm, mushy sand plastered to the baby's scalp, filling the pockets and hemlines, and weighing down the towels. It's the futility of rinsing your feet and then stepping right back into wet sand; dipping them in yet again, only to have them soiled in an instant. It's the leaden heaviness you feel as you board a bus, dragging sodden robes and grimy picnic leftovers in sand-filled shopping bags, and sitting through the ride home with tired, gritty kids all over your lap.

And though all the poems describe warm sand between your toes, when you've got to plod through that scorching stuff barefoot, it hardly feels poetic.

Once your shopping-bag handles have torn, though, and you've scooped up the sand-coated paraphernalia; once all that is behind you and you've made it into the water, well *then*, I'll admit, it's heaven on earth, or at sea. There, standing a few inches into the frothy ruffles edging the deep blue waters, there, gently swaying with the rocking waves, it's simply delightful.

There, the jarring noise ebbs into the distance, and all you feel is warm gentleness engulfing you again and again. Although there are children and teenagers, grandmothers, and middle-aged women jostling and thronging, flinging wet, sun-dappled arms out in front of you, you don't see them. You stand there, mesmerized by the lapping waves, letting the breeze caress your face, while your feet dissolve into a warm tunnel of slippery sand.

Suddenly you are alone, at one with the roaring water, a silhouette against the cerulean horizon. There is no past and no future, only the inebriating sensation of joining nature, of being submerged in it, and imbibing its intoxicating beauty.

Your body rocks with the slow rhythm, and you feel the tranquility settle over you, as the tension inside slowly dissipates into the far-off distance. A million miles away from the frenzied pace of everyday life, you feel like a newborn infant gently being lowered into a warm, soothing bathtub.

It's paradise. Pure, unadulterated beauty. But paradise, I guess, doesn't come without difficulty. At the beach, I've come to realize that "pure unadulterated beauty" is somewhat of a paradox, an illusion.

In all the poems I've read about the undulating waves, the tide and the shore, in all the breathtaking paintings and stunning snapshots of sunset over the sea, of sunrise mirrored in gold-tipped waves, I haven't tasted sand on my tongue, or gotten stung by a jellyfish. And yet those picture-perfect scenes are lacking a dimension that only the original can afford.

Reading about the sight, the sound, the smell of the seashore, seeing it stilled for posterity on a piece of Kodak paper is synthetic beauty. It can be enjoyed in a plush armchair, shielded from the searing heat, away from the smothering humidity, and yes, the inescapable, all-pervading sand. The heart of it, though, just doesn't come close to the real thing.

And it's the same with *Shabbos* and *Yom Tov* and Eretz Yisrael. It's the same with Torah and *chinuch*, and *kedushah*. Each and every facet of *Yiddishkeit* is a multifaceted gem, a warm radiant ray of sunlight, a fresh tantalizing waft of pleasure. And a lot of hard work.

Shabbos comes with sweat and preparation, *Yom Tov* requires careful menu planning and time-consuming cleaning, constructing, instructing, and conducting, depending on the particular *chag*. There's a lot of mundane shopping, and stopping, many sleepless nights, and tiring days.

Only someone who's worked toward it, though, can fully appreciate the resplendent beauty of a *Yom Tov seudah* accompanied by harmonious *zemiros* and *divrei Torah*. A guest witnessing the scene may perceive the experience with reverence and awe, perhaps even more reverence and awe than those on the inside, actually savoring the joy. But that spectator is getting a very shallow glimpse.

Visitors to Eretz Yisrael will feel uplifted just by breathing the very same air that everyday dwellers don't pause to think about. Still, only those who have bumped and tumbled a bit along the narrow, rickety roadways of living in the Holy Land can truly appreciate the richness of the gift. Those contending with the trials of cramped living quarters and the constant, hovering threat of war most richly experience the privilege of living in the King's palace.

Living, in the deepest sense of the word, is like visiting the beach. If you haven't gotten your feet wet, you haven't experienced real beauty. And in order to get your feet wet, you've just got to contend with the sand.

Teamwork

One advantage of having Hebrew-speaking neighbors and friends is being able to write about them without any qualms. Actually, most of them feel quite honored to serve as the subject of my introspection, which is why I told Meshulam I'd be writing about him.

He took his arm off the ladder he'd been leaning on, and looked up at me from the pad he'd been scribbling his figures into, with a kind of amused look. Winking with good humor, he checked his splattered green overalls and surveyed the general chaos in my front hall, trying to discern if I was serious.

"Is that how desperate you are for a scoop, that you broadcast your *shiputzim* in the newspaper?"

Shiputzim is the basket term used by Israelis for all and any renovations. To me, the term renovations brings to mind serious construction. The paint job and household repairs Meshulam was about to execute hardly justified the description. I didn't bother trying to find a more moderate adjective, though.

Israeli workers take a lot of pride in their work. When they apply a fresh coat of paint to your dingy whitewash, fix your running toilet, drill some holes, and install a few rods so you can hang laundry when it's rainy outdoors, they expect that they've given you a new lease on life. The least you can do, besides pay them, is give proper respect to the job.

So I did. I went along with his spiel and told him that I thought the local current events, going on right under my own roof, were earth shattering, perfect material for the front page. He chuckled, and as far as he was concerned, the joke was over. But I'd had something else in mind, and while he instructed his crew, his voice echoing in the dining room emptied of furniture, I mentally filed away his attitude, his smile, his good humor, and, most importantly, his line.

I've had many workers cross my threshold since we've settled in this country. Half of life, I'm beginning to think, is spent breaking things, and the other half repairing them. It's not just things, either. It's people and relationships and *middos*. But talking, as I am, about the things, I've learned a lesson or two on either side of the division. I've learned a lot from inflicting damage, and I've learned even more from trying to repair it. Or calling on others to do so.

Most of the lessons I've learned were practical. Get an estimate before you let the worker start. Get a second quote to compare that with. Never seem overly eager, terribly desperate, or too willing to pay the quoted price. You've got to know your cards.

In the United States, or across most of the globe for that matter, prices are generally fixed. Unless you're really feeling a pinch in your purse, it's not accepted custom to visibly frown at a price, never mind haggle. Around here, however, prices fluctuate. They vacillate with the mood, the customer's accent, the general vibes exuded by the particular patron with regard to his or her level of naivete or thriftiness. The first price, I've learned, is an invitation for negotiations.

So when Meshulam walked past my doorstep, speckled overalls, broad Yemenite smile and all, I knew enough not to fall for the ruses. When he puckered his brow and drummed his fingers against his forehead, clucking his tongue in concentration, I assumed it was a show of trying to reckon the best price he could give us. I tried to convey some apprehension. Remembering my tendency to give workers the impression they've been hired, before I've formed my own opinion, I threw in a question or two, if only to give voice to some hesitation.

I saw him smirk, as if he recognized my tone, wavering between accusation and restrained excitement, and for the first time of many, he assured me,

"*Giveret*, what's your name," and here a quick glance at the plaque on my door, against which he stood, "*Giveret Feig, tish'ali et* *kulam. Ani **b'ad**, ani lo neged.* (Ask anyone, I'm on your side. I'm not the opposition.)"

His eyes sparkled with good will; they looked like anything other than the eyes of someone trying to pull the wool over someone else's.

"You can take me. You can take someone else. You can call me next week. *B'ezrat Hashem*, you can call me next year. I don't care one way or the other. Believe me, I don't. *Hakol mimenu* (Everything is from Him)," he gestured heavenward, and I instinctively followed his gaze. "But do me a favor. Ask around, they'll tell you. *Ani **b'ad**,* I'm on your team, I want your house to look nice, I want you to be able to afford it, I want you to come out happy. *Ani lo neged"* (I'm not the opposition).

With that, he picked up his clipboard, his workbox, handed me his card, and left. I grabbed a pen, scribbled down, *ani b'ad, ani lo neged.* I knew I would call for another estimate. And I knew Meshulam would be back.

He came punctually at 8:15, handed snacks out to his workers, provided instructions peppered with some good-natured banter, and offered to drive us to choose a replacement faucet or a new fixture, or whatever materials the morning tasks required. And whenever we'd question him about a discrepancy in prices, the difference between two tiles, the reason he recommended one brand over another, he'd remind us, only half in jest, "*Shichachtem kvar* (Have you already forgotten)? *Ani b'ad, ani lo neged.*"

He came, showered and changed after his evening *shiur*, his tanned complexion making his white shirt look almost fluorescent, and he surveyed the day's work with a satisfied smile, sometimes shaking his head in disapproval, and marking a note on his clipboard. He listened calmly to my complaints, his eyes glinting with that indulgent smirk, displaying the patient understanding of a tutor for a third grader frustrated with math homework. My husband asked him if we could pay him with a check, and predictably, he smiled, "*B'vadai bachur'chik* (Certainly, young man); *ani b'ad, ani lo neged.*"

He's left, so has his crew, and the repaired items have managed to begin their breakdown again. Like I said, we're either in one phase or another of the breakdown-repair cycle. But I haven't forgotten his line. *Ani b'ad, ani lo neged.*

In this age of dog eats dog, of bottom-line motives, of cunning marketing techniques, we've become accustomed to looking for the fine print. We've become mistrustful of small talk, of friendly inquiries, of ready smiles. "What's the catch?" our minds snap, "How much will this cost me?"

It's all fine, in keeping with *Chazal's* advice of *chashdeihu*, but somewhere along the way, we seem to have dropped the *kabdeihu.* Sometimes we view the people around us, the ones we act and interact with, colleagues, *mechutanim*, employers, employees, our children's teachers, our students' parents, and sometimes even our closest ones, as if they were competitors, outsiders to be squinted at with cautious suspicion.

Why did s/he do, say, call, not call, remember, forget? What could they have meant? Why didn't they ask, promise, answer, buy, return, come, go, the way logic, meaning us, would have dictated? We rack our brains, turn the scenes over in our minds, draw conclusions, add commentary, create comparisons, all on the premise that the significant other must have had something, some malicious intent, up his sleeve, down our back.

Sure there's a place for prudence, primarily where the stakes are high, financially, healthwise, or other. What danger do we risk, however, when we give in, accede, trust, treat people around us with confidence and respect, with willingness, and acceptance? What is this irrational phobia we have of being exploited?

No one can be taken advantage of if he chooses to give freely of his advantages. Imagine what the world, what families, schools, *Klal Yisrael* could look like if we dropped our guard long enough to convey Meshulam's message: *Ani b'ad, ani lo neged*, I'm on your team, with you, together. We're not out to prove each other wrong, but to share the taste of success. Picture what a different rapport we could enjoy with our children, our students, our daughters and sons-in-law, if our words and actions relayed our faith that they too, were *b'ad, lo neged.*

I know I risk saying this above the obliging chuckles of some seasoned businessmen. I know they may be amused by the fanciful wishes of a gullible lady, taken by some socially adroit handyman. But I don't care.

We've gotten a top job at reasonable, if not bottom dollar. We've made coffee, listened to *berachos,* exchanged compliments, enjoyed some hearty humor. We've stood firm, and still understood, disagreed in agreeable tones, and we've sent Meshulam a whole lot of customers.

What should I say? *Ani b'ad,* I'm all for it.

Parenting on Paper

Sometimes I wonder what ever happened to all those brilliant ideas, to those sure-fire solutions that I used to spout a dime a dozen, at the tender age of 12.

It was in seventh grade, I think, that a group of us, confident and boisterous, would stroll home from school together, bookbags slung over our shoulders, hair bouncing in the breeze. On the way home, as a sort of game to make the walk more stimulating and fun, we'd play "situations."

One of us would pose some very difficult classroom situation, and the rest of us would sink into a pensive silence as we pondered the possibilities.

"Suppose you caught a student eating a cookie behind her social studies book," went a typical round. It didn't take a minute, and the brainstorms started coming fast and thick. First came the don'ts, as we knowingly vetoed all the unproductive approaches that any teacher we ever knew had unsuccessfully tried in a classroom of ours.

"I would *not* say, 'Bring that cookie up here.' That could turn the teacher into the fool if the kid just shrugged or denied she was eating."

We were aware of all the potential pitfalls. We knew all the booby traps set up for teachers, and carefully sidestepped them. We took every eventuality into account, and we came up with some ingenious tactics. They would have done well to invite us as a panel to any "How to Handle Typical Classroom Disturbances" seminar.

We accomplished great things on those walks home, we budding teachers. We developed a foolproof anticheating system, invented an extra credit program that would motivate even the most uninterested student, and devised a novel method of presenting rules of *tzeniyus* (modesty) in a way that wouldn't invite an explosive reaction during the recess break.

The dares became more challenging with each walk home, but we experts were never stumped. Sometimes one of us came up with an idea that the rest of the group discarded as flimsy, and at other times, a really clever solution prompted a shower of sincere admiration.

After a while, we had exhausted every topic from homework to note-passing, and we only had one question that we were hard put to answer: Why hadn't all our own teachers come up with all these marvelous ideas?

Then we advanced to the realm of motherhood. Of course we only tackled problems that pertained to children 12 and 13 years old. But again, we had an impressive array of ideas under our belts. We had a ready supply of situations, our experience as children provided them daily, and we knew just what the ideal mother would do to get out of the dilemma respectfully while placating the child at the same time.

Sometimes, one of the group posed a really tough situation, and we had to admit that motherhood wasn't as easy as teaching. In general, though, we were full of confidence about our problem solving abilities, and the walks home were a thrill we looked forward to every afternoon.

It's a shame we didn't think of writing down our brainstorms, of documenting our tips and ideas into some kind of handbook, entitled "Guide for the Perplexed Educator" or maybe "Everything You Wanted to Know About Handling Children Under Thirteen."

Some days I find myself really wishing we had. How I would love to browse through a catalogue of fool-proof ideas, one more attractive than the next, tested and censored by the real experts in the field.

Some days I really wonder if I've regressed in my educational prowess, if the ever-forthcoming wellspring of ideas I had at 12 and 13 has actually gone dry.

How is it that a person who has thought of THE solution to every existing problem, cannot think of how to wean a 3-½-year old from his habit of hitting, or what to tell a 5-year-old, begging sweetly from her bed, "Pleeeeeease, Mommy, one more cup of water; I'm so thirsty, I can't fall asleep."

Should the hitting be treated strictly? Should hitting-free behavior be rewarded? Timeout? Perhaps a story related to hitting? And then maybe the hitting was an expression of distress? Perhaps someone was bullying him in kindergarten? What about the innocent cup of water? I have nothing against providing my children's basic needs, and water at bedtime is not even harmful to the teeth.

The problem is that when I give in, I suddenly hear a chorus of voices chirping their older sister's refrain. And that tomorrow night, we'll be haggling over a third cup. On the other hand, what if she really *is* so thirsty that she can't fall asleep? It's a hot night, and I didn't actually *warn* her that there would be no drinking after lights out. It's so complicated! And to think that all this was once so blissfully simple and clear cut!

I try to rack my brains. What did we kids say about children whose unfaltering response to any request is, "Why?"

"Please go brush your teeth." "Why?" "Please stop dragging the baby around." "Why?" "It's time to be heading home now." "Why?"

We certainly would not have advocated the stodgy, "Because I said so and I'm the mother" school of thought. Had we advised ignoring, repeating the request, smiling, or actually explaining the reasoning behind the directive?

It seems to me that so many new options have mushroomed since those days when we had everything so down pat. Had we perhaps had the advantage of seeing circumstances from the twenty-twenty vision of childhood? Had we, as youngsters, better understood the motivation behind kids' behavior; when they were begging for intervention, and when they had to be left to their own devices?

Maybe.

But I still like to think that hindsight offers a broader lens, one which highlights a lot of subtle details, and focuses on background a lot more sharply than the zoom lens of the present. I like to hope that age has somehow tuned my senses so that previously indiscernible sensitivities have now become important factors to be taken into account.

Time has a way of smudging black and white, creating a terrain of gray that sometimes belongs with the black and sometimes belongs with the white, sometimes with a little of each, and sometimes with just a touch of one or the other.

As an adult, I have somewhat learned to temper my need for immediate gratification, and I can appreciate that many times, the crystals that grow over time, in a carefully monitored climate, far outlast a quick-fix solution plastered on the spot.

I also know that what works like magic on my neighbor's kids just won't budge mine a single inch, and that the method that went over so beautifully last week with my own, may completely backfire tomorrow morning.

True. It's all true. But if I happen to spy a group of all-knowing seventh graders in animated discussion on their way home from school, I still think I'd slow my pace and try to catch some pearls of wisdom.

Pony Tales

If one can tell a person by what he discusses, then the weekly or biweekly splash of advertisements cluttering the mailboxes of any given neighborhood can presumably serve as the pulse of the community. Thumbing through the pamphlet that circulates ours, one knows one thing for certain: We belong to the people of the Book.

No dizzying shoe knockouts, or mad bashes for you in these leaflets. Of course, there'll be announcements declaring the cheapest prices on coats, or the best buy on the sturdiest furniture; those are indicators of any young flourishing community. The bulk of the ads, though, offer you the opportunity to open the cache of some as yet undiscovered source of wisdom, over the span of two or three or ten courses.

If you have the time and the means, you can learn reflexology, music, special education, graphology, English, or *safrus*; you can tap the wellsprings of proper nutrition, child rearing, informed marketing, interior decorating, or computer programming, all within a relatively short period of time.

Since I lack both the time and the means, I usually skim over these quarter-page ads before I can even consciously internalize their content. Though the idea of amassing knowledge in some new intellectual realm tempts me like a good square of chocolate, I am of the opinion that a little of either of the above tends to be dangerous. So I steer that curious child inside me away from wistful appeal, and turn toward some more practical information, like where I can get lens solution for half price.

A couple of months ago, however, as I was browsing through the paper, something about a particular ad made me pause before I flipped the page. *Bibliotherapy — learn how to use the most powerful tool at your disposal: stories.*

Now stories were nothing new to me. I'd been spinning them since time immemorial, and I was your first customer for the written variety, regardless of the time of night or day.

Here was an opportunity to polish a skill I already had, and personalize it to help my children deal with their everyday challenges. I was nearly swayed. When the words "sibling rivalry" jumped out at me from the list of the "everyday challenges" that effective storytelling professed to uproot, I was sold. I jotted down the number near the telephone, and in no time I was enrolled.

I had been at war with fighting (sounds like an effective technique, doesn't it?) for the past few years. I had begged, cajoled, ordered, demanded, commanded, intervened, ignored, and then started again from the beginning of the list. I had made contests and compromises, and had consulted many an authority on the subject. In vain. So when I spotted this ad, it was like discovering the promise of an unexplored vista.

Equipped with a brand new notebook and pen, I set out to the first session, eager as a child on her way to art lessons. The introductory lesson had me intrigued. Although the instructor valiantly tried to keep my creativity in check, insisting that this was only the barest presentation of the principles, I felt the unleashed ideas coursing through my veins, nudging my mind, tickling my thoughts. I had never been good at sufficing with theory, and now too, I was just itching to get home and put my raw skills to test.

So as I puttered about my daily tasks, checking rice, depositing a check, sweeping under the beds, my thoughts took on a life of their own. It was hard to tell who was more excited at the prospect of the story, my junior audience, or myself.

I spun the tale around an imaginary family of ponies (animals were supposed to be the most neutral catalysts to drive a point home, and anyway, what could be a better way to address a "pet peeve"?).

I already envisioned the happy ending in my very own home: an atmosphere of loving harmony and peace, undisturbed by the strident battle cries invariably peaking with the ever-grating "Mooooooooommmmy!"

My little charges were perfect bait. They listened attentively to every detail, their eyes gobbling every nuance of the fantasy. I swallowed a smile as I watched an expression of consternation pucker two sets of brows as they listened to the description of the two ponies, tangled in a ball of vengeful fury, rolling over and over again in the muddy barnyard.

Bringing the story to a dramatic climax, and then steering it toward a soft ending, I felt a surge of accomplishment. I always love the island of relaxed togetherness that storytelling provides; it sort of puts reality off the hook for a while, without eliciting the annoying busy signal in the background. This time, however, there was an added dimension; I was curious to hear the kids' reaction to the indirect therapy I had just administered.

Rivky looked thoughtful, which is just the effect I had been hoping to achieve. I didn't probe. Long before story therapy, I remember

Rabbi Josh Silbermintz admonishing B'nos leaders never to third degree kids about the moral of the story. So I kept quiet.

Rivky, however, didn't need a penny for her thoughts; she was ready to share her impressions for free.

"Ma, what are ponies?" she asked.

When she saw my expression, I guess it must have been, well, kind of surprised, she quickly amended, "No, I know what they *are*, but are they horses' cousins, or horses' grandchildren?"

I almost heard my ego land on the floor. So much for story therapy. There's nothing like a child to send some of your nicest theories plummeting. I sat there in disbelief as my tale spurred the next argument over whether ponies were the relatives or the descendants of horses. And I thought to myself in a kind of disengaged amusement, that it would make perfect story therapy for adults.

I don't know if it's fighting on *HaKadosh Baruch Hu's* agenda, or what, but we've been hearing an awful lot of stories lately. Stories with happy endings, many without, some of them terrifying, some hair raising; all of them extraordinary.

And like the kids, we've been asking questions. "What are ponies? How many people were killed? How old were they? Where was the bus going? How come they couldn't trace the phone calls?" A bunch of irrelevant, extraneous, impertinent questions. A bunch of off-the-mark, besides-the-point, childish commentary.

There's a reason the headlines are reaching us every day, and it's something beyond the advances in modern communication. There's a reason for that too, after all. There's Someone designing the plots with each of us in mind, tales individually customized to each attentive listener.

And the story is not about ponies, or about bombs, or tyrants, or accidents or terror. The story is not about Bush or Sharon or Arafat. It's about us. It's about fighting. It's about overcoming animosity, and improving our *tzeniyus*, its about self-checking our integrity and perfecting our *Shabbos* observance. We each know what it's about.

And unlike my own little fantasy, the story is real, and it is only coming to its climax. The ending is up to us.

Sweet Dreams

For some reason, I've been thinking of Mrs. Travis lately. I have a feeling it has something to do with Fantasia, but then you probably have no inkling of what I'm talking about. Unless, of course, you happen to have been in Mrs. Travis's class.

Creative writing is a subject that makes 90 percent of your average student-population groan, 8 percent glad for the reprieve from math and history, and 2 percent glow with excitement. I belonged to that 2 percent. So did Mrs. Travis.

She never came up with stodgy topics like "How I Spent My Summer Vacation," or "Lost in the Forest." She would walk purposefully to the front of our eighth-grade classroom, lower lip sucked into a glimmer of a smirk that matched the glint in her eye, and post the title on the board with a flourish. Then her smirk would turn into a broad smile, inviting our eager response.

"How to Nag Effectively," "The Art of Professional Eavesdropping," and "Fifty Uses for a Toothpick" (a hundred for the really inspired) were a sampling of her brainstorming starters.

The title I really remember is Fantasia. I recall squinting up at the board a second time to see if I had gotten it right, and then sliding forward in my seat, waiting for an explanation.

Fantasia, Mrs. Travis described, was a place where some fantastic dream replaced reality. Fantasia was a place where the word impossible wasn't listed in the dictionary, where reasonable limits didn't smother anybody's wishes; fairyland, if you may.

What Mrs. Travis wanted was our personal idea of Fantasia, and the reasons we had chosen the particular aspect of fantasy come alive.

There was some squirming and grumbling, the rattle of pencil cases and the decisive sound of papers being shuffled and then straightened on some desktops. I got into my favorite position, legs crossed under me, head cradled in palms, elbows on my desk (Mrs. Travis was kind enough to overlook table manners), and stared at some impertinent notice on the wall, freeing my mind to explore Fantasia. Then I began scribbling fast.

Fantasia was a place, in my humble eighth-grade opinion, where the need to sleep was extinct — exclusively for the lucky cardholder, of course. In Fantasia, you never ever tired; you simply went on and on with abundant energy and lucid mindfulness, tackling one conquest after the next. While the entire populace snored uselessly, squandering priceless stretches of life, you expanded your horizons, finished neglected projects, read, wrote, built, sewed, cooked, tidied, whatever at all you fancied.

Of course you spent your waking hours running errands and cultivating interests that needed the backdrop of a wakeful community, like shopping for instance, or talking to a good friend. All the while, though, you didn't feel that nagging anxiety of that which had yet to be seen to; you knew that in another few hours you'd have a nice block of peace and quiet to accomplish all you had left to do.

Don't forget the small, but significant gains accumulated on account of tasks like getting ready for bed, alarm-clock setting, *Krias Shema*, as well as bed-making and linen-stripping, tasks which would be rendered obsolete by the very exclusion of sleep. No insomnia, no nightmares, no waking up frantically twenty minutes late.

And perhaps the very sweetest part of the whole deal was the fact that nobody else was party to the secret of your productive nights. Nobody knew about those extra hours in your account, no one plied you with their own surplus of duties and obligations "since I've noticed you get along on no sleep." It was pure bonus, net fantasia.

So much for an eighth grader's fantasy. To think that I had craved all this way before the advent of test-marking, newborn colic, late-night ironing, and early-morning appointments. Once all that came around, I found myself wistfully remembering

Fantasia, longingly stroking the memories of the place I had concocted back then in Mrs. Travis's class.

More than once, I've found myself yawning over a pot of simmering applesauce, surveying stacks of pots and pans, piles of laundry, unfinished Purim costumes through a mist of tearful tiredness, yearning for a free ticket to Fantasia — one way, please.

More than once, I've paced the dining room with a screaming infant, lain beside an insistent 6-year-old, scoured encyclopedias for an older one's report, taut with the tension of all that had yet to be finished before I could call it a day.

On those nights and on so many others when I've turned the key in the keyhole at 1 o'clock in the morning to face the pre- and post-supper chaos abandoned by an overwhelmed babysitter, I've found myself wishing that I could somehow crawl into the smaller-than-life characters in my preteen handwriting and join Fantasian existence.

No one ever put any limit on wishes; as long as they don't bother you or anybody else, you're entitled to wish all you like. Not that these wistful cravings get the test papers marked or the laundry off your bed when you'd like to make a beeline for it. Not that they solve insomnia, or return telephone calls, or send an emissary to perform errands the next morning.

Sometimes though, wishing just helps you get through that moment or two of helpless hysteria; sometimes Fantasia is the only escape from the state of overwhelmia, a condition that, at one point or another, plagues most mortals.

Only sometimes, though. At other times, I think of Fantasia and shudder. I think of our lives, one big run-on sentence, incoherent and unpunctuated, one giant mess of days running into one another, tumbling over one another endlessly. I see the spreading continuum blotting the borders of day and night, smudging the outlines of significant events, blurring the distinct beauty of each snapshot of our existence.

There's something about waking up to a new day, and it isn't contingent upon whether or not you are of the variety that leaves dishes in the sink overnight: something brand new, and undiscovered and challenging all over again.

There's something about sleep that puts a crisp new sheet of wrapping paper on the gift of life, something about saying *Modeh Ani,* even if your voice is trembling with a suppressed yawn, that lets you delight in tearing open that wrapper, undoing the curled ribbon, and reaching inside.

There's a magic quality to morning, the seeping sunlight, the birds chirping, the vigorous stretching, that makes yesterday seem miles away, that dissolves harsh words uttered in the dark of night, and laughs gaily at fears inflated by the pump of overtired speculation. There's something about the breaking of dawn that breeds forgiveness and hope, that punctures the bubbles of anxiety and loneliness, that makes matters seem so simple and clear and light.

It's the blessing of fatigue and the ensuing sleep, however short and insufficient, that allows us to start again, to open our eyes and see the people around us from a new angle. It's the inevitability of exhaustion that grants us the gift of pausing before we plunge ahead relentlessly, of winding up our affairs once every twenty-four hours so we can keep some sort of tab on our progress in this world.

And the constant struggle of having to fit, stuff, and shove more than can be contained in our waking hours is a small-scale reminder of the finite quality of our time in this world, of the need to sort our tasks, and tackle priorities first.

Fantasia, I've come to realize, is not about an ever-vigilant existence in some contrived paradise. It's the solid reality of missing shoes and honking horns diffusing the irrational tears of ghostly hours. It's the daily unfolding of the *birchos hashachar,* the unfailing predictability of morning's appearance amid the terrifying flux of a world fraught with personal tragedies and global insecurity. It's the blessing of pacing our bodies for the forced recess of cleansing our souls in the stillness of night.

And so, if the assignment is still up for revisions, Mrs. Travis, I'll take mine back. Fantasia, I'd write, is the magic of dawn and dusk, right here in the world we live in. Fantasia is pure sleeping beauty.

Headlines and Deadlines

*N*ot that anybody asked for my endorsement, but I think that the Jewish calendar reflects the most exquisite design of perfection. A year isn't a serendipitous slice of life, a hodge-podge of 365 consecutive days. A year is a complete experience, a full circle, a prize-winning composition of thin, soul-stirring notes rolling into explosive song.

Each time has its own mood, its own texture, its own set of sights and sounds, smells and tastes. Each period has its own very unique appeal through some facet of the human experience.

Think of *Yom Kippur* and *Succos*, *Tu B'Shvat* and *Tishah B'Av*. Picture *Purim* and *Chanukah*, *Sefiras HaOmer* and *Aseres Yemei Teshuvah*. Take a deep breath and smell the *b'samim* of *havdalah*, feel the shooting potency of *marror* in your nose. Listen to the squawking of *kapparos*, the roar of *birchas Kohanim*.

And then there are the times in between, the regular days, whose characters are forged primarily by what they are not.

Like *Motza'ei Pesach*.

No, I don't mean *Motza'ei Pesach* per se. I'm not talking about the merry clattering of crystal and stainless steel finding their way back into boxes and attics and basements. I'm not talking about the boisterous interaction of children and adults, the reckless ripping of tape and aluminum foil, the noisy banter as jokes and instructions and chocolate are dispensed without heed until the wee hours of the morning.

I'm talking about the blessed quiet after the blessed storm, the very mundane Monday or Tuesday or Wednesday morning after all of this hectic activity ceases. After the dishes are back into place, and the people too. After the last dishtowels are laundered and the tablecloths ironed, and the *Pesach* closet locked until next year.

Suddenly you stand in your kitchen, right near the window, and you hear the clear trill of birds chirping, notice that the tree in the front yard is starting to show some tiny green buds. Suddenly you are in the car, or on the porch, squinting against a sudden burst of sunshine and you realize that you have nothing absolutely pressing on your immediate agenda.

And after all that whirlwind and all that activity, after all those guests and all those menus, after all that scrubbing and rinsing and peeling and clearing, I'll tell you, it's a boon.

Just the ordinariness of breakfast and lunch, the house all to yourself, the hum of the washing machine taking its time. Just the predictability of departures and arrivals, of mealtime and bedtime, of homework and housework. Just the leisurely pace of it all, like the soft, surreal sensation of padding on carpet after a vigorous workout on the treadmill.

Not that I don't love *Pesach* or the hectic weeks preceding its arrival. Not that I don't revel in the sense of renewal, in the fresh smells of paint and bleach and carpet shampoo wafting in the air. Not that I don't relish that vigorous sense of mission and accomplishment, the sweet stretching of strained muscles after a full day's work.

I do.

Still, when it's all over, when it's all been unpacked and unfolded and thoroughly experienced, and then packed up and folded and stored, it's like a music tape that has to rewind back to the beginning, quietly and steadily, before you can enjoy it again.

Which is just what I was doing last Thursday morning as I sat at my kitchen table, lazily eyeing the plastic ivy crawling out of the gray ceramic vases on either side of my kitchen clock. Never mind that there was *Shabbos* to prepare, and some neglected chores to be seen to; that was routine.

At the particular moment all I felt was the blissful simplicity of my agenda, the absence of anything imminent jogging my mental accelerator to lunge ahead at full speed.

Instinctively, I shuffled through the pile of mail at the edge of the counter. What was a private bowl of branflakes worth if I didn't have something to read while I savored the moment of leisure?

I picked up the full-color magazine eagerly and then put it down, disappointed. No, I hadn't been hunting for advertisements. I was more than satiated with shopping for the time being. Where was my Thursday-morning prize? I wondered in annoyance as I carefully sifted through the pile again.

A handful of routine bills, a plastic-wrapped solicitation brochure, a pink flyer promoting some extermination company. Where was my *Bayit Hayehudi,* my weekend reprieve, my regular dose of inspiration? I pictured the glossy cover, wooden house amid greenery dotted with pink flowers, pleasant blue sky creating the background for the black lettering on the top. It was right there in my mind's eye, so vivid, I could almost reach out and turn the page, yet it wasn't there.

I should get up and find those *Erev Yom Tov* issues that I never got a chance to finish, I thought halfheartedly. The idea was as appealing as walking to the grocery for a sugar cube, while the coffee turned cold. What could have happened? I speculated, tapping around the pile again, as if the elusive subscription might suddenly appear if I was insistent enough.

This was really ironic, I mused; just when I was about to forgo discipline and indulge in the privilege of reading over breakfast on a Thursday morning. Maybe there was some problem with the mailing, I pondered. Reluctantly, I picked up the advertising circular and turned the pages impassively, like a kid picking at leftovers.

And suddenly I sat up straight.

*Funny, who do you think the Bayit Hayehudi **is**?*

A bunch of women, just like yourself, mothers and teachers, professionals and homemakers, all who have just landed and are dealing with post-*Pesach* jet lag along with the rest of us.

You *didn't write this week, did you?*

"Of course I didn't," my tone turned defensive. "It's all of two days after *Pesach*. When do you propose I should have written: on *Isru Chag* or on *Chol HaMoed*?"

I shoveled the last of the soggy branflakes into my mouth and collected the plate and spoon purposefully. Lest this annoying accuser catch me taking a coffee break.

It had been enough of a challenge weaving my writing through my *Erev Pesach* schedule, I thought defensively, as I rinsed the spoon and wiped my hands.

O.K., O.K., no reason to get all worked up. Begrudgingly, I smiled, ashamed at having played the little girl sulking at a joke.

Some joke!

True, it was only two days since *Pesach*. And yes, it would have been unthinkable to sit down in front of the computer either yesterday or during *Yom Tov*.

After all, there were so many deadlines one could handle *Erev Pesach* without the thought of cramming in yet an extra article. All that was perfectly understandable. What eluded me now was: Why hadn't all this logic dawned earlier, when I'd been searching for my food in print?

It was the TH factor at play; the difference between TH*em* and *me*. *Them* was a magazine, not a person. *Them* was *The Editors*, some kind of an establishment, some kind of professional concern who was there to serve my needs on a constant and continual basis. And *Them*, of course, was expected to function without skipping a beat.

Me was a different story. *Me* was a mother. *Me* had a teething infant who screamed around the clock, and a nephew in the hospital over *Pesach*. *Me* was an exhausted lady who needed to get her bearings before she could think of sitting down at the computer. And *Me*, of course, had to relax with the *Bayit Hayehudi* while she got her bearings.

It's amazing what two little letters can do to an attitude.

And the TH factor isn't limited to writers and housewives. It's the way we relate to our principals and our *askanim*, it's the way we view our teachers and our caterers. It's the way we talk about "The School System" and "The *Kiruv* Movement."

It's the way we balk at "another day off," when Them are the teachers, the way we criticize the curt manner or the long lines when Them are the volunteers and the doctors. It's the way we grimace at anything less than perfection when Them are the florists, the carpenters, the seamstresses.

And it's the way we understand that "a young couple should spend their first *Yom Tov* with the wife's parents" when Me is the wife's parents, the way we maintain that stores should extend credit to their customers when Me is the customer.

Let's not kid ourselves; there are no two camps. We are all Them and we are all Me. It only depends which side we happen to be peering in from at any given moment.

So next time, before we come marching in with grudges and complaints, before we come armed with accusations and demands, let's remember the *Bayit Hayehudi.* The place where Them and Me merge, and TH stands only for True Harmony.

The Great Unknown

She'll never know, I thought to myself, as I waded across her dining room, wet skirt slapping against my knees. Over two hours had passed since I'd been summoned to my sister-in-law's fourth-floor apartment by a frantic neighbor, and still, I was far from finished.

Actually *I* was finished; it was the apartment that required some serious overhauling to get it back to its original state.

The boiler on the roof of the building had burst, and by the time the neighbor on the second floor had tracked me down to tell me that the roar of gushing water could be heard from my sister-in-law's apartment, I knew it was serious business.

My sister-in-law was abroad with her family, and was scheduled to return in two days' time. When she had asked me, before leaving to the airport, if she could leave my number with her neighbor "in case of emergency," I had chuckled in response. "With you and the family on the other side of the ocean, exactly what kind of emergency are you anticipating?"

Well, now I knew.

I'd made quick arrangements, and had arrived on the scene of the flood, equipped with boots, a wet vac, and a sponga stick. And as I started off saying, I'd been working relentlessly for a couple of hours, when I stopped for a moment to assess the extent of the second-degree damage inflicted on the apartment.

Endless, it was endless. Although rivulets of water cascading across the kitchen and hall floor of an Israeli apartment are usually a healthy sign of a robust *balabusta* at work, even a born and bred *sabra* would have stared in wide-eyed horror at the devastation wrought by this flood.

The toys were floating in the water, as were the chairs, throw rugs, and plants. Not to speak of the electrical appliances like the vacuum cleaner and the radiator, that were almost completely submerged in water. The ceiling was a horrific sight, huge faults dividing it like the plates in an earthquake zone.

I made a mental note to call a painter, as I emptied the washing machine of the towels I had put in, and filled it with a load of soaking bedspreads. Thumbing through my sister-in-law's personal phone book, I jotted down the numbers of a painter and an electrician. Then I got busy emptying the lower cabinets of her dining-room buffet, gingerly laying out one item at a time on the towel-lined dining-room table to dry.

I made a quick calculation of the family's return date, and the list of chores that had yet to be completed if they were to arrive to home, sweet home. As things stood, it seemed more likely that they would experience somewhat of a bittersweet homecoming.

It was precisely then that the thought passed through my mind, *She'll never know.* Sure, she'll hear there was a flood, and she'll notice all the aftereffects of it on her usually perfectly maintained home. She'll see water rings in some places on the walls, and she'll realize that the Oriental carpet had become slightly rippled.

She'll probably cluck her tongue in dismay at the discolored legs of the dining-room table, and she'll swallow her annoyance at the tablecloths folded in the cabinet where the photo albums belong. Her neighbor will listen sympathetically to her tale of how difficult it was to come back to such damage and disarray, how hard it was to arrive home in the wake of the flood.

And of course, it goes without saying, she'll thank me profusely for being there, for getting the water out, for administering first aid on her apartment in her absence.

But she'll never know. She'll never know what the apartment looked like when I first arrived, how it looked three hours later, and then the next morning, after a night of wiping, emptying, folding, painting, varnishing, and wiping again.

There's just no way she'll know how many calls to the babysitter, visits to the hardware store, urgent messages to the handyman, and trips to the dry cleaners the whole two-day operation entailed.

She'll never know how many times my weary eyes stopped to survey the progress, and how many times I was almost tempted to leave well enough alone. But I didn't. I aimed at getting the place back into perfect order, because I knew what it meant to my sister-in-law.

I also knew that as perfect as things would seem from my vantage point, they'd seem more like well enough to the owner of the home who was familiar with every corner and was expecting to find things as she had left them.

Not that she was an ingrate, or a killjoy, or even the critical type. Not at all. She was just perfectly human, and tended to see things in relation to what she was used to, to what was normal, expected, comfortable, routine. Like me. Like many of us.

How often do we get to be backstage, cleaning the flood, clearing away every vestige of water from someone else's home? How often do we get to see what goes into it — rather than what comes out of it?

Most of our everyday dealings bring us into contact with people who are doing something for us, something that requires a lot of big and little details we'll never know about.

Who'll ever tell us that the green suit we gave in to the dressmaker last week for alterations had to be taken apart four times before the darts looked satisfactory? Who'll ever make us aware that our daughter's kindergarten teacher was up until 3 a.m. because someone misplaced Chany's cape and crown the night before graduation? And who'll ever disclose the secret behind the neatly stocked shelves in the *Pesach* grocery; the hours upon hours of cleaning, sorting, unpacking, and organizing that went on before the doors to the humble-looking, slightly cramped store were able to open?

Most probably no one. And most probably we'll notice that the hemline on the suit was puckering, that Chany didn't seem to know the motions, and that the lighting in the *Pesach* grocery was really dim.

No matter that we think of ourselves as courteous, positive, appreciative people. No matter that we do pay the dressmaker, thank the kindergarten teacher, and smile at the grocery owner. We still won't ever know what went into it to make it happen, how many efforts were expended to make it this good, and how many hindrances were strewn in the way.

We may have asked a neighbor on her way to the supermarket to pick up a roll of aluminum foil and some detergent for us. When we find the shopping bag with the items and the receipt slung over the doorknob, we'll never know that the aluminum foil had been left in the taxi and had warranted a half a day of playing cat and mouse, before it had landed on our doorstep.

And when we analyze our teaching schedule, neatly printed out on a sheet of paper, we won't ever know that the secretary had confused our preference for Tuesdays and Thursdays with someone else's Mondays and Thursdays, and had been forced to rearrange the whole schedule.

That's as far as the human beings in our life are concerned. And it's much the same with the thousands of big and little acts of goodness bestowed upon us from Above.

As we dart across the avenue in a rush to make the trimming store before closing, we won't ever know that we have just escaped a tragic accident, and that some heavenly defense in our favor precluded the tragedy at the last second. We *may* notice, with a trace of annoyance, that the trimming store was closed despite our efforts to get there in time.

Here and there we catch glimpses of *Hashgachah Pratis*, and we constantly thank Hashem for "the miracles You perform with us daily," but how often do we really, deeply, *feel* those miracles? How often do we stop to contemplate the many things that could have gone wrong, that should have gone wrong, but didn't?

It's not that we're ingrates, or killjoys, or even critical. But like my sister-in-law, we're very much human, and we expect to find things as we left them (when we leave them in order, that is). We tend to see things in relation to what we consider normal, expected, comfortable, routine.

Sometimes, we've got to step backstage, and see the frantic flurry of action behind the perfectly, or not-so-perfectly coordinated scenes. Sometimes we've got to use our multiplication tables to figure that whatever we see in front of us is in fact that many more times more difficult, tedious, and involved than we may realize.

And many times, all the time, we've got to cultivate our sense of gratitude, of appreciation, of thankfulness, for all those details we'll just never, ever, know about. Whoever said that ignorance was bliss?

Messy Musings

You're sorry about the mess, oh are you? Well, without even brainstorming, I can give you a handful of solid reasons why you shouldn't be. Unless of course you meant that you were sorry for yourself. In which case I might be able to be of assistance too.

If I look kind of perplexed, it's because I'm pondering whether you're sorry that your kitchen looks as if you're in the middle of making *challah* and *kugel* and *cholent*, when in fact you are, or if perhaps you're apologetic that your toddler appears to have been fishing in the toilet bowl instead of having been engaged in a nice, respectable activity like reading a book. And then, maybe you suspect I feel slighted by the fact that the noise level in the background almost drowned out the sound of my knocking.

Well, let me let you in on a secret. *Shabbos* isn't a very selective guest. She's visiting my abode too, and I'm also trying to get my culinary act together. The way I look at it, it's have the mess now or have the mess later. And I prefer now, although I must admit, sometimes it's both. There's no magic formula I know that creates delicacies without creating dirty bowls, cluttered sinks, and mounds of peels. And I have yet to see a happy toddler who looks like Prince Lord Perfectdale.

So if it's any normal mother of children at the door, she's taking great comfort in the familiar sights and sounds of a live and kicking household. She's heaving a mental sigh of relief that glasses break even in the best of homes, and the stapler gets misplaced, and the kids line up the chairs to play train right in the middle of the kitchen where the soup may have just boiled over. And no, apparently the children in this house, like in hers, do not take out only one toy at a time despite repeated admonitions to the contrary. You've just made her day, so please, don't be sorry.

In the event that it's your newly married neighbor knocking, the one who still keeps a doily on her table and microwave when they're not in use, which is presumably more often than not, well then I'll concur, she may be doubting your managerial capabilities. She may be smugly doing a mental edit on the scene in front of her, as her mind's eye pictures herself as the mother.

So as I said, you may be feeling sorry for yourself, but don't you utter one word of apology to your visitor. She's reveling in the fond illusion of her own housekeeping prowess, so you needn't feel the slightest regret. What bigger pleasure can you have brought to a member of the human race, especially one new to the married ranks, than affording her the sentiment that she's one up? And besides, ten years down the line, on some hectic Thursday afternoon when she's wondering whatever happened to her standards of old, perhaps she'll remember your unapologetic welcome and she'll take consolation.

If it's a male, your uninvited guest, a married one to be exact, you've really hit the jackpot. Promoting familial harmony is one of the greatest feats, and here it is, literally knocking at your door. It's a no-lose situation.

Assuming his wife is a woman with some tolerance, ambition, and a few children, or a full-time job, then without entering their abode, I'll put my stakes on the probability that, add or take away a pot or a briefcase, your house is a familiar sight. If he's been wondering aloud as of late, how other homes run, if the coats get flung on the floor, and whether supper isn't always on the table on time, then lingering in your front entrance while you sign the receipt book, or call someone to fetch the drill, has given him his answer.

And *if*, by some stroke of rare fortune, his wife inhabits the scantily populated realm of superwomen; if in his home the food's neatly packaged in containers by the time he steps through the door, the kids are bouncing in their pajamas freshly bathed, his supper's set out on a place mat with a napkin gracefully twisted in a sparkling glass (no disposable for him, oh no!), and his wife has only tales of gladness to regale his soul, then visiting your home will earn his better half a sincere compliment. A tribute for which, she'll never know, you get the commission.

So, no, don't you tamper with your reward for any of the above by offering a flimsy attempt at inferring that this fateful moment in time happens to be the one exception to the norm, which is, of course, perfect order. Chances are, your visitor won't believe you. And you'll have forfeited your opportunity to assuage someone's ego.

Next time that apology springs unbidden to your lips, tuck it under your tongue and save it for the people closest to your heart, for the times you truly hurt someone's feelings.

And as for your own wounded ego, if that's what you had in mind in the first place, perhaps it would help to tack a reminder in some conspicuous spot: "The housewife who makes no mess does not usually make anything."

Sold!

It started innocently enough, the way these things tend to begin. When the doorbell rang on an ordinary Monday morning, I had no reason to suspect that it was anybody other than my next-door neighbor borrowing a cup of sugar or returning three eggs. "Just a minute," I called breezily, as I lowered the volume on the stereo, and hurried to open the door.

That was mistake number one. It always is. Somehow I never remember about the peephole rule until I am squarely facing some odd character at my doorstep.

This time the man was short and stocky, his facial veins bulging with exertion, as he heaved a rolled-up carpet to its full height, and propped it against the wall so that it was leaning on the doorframe. If I had harbored intentions of closing the door, it wasn't a feasible option any more.

"Carpet, *Giveret*," he announced.

"You must have the wrong address," I informed him. "We haven't ordered any carpet. I'm sorry."

The fellow, though, seemed unperturbed, and made no sign of budging either himself or his carpet even an inch.

"These are Oriental carpets, *Giveret*, made of the finest quality English wool. I'm selling them at rock-bottom prices. It's a real one-time opportunity. Compare them at any store. You'll never beat the price."

"How much are you selling it for?" I asked.

That was mistake number two. As soon as the words were out of my mouth, I would have done anything to take them back. What I should have said is, "No, I'm not interested." Period. No questions, no explanations, no apologies. I didn't *need* a carpet. I didn't *want* a carpet. I had never harbored even the remotest thought of buying one.

But like the peephole rule, my logic came lagging in a little late. What I could have and should have said were things of the past. My carpet vendor had this gleam in his eye, and I could tell that as far as he was concerned, the carpet was as good as sold. He began unrolling the prize, assuring me all the while.

"These usually go for 800, but for you, *Giveret*, I'll give it to you for 400."

I almost asked him if he meant *shekels* or dollars, but I bit my tongue. There I was, going for the bait again. Say *I'm not interested*, my mind commanded, but I just didn't have the heart to interrupt the fellow's enthusiastic wishes for mine and my husband's continued health and happiness, and the prosperity of our family forever after.

The carpet was now unfurled in all its glory, and I almost leapt for joy. It was a paisley design colored in the brown and gold family, an obvious clash to the mauve upholstery on my dining-room chairs. Anybody, even the most enthusiastic Sephardic carpet merchant, could see that the carpet would be an eyesore in my dining room.

I quickly grabbed at the excuse. "It's really beautiful," I complimented, running my hand over the soft wool, "and the price does seem very reasonable. But it doesn't match the room."

For a moment, the carpet vendor wavered, as he made a lame attempt to convince me that brown was a neutral color, and why, what color were my dining-room chairs? I was not about to lose my turn a second time. I firmly reiterated that I simply would not consider brown in my dining room.

That was strike three, although I didn't know it at the time. For the time being I was off the hook, liberated, and I was smug with relief, as I offered my apologies and wished the fellow success with his sales.

It was only a week later, the incident completely forgotten, that I was made to face the grave consequences of my gracious dismissal. Again, it was an ordinary ring of the doorbell, and again, I had the door opened before I remembered to check the peephole. My heart dropped when I recognized my visitor: same face, same voice, same carpet.

"This time I got one just for you, *Giveret*. I had the factory custom make it in shades of mauve and pink especially for your dining room."

There he was, heaving the roll into my front hall, beaming with pride, heading straight for my dining room. I stood there, twisting the dishtowel in my hand, fumbling for something, anything, to say that would get the fellow and his carpet out of my house.

"I don't have any money, sir," was the first thing I thought of. I knew it wasn't very good, but it was better than "I'll have to think about it," which I knew would prompt a replay of the scene on yet another innocent Monday morning.

"Oh, that's no problem, *Giveret*. Check, Visa, I'll take anything. I usually prefer cash, but for you, *Giveret*, you deserve this carpet. It was made for your dining room."

"We don't write checks, and I don't have a Visa card either." I was desperate. He was too busy flattening the carpet on my dining-room floor to respond, though.

"If you want, you can leave it here as a present," I joked feebly.

"Hm, *Giveret*, I've never done that before, but with such a beautiful carpet that blends in so perfectly, you know what? I'll leave it here. I know I can trust you. I'll come in two or three days for the money."

I wanted to ask him how he knew he could trust me, when I couldn't even trust myself to keep a stranger out of my own home, but I kept quiet. I was too frantic pumping my mind for some way out of my predicament.

Why does this always happen to me? I moaned inwardly. I was willing to bet that this guy hadn't managed to get his carpet even one tile past any of my neighbors' doorsteps. They must be in cahoots, I decided, this man, and that lady who came around with cosmetics last month, and the towel peddler who wheedled me into buying a set of bath sheets *Erev Pesach*.

They must just know that the lady on the third floor of the corner house is easy prey. No wonder they were all so willing to halve their prices "just for you." After all, how many customers did they come across who fell for their bait, hook, line, and sinker?

The guy was sweating at the temples, pushing and tugging, trying to slide the carpet into place beneath my dining-room table and chairs. In a brief moment of weakness, I even managed to glance down and admire the rich aura that the tapestry lent to the room. And in the split second it took me to recover my wits, the man was off the floor and hustling through the doorway, telling me he'd be back, and that I, *Giveret*, should enjoy the purchase in good health.

Well, well. I'd always secretly prided myself on my inability to say no. Although I referred to it as a weak point, frankly, I liked to think of my tender side as a sort of noble trait inherited all the way down from Avraham Avinu.

I was the sort who always bought a cup of lemonade at the 8-year-olds' makeshift lemonade stand, and who couldn't turn a raffle book down, even if it was the fifteenth one in the span of an hour. Not that I particularly liked lemonade, or that I ever won a raffle. I just found it too difficult to diffuse the eager optimism on those children's faces with adult pragmatism.

It wasn't only children, mind you, either. Over the years, I had collected an impressive assortment of tapes, books, wall hangings, and ointments, that had one thing in common. They served absolutely no purpose in my home, other than the sole role of reminding me of my virtuous weak point.

My indulgence had never taken me this far, though. To humor someone on a blustery winter day, and buy a tube of hand cream, was one thing. To watch your dining room undergo a metamorphosis in front of your eyes, while you stood by in passive silence, was quite another story. Not a very admirable one, either.

Being nice did have a limit. There were other people in my life whose feelings took precedence over this total stranger's. Like my husband, who would have to handle the embarrassing job of getting me out of the pickle.

It suddenly struck me as it had never hit me before. One needs to know how to keep the door shut. One needs to learn how to say, "No, I'm not interested." Absolutely and unequivocally. Not always were pleasantry and generosity the compass by which one's moral standards were to be determined in times of doubt and uncertainty.

Yiddishkeit definitely called for a staunch stand at times; a stand in which one didn't violate one of the three cardinal rules: Don't open the door. Don't ask questions. And if you've trespassed the first two, then number three may save you in the nick of time. Don't offer reasons or excuses.

The *yetzer hara* is a pro at making housecalls to unsuspecting customers like me. He knocks at the door selling a variety of wares in the form of practical suggestions, and attractive offers. And if we're not wise enough to look through the peephole and identify him at first glance, then we risk falling for the bait.

Once he's engaged us in discussion, he's won half the battle. At that point, our only hope is to retreat and say three words: "I'm not interested." If the *yetzer hara* starts again with his sales pitch, we've just got to stick to that boring assertive, no-nonsense refrain for as long as it takes him to back off and look for a better address.

It took the carpet incident to teach me the third inviolable rule. Don't, by any means, offer any reason or excuse for your flat refusal. Don't let him in on your rationale, because he'll come up with a hundred and one plausible counterarguments to prove you wrong. Tell him the carpet doesn't match, and before you know it, he'll be hauling a perfect match straight into your dining room.

That's how it is with these fellows. They're trained to do their job well. And we've got to do ours. So I'm learning how to say, "No, I'm not interested." Slowly. But that's okay. After all, it takes time to get rid of the dust that's been swept beneath the carpet for so many years.

Living Disability

re you suffering from the following symptoms? You may be afflicted by a recently diagnosed disorder estimated to plague a large percentage of society, with females being particularly affected. While the symptoms range, and may affect the male sector with a completely different set of manifestations, the following description will be focusing upon the disorder as it influences the female gender. Studies have shown a sharp rise in the prevalence of symptoms at this time of year, and experts hypothesize that the widespread "pre-Pesach fever" is somehow playing an important role in the swelling numbers.

"Chametz on the ceiling?"
There was sheer frustration in his voice
And from the heights of the ladder
And the depths of my haggardness,
I mumbled tiredly,
"Part of the pre-*Pesach* protocol."

I was scrubbing the light fixture,
My schedule in shambles,
bedtime routines
severely curtailed,
the basics just about clinging together
with the fragile pins of the family's forbearance.
Pesach is *Pesach*.
No shortcuts.
No nonsense.
How?
Why?
When?
These questions lose their validity,
In the sheer urgency of the race.
Schedule?
Bedtime?
Proper meals?
They've just got to find their place
somewhere
between the silver and the windows.
Extras
say— like bedtime lullabies

and leisurely outings —
Must fall away
In the face of the basics,
like organizing the albums
and washing the curtains.
That's *Pesach*.

But just the other day
I was pacing my kitchen
opening my pantry,
perusing the refrigerator —
searching the cabinets —
agitated.
Looking for something,
but not quite knowing what.
Until it dawned,
something I'd heard in the distant past —
a thought I'd once come across
Suddenly flickered vaguely in my consciousness.

"When you're plagued by an inner need
to replenish,
to fill up,
to be satisfied,
When you're hot in search
of some elusive something
to still some indefinable craving,
that need isn't hunger.
It's something a lot deeper,
a stirring of the soul,
searching for inspiration
an expression of the spirit,
seeking true sustenance."

Don't quiet those pangs
with a slice of cake.
Don't silence those pleas with a bag of potato chips,
or leftover dessert.
Lest your *neshamah* retreat,
into the far-off distance,
invisible,
faint,
like the ring of a cordless phone,
beneath a pile of laundry.

What about my cleaning craze,
my drive for perfection,
hands raw from ammonia and bleach?
From whence come the ambition,
the adrenaline,
the perseverance
for this draining pursuit?
Perhaps the phone's been off the base,
for too long,
Perhaps I can't hear it
ringing any longer,
Perhaps my *neshamah*'s been begging
for reform
A drastic overhauling,
some real honest scrubbing and stripping
whitening and washing,
And I've been fool enough
to exchange all that
for a bunch of
physical work.
And shallow enough to think
I was feeling fulfilled.
Not *davening* —

Because the curtains had to be washed,
Dishing out the minimum
Of T.L.C.
and plenty of the opposite (Tense Loud Criticism),
in the name of order.
Did I say order?
I guess I'd change that to
DISorder,
I've been living disabled.

Integrated Math I

With all due respect,
for well-honed intellect,
for accuracy,
exactitude,
and mathematical aptitude;
with all the rightful regard
for abstract science,
for intellectual defiance,
for the importance,
the practical use
of proving an angle acute
or obtuse,

I find the system faulty,
hazardous in fact
when applied
to the delicate act
of living.
With no intent of treason
to the higher schools
of logic and reason,
I find I often
learn,
everyday events,
to the point of
paralysis,
spurn,
good sense
for incisive analysis,
Wield logic's knife
Upon facts of life,
Husband and wife,
Crisis and strife,
in my persistent,
resistant,
obsessive,
depressive,
all-destructive,
counterproductive,
horribly gnawing,
conclusion drawing,
quest
to figure out,
Why?
Why am I so tired?
So lazy
So fat?

Why am I this
The other
And that?
Why is my child
So wild?
My papers
not filed?
the bathroom, untiled?
Why is it so noisy,
So dirty,
So late?
Why am I at 30
stumped by tantrums
He's still throwing,
(But why?)
At the age of 8?
Why's the bill missing,
The kettle not hissing,
The 2-year-old biting
The boys always fighting?
Why, why, why,
The brutal
Futile
Tormenting
Unrelenting
Attempt to prove,
Remove,
over and out,
the self-imposed doubt,
regarding
the fact named I.

With all due respect
For geometrical designs,

Like triangles
And lines
Whose proofs
are conclusive,
nonelusive,
the inner confines
of human designs,
are far too tangled
multiangled
exquisitely spangled,
to explain
with theorems
and postulates.
Every person
is a bottom line
Given,
G-d given,
Whose behavior
Ought to be driven,
Not by abstract theory,
But the very real query,
"How?"
This
Or that actuality,
Being a reality,
How can I change
Rearrange,
Effect, direct, inject
Pursue, undo,
Uncover a clue,
not reasons
To explain mortal ailings,
proofs
To support

Our human failings,
But for ways, means
To inspire our desire,
To reshape
Our soulscape,
Spiritual logic
Is not about
learning
To prove,
But about learning,
burning,
yearning
to
*Im*prove.

Self-Service

I'm not what you'd call the life of the party. In fact, I'm not usually *at* the party to begin with.

"Don't you want to come?" friends will cajole, "You know, just to get out a little?"

"Yeah, maybe, I'll see," I reply vaguely, trying to inject some glimmer of eagerness into my tone.

It's no use. My ambivalence goes about as undetected as a mouthful of stolen cookies behind a guilty smile. I may as well come out and say it; there is no hope I will be at that party.

I hate to sound like an incurable hermit, I really do. It's just that after a full day of chasing the ball, my modest idea of entertainment is to finally clasp it within my arms, firm and round and still, against my racing heart.

Though it never really works out quite that still, evening is the closest I ever get to reaching that elusive finish line. It's the only time I ever get to grasp that slippery ribbon and tie a knot, albeit a very temporary one, on the parcel of my existence. And when those few, fragile hours finally settle upon my household, I like to be there to enjoy them.

So parties are definitely not my cup of tea.

Sometimes, however, you just can't refuse. When all your friends are volunteering to sell tickets, when all your neighbors are offering to make miniatures and to recruit sponsors, the least you can pledge is your unswerving commitment to attend the affair. So I did.

Maybe I'll even enjoy it, I mused skeptically, as I studied the two-page spread announcing the auction. Unprecedented selection of items! Mouthwatering refreshments! Separate *milchige* bar! Split the pot! Renowned graphologist on the premises!

The last splash finally kindled some excitement. I was as much a raffle winner as I was a party-goer, and I could think of some easier ways to procure a cheese Danish than spending your night at a party. But a graphologist on the premises, *that* held allure.

Apparently, I wasn't the only one who thought so. From the lines snaking out of the graphology booth, it seemed I'd have to wait at least an hour if I wanted to get a reading. The booth was even more crowded than the beckoning reception tables at the center of the hall. Impressive.

I parked myself at the back of the line.

There was an excited babble permeating the crowd, as people clutched the samplings they had brought along to present. It was amusing to behold a bunch of adults infused with the nervous restlessness of fifth graders waiting to hear their parts in the school play.

"She's printing out the assessments on her laptop!" I heard a plump woman report, in rapid Hebrew.

A slight, fair woman in a pinstripe blouse and navy skirt walked slowly out of the booth, eyes swiveling back and forth like twin cursors over a printed page. A faint smile shaded her features as she halted unwittingly in her tracks to better concentrate on what she was reading. She seemed pleased.

The line inched forward ever so imperceptibly.

"Look around," a broad-shouldered woman ahead of me complained. "Everyone seems delighted with their results."

She sounded downright disappointed.

"The whole thing is a farce," she continued. "That's not what I'm waiting on line to hear, flattery."

"What are you waiting to hear?" the woman behind her challenged in innocent wonder.

"I want an honest evaluation," the first woman replied. Her tone was just a decibel short of impatience. "A graphologist is supposed to help you see your blind spot, the part of you that your one-sided perspective conceals."

"Ah," answered the other woman, her response saying she had understood, her perplexed expression confirming quite the opposite. If she had wanted an ego booster, she wasn't going to let on to this imposing woman who thought it so disdainful.

The broad woman, dressed in a dusty green suit, pulled out the two sheets of paper she had brought along and held them at arm's distance. I tried to get a glimpse of her drawing.

"Excuse me," a charming brunette, pocketbook slung over her shoulder, tapped me lightly. "Do you mind if I get ahead of you? I was further down the line before, but I left my place for a few minutes so I could put in some bids for the auction."

"Fine," I answered distractedly. I don't think I even heard her lengthy explanation. I was busy craning to see the elusive paper a yard down.

"Do you mind —" I heard her lilting voice weaving in and out of my consciousness, as she approached the next few women on line.

My attention was riveted to the drawing. It looked like a sketch of a rowboat on a lake.

"Excuse me, do you mind —"

"I actually do mind," asserted Mrs. Green Suit.

The brunette looked slightly shocked. She hadn't anticipated a snag. Neither had I.

"I mean, we've all come to put in bids, and we're all waiting our turns on this line. What makes you think you deserve preferential treatment?"

The smiling woman stood there for a moment, unnerved.

"Can't you be understanding?" an indignant woman came to the brunette's defense. "Maybe she has some emergency at home."

The defendant looked exonerated.

"Nobody forced her to come to this auction," Mrs. Green Suit muttered.

The rowboat fluttered to the floor, and some quick hands stooped to retrieve it, grateful for the diversion.

"Yes," chimed in someone from the jury, "if she was pressed for time, she could have skipped this booth. It isn't fair to inconvenience everyone else."

I stood at the sidelines, faintly amused, as the seething cluster moved forward into the space that had cleared. The incriminations were turning sharp. So were the rejoinders. To think that these women had been keening for an honest analysis of their faults just moments ago.

Talk about blind spots.

We all have them, individually and collectively. And if there ever was a scene that staged the satire for the collective variety, it was this clash in front of the graphologist's booth.

Self-awareness. It's the religion of this century, the order of the times. You've got to get to know yourself.

You've got to be aware of your ins and outs, your faults and virtues. You have to know if you are a thinking type or a feeling type, if you are an introverted sensory, or an extroverted intuitive. It's the only way to improve, the only way to be a parent, a spouse, a person, in this enlightened generation.

And if you need help figuring yourself out, there are tools. There are self-checking questionnaires and there are awareness groups. There are Rorschach blots and emotional IQ tests. And there are graphologists.

Apparently, we all want to know the truth. The truth, the whole truth, and nothing but the truth.

Not from just anybody, though.

Not from our spouses, our parents, our neighbors. No, thank you. Not from our colleagues, our employers, our children.

Definitely not from our in-laws.

There's a halo of novelty that surrounds anything related to psychology; an aura of sophistication and enlightenment that throws an iridescent light on introspection and analysis. As long as it's solicited, it's fine.

Just don't give me any criticism. Don't give me your opinion, your blame, your unbidden advice. Don't even insinuate that I'm being inconsiderate, unrealistic, irritable, petty, cold.

Sorry. Plain old *mussar* is out of business.

And it's a shame. Because it still is the most honest reflection of where we stand.

We don't even have to wait on line. All we have to do is listen, tune in to the feedback we are getting from those closest to us. All we have to do is perk up our antennas to the vibes around us, to the messages we are receiving, and swallow that immediate impulse to come to our own defense.

There is no graphologist who can zero in on our blind spot like the people around us. There is no analysis that can point out our rigidity, our inconsistency, our overbearing tendencies like the unadorned assessments of our spouses, our children, our relatives, and friends. There is no one who can highlight our impatience, our indecisiveness, our irresponsibility like the clerk in the post office, the taxi driver, the saleswoman in the store.

All we need is courage and candor and commitment. Courage to put our insecurities aside, candor to admit to our fallacies, and commitment to improve. And then we need the big C, creativity. We need to be able to blot out the setting, the roiling emotions, the person in front of us, and see those offensive accusations shrink into an objective printout on a crisp sheet of paper.

Criticism is never pleasant, but graphology is fun. So let's take up the art. It's all a matter of how we read the script.

Tooth Rush

Yesterday,
    You couldn't talk to me,
    I must have appeared
    Weird.
    Cheeks sucked inward,
    Eyes squinted
    Mouth puckered
    Into a whining,
    Whistling
    Little hole.

But I

Was oblivious,
Sucked away
In a vacuum of pain,
It was
Like chewing aluminum foil,
On a fresh filling,
Like spraying cold air,
On an exposed nerve.
No, worse,
It was a shooting,
Throbbing,
Breathtaking,
Pain.
Stinging,
Wringing,
Agony,
Drilling tunnels
Down into my jaw,
Radiating
All the way
Out to my ears,
All the way
Up to my eyes,
Nothing,
Not even Advil,
Helped

By late afternoon,
I was desperate,
Jabbed the buttons,
On the telephone,
Listened to music
While I held,
Waited

For an appointment,
How about
next Monday
10:30?
Oooooooh,
Isn't there anything
Sooner?
Hmm,
How about
Tomorrow morning
At 10?
Yes, tomorrow morning
At 10,
Should we call
To remind you?
You won't *have* to
Call
To remind me.

That was yesterday.
Eons ago.
Planets away.
This morning
The sun tickled me
On my face,
Woke me up,
Singing,
I got busy,
Filling bottles,
Finding shoes,
Frying eggs,
Served, scribbled, signed,
Curled, combed, kissed,

Silence.
For a split second.

Then,
Flapping linens
The swish of laundry,
Running water
The clatter of bowls,
All but forgotten
Anything of teeth,
Of pain.
Of holes,

Ten o'clock came
And went.
Without advent.
The dentist's office
A wispy memory,
A blurry dream,
As far away as
Yesterday's pain.

10:05,
A benign ring,
Jarring
Marring
The tranquility,
You've got an appointment,
Ma'am.

But,
But,
I've got plans for this morning,
Things to do,

To write,
To care,
Who has an hour
To spare
In the dentist's chair?

Didn't you say
It was an emergency?
I did.
It was.
Yesterday,

When I couldn't think
Blink
Drink
When pain pushed me to the brink,
Made me utter
A hasty vow,

The pain's gone,
Now.

Sorry, Ma'am
Really am,
But
You've got to keep
Your appointment
Today,
Or pay
The cancellation
Fee.

I went
Paid every cent,

Came home utterly spent,
Still, I felt like a queen
With my crown,
Master, sovereign,
I had acted on pain,
Gotten to the core
When it hurt
No more.

Not that I
Ever
Would have gone
To fill
A tooth
Of my own free will.
Not that I
Ever
Would have found
The time to spend
The money to pay
One sunny day,
If I hadn't made
An appointment
Right away.

If we don't
Get to the root,
While the pain is acute,
Make that appointment,
Have a secretary write it
Down.
Chances are slim,
Grim
That we'll ever

End up
With a crown.

Optical Delusion

I remember the card my mother gave me on my 10th birthday. It had two yellow daffodils on the outside, nestled against a background of dark greenery, ferns perhaps. On second thought, it was something softer, blurrier, less distinct. It was a lot like my mother, the card, cheerful, alive, and warm in an unpretentious way.

Inside there was a simple *Happy Birthday* inscribed, with plenty of room for personal wishes. I've always preferred cards like those. Messages like "There's no daughter like you" or "You are the sunshine in my life" should be written in a mother's, any mother's, neat handwriting or sloppy scrawl. Reading them in Hallmark's professional calligraphy is something akin to getting a hug delivered by a robot.

"Ten years old?" my mother wrote, *"It seems like just yesterday that I held you in my arms for the first time, tiny and adorable ..."*

The rest of the two sides were filled with love and hopes and wishes, but I remember pondering those first few words. Just yesterday? Did my mother really mean that?

Ten years, to me, epitomized the concept of a long time. I had been a baby; I had learned to walk; I had graduated pre-1a, learned to read and write, add and subtract. In my long life, I had undergone a series of hair-styles from a short pixie to pigtails, a ponytail, and finally, a sophisticated pageboy. And at 10, I already had five siblings younger than I was.

It must be the way mothers write, I concluded, a poetic expression of fondness.

Well, I've come to question my conclusion since. Time has a way of turning babies into teenagers and young brides into grandmothers while they are busy just trying to put their lives in order. The clock has the most innocuous way of sending people off on errands, making money, spending it, anything really, to keep them distracted while they are involuntarily being propelled upward on the ladder of age.

No one notices the growth in his own garden. Hard as one may stare, one never gets to see the baby putting on the ounces that turn into pounds, never does get a glimpse of hair inching out of the follicles, or wrinkles suddenly appearing the way they do in the bath, at the onset of any particular birthday. It all happens ever so gradually, ever so subtly, deceptively blurring the borders of stark transformation.

So it hits me most when I return home. Leaving your hometown is like inserting a pin into the unfurling ribbon of time. You come back and you look for your contemporaries, neighbors and acquaintances, relatives and friends, right where you pinned them, somewhere close to the beginning of the strip, and there are new people, strangers, taking their place.

You look a little closer and you recognize those imposters as your students, your campers, your nieces and nephews and baby cousins who have suddenly become teachers and parents, uncles and aunts. You meet young women pushing baby strollers and you half expect them to be your mother's friends, see the store owner you remember, still sporting a pitch-black beard, and never even harbor the thought that it might be his son.

It takes some time until you realize that the pin you had stuck in for reference has slowly and steadily advanced in your absence, shifting everyone's status, including your own.

Which is not always a very, shall we say, comfortable, revelation.

Sitting around the table at a recent Bar Mitzvah, I found myself discussing current Jewish literature with a young aunt of mine, the youngest one in fact, who's always been up to par with the press.

"I'll tell you the truth, Malky, I don't read much lately."

My eyebrows must have expressed what I was thinking. This aunt of mine and me, we'd always shared a secret rapport, namely the love affair we had with words.

I didn't even bother asking her if it was her busy schedule that precluded her from picking up a book. A fellow addict, I believed that a bookworm who didn't have time to read was about as likely as a chocoholic who couldn't find time for a chocolate bar.

"Believe it or not," she was quick to explain, "it's my eyes. At first it really didn't affect me, but you know, it's wearing me down, reading with a book at arm's distance."

Oh. I looked at her again, my youngest aunt, and I almost felt an invisible belt move under our feet. There. We'd both been transferred to a respectable new spot on the ribbon.

Still, I didn't understand. "Chedva, why do you have to hold the paper at arm's distance?"

She looked at me strangely.

"Time doesn't sit still, you know. You can stand up for me; I'm joining the club." She chuckled an attempt at lightheartedness.

Yes, yes, I nodded. I had understood. And I hated to press her, but I had apparently missed something.

"Why don't you wear reading glasses?" I dared the simple question.

"Reading glasses?" The words shot out of her with an unwitting shudder, "You've got to be kidding! I want to stay young."

You've got to be kidding, I thought in amusement. Kidding yourself. But I didn't say a word.

There's no sense rubbing a sore point, even if from your vantage point you can't appreciate the tenderness. So until I owned a pair of bifocals myself, I wouldn't even attempt to challenge her logic.

In the privacy of my own heart, however, I couldn't help smiling. As if not getting glasses would in any way alter the inescapable fact, as if not wearing them reflected that she didn't have use for them.

Here was a person who'd been addicted to the written word. Anything in print, from shampoo bottles to solicitation letters, had been virtual food on which to feast. Neither deadlines nor tiredness had stopped her from devouring paragraphs, slurping stanzas, snitching pages. And all at once, she had encountered an obstacle serious enough to hamper her relentless pursuit. She had come up against a roadblock, an encumbrance larger than nature: the denial of it.

A simple pair of glasses would have instantly renewed her membership to the reading ranks. But getting them would mean, in her lingo, voluntarily signing herself into a club she didn't quite feel ripe to join. Wearing those obtrusive magnifying lenses would be conceding, passively putting out the white flag without putting up a fight.

As long as she didn't sport those glasses, there was still some glimmer of hope that she would remain perpetually young; after all, as long as there was no solution on the horizon, there couldn't possibly be a problem. Solutions always came hot on the heels of problems, didn't they?

Well, they either did or didn't. But if they didn't, that left you with only the problem.

No one's difficulties were ever solved by wishing them out of existence. No challenge, physical, financial, or emotional, was ever alleviated by making believe it didn't warrant help.

No one likes to make waves, especially on his own peaceful turf. *Don't tell me about problems*, we like to think unreasonably, *just let things ride and I'll be fine.* In our desperate pursuit of harmony, we fail to realize that waves are inherent to the ocean. We don't *create* them, they are there; we either go under them or over them.

And going over them means getting glasses. Or advice. Or help. Riding the tidal storms of life means admitting when we don't see, or our children don't see, and seeking out the prescription we need.

Turning a blind eye to one's problems is the worst form of visual impairment. In this world of vanity and falsehood, we may look better without the bifocals. We may even be able to fool everybody pretty successfully. Everybody, but our own selves.

So if you're reading this at arm's distance, get those glasses. They aren't a sign of growing old; they're a sign of growing up.

Paid Waiting

I always find amusement in the mixed volley of messages and cryptic comments crackled over the Israeli driver's radio. It's a combination of boredom and camaraderie that inspires the tone in these radio conversations between drivers, and the sum contents of them amounts to a large number of good-natured gibing, some sincere empathy peppered with advice, and not a negligible percent of just plain gibberish.

And since my taxi excursions are usually about five minutes long, too short to begin any serious introspection, yet too long to keep my mind idle, I usually find myself listening to the exchange going on. I must admit, I would probably do better with a pocket-size *Tehillim* in my purse, but then last week I did overhear a line that has become a meaningful motto for me.

We were waiting for a light to turn green, the driver impatiently tapping a tune on the window, when another driver barked his short-tempered litany into the transceiver, addressed to "whomever it may concern."

"I'm waiting at 41 Rechov Yerushalayim for almost five minutes, honking my horn. I'm just about to pull away when the lady shows up, dumps a shopping bag on the seat, and tells me she'll be back in two minutes with the rest. What does she think, I have all day?"

There was some static, and then came the indisputable response.

"*Mah habaayah? Tadlik moneh v'chakeh b'savlanut!*" (What's the problem? Set the taximeter, and wait patiently.)

In contrast to taxis that charge a set rate for all local calls, and whose drivers, therefore, bless a trip that takes the minimum amount of time, the Israeli driver's pay depends on the duration of the drive or, alternately, on the duration of the wait.

Theoretically then, it really should make no difference to a driver if he's careening around corners, wheels rolling toward his destination, or if he's sitting and smoking a cigarette, waiting for some woman to finish lugging her packages, and fold her stroller.

Theoretically. *Sabras*, though, tend to be temperamentally irate, and watching someone take her good old time, while they are sitting with their thumb on the horn, is wont to get the better of them, or rather, to bring out the worst in them. Sometimes they need a gentle reminder over the radio to "turn on the meter, and wait patiently."

Like all of us do.

How many times do we get stuck in the traffic of life; how many times are we forced to put up with a "passenger's" insensitivity, clumsiness, forgetfulness, and any other of the many far-from-pleasant character traits that plague humanity?

How many times do we make trips for nothing; how many times do we find ourselves honking until we're blue in the face, without receiving more than a noncommittal nod in response? And how often do we drive around on call after call, from the crack of dawn until midnight, without receiving as much as a peep of appreciation in return?

What we tend to do is get angry, impatient, frustrated, insulted, tense, anxious, and vengeful. What we ought to do is to keep one message crackling over our radio system.

"Mah habaayah? Tadlik moneh, v'chakeh b'savlanut."

After all, no one here is running an independent business. We're all employed by One Boss, driving for one cause. We're dispatched on calls throughout the day, and some go more smoothly than others.

But the meter is always ticking. Gauging our progress, calculating our rewards, doubling and tripling the roster of our personal earnings in terms of *kapparas avonos*. The trips that are the most winding and tiresome, the calls that test the threshold of our patience and tolerance, those are the "big trips," the kind that taxi drivers vie over.

When a colleague at work makes a joke at our expense, when the orange juice spills in the freshly cleaned refrigerator, when the repairman doesn't show up after a full morning of waiting, it's normal to get a little frazzled.

We're all human. It's tempting to retaliate with a cutting remark, to work ourselves into a frenzy, to rehash the utter unfairness or the ridiculous waste of time.

But then again, if we can contain ourselves long enough to keep our tongues in check and take our hands off the horn, we may be able to discern the faint sound of the meter ticking.

I've tried it. It really works. Forget the neighbor, spouse, child, student, boss, or in-law; let yourself disentangle from the messy kitchen, the provocative argument, the depressing flop, and watch those big, luminescent numbers rapidly switch, grow, rise in value. Those numbers are what count. Those digits are what sum up our productivity in this world and assess our profits in the world to come.

It's hard work, and it takes getting used to, but ever since I've been in that taxi, I've tried applying the principle: *"Tadlik moneh!"*

It pays — in full.

Relationships

Accounts Payable

*F*ree rides are an expensive proposition. What they don't cost in money, they cost in time and convenience. If you've ever tried hitching one, you know what I'm talking about.

Sure, you can come with us, but we don't know exactly when we're leaving.

Call in about fifteen minutes.

Oh, no, we aren't ready yet; we should leave within the hour.

We're leaving this minute; can you be waiting at the corner?

Sure, sure, anything. What don't you do for a free ride?

It isn't only rides. Try getting an opinion, an estimate, a tutorial session, gratis. Not a serious job, of course; just a quick look, a general idea, a few lines.

You may have a cousin who's a carpenter, a friend who's an editor, a neighbor who's a play therapist. They may be the nicest people with the best of intentions. They're also busy individuals, parents, jobholders, service people. They want to help you, they really do. You just won't get the same commitment a dollar will buy.

Money has binding power. Even $5 earns you consumer's rights, turns you from a beneficiary into a benefactor. It buys you your dignity, your sense of proprietorship, your independence. A pretty worthwhile deal, in my opinion.

Which is why I like to pay my way, thank you. Hire a baby-sitter rather than take advantage of a neighbor, call a repairman rather than rely on my nephew's good graces. Tell me what it cost, and I'll be happy to oblige.

Last week, when I needed to spend an afternoon in Tel Aviv, I put my policy into effect. The older girls were thrilled to spend their afternoon with friends, the boys would be in yeshivah. The younger clan posed the problem.

All my attempts to locate a responsible baby-sitter failed. The woman I generally use was out of town, and her daughters couldn't help me. Baby-sitters are a hard-to-come-by species all year round. With finals and state exams to study for, finding one was an impossible feat.

I was beginning to get really discouraged, when I suddenly remembered the baby-sitter in the next building. True, she usually worked morning hours, but I would explain the urgency of the situation.

And I would pay her, of course.

"Hm," she sounded hesitant. "How many children?"

"Three," I said, holding my breath, "But the two girls don't need much. They usually play together quite nicely."

I heard her uncertainty as she considered the proposition. There went her afternoon nap, her list of errands, her plans to do anything of consequence all Tuesday afternoon.

"I'll pay you, of course," I interjected quickly, trying to tip her deliberations in my favor, "whatever the going price is for afternoon hours."

"Tomorrow afternoon, until about 7, you say," she calculated out loud, disregarding my mention of remuneration.

I hung quietly on the line, nervously doodling threes all over an envelope, as she mentally fiddled with my request.

"O.K. I'll do it."

I exhaled with relief.

"But please don't tell anyone. I don't usually accept afternoon jobs."

"Of course," I gushed in compliance. At that point, she could have asked me to move a mountain.

At 7:30 the next evening, I stepped off the bus, tired, disoriented, checking my watch in disbelief. There is something about spending that hour between dusk and nightfall on a dark bus that makes you lose your sense of time. The little ones were usually fast asleep at this hour. It seemed like an eternity since I had left the lighted streets of Tel Aviv.

Squinting into the mirror plaque on the baby-sitter's door, I tried to smooth my disheveled appearance as I knocked. I listened to the sounds of running water and the patter of feet, then the turn of the lock, and a weary smile. Three little displaced persons were sitting in the front hall, washed and combed, waiting for their mother.

"There was terrible traffic on the way back," I apologized as I scooped up my bathed booty into a sweeping hug. "I can't thank you enough."

I fumbled for my wallet with my free hand and pulled out two bills, a hundred and then a fifty, which I handed to the baby-sitter.

"*Mah pit'om?*" she protested, sticking the fifty into the hood of the baby's stroller, "It's 100 *shekels*; not a penny more."

"But I told you I would pay the afternoon rate. I know what it means, working during off-hours."

"I don't *have* an afternoon rate," she countered emphatically. "I work for 7 *shekels* an hour, 6 for a third child, and that totals exactly 100 shekels."

"But I want to *pay* you for making the exception," I almost pleaded, as I handed back the fifty. The limp purple banknote fluttered to the floor.

"You're confusing two accounts," she told me with typical Israeli forthrightness. *"Choivos darf men tzulen; toivos darf men shuldig bleiben."* (Debts are meant to be paid; favors are meant to be owed.)

I looked at the bill on the floor, and considered leaving it there. Then her words penetrated, a minute late. I stooped to pick up the money, thanked her profusely, and freed her of my charges.

Tovos darf men shuldig bleiben. I chewed the sentence over in my mind. It didn't taste very appealing.

This lady, a woman whom I had never paid much more than a perfunctory nod when I passed her, had tended to my three children all afternoon. She had fed them and played with them and showered them clean. And all the while, I had felt completely at peace.

I wasn't taking any free rides. I had 150 *shekels* in my purse. A hundred for the job; 25 for the off-hours, and another 25 to wipe my ledger clean.

Flawless math; it was the accounting that had been faulty. Gratitude, the baby-sitter was telling me, was not about clean ledgers. It wasn't about 50 *shekels* either. It was the art of remaining beholden, of acknowledging that you were the recipient of a favor.

The hundred *shekels* were her due; debts had to be paid. For a measly 50 *shekels*, though, she wasn't ready to auction off the favor of having given me her entire afternoon. All she wanted was my genuine appreciation.

We all love being the benefactors. Paying empowers us, neutralizes the vulnerability of having to ask another human being for something. As long as we pay, we can tolerate someone scrubbing our stoves for us, ironing our shirts, making supper for our families.

Sometimes, though, circumstances force us to be the beneficiaries. "I'll pay," we offer benevolently, proffering the magic bills that we think will bail us out of indebtedness. Not always, however, are the things we need from others the stuff that money buys.

Sometimes, whether we like it or not, we've got to accept a free ride. Time and inconvenience, emotional and physical energy, embarrassment and anxiety aren't things that bills can gloss over. Even if we've paid the token $10, we might be getting a free ride. Knowing that is part of being human. And integral to being Jewish.

A Jew is beholden. Period. We owe our lives, and we owe our souls. We owe our health, and we owe our success. There is no currency that can pay for the gifts of strength and sanity, friends and family. Our existence is rooted in gratitude.

And gratitude isn't a thing. It isn't silver and it isn't silk; it isn't a present and it isn't a check. It isn't that uneasy feeling that we try to smother by sending elaborate gifts and arrangements.

It might be a card. Or a poem. A phone call. Or a letter. It might be a favor a few months down the line. Or a heartfelt *tefillah*. Gratitude is anything that blooms from the humble, heartwarming knowledge that someone else has done us a good turn.

Gratitude doesn't cost money. It's pride that costs.

So keep the difference.

You'll be a richer person for the change.

Broken Telephone

I confess. There are times I catch myself talking to myself. There are moments, when no one's around to question my sanity, that I let down my guard and simply engage in serious discussion with yours truly.

And I'm not ashamed to admit that I've come to some very enlightening solutions to some very challenging issues during these one-sided monologues held in the privacy of my kitchen or laundry room. Sometimes, talking to one's self, or thinking aloud, as the more self-respecting members of the club refer to it, can be surprisingly productive.

Still and all, that's not usually what I have in mind when I dial my sister's number overseas. When I am finally over the bath and bedtime hurdle, the second supper shift, and the homework hassle, I spend a moment just savoring the blessed peace and quiet that has descended upon my household. Then I grab for the cordless phone in the hope of tackling my supper dishes in the company of my sister abroad.

In my mind, all the day's events clamor for first place in the conversation, and as I hear the familiar ring, I'm already formulating the beginning of our chat. I can almost hear my sister's enthusiastic response to my description of the baby's latest antics, and I imagine her cluck-clucking in empathy as I recount my miserable attempt at shopping with my clan.

As the phone rings another couple of times, I continue to indulge in my imaginary dialogue. By the time I actually hear the slightly frazzled "Hello" on the other end, the words virtually pile out on their own.

"Hi, Chaya Rivky! Boy, am I glad you picked up! I'm waiting all day to talk to you. You can't imagine what an afternoon I've had—"

"Malky! Hi! How are you? *Uh oh, Ruchala, is that your aleph–beis sheet that Shimmy has in his mouth?*"

"Don't ask what possessed me to attempt a trip to the shoe store with a bunch of cranky kids."

"*Oy vey*, you tried going to the shoe store with all of them? *Dina, I said no going to the refrigerator without permission. What do you want? Orange juice? Milk? No, soda is for Shabbos.* What were you saying?"

"So I got onto the bus, I mean first I waited twenty minutes *until* the bus came."

"I don't believe it!"

"You're talking to me?"

"*Wow! You drew that yourself? I can't believe it! You colored that red and yellow umbrella all by yourself?!*"

"Hello??"

"Yeah, yeah, I'm so sorry, Dov Ber just walked in holding his masterpiece from kindergarten. So you were on the bus?"

"No, wait, I wasn't on the bus yet. As I'm standing there trying to fold the carriage with one hand, while my other hand is firmly holding Gitty so that she doesn't step off the curb, Tzippy remembered that she needed the bathroom."

"Oh no, after all that waiting. You must have been ready to give up and go home. *Oy*, one minute, that's Suri's van beeping. I'm so sorry, just hold on one minute. I'll get her and I'll be right back."

By the time my sister is back on the line, the realization is slowly setting in. Whether I like it or not, I've got to face the fact that I'm talking to myself at the princely cost of 13 cents a minute. As an added bonus for the same price, I'm connected to the cacophony of sounds that have accompanied me from dawn to dusk today. ("She took mine!" "He has a bigger one!" "Maaaaa!!")

Like I said, I'm open to the advantages of talking to myself. I also love listening to the lively collage of sounds that turn a house into a home. At this hour, however, I've had my fill for the day, and I'm valiantly trying to turn my *home* into a *house* again. And while I'm at it, picking up shoes, signing homework pads, and drying dishes, I'm itching for some satisfying, two-way adult dialogue.

What I've forgotten to take into account is the seven-hour time difference between us. While my watch is nearing 11, ushering some serenity into my domain, my sister's clock is striking 4, heralding hecticness at its height.

So I continue telling myself about my unsuccessful shopping trip, and regaling myself with my 3-year-old's latest witticisms, while she puts carrots into her food processor, instructs her cleaning lady, and breaks up a fight. When her 4-year-old drags the box of *Purim* costumes into the kitchen, we both know it's time to end the phone call.

"I'm so sorry, Malky. I see it's just not a time to talk. *Bli neder*, I'll call you when it quiets down around here."

That's scant comfort, and I know it. When the telephone breaks the early-morning silence at 5 to 7, Chaya Rivky's brood is blissfully asleep, and her kitchen has taken on a semblance of order. She wants my recipe for cupcakes, and my opinion about switching Ruchala's class.

It's still fairly quiet in my home, so I can carry on the conversation while I get breakfast ready. She starts telling me about a *shiur* she attended on the topic of priorities, and we're just about to plunge into an animated discussion when my little daughter shuffles into the kitchen to wash her hands. Talk about priorities!

"*Good morning, Tzippy! I love that smile on your face! Come, let's wash negel vasser.* Yeah, I'm listening."

"It's just so unbelievable the way we get so sidetracked by such unimportant trivia like —"

"*Yanky, wow! You're already taking off your pajamas. Here's your shirt. Let's see if you can get dressed before the timer rings.* What were you saying?"

"The speaker was really good. She gave such pertinent examples."

"Like? *Oh no, no stickers before everybody's dressed and ready.* You know what, Chaya Rivky, this is ridiculous. I know it's quiet on your end, and when it's 12:15 a.m. it's a little hard to envision your sister in the middle of the morning rush, but I'm afraid I'm gonna have to —"

"Mommy, Moishy's on the counter trying to take sugar!"

That ends all the niceties, as I cut my apology short and dump the cordless onto the bed.

When am I ever going to get to have a decent conversation with my sister? And it isn't only her. It's my mother, who's always either teaching or supermarket-shopping whenever my kids happen to be miraculously not fighting or in need of my supervision.

Or me, who's in the middle of baths when my mother's got twenty minutes to shmooze before she's off to some appointment. And it's Rochel, my friend since third grade, with whom the telephone is my sole connection. When I finally indulge and call Rochel, our exchange usually sounds something like this:

"Hi, Rochel! How *are* you?"

And Rochel, good, old, natural Rochel, hisses something into the receiver, which I construe to mean "My boss is in the office now."

"Oh, so you can't talk."

"Uh hu."

"Oh, I'm so disappointed! So when should I call you?"

"Right, uh hu."

"Okay, I get the picture. You really can't talk. Call me whenever you can."

Whenever she can, of course, is either 6 o'clock Thursday evening or when I happen to be out, or sleeping.

No one is to blame, of course. It's just part of the difficulty of being situated at opposite ends of the globe. When it's pitch dark outside, and all you hear is the even breathing of your sleeping angels, it's a little hard to imagine your friends running their errands, or your mother serving supper. ("Which person with any consideration calls a busy household smack in the middle of supper hour? Don't they know it's not a time to talk on the telephone?")

And when you're coaxing your charges to get their pajamas off please, on a lazy Sunday morning, it takes some imagination to realize that the mothers on the other end of the ocean are requesting that the pajamas go *on*.

It isn't just a matter of adding or subtracting the seven hours. It requires some more advanced arithmetic like taking all the factors into account, and figuring if the person you're about to phone will be as available to talk as you are.

And as I'm coming to realize, it's a skill that isn't solely confined to trans-Atlantic phone calls. Channeling into the next person's zone is really an integral part of the art of communication

It may not be a time zone that separates two people. It may be an age zone, a stage zone, or a circumstance zone, but there are always facts of life that make your friends' needs, preferences, and schedules different from yours.

And like with the overseas phone call, it would be so helpful if we'd make some calculations before we launch into conversation with whomever it may be. What zone is he or she in right now? What challenges is she dealing with? What does the *other* person want to talk about, or perhaps he prefers not to talk at all?

He or she may live next door to you, or even in your very own house, but the fact that she is single or elderly, tired or disappointed, may take some extra sensitivity on your part. Tapping into the other person's range of interests, and pinpointing the right time to say the right thing is all part of the challenge.

So next time you want to engage in conversation, *do* talk to yourself first. Otherwise, you may just encounter a broken telephone.

Health Warning!

Our local dental clinic is situated about thirty yards from the neighborhood grocery, but you would never know. The minute you walk out of there, it seems, you forget the bold poster that has silently admonished you while you waited in trepidation for the dentist to tackle your cavities.

All those pictures of fruits and vegetables and nuts are fine for the dentist's office, but a quick survey of the display near the grocery checkout counter will give you a fair idea of the most popular items sold: coated wafers, nougat rolls, gumballs, lollies and assorted jellies in the most outrageous colors and shapes. For those willing to spend a bit more, there's an array of powdered doughnuts and heavily glazed Danishes.

It's hard enough for a grown adult to pass by these temptations; approaching that counter with a child is an activity doomed to one of two failures. Either the child walks out stomping and grumbling, lagging behind a tight-lipped mother feigning indifference, or else he or she is happily munching, chewing, or at least gleefully clutching something to munch or chew on at some later point in time. In this case, Mother appears either defeated or resigned, depending on the amount of erosion she's undergone in her childraising career.

Children are experts at wheedling their parents into buying things. They know just when to remember old promises, when to pledge new promises, and how to effect a number of other potent strategies that make their parents' convictions suddenly seem excessively stringent. So up until here, it's all pretty foreseeable.

The thing I find amazing is the quantity of nosh purchased by mothers independent of their persuasive progeny, the volume of unadulterated junk filling the carts of reasonable, unaccompanied adults.

"Oh this?" they'll say, "It's for Shabbos," and then surveying the growing pile, they'll add, "and you know, just to have in the house."

Which, I've come to realize, is no "just." The sweets industries have long outstripped Johnson and Johnson when it comes to household first aid. From boredom to sibling rivalry, whatever the crisis, a bag of nosh faithfully remedies the situation. Half a dozen freeze pops can get a room cleaned up as instantaneously as a wafer can console a 2 year-old griping about almost anything in the world.

And any time you need some instant peace and quiet, just about any sweet of your choosing will keep kids of all ages blissfully entertained for as long as it takes them to eat it. It keeps mouths and hands out of fights, and it certainly is a lot easier than telling stories or supervising finger painting.

The key words are quick and gratifying. Doling out nosh is hassle free, requires zero creativity, and is almost guaranteed to achieve instant results.

And if I may be so bold, it's not a solution limited to the junior division.

A handful of cookies takes about half the time to consume than a cucumber and carrot takes to peel, certainly a lot faster than washing for six-grain bread. And anyway, who's in the mood of carrots and six-grain bread, when you're down and out and scrounging around for an instant energy booster?

Almost no one. But like that ominous sign in the dentist's office warns, "The moment you finish consuming your candy bar, your candy bar starts consuming your teeth." Forget about your conscience.

One hour, nay, ten minutes, after that foil wrapper is disposed of, you have nothing but a faint sense of unrest, which usually sends you diving for seconds. That's more than you can say about vegetables and whole wheat bread.

And even if you do feel rather contented by the snack, just the image of that candy bar gnawing insidiously at your teeth, and settling down comfortably inside you, is enough to get you down.

To think that we do this to ourselves and our kids in the name of goodness. We, who sterilize bottles and keep poison safely out of reach, who expend so much time and money toward healthy habits and fitness. But no, I'm not writing for the health department; I'm not that great myself, and I have sparse hope in my ability to convince people to snack on organic bananas.

I'm targeting the food we feed our minds and hearts, the junk thoughts we so readily dispense to make our loved ones feel instantly better. I'm thinking in horror of all the mental sweets we pop without even thinking, those negative, self-pitying, condemning messages that we dwell on to assuage our feelings of anger and disappointment.

In life, we're constantly up against big and small stresses. And from stalled cars and unmade beds to difficult relationships and monetary hardships, it takes a lot more discipline and fortitude to feed our minds with healthy, energizing thoughts than to lunge for some sweet morsels of self-righteous indignation.

It's a lot easier to stage ourselves as martyrs, suffering victims, and put everything and everyone else in the bad book. To convince ourselves that we've gotten a sour deal, that we deserve better, that we're putting up with more than we should.

Like nosh, these reactions take no time and even less effort to cultivate. And they taste good while we're chewing on them. They quench our appetite for confirmation, for sympathy, for a few moments of some good hard-earned misery.

The second we finish consuming these thoughts, though, they begin consuming our happiness. They gnaw at our minds and hearts, eat away at our insides, and send us plunging desperately for more. They create big, aching emotional cavities of bitterness and resentment, and make a wreck of our spiritual figures.

That's not the worst of it though. The real harm is done when we unwittingly serve them to others. Not just any others, but our children and siblings and closest friends. In our well-meaning attempt to offer support and encouragement, we sometimes grab for a quick fix, and dish out discouragement instead.

"Oh don't tell me you took that extra afternoon job. Why didn't you just tell your husband you couldn't do it? You're so overworked as it is!"

"I can't believe you're missing it again. Can't you find someone else to tend to your mother for a few days? Where are your sisters?"

We mean to be nice, we really do. We want to convey our understanding, express our heartfelt empathy; more than anything else, we want to help. Which we're welcome to do, if we can.

Many times, though, we can't. Many times the burdens our dear ones have to contend with aren't parcels we can carry in their stead. So in our desire to whisk out some instant solution, we offer a candy bar. We pull out the same junk we placate ourselves with when we're up against some dispiriting eventuality, and with the nicest of intentions, we wreak some very serious damage.

Our children may reassure us laughingly that they don't mind; our friends may defend their siblings and say it's the least they could do for a parent. Don't be fooled. It's the candy bar law in effect. Your comment may be momentarily soothing; it only begins its insidious damage later.

Most people prefer to engage in self-pity in the privacy of their own hearts. So when the difficulties rear their head again, your words will be there to add fuel to the festering resentment. And the last thing we want to do is to foster ill will and discord in our loved ones' lives, to be the catalysts for unhappiness and bitterness and friction.

So let's take those extra few moments of forethought, of sensitivity and restraint, to proffer a helping of real food, of honest, nutritious support. The kind that provides lasting energy, not the achy, sullen feeling that follows a dose of empty calories. Let's swallow the temptation for candy, and say what we truly want to say.

"I really admire your devotion; I'm sure it doesn't come easy."

"I can imagine how terribly difficult it must be for you to miss that; Hashem counts every drop of disappointment."

The trick is not to do away with the empathy. It's learning to emphasize the difficulty, rather than the unfairness; it's giving credit rather than criticism. Encouragement gives the other person a lift without putting others down.

I'm not sure how much reckoning we'll have to do for the havoc we wreak with our family's teeth. When it comes to food for thought, though, let's be careful with what we dispense. Emotional dental work can be very costly; we don't want to be billed for ruining anyone's smile.

The Yes Mess

I don't usually use this column as a forum for my personal correspondence. Not any correspondence, and certainly not apology letters.

Come to think of it, I'm hard pressed to remember the last time I've written one at all. Apology letters were those neatly penciled notes written on behalf of the entire class, and formally tucked into an envelope in the hope of appeasing a mortified substitute. Or those contrite lines written to a parent and then gingerly tucked under a pillow in a quivering mixture of eager anticipation and nervous apprehension.

In any event, these apology letters were usually of pretty private content. Those to whom they were addressed could surely appreciate the sheepish smile between the lines, the courage behind the admission of guilt, the vulnerability risked by claiming fault and promising change. Apology letters were never the type of thing you presented with a flourish, let alone showed anyone other than the intended recipient.

Which is why, I guess, I've graduated to the less formal alternative of verbal apologies. Subtly inserted into the natural interchange of words between people, apologies are less daunting. You don't have to put your innermost feelings into a bottle and toss them off to the waves. You can gauge your partner's expression and wait for the right mood, the opportune moment, the ideal setting. And you get immediate feedback. There's no walking on tiptoes while you wonder anxiously, did s/he read it yet?

Most of all, the unwritten apologies leave room for amendments at the end. They allow us the combined luxury of expressing our remorse and remaining in the right.

"I'm really sorry I never got back to you," we'll start out, *"but you can't imagine what was going on here this week."*

"I apologize for getting so worked up, *but the reason I got so upset is ...*"

To be perfectly honest, something about the ambivalence of these statements bothers me. Apologies that come hobbling in on crutches of self-defense are like fractures that haven't quite fused yet. If they can't stand on their own, and they still hurt, there's no sense making believe they're healed. A little time and a lot of self-effacement is usually in order.

Sometimes, though, these limping apologies only worsen with the passing of time; sometimes they are the complications of what should have been a clean break, ages ago. So let me apologize.

I don't recall exactly what time Devorah first called, but I had definitely been thinking that another pair of hands would be warmly welcome. Or an extra twenty-four hours somewhere in the ensuing week. I was late with my writing, overdrawn on my commitments, and trying to tend to several inpatients, while I served the second shift of supper.

I hopelessly looked for a relatively quiet corner where I could hear what Devorah was saying. She was calling from overseas; she definitely deserved the courtesy of a calm connection. I motioned for someone to rock the baby, while I shut the tape recorder.

In the meantime, Devorah introduced herself, and politely asked if she wasn't imposing. She wasn't, I reassured her. I always loved connecting with the other side of the ocean. Only if she wouldn't mind calling back in twenty minutes or so, things would be a trifle quieter.

"Sure," she said, pleasantly, "I can call back later than that too, if that's better."

"No, no, twenty minutes should be just fine."

Which it was. Devorah wanted my permission to use several songs I had written years ago in my capacity as a day-camp counselor and teacher. I answer enthusiastically in the affirmative.

Having someone enjoy something I'd composed years ago afforded me a pleasure akin to that of dividends coming in on an investment long forgotten. It was like the joy of taking out a box of used clothing and finding they were in perfect condition to give to an excited recipient.

"Sure, sure, you can gladly use the songs. I don't mind at all; in fact I'll be thrilled."

So far so good. Then came the hitch.

"We'll be holding a *Yom Iyun* in about two weeks on the topic of *nesinah* (giving). Do you think you can fax me any songs you have on the topic?"

Lurch. The songs were somewhere in the back of my file, among hundreds of assorted poems and articles. I wasn't even sure if I hadn't lent the file out to someone else. *Nesinah*, I did a quick mental check. I had songs on appreciation, on *shemiras halashon*, on *tefillah*. I had theme songs and team songs, slow songs and fast songs. I tried to desperately remember one connected with the idea of giving.

"I'll check," I promised vaguely, though my earlier enthusiasm had markedly waned. Checking wasn't a matter of scrolling down on a neat list of computer files. Checking would mean sitting cross-legged over cardboard files, riffling through pockets of extraneous nostalgia before I hit upon the songs in question. Then, it would entail combing through the material to try and find something appropriate.

I didn't want to renege on my word, though. I had wanted to help. And why shouldn't I, if I might have just the perfect song in my possession?

Now, in retrospect, I can think of a few viable reasons. Like the neighbor's children staying in my care; the cases of bronchitis on my own home front, the two evenings out of town within three days. The laundry waiting to be put away, the urgent errands that couldn't be postponed, the *sheva berachos* taking place in my home later that week.

I should have said so. I should have said, honestly and openly, that I couldn't recall any particular song on the topic. I'm sure Devorah would have understood.

For some reason, I didn't. I kept putting her off the way you'd snooze some inanimate alarm clock, with no solid sense of when you'd actually be rolling out of blankets.

Tomorrow. *Motza'ei Shabbos*. Yes, *bli neder*, just remind me.

Every time I heard her voice, sweet, tentative, apologetic, I'd re-experience that initial lurch followed by a wave of what felt like my conscience doing hiccups. I had the vague sensation of having misled her, of having made her weave through some crazy maze together with me, only to concede, halfway through, that I was just as lost as she was.

"When do you think you can fax them?" she asked, no edge of impatience apparent in her voice. That made it even worse; I felt doubly ashamed to resign.

So I dragged her along with me for about a week or so, in and around my hectic schedule, under and over the challenges of the week. I don't know who was more hassled by the ride, she with the dread of hanging on to my elusive back, or me with the ever-mounting guilt, the niggling responsibility to get her to the other side of the thicket.

She called back. And she called back again.

And please could she call back in another two days? By then, I'd surely have it. Such a simple request really; it was growing ridiculous. Couldn't I just fax the papers?

Sure I could. I *would*. After I met my writing deadlines and took the baby to the doctor. After supper was cleared away and the soup cooked and the trip to Tel Aviv over. As soon as I had an hour or two to locate the file and sort the papers and rewrite the material.

If you want to know the end of the story, yes, we made it. We both made it by the skin of our teeth, but it wasn't what I'd call a success. Devorah got a song, some kind of old excerpt just barely in step with her theme, just barely in time for the deadline. And I sat over a fax machine, just barely clipping earrings to my ears with one hand, just barely stuffing my feet into high-heeled shoes and flying out to the bus stop.

I'm sorry. I am. Without appendages.

I'm sorry for letting you hang in there, holding on to a thread of disillusionment, dangling from it, tangling around it, meshing both of us into a web of unnecessary anxiety. I'm sorry to you, and I'm sorry to your many predecessors over the years who waited for games and ideas and poems and speeches, that just about materialized in the nick of time.

I'm sorry, not for letting you down, but for letting you on. For acceding to unrealistic deadlines, and to the uncensored desire to be the ever-helpful savior. For writing checks with no backing and then having them bounce in your face and mine. Or having to dig into some other innocent people's resources to bail us both out.

It's so easy to say yes. We all love feeling generous as we dole out affirmative answers. Holding generous as we dole out affirmative answers. Holding others hostage to our good intentions, though, is not benevolence. It is inconsiderate and misleading. If we want to give in the true sense of the word, we have to learn a simple bit of logic; you can't be here and there at the same time. It's always a matter of saying yes to *something*; it only depends what we choose that something to be.

So, there, that's my apology to you, Devorah. Don't hesitate to ask again: I'll be happy to help if I can. And if I can't, well, then, I'll say I'm sorry. An apology, I've learned, is not only the nicest way to have the last word. Sometimes it's the nicest way of having the first word.

In Tribute

*L*ast week was the big week. We parents actually made it into the *Aseres HaDibros*. And for some reason, I felt this childish impulse to keep drawing attention to the fact. "Who's going to bring Mommy a cup? Come on, doesn't anybody remember what it says in the *parashah* this week?"

I know that respect is a lot more, well, respectable, when it is commanded, not demanded. And I generally do try to be a little more discreet about imparting lessons of life. I guess I just couldn't forgo the temptation of reminding myself and those around me that my simple everyday requests, my right of way in this household, were endorsed by none other than the Master of the World, engraved alongside the most basic fundamentals on the *Luchos HaBris*.

So I enjoyed my day in the sun. It was nice bathing in that warm glow of feeling appreciated, knowing I occupied such a prominent position in the hierarchy of Judaism. Until a dismaying thought began merging with those caressing rays, turning the halo into an uncomfortable sort of spotlight, making me suddenly cognizant of the fact that my day in the sun also happened to be my day as a daughter.

Modern psychology has given birth to a brand-new notion: reparenting. You know those disgruntled, aggressive, unhappy, manipulative adults? Well, psychology has some news to offer them. The bad news is, that as they grew up, they weren't properly parented, which is why they feel, behave, react the way they do. The good news is that they can be reparented.

With the help of a competent therapist, trustworthy friend, or supportive family member, they can reestablish the components of a healthy relationship and have a second chance at being parented.

I've never tried it. I'm fortunate enough to have been parented properly the first time around. I'm lucky enough to have been showered with love and empathy, swaddled in abundant layers of protection from harmful influences, physical and spiritual. But bathing in the sun, almost singed by it, as I was this *Shabbos*, I was driven by a passionate desire to check the psychology books, if perhaps there existed a possibility of rechilding.

Perhaps there was some way I could go back and rechild my parents, making amends for the thousands of mistakes, the mumbled comments, the thoughtless requests, the unfair expectations. Perhaps there was some way I could rewind and fix up, apply some spackling and a fresh coat of paint on some of those moments I recall with a sense of deep shame and regret.

Well, no, sorry, there aren't really second chances being offered, it's one childhood per lifetime. But I feel compelled to write the tribute that was never written, the tribute every parent who is also a child mentally pays dozens of times each day as he or she faces the myriad challenges of guiding youngsters who don't seem to appreciate being guided; feeding, bathing, dressing, waking, taking, kids who seem bent on proving Newton's law that every action evokes an (equal and) opposite reaction.

A tribute for pacing the floors, bleary eyed with exhaustion trying to quiet colicky cries, for stripping sopping sheets at 4 o'clock in the morning, and tucking a cranky, ungrateful child back into a fresh warm bed, for dashing out to the drug store in the middle of suppertime to get calamine lotion for poison ivy, for painstakingly applying patches to lazy eyes. It sounds terribly selfish to say this, but I never thought any of this was anything special. If truth be told, I never much thought about any of this at all.

It sort of seemed self-understood that by some natural law of biology, parents would want to do all this for their offspring. It never occurred to me that fatigue and stress, worry, exhaustion, and pressing priorities could play a lot of tricks with this natural desire. It never dawned on me that parents needed sleep like any of the rest of us, and that inconveniences truly messed up their day.

What about food, clean laundry, ironed shirts? Well most kids would say just that: What about it? So this tribute is for scrubbing stains, pairing socks, for untangling *tzitzis*, sewing on buttons, fixing hems. Always, constantly, without fail. For putting the laundry back in the drawers faster than they could empty, for patiently washing all the items thrown in the hamper just because they were easier to dump in there than to hang up.

For peeling, cutting, blending, frying, for washing the pots and dishes and silverware, and then doing all of this again and again like a never-ending repeated decimal. For serving supper in a million shifts, for rewarming portions, and contending with the clatter and bang of opening cabinets and the creaking of the refrigerator door after all these shifts were completed.

For driving carpools to and from school rehearsals, classmates' Bar Mitzvahs, not to mention the regular thankless Sunday chore of shepherding kids to and from their assigned destinations. For finding the right boots for the right feet, for replacing lost rubbers, for labeling brand-new mittens and scarves and then having them get lost, never to be claimed in the school's lost and found.

For wiping the trails of sticky ices all the way out to the back porch and front patio, for supplying ideas and help, and papers and the bathroom (and the ensuing cleaning of it) for the backyard day-camps, for trying valiantly to come up with some reasonable suggestions for the whining chorus of, "What should I do?" or "There's nothing to eat."

All this is in the way of physical sustenance, and it's not a fraction of it either. We've got our parents to thank for buying our annual school supplies, remembering to put $2.50 for the teacher's present in our pencil case, getting rid of rotten apples in briefcases, replacing broken frames, scratched lenses, and torn sneakers.

And then some more. For teaching us to ride a two-wheeler, for buying the two-wheeler, for providing the training wheels in life while giving us the illusion we were riding by ourselves. For going that extra mile to get the nicer graduation blouse, the pants that didn't itch, the hat that all the boys were getting.

And there are the apologies. For the constant pressure of being measured against our friends' parents, or our utopian perception of them. For the rejection of having a genuine inquiry about our day tossed back with a flat "nothing," for the annoyance of having every personal phone call interrupted with "Ma, who's on the phone?" or, worse yet, "So can I sleep over at Devorah's house? Yeah? Yeah?"

For the slammed doors, the late homecomings, the bringing home of uninvited guests, including goldfish, rocks, and bags of junk. For the procrastination at bedtime, the unmade beds, the homework assignment remembered at 8 o'clock in the morning, "And, oh, Ma, I'm supposed to bring a nosh for twenty-eight kids, but not popcorn or anything else we have in the house." For bringing up old forgotten promises at the most inopportune moments, and for forgetting our own promises once we'd cashed in on the incentive.

For scowling at the brand-new outfit, for refusing to wear the jacket from last year and for turning and fidgeting and jumping around, making shopping and trying on impossible. For grumbling about setting the table, for pushing away the vegetable soup, for forgetting snacks at home, and missing the bus. For losing the list on the way, and leaving the change in the store.

For sharing our frustrations in the most unacceptable ways, and saving the really gratifying moments for friends. For divulging secrets, and for keeping secrets, for begging and whining and deliberately playing on the most vulnerable spots.

For the refusal to admit being wrong ("What did I do?"), for the begrudging "I'm sorry" when we did admit it, for taking things without permission (also, incidentally, an infringement of another one of the Ten), and for persisting with the annoying "But why?" when the answer was self-evident. For fighting, and teasing and bossing our siblings, the screaming and chasing and squabbling that could stretch the most patient parent to the fraying end of the rope.

When I think of it, I am staggered by the enormity of it, this huge debt, the biggest debt we owe to any human being in this world, for our existence, our sanity, our confidence, our hopes, and our memories. For our perception of *Yiddishkeit*, of *tefillah* and Torah, for the flavor that will forever accompany every day on the Jewish calendar.

For the pain of the perpetual struggles writhing beneath the surface of the deceptively smooth-running household, the clashes between obligations and aspirations, the conflicting demands of three generations. For the constant quandary of how much to overlook and how much to oversee, of when to understand and when to stand over, when to give up and when to give in.

For those moments we never knew about, those moments of guilt, of indecision and doubt, those moments of crisis and tension, frustration and failure and dashed dreams. For those tears, those salty, choking tears of disappointment, of prayer, of fear, of humiliation. For the bottomless reservoir of patience and perseverance that we mercilessly plumbed time and time again.

For all this, and for so much more, and for everything else is this tribute. For every single father and mother who have raised a child, have trained him, and dressed him and fed him, prayed for him, taught him, and loved him. For every single son and daughter who can still grab those last few years and rectify a thing or two is this tribute. And for all the rest, I, we, all of us, who have forfeited our chance to rechild our parents, with this tribute we plead to be able to amend the fifth.

Language Arts

*I*t's called "Lady Language," and it's downright confusing. The incredible thing is that we women seem to have a perfect command of it, despite it being the most contradictory, long-winded, illogical form of communication there is. What's even more incredible is the way we expect our better halves to follow its unpredictable pattern of senseless rules, and we even question their straightforward logic when they fail.

It would be way too complex to ponder the language in its entirety in a few scanty lines. If you want to know what I'm talking about, though, I'll offer you a sampling of one of its very popular usages, centering around one innocent theme: You think, I think.

She: "You think I should order supper tonight?"

He: "No, I don't think so."

She: "O.K. (resigned, insulted, resentful), then I guess I'll *make* supper."

Now, if you'll ask Mr. and Mrs. for the content of their above one-minute interchange, you'll get quite a varying version of the dialogue. Mrs. claims that she asked her husband if she could buy supper, to which he responded in the negative. She also thinks she very obviously told him that she was unhappy about the unfair response. Mr., on the other hand, will have an entirely different account. According to his recollection, he was asked if *he* thought supper should be bought, and his perfectly honest opinion was that it shouldn't. To which his wife, of course, readily agreed.

Just put a woman in Husband's place. Any woman will tell you that a question prefaced with "You think." is not meant to be a question at all. It is a thinly disguised way of asking for the listener's validation. It's a way of presenting an idea, opinion, or request for which we not only want permission, but an unequivocal ruling that we absolutely cannot do without whatever it is we are contemplating.

Sometimes we even include an appendage that sounds like a reasonable claim to cancel the idea. That makes it even more confusing. But of course it's clear to us women that the listener is supposed to offer a sound refutation of the dangling question mark.

"You think I should buy that outfit, *or you think I could still find something cheaper*?"

Any female knows what the one correct, anticipated response is. "Of course you should buy it. In fact, you should *grab* it! A three-piece suit at that price? Where are you going to find something cheaper? And even if you do, it'll never be the same quality."

"You think I should serve on paper goods — I mean nice paper goods — *or china would still be more proper*?"

Mrs. Baalas Simchah has her stand quite clear. She plans to keep her china safely stowed in the breakfront, where she'll be spared the job of washing and drying stacks of soiled dishes at some hour way past midnight. More importantly, though, she wants *you* to agree with her, to vehemently discard any notion of using china as ridiculous, completely out of the question, and tell her that paper goods is the only way to go.

And Mrs. Baalas Simchah's married daughter, friend, sister, or neighbor knows all this without even pausing to think. There is no decoding, no misreading, no throat clearing. This is a natural conversation, one that repeats itself countless times in the day, revolving around different issues.

And those are all the clear-cut ones. It shouldn't be that difficult to teach people, even those not belonging to the gender fluent in "Lady Language," one universal rule: "Any opinion starting with 'You think ...' should be treated as a request for permission, consent, or validation."

The problem is that the rule isn't universal. We women know how to complicate matters.

"Our budget really *is* tight, now that the rent has been increased. You think I should cancel the cleaning lady?"

Please. Don't anyone say yes to the proposal. The question was never meant to be one, and the cleaning lady is not up for grabs. She never was for one single moment. "You think" in this case was an abstract offer meant to convey: "I am really taking this seriously," and no less important, "Please, don't take me seriously."

"I really tried finding out about those cheaper rates. You think I should still try to get the company's number in Arizona?"

In Lady Language this is an explicit invitation for refusal. Please tell me I've tried hard enough, and that it isn't necessary to pursue it any further. In fact, I would really like to hear that the long-distance inquiries aren't even worth my time and energy.

So the questions are usually statements, and the statements most often indicate questions. "You think I shouldn't?" (as in, "So you think I shouldn't go to the N'shei play?") translates as "I think I should," and "I think I should" (as in, "I think I should really lose a few pounds."), warrants a "Oh, you really don't have to."

Then there's the intonation. If there was any way to provide rules up until here, then here it's totally useless. You simply have to look into her eyes, listen for voice fluctuation, and be endowed with some heavenly assistance to figure out the obvious. What does Lady want this time?

"I can't find a babysitter for the evening of the Schreibers' wedding. I'm thinking of staying home."

Does she mean she wants to be convinced that her presence is of utmost importance to the Schreibers' absolute happiness, or does she mean that this is the perfect excuse to get her off the hook so that she can stay home and organize the closet? Does she want him to get his *chavrusa*'s daughter to babysit, or — just a minute! Perhaps she is actually asking *him* to babysit?

How about, "I'm thinking of calling a plumber to fix the clogged drain."

O.K., so she's thinking of calling the plumber. She's said as much. Is she insinuating that she truly understands the fact that he is too busy, and perhaps too respectable in her eyes, to be fiddling with pipes? Or is she presenting a polite ultimatum aimed at getting that clogged drain cleared, *today*? Or then, maybe she's only making a simple appeal for some cash.

Whatever the correct answer, there's one word of caution. Just because the right choice this time was A, don't try coming to any quick conclusions. Next time the very same statement may be an attempt at eliciting answers B, C, or D, or perhaps "none of the above."

So tell me, now that you know some of the stuff that comprises Lady Language, not that you haven't spoken it all along, but now that you've gotten to hear some of it in all its simplicity, *what do you think?*

You think it's reasonable to assume that any nonfemale can master the language with ease?

Blind Spot

Sometimes I wonder if there's an unwritten script mothers the world over go by. Or perhaps it's just in our house.

"Why is the empty tissue box sitting on the toilet?" I sigh, as I toss the box into the wastebasket. "When you see that the tissues are finished, you replace the box."

I don't know why I haven't given up yet. It must be that inborn maternal optimism. Perhaps, I reason, if I repeat the rule often enough, it may penetrate.

My progeny, though, disprove my hypothesis. It isn't that they don't know the rule, or even that they've forgotten. It isn't that they don't believe in throwing things away, or that they don't want to pitch in.

It's just that they didn't see. Didn't see that the tissues were finished. Simple as that. It isn't only tissue boxes. It's missing buttons, loose covers, dripping containers. It's overflowing vacuum cleaner bags, unlined garbage cans, towels strewn on the bathroom floor.

Nobody means to leave them missing, dripping, sticky. Nobody deliberately wants to break the vacuum cleaner, soil the garbage can, step on the towel.

They just didn't see. Didn't see that there was no bag in the garbage can. Didn't see that the towel was on the floor. Sincerely and honestly didn't see.

"But you stepped on it!" I moan in exasperation, "How can you step on something and not see it?"

They look at me, contrite, and a little dumbfounded.

"I stepped on the towel?"

At that point I know that anything I say will be futile. But I can't help it.

"How come I'm the only one who sees things in this house?" I mutter as I shake the towel and emphatically smooth it over the rod, so it will stay there for a while. "You have to *learn to look.*"

The words always strike a familiar chord. They seem to echo after me, a trifle mockingly, like I'd have heard them somewhere before.

I have. Many hundreds of empty tissue boxes ago, I have. Same scene, same script, different role. I was the child then, carefree, happy little girl, sprinting out of the light-blue tiled bathroom without a burden in the world. Who paid a thought to cardboard toilet-paper tubes when there was so many more exciting things going on?

My mother, I guess.

"Come back," I remember her calling after me. "Do you see something you forgot?"

"Forgot?" I stuck my head into the bathroom, puckered my face, bewildered. My friends were calling me. What could I have forgotten in the bathroom? I shrugged.

"When you see that the toilet paper is finished, you throw out the tube and put on a new roll," my mother reminded me patiently.

I was halfway down the stairs already.

"Oh," I blurted in apology, " I didn't see it was finished."

"That's the problem," I'd hear my mother, more to herself than to me. "Why am I the only one who sees things?"

Why indeed? I'd often wondered about it myself. How come mothers always found the scissors, the stamps, the elastic, exactly where they said it would be, after children turned up empty handed from the search? How come half a dozen youngsters could come home from school, walk up the driveway, right up the steps, and skip the fruit order waiting to be hauled into the kitchen?

It was a mystery I was hard pressed to solve. Mothers must have been endowed with some kind of special vision, I concluded. That absolved me for quite some time.

Until I became a mother.

It wasn't a matter of vision, I found quickly enough; it was a matter of *super*vision. It wasn't sight; it was *fore*sight. When you're the one in charge, you learn to see rather well. When you're going to have to scrub that garbage can, you *look* before you dump an oily tuna can full of peels. When you're the one who contends with the stains, you *notice* that the apron is torn, that the ices are dripping, that there's some sticky black gook on the park bench.

Kids are a busy breed. They've got papers to cut, dolls to dress, collections to count and organize. They've got friends to impress, promises to keep, choirs to practice for. How the bananas made it into the basket or how the filthy, creased, Shabbos shirt became pressed, stark white are not usually questions that haunt children. So no, they really couldn't give a hoot to a plastic cup on the floor. Even if they have to kick it all the way across the kitchen and down the steps.

Not to worry, though, all kids grow up. For better or for worse, despite and albeit their parents' worries, all kids eventually learn to see. And contrary to what we would like to believe, it has very little to do with their mothers' tirades.

Give them a few days in a brand-new apartment of their own, and wonder of wonders, they'll be picking up the shoes, closing the lights, refilling the water in the pitcher. Give them a few years, and they'll be repeating your refrain. There's nothing like responsibility to do the trick.

Yes, all kids grow up where tissue boxes and towels are concerned. It's frightening, however, how many of us can remain frozen in childhood oblivion, where people and circumstances stand.

"I didn't see," we claim, "I didn't know." Didn't see that the person who usually sits next to me in *shul* was absent for the past three weeks; didn't notice there was a new family on the block. Didn't know that they were struggling with *parnassah*, that their daughter needed a *shidduch*, or that the mother was bedridden all winter.

I would have done something; I honestly would have.

But I didn't know.

We are each individuals, and we are each part of a bigger picture. We teach in schools, attend functions, *daven* in *shuls*. We belong to a family, a neighborhood, a community. We belong to *Klal Yisrael*. It behooves us to see.

To see the tension behind the terse manner, to see the pain behind the taut smile. To see those who are there and those who are not there. And those who are there, but not there. It behooves us to notice when a neighbor is going through a crisis, when a student is begging for recognition, when a colleague is in need of support.

It's so easy to get wrapped up in our own affairs. Like the kids, we're a busy breed. We've got appointments to keep, lessons to prepare, *simchos* to attend. We've got houses to run, jobs to maintain, our immediate families to care for. It isn't any wonder that sometimes we don't see.

But like all good mothers can tell you, *you have to learn to look.*

Very few people wave a red flag when they are in crisis. Very few individuals will phone to ask you for a meal, a phone call, a visit. But if you take that moment before you run off, if you pause to look, you may see an empty box, silently pleading for a refill.

Seeing isn't a matter of vision; it's a matter of *super*vision. It isn't sight; it's *fore*sight. When you're in charge, you see. When you feel personally responsible for the family called *Klal Yisrael*, you learn to look. You learn to pick up on cues, notice leads, you learn to listen in for the subtle nuances that tell you there is something you can do.

And you try to do that something. It doesn't have to be something big. Pick up a telephone. Jot a note. Send over some salad, some cake, some flowers. Offer to run an errand, to pick up some bread and milk, to baby-sit for an hour. If you can't offer anything else, then smile.

But don't say, "I didn't see."

Because *Ahavas Yisrael* is the belief that we all belong to one family.

And seeing is believing.

Price Tag

Sometimes, my Israeli neighbors think I'm odd.

"You're taking your daughter to America, and you aren't taking her to see the Statue of Liberty?"

What should I say? I might appear poor and tired and huddled by the time I land at John F. Kennedy International Airport, but the dour interior of the famed sculpture is hardly my idea of a haven. The last time I climbed all those steps was on my fifth-grade school trip, and believe me, I don't remember ever being as uninspired by stories.

So no, I don't intend on visiting there with my daughter.

"Don't you want your kids to see what you grew up with?"

Yes, I do, surely. But I didn't grow up with the Statue of Liberty. Or the Manhattan skyline. Or Fifth Avenue. I grew up with my parents and siblings, aunts and uncles, and lots of cousins. I grew up with a big playroom, a sunny dinette, a weeping willow tree in the backyard. Those are the things I want my children to see.

And if an itinerary abroad won't do without an outing, then Amazing Savings tops the Statue of Liberty any day.

The closest my Israeli-bred children have ever gotten to a close-out store is the two *shekel* place, where for some reason, almost nothing cost two *shekels*. For the same reason, I suppose, the items on display are either ridiculously colored, impossibly junky or out of stock. Aisles of sturdy cars and trucks, dolls and accessories, ceramic and crystal, all bargains, constitute fairyland to them.

So when we set out to Amazing Savings together, on the last day of *Chanukah*, my daughter and I were brimming with expectations. We weren't disappointed. The place was just as I had remembered it, teeming with shoppers, packed with merchandise, alive with announcements.

"Look, Ma!" my daughter marveled, "Tiny socks for the baby." She held up a pair of striped booties. "Should I put them into the cart?"

"They're cute," I smiled, "you can put them in."

"A thermometer, Ma. Ours broke before we left, remember?"

"Yes, you can take it. Even two. Oh no, they're Fahrenheit, I forgot." I was studying a set of pots on sale, trying to figure out if they would complement my *Pesach* collection.

"This is so cute for Fraidy's kids," my daughter gushed, as she dragged me to a wooden workbench replete with tools.

"Or maybe this; we have to buy them presents, don't we?" She was almost delirious with the thrill of all the bounty at her fingertips.

Admittedly, so was I. When was the last time I had gotten to carelessly fill up a cart with all these nonessentials? When was the last time I had had the leisure of browsing through a store without the built-in guilt alarm ringing insistently at the back of my conscience? It took me a few minutes of habitual watch-glancing to realize that I could simply shut the nagging mechanism, and slow my pace.

"Can I have these markers, Ma? All my markers are dried out, and anyway, we're missing half the colors. Please?"

I didn't remember missing half the colors, but I relented. What was $2.99 for a good set of Crayola washables? You couldn't get them for double that, back in Eretz Yisrael. In fact, you couldn't get them at all.

My daughter giggled with abandon as she threw the package on top of the foil pans. She leaned one leg and an arm on the metal frame of the cart, and skipped along, scooter style, gleefully tapping the items we passed. I was going to say something motherlike about the cart being difficult to maneuver with all her weight on one wheel, but I let it go. This was supposed to an indulgent trip. I wasn't going to spoil it.

We oohed and aahed over some paper goods, debated the wisdom of schlepping back plastic containers, and tossed seven friction-operated racing cars into the cart. She said *s'lichah* (excuse me) to a gray-haired woman, we both laughed heartily at her mistake, and we met an old classmate of mine. This was fun, this trip to Amazing, though I was beginning to wonder about the savings.

That's when we spotted the infant seat.

It was an adorable lavender and pink infant seat, Fisher Price, I think, perfect size for playing pretend. The light-blue box featured a picture of the cutest-looking blonde doll sucking a matching pink and lavender pacifier. Gitty stopped short. I saw her stare lovingly at the box, imagining her favorite doll ensconced in the pastel perch.

She looked at me, trying to assess her chances.

"Can we buy this, Ma? It's so cute!"

"It's adorable," I admitted, as I turned over the box to find the price — $10.99. This, after the markers and stickers, a box of colorful paper clips, a personal diary, and a set of play accessories in a gingham zippered case.

"So can we buy it?" she asked hopefully, her hand on the box.

"Hmm," I mused, my elbow leaning on the handle of the shopping cart.

"Look, Mommy, it comes with a *motzetz*, and you can make it sit or lie down."

"Hmm." This was a hard one.

"You know what?" I suddenly had a brainstorm. "How about buy-ing this with the twelve dollars you received from both *zaidies* over *Chanukah*?"

Gitty let go of the box, stunned.

"*Vus* (What)," she spluttered,

"*Mit **mein** gelt* (With *my* money)?"

The infant seat was a dream; pretty, feminine, adorable. It had the matching pacifier and it changed positions. Her doll would fit inside perfectly.

But, *Vus, Mit mein gelt*?

The question shot straight out of her eyes, struck my funny bone, and whizzed right past me. Then it ricocheted back, grazed my mind, and lodged itself right inside my conscience.

Where it's remained ever since.

All of us, children we are, on a grand spree. We want life, we want health, we want families. All we do is ask, hang a pair of pleading eyes, look a little wistful, say that what we have is good, but not good *enough* really, and can we please have more?

Sure, He says, this is your trip. You want life? Put it in the cart. *Parnassah*? That too. You can take *gezunt*, yes. And a family, yes.

Yes.

We smile.

Then we hear about Torah. We see it in gold and silver, wrapped in a pretty window box. We stop in our tracks. *Kedushah*. Purity. *Tzeniyus*. A life of meaning, of transcendence, of sterling beauty. We look at the picture. We see wisdom. And peace of mind. *Nachas*, too. And depth. Happiness. True, guaranteed happiness.

So can we buy it?

Hmm.

How about getting it with those Italian summer outfits for the kids, with the annual vacation, with the custom *shaitel*? How about paying for it with the sweet table at the *sheva berachos*, the Borsalino hat, the hours on the telephone?

Vus, you can't be serious.

*Mit **mein** gelt?"*

It's all very well when we hear a nice speech, watch a moving presentation, read a poignant account. It's all very stirring, thrilling, uplifting. A lifetime of Torah. The *Rosh Yeshivah's* son. The best boy in Lakewood. It isn't very hard to want all of that.

But please, *you* pay for it.

You don't mean for *me* to pass up on charisma, on chic, on impeccable manners. You don't mean for me to have to give up the wedding of my dreams, the in gown, the best photographer. You can't mean it. That's *mein gelt.*

We want *kedushah.* Sure. It's our stronghold, our trademark, *mamleches kohanim v'goi kadosh* (a kingdom of priests and a holy nation). It's our shield against spiritual warfare, the invitation for the *Shechinah* to dwell among us. It's our warranty against tragedy and illness. What's a *Yiddishe* family without *kedushah?*

Just don't ask me to pay for it.

Just don't make the *mechitzos* so impermeable, I can't see the dancing; don't censor the tunes for the production after I've worked so hard to find them; don't tell me not to go the concert, when everybody I know is going.

Careful.

That's *mein gelt.*

Shavuos is approaching. We want that box. There are some very good things inside. *Shalom bayis, tzeniyus, kashrus, Shabbos.* It's all included in the package.

Can we have it?

Sure, He says, you can have it, every one of you.

Mit dein gelt.

If Life Gives You Lemons ...

In Eretz Yisrael it's easy to learn. If you're only willing to be educated, then there are plenty of people around ready to do the job of teaching you.

From the *savta* on the local park bench who instructs you how to better protect yourself against the elements to the taxi driver who recommends the cheapest shop for produce, everyone is eager to impart some wisdom. The subject matter ranges from the Hebrew language to economics and psychology, and is most often from the homegrown variety of knowledge.

In the course of years since I'm living here, I've learned how to make a hat out of a napkin ("That baby's head is exposed to the sun! Don't you have a napkin? I'll teach you how to make one into a hat."), what strain of apples are best for baking, and how to pronounce my own children's names. But I never expected to glean one of my profoundest insights from a simple electrician. Which I did.

It was the hottest *Shabbos* of the year, if not the decade, and my relatively new air-conditioning unit had decided to go on strike. I was steaming, literally and figuratively. The thing had only been installed three weeks earlier, and already a part had been replaced.

"Lemon," the electrician had declared. "It happens once in every few hundred machines. This time though, I assure you, *Giveret*, the part is brand new. Perfect condition. You should have no problems."

But I did. In fact, it was problem after problem with this leaking, vibrating, overheated appliance, and now it had quit on the hottest Shabbos of the year. I valiantly tried to keep my cool. With everyone's windows plastered shut against the heat wave, I didn't even have company for my misery, but somehow the joy of *Shabbos* managed to tide me over the afternoon. The minute *Shabbos* was out, however, I had that electrician on the phone.

"Tell me," I fumed, "why this brand-new machine has not given me one day of satisfactory service? I want you to tell me the reason."

There was silence on the other end, as if the guy was contemplating if the time was right for his reply. "Look, I can explain it this way or that, but you really want to know the reason? The *real* reason?"

"Yes, the real reason," I echoed tersely. This guy was really annoying me.

"You might not like it, and I truly do regret that you had to suffer through such a boiling-hot *Shabbos*. It must have been really stifling —"

"But?" I interjected, my voice a trifle mellower. His sincere empathy had blunted the cutting edge of my accusation. Now I was downright curious.

"But, *yesh Abba shedoeg b'shvili* (There is a Father Who worries on my behalf). If they made those parts the way they should, I'd be out of business. I'm not into the big money like installing central units and all that, but Hashem never lets me down. There are always visits to customers like you. As for you, *Giveret*," he was quick to console me, "I'm sure there's a reason you were supposed to sweat through this afternoon. After all, He's your *Abba* too."

I was touched. My hostility had melted like an icicle in the sun, warmed by the rays of his simple but genuine outlook on life. The article in question happened to have been a malfunctioning filter, but his explanation had transcended carpentry or electronics.

"*Yesh Abba shedoeg b'shvili.*" His words resounded in my ears. It wasn't the deepest insight I had ever heard regarding *emunah*. As a teacher and as a pupil, I'd furrowed through many a profound saying on *Hashgachas Hashem*, or on the inverse relationship between *hishtadlus* and *bitachon*. I'd delved into the *pesukim* and *midrashim*,

I'd read stories and written songs featuring different aspects of faith and trust. But this guy was different. He was real. He was dealing with a filter and a customer in the world of hard reality. He wasn't at a podium, he wasn't even wearing a suit, but he was discussing *emunah* as a phenomenon as natural as voting and antibiotics and inflation. I had been toting synthetic *emunah*, observed and cultivated in the lab, while he was living the natural brand, a simple reality he imbibed with every breath.

I thought about comments I'd heard and made over the last day or two, and suddenly I was ashamed.

"The Palestinians are finally piping down with their attacks. I guess the only language they understand is their own — terror," in regard to Sharon's hard-line policy as of late. Or,

"How could I have forgotten that the florist moved her shop?" as I bristled at the inconvenience of having to locate the new branch.

"You're sure he's a top doctor? Why can't he figure out the reason for the recurring infections?"

Of course I *knew* there was one Boss Who had this world mapped out to precision. Somehow, though, when I'd encountered the bumps and lurches along the way, human tendency had me tighten the grip on the steering wheel and check the dashboard, or else honk reproachfully at some reckless trespasser.

Whether fretting over fruitless shopping trips or unsuccessful *shidduchim*, I'd repeatedly overlooked the sentiment that *"yesh Abba shedoeg b'shvili,"* and that the minor potholes in the roadways of life were, too, manifestations of His concern.

Sure, like any good believing Jew, the term *"bashert"* was part and parcel of my phraseology, liberally sprinkled through my daily conversations. I had failed though, to incorporate the concept, to realize that *"bashert"* meant that nothing and nobody in this world ever suffered at the expense of something else. All aggravation, big and little, was especially designed for the advancement of good in this world, and every person affected along the way was specifically benefiting. *"Bashert"* wasn't an afterthought or a condolence or another way of looking at it. *"Bashert"* was a reality that reflected the Omnipotence of a Master Planner, and the individual attention of an *"Abba shedoeg b'shvili."*

The guy may have given me a lemon of a filter, but he had certainly taught me something on the way. He had twisted the old proverb to teach me that if life handed you a lemon, then either in this world or the next, there was lemonade in the making. And so I paid him his fair share, and although the air conditioner has not quite had a storybook ending, we've been living happily ever after.

Buggy Monsters

If you've ever wondered whom the big black rubber arthropod lurking on the substitute's desk was modeled after, you've got to come to Eretz Yisrael and meet a "juk."

When I first beheld the real live version of the unsightly creature racing across my dining-room floor, I was, indeed, ready to place a substitute in my stead. Only this thing wasn't rubber, wasn't stationery, wasn't a joke; the only thing it had in common with its inanimate counterpart back in the States was the word association it evoked: chutzpah.

I've since come to view the thing in a more philosophical vein. If this universe was designed so that all things positive have a negative reciprocal, then this repulsive creature certainly countered the depth of beauty and dimension that characterize the physical and spiritual landscape of our beloved land.

That first time, though, all lucid reasoning went over my head, as the winged, brown, oversized cockroach zigzagged underfoot. And though I generally scoff at tales of shrieking women reeling in panic at the sight of a bug, this was no bug! Swallowing my pride, I got onto a chair, my eyes vigilantly tracking the invader, until some able-bodied troops arrived on the scene.

"Ask the Israeli neighbors," my husband advised, after I'd gotten over the initial panic. "I'm sure they'll have some suggestions."

Which they did, albeit not of the sort I'd anticipated.

"Oh, that?" Most of my neighbors responded in the offhand sort of manner I would use to dismiss inevitable pests like mosquitoes near the swimming pool, or moths in the *succah*. "You can try some insecticide. But don't worry, you'll learn to live with them."

Poor solace, I thought. If I hadn't been worried to begin with, the prospect of "learning to live" with those flying, leaping, ugly, two-inch waterbugs certainly did the trick.

Appalled, I trooped all the way up to the fourth floor in search of some helpful advice, or at least someone who would identify with my alarm. *Sephardim* have a way of playing up the drama, I thought, confident that in that fourth-floor dwelling, heavy with the pungent fragrance of Oriental spices, my problem would receive the utter consternation it deserved. My confidence was well placed.

"*Ima'le*," ululated my neighbor, hands flying to her cheeks, in the traditional pose of maternal concern. The melodramatic wail, that ordinarily grated on my ears, surprisingly afforded me with a faint sense of satisfaction. I stood there, amused, while she enacted some of her own experiences with the despicable insect, and suddenly, I felt quite stoic in comparison. This was definitely the right address if I had been looking to combat complacency.

What I remember about that visit to my neighbor, however, is not the relief of being understood, or even the indulgence of feeling relatively composed in the shadow of her hysteria. What I remember is her elderly mother's keen postscript.

Sitting at the kitchen table, peeling some vegetables over yesterday's news, her mother, a slight Moroccan woman, listened quietly to our exchange. Her profile intercepted a ray of morning sunlight, so that her wrinkled, olive-skinned complexion appeared radiant.

I thought I detected a hint of a smile playing on her thin lips, as her gnarled hands dropped the tiny sharp blade which she'd been using to pare the greens. Then she looked up intently, and though my memory's made a blur of whom her gaze was fixed upon, I like to assume it was me she was addressing. Quietly, in stark contrast to her daughter's shrill tone, she said, without a trace of reproach, but with the soft wisdom of having lived a lot longer than both of us put together:

"Listen, *motek*, it isn't pleasant, but if you want to get rid of an unbidden guest, it's got to first make its appearance."

That was it. One line of wisdom from a Moroccan woman, in regard to a fleeting creepy crawler, but it's helped me face bugs of many kinds ever since.

I don't know about the rest of humankind, but I generally like to live under the pleasing illusion that I house within my personality no trait worthy of ruthless extermination.

Of course I'm not naive enough to actually believe I was fashioned devoid of failings; I simply prefer to think that my shortcomings fall within the category of the forgivable, the reasonable, or at the very least, the easily correctable. The notion that there's any part of me that's truly despicable is a thought I am not fond of admitting.

Not that I have ever been your perfect angel. As a child, I could pout and shout, lie and cry, indulge and insult. Still, I always harbored the dream of becoming a great, pious, kind individual. Once I crossed the line into adulthood, once I left the scrap paper draft behind and began the first, brand-new pages of life, I expected that all the sloppy childish nonsense would remain forever buried in the wastebasket of the past.

As I set the table for those beautifully prepared meals for two, as I serenely wheeled the brand-new stroller with my little princess tucked inside, and later, as I remained cool and composed during a full-blown tantrum by my thrashing toddler, I was almost convinced that I might make it through life, not beleaguered by those frightening failures they described in the books.

Those first-timers really knocked me flat. When, sooner or later, I was provoked to think or say or do something that burst my illusion of being the generous neighbor, considerate spouse, or even-keeled mother, I felt the startled horror of that initial encounter with a *juk* on my home frontier.

Like that audacious bug disclosing its ugly presence in my picture-perfect abode, the appearance of these detestable traits dissolved my idealistic dreams of effortless harmony and seamless perfection. Though not quite as dramatic as my encounter with the multilegged cockroach, these collisions with myself, lashing out in anger or bristling with resentment, adorning the truth, or being rocked by envy, all shared a dimension. The dimension of startled dismay at facing an unbidden guest.

As I continue through life, there are forever new firsts to scale, forever the discovery of thus far unseen bugs. And each time, after I recover from the initial horror that there still exist unseemly motives running loose across the polished floors of my inner dwelling, I know I can choose between the suggestions offered by my neighbors.

I can "learn to live with them" in the resigned complacency of growing older and replacing rosy dreams with rude awakenings. I can get off the chair, loosen my grip, and give up. I can let my shoulders sag and say, "Oh well, what did I think, I'd be perfect?"

Or I can recognize the wisdom in the advice of that old Moroccan woman, that "if you want to get rid of an unbidden guest, it's got to first make its appearance."

If we really want to get our properties clean, then we've got to welcome those unwanted visitors. Every time we fail, it's one less cockroach lurking in the recesses of our soul, one more opportunity to exterminate something that's been festering inside us.

Every time we catch ourselves behaving unlike the spouse, parent, in-law, teacher, grandparent, or person we've dreamed of being, we have the chance to track that behavior, to find out where it's coming from, and weed it out of our lives.

So next time you stumble upon some unkempt spot in your inner landscape, take the rake, the shovel, the hoe; try some insecticide, anything indeed, but don't "learn to live with it."

And more important yet, don't let it bug you!

Breakthrough

"Why do I have to stand like a policeman?"

The truth is, I don't know. Why *do* I have to stand like a policeman? Lately, I've been pondering the question aloud. About the pettiest of issues, to boot. About bedtime, about homework, about personal hygiene. And about nosh.

Believe me, when educators spoke of the importance of setting policies, I never suspected they meant something as trivial as the consumption of nosh. My opinion has always been that while there are certain issues policies resolve, there are an equal number of them that policies create, and the nosh issue seemed much like the latter.

So I never set too many rules. Without too much talk, I thought I would simply allow potato chips and pretzels during the week, and save the real junk for *Shabbos*. In my naivete, I assumed that's all there was to it. If the snacks were available in quantity, and were readily accessible, I reasoned, they would lose the coveted property of stolen waters.

I couldn't have been more mistaken. While my kids approved of my laissez-faire attitude, they completely disproved it. The nosh was there for the taking, and they would have lots and lots of it, self-service, anywhere, any time. A situation that found me patrolling the kitchen, policing the offending cabinet, an activity I wasn't particularly fond of or good at.

"How about installing a lock?" a friend advised me.

A lock on a household pantry? I tried to hide my contempt. It sounded like the kind of thing that belonged in a prison, not a home. I mean, how was I going to teach the kids trust, if I couldn't convey my basic confidence in their ability to exercise self-control? And talking of self-control, how would they become adults with inner restraint, if I made my rules ironclad, literally?

Well, like so many other ideals, my stand on the issue has taken a shift. I'll never know if it was the rationale that preceded the change, or the other way around, but I've become a staunch advocate of household locks.

Pedagogues nowadays are into all kinds of aids, visual, tactile, auditory. No one seems to be too concerned that the use of these props will lead to lifelong dependence. Young children, they say, seem to need help integrating concepts. I've decided the same is true of values.

Most convincing of all, though, I've found locks to be self-eliminating. For the first two weeks, I had the kids dragging the stool to the cupboard and fiddling with the lock. I heard the boys conspiring to figure out the combination, and the toddler rattled the doors back and forth in an incessant effort to defy the stubborn metal bolt. There was a lot of initial balking, but by the time

I considered removing the point of contention, I realized that the resistance had abated.

It was one afternoon, when my daughter requested an afternoon snack, that I noticed I had forgotten to lock up the last time around. What amazed me, completely astounded me, was that no one else had. Noticed, I mean. To think that the pantry had been open for a day and a half without anybody even attempting a raid!

I haven't removed the lock, but for the most part, its appearance seems to be deterrent enough against prowlers. Not that they've lost their natural craving for the stuff inside; they simply seem to have become accustomed to the fact that the contents of the closet are out of bounds.

If they only knew the truth.

If they only knew that I've become lax about aligning the three gears on the small lock first to open and then to close the little gadget each time I hurry to fetch a few crackers, or to return a bag of cookies to the cabinet. If they only knew that the impenetrability of the nosh trove was no more than a fragile illusion they could easily expose. One jiggle, one turn, and the sham would be uncovered: Welcome to candyland.

So far though, no one has tried. Which I'm actually quite pleased about, given my poor rating for consistency. The thought, however, frightens me. This innate human passion, so easily trained into docile submission, scares me, when I think of all the locked doors we've despaired of ever opening.

Deep within our souls, most of us have fanned flames that have been extinguished at some point along the way. Somewhere in the process of growing up, failure slams its weight on our ambition, crushes some of our morale, brings tears to our eyes. We rush enthusiastically into success, thrust our hand out to scoop up the booty, only to endure the splitting pain, the tear-jerking humiliation, of crashing into an opaque barrier.

Disappointment, however, has a fading quality. It's frightening to see how quickly human fire can shrivel and die, how quickly that red-hot spark of yearning and determination can turn into a charred coal of resignation, black and smoking and defeated.

We've each encountered our own locked doors, sometimes created by the hand of fate, sometimes our own imperfections. The accompanying challenge lies in figuring out which doors are indeed impermeable, which entryways circumstance has locked shut, and which hinges can be oiled with elbow grease, so that they will suddenly swing open with ease at some unexpected moment after months of unsuccessful trying.

There is no one rule, no identifying sign that marks those doors. It's trial and error, a lot of sweat and tears.

And prayer.

Yes, prayer.

If there's one door that forever can be pried open, if there's one lock that invariably gives, if there's one gate in life that spares us the excruciating decision of whether or not to keep knocking, it's prayer.

We've learned it in first grade, sung it, cheeks flushed pink with the innocent excitement of receiving a *siddur* for the very first time. We stood there enchanted, wide eyed with wonder at the magnitude of the gift, at the power of the key entrusted in our hands. And ever since, we've taught it, repeated it, listened to it. *"Ein tefillah chozeres reikah,"* no entreaty ever goes unanswered.

We know it, the profound simplicity of it, and the simple profundity, yet sometimes we very plainly forget. Forget the magic of those giant doors, forget that the little key we wield, will, must, *has* to fling them open wide. And sometimes, we drift in the unfocused way we sometimes hold a ringing receiver on one ear, while our minds wander off, and then, in a sort of startled way, say, "Oh, I'm so sorry I let it ring this long; I forgot I even dialed."

A lot of the time, on the other hand, we're passionately aware. At those times, we come gasping to the entrance, clutching our requests, rapping desperately on the solid door until our knuckles turn sore. Cheeks burning with anxiety, palms sweating with tension, we take that key out of our pockets, and turn it in the lock, our insides pulsing with the hope that our efforts will yield results.

When that key gets jammed in its groove, we begin knocking, first softly, then a trifle harder. And when our polite knocks aren't heard, we do what we do when we're locked out of the house past midnight, and we *know* someone is inside; we begin ringing, banging, rapping on the windows, gathering some more voices to join us.

And often, we get discouraged. Our voices hoarse, our knuckles chapped, we stand in front of the door, doubtful, disheartened. Names for which we have implored so desperately for are crossed out, opportunities we've dreamed of elude us, our hope begins to falter, to flicker and die in the whipping winds outside that door.

We keep knocking, but it's a different kind of knock. We've lost that surety, that innocent belief, that indefatigable trust that no matter what, those doors will give.

"Only *tefillah* can help," we sigh, about this thing or that, and in our heart of hearts, something has been snuffed out. In the most imperceptible way, we've crossed some invisible line from real, convincing hope to a last-ditch effort at optimism.

If we only knew. If we only knew that if we stood there long enough, we would discover that the lock was never even snapped shut. If we only knew enough to return, time and time again, to keep rattling those doors, keep picking that lock, we'd be there to experience the sweet, startling surprise of having those doors swing open in a moment of stunning revelation.

We each know what we need, what we want most. We each know someone who needs something even more critically than we do. Let's not lose hope. The door may have been closed every time we turned the knob, all the statistics may lock us out, but let's not forget two very important things: *tefillah* and the genuine belief in its power. Every Jew has access to the combination.

Playing It Right

It looked exactly the same as it had back then. But the thrill was gone, vanished together with the challenge. It was a navy, hard-plastic square case, snapped shut for easy portability, marked with raised white lettering underlined by a double line for emphasis. Hi-Q.

Back then in those precomputer days, when good old-fashioned board games kept kids occupied, I spent many a bedridden morning or bored afternoon trying to beat my highest Hi-Q score. The objective of the neat little game was to remain with as few pegs as possible on the board.

The ultimate goal was to be able to boast an empty board, except for one peg in the center. Attached to the game was a little leaflet with a key for evaluating the player's prowess: Three pegs scored excellent, two pegs was outstanding, and a single peg left in the center of the board constituted genius.

Usually I wavered somewhere between excellent and outstanding, and was determined to earn the coveted, but elusive, title of genius. And so, driven by the challenge and the will to succeed, I sat, lips pursed in single-minded concentration, weighing my every move.

In pursuit of my goal, I carried the little case along with me on trips, and brought it to the dentist's waiting room. At 8 years old, I thought it to be the most brilliant puzzle around. And so, when I spotted the game, looking very much the same, on the shelf of a discount store some twenty years later, I jumped for it.

Fingering the case with nostalgia, I couldn't wait to sit down at the dining-room table for a stimulating round of what had been my favorite game. I felt an impatient, childish impulse to get my work done, so I would be free to challenge myself, chucking off pegs with deliberate deftness.

Well, I was disappointed. The game was the same, but I suppose *I* had grown. After two or three tries, wherein I managed to alternately score "excellent" and "outstanding," I mastered "the trick." There was a pattern, a sure-fire, no-fail technique to the game. If you followed that strategy carefully, you were inevitably left with a single peg in the center: genius.

I should have been thrilled. After all these years, I had finally hit genius. And now I could accomplish the feat again and again. As many times as I wanted to be a genius.

The heady feeling, though, was gone. That wonderful swirl of ecstasy, that gush of triumph, had somehow vanished, together with my new discovery. I clasped the case shut, slid it to the middle of the table, and wistfully ended my Hi-Q career.

If I had mastered the trick, there was no point in playing the game. So I put it aside for my 9-year-old son, who could still relish the crisp challenge.

Sighing with the anticlimax of dissolved anticipation, I surveyed the dining room, fumbling for something to do. Not that I was wanting for chores that could occupy the empty slot of time. Time has a way of being instantly filled, never leaving much of a vacuum to fill. I had been looking forward, though, to the thrill of competing with myself, and found myself absently scanning the room for some substitute activity.

It was then that my eyes hit the *Sefiras HaOmer* chart. As my gaze rested on the bold lettering, I noticed some faint notations penciled in on the side of the chart. It was a list of goals I had been trying to achieve in preparation for *Shavuos* last year. Or had it been the year before? I didn't quite remember. What struck me was the nature of the resolutions crowding the margins of the chart.

The very same issues I had been struggling to overcome whenever it was that I had put my aspirations into writing were as pertinent today as they ever were. Not one of the goals I had set for myself was irrelevant now, as my eyes beheld the faint markings of hope, of promise, and commitment.

Only seconds before, I had been bemoaning my lost challenge. Here it was staring me in the face: spiritual Hi-Q.

The perpetual struggle to drop all the extraneous pegs, leaving only One in the center of our lives; the ongoing challenge of skipping over obstacles and removing hindrances, until there remained The One and Only Central Point, Focus of all focuses, Purpose of all purposes.

And unlike its physical counterpart, although I've been playing the game for some decades now, I still haven't mastered the trick, still haven't come up with some flawless formula that ensures I will emerge a genius. Each time around there are new nuances. Each time I battle with unfamiliar loopholes, brand-new challenges.

It's a tricky business, this task of uprooting and obliterating undesirable traits, of keeping one's sights ever on the Center, ever on the goal. And as many times as I triumph, I can't seem to reach a level of everlasting victory, a feeling of finally having uncovered a technique to transcend my internal struggles for good.

No matter how many rounds I play, I can never relegate my success to previous victories; I can never remove my pegs with the well-oiled ease of an almost distracted player. And sometimes, after a particularly difficult round, I nearly droop with discouragement.

The list on the *Sefirah* chart seemed to encapsulate the constancy of this unrelenting upward climb. Yet unlike the acute frustration that often fills me, I was suddenly sparked by a new insight, a fresh flash of inspiration.

What had previously crept into my heart as the insidious worm of despair now seemed to take on the appearance of a delicate silkworm, inching its way ever forward, spinning silken strands of breathtaking beauty with its ceaseless perseverance.

Avodas Hashem (serving G-d) wasn't meant to be depressing; it was meant to be uplifting. There is exhilaration in the fact that one never outgrows the challenge of trying yet again. A Jew's life is infused with meaning precisely *because* there is no quick trick to attaining spiritual genius. Indeed, *Avodah* is the name of the game.

Making the Mark

We must have been rummaging around the attic for some old notebook or something, when we hit upon it: a box with some relics of my mother's high school days. Archeologists could not have been as thrilled. Fancy, unearthing your mother's autograph book!

It was a burnt-sienna velvet rectangle with the word *autograph* embossed in gold on the front cover. Come to think of it, it may have been burgundy. But it was velvet, for sure. Dated elegance.

"Ma, can we open it?" We had asked, toppling over each other in a frenzy, as we scrambled down the rickety wooden ladder. It wasn't every day we hit a find like this, a dusty diary that held the key to our mother's youth. So it wasn't a diary; it was an autograph book. It was just as well.

My mother, I remember, punctured the drama of the moment.

"There's nothing that private in there," she chuckled, easing the jammed zipper around the corners of the pad. We were hardly convinced. And anyway, just the thought that these inscriptions had been penned by teenagers who were now mothers and grandmothers made us jittery with adventure.

"Roses are red, violets are blue, but there's no one in the world quite like you."

"May your life be like arithmetic; joys added, sorrows subtracted, friends multiplied, love divided."

"Don't suck lemons; suck ceed."

Oh, so those wishes were *that* old!

There were some mushy love notes, some attempts at humor (Don't open this until your ninety-first birthday ... Ha, ha! Curiosity killed the cat!), and a few succinct signatures. At some point about halfway through the book, the messages changed their tone. The penmanships turned into mature script rather than the childish print. And the content of the inscriptions was noticeably more personal and reflective.

There was one pun in particular that seemed to characterize the transition from frivolous eighth graders to introspective seniors. It came either at the beginning or at the end, but almost every entry included the somber admonition.

"Graduation is going from a life of tests to the tests of life."

I liked the twist, and when my own turn came to sign autographs, it was a good line to fall back on. It had a mature ring, a life of tests to the tests of life.

If it was meant to sweet-talk anyone into savoring midterms and finals, though, it fell short.

Oh, I loved *studying* for those tests. I loved sitting around with a friend on the bed and on the carpet and on the couch, anywhere except the desk that was meant for no-nonsense learning, and whiling away hours over barbecue corn chips and *historia*. What wouldn't I give to be able to relive those hours?

Still, when I walk past the bus stop early in the morning and see those groups of high school girls feverishly cramming the last of the facts as they wait for the bus, I can feel a flutter of tension flit through my stomach. They stand there in groups, pumping each other for information, nervously rambling off answers, frantically flipping through source sheets, their freshly groomed appearances standing out in stark contrast to the dark circles around their eyes.

And as I brush past them, on my way to tackle the tests of life, something inside me exults over my part in the pun. Don't anyone delude me into romanticizing about a life of tests.

I've got my own challenges to deal with. But I don't have to sit in a chair facing a grim-faced *Navi* teacher, and quell my rising panic over names that have eluded me. I don't have to plumb my mind in desperation for the missing variable that will help me decide whether a or c best describes a totalitarian government.

And I don't have to endure the ordeal of sitting in an unfamiliar classroom, near unfamiliar girls, under the supervision of an unfamiliar proctor.

It was part of the policy back then in my days to shuffle the classes in honor of finals. Ninth graders sat along eleventh and twelfth graders, *Halachah* alongside *Chumash*, *Dikduk* touching shoulders with *Mishlei*.

"Just to eliminate the temptation," our principal explained. Why should students have to deal with the enticement of looking over their shoulders, of winking questioningly to a friend, of noticing a phrase they'd been hard put to remember? Why should teachers be put into the uncomfortable spot of policing their students, of suspecting foul play?

Not that any of us ever considered blatant cheating. We just found comfort in weathering the storm together. There is something reassuring about knowing you aren't the only one balking at question number three, something mildly soothing about the mute scratch-scratch of pens tackling the same test as you are.

And then there were the inadvertent tip-offs. If you tuned in to the verbal volley long enough, you were bound to pick up helpful information.

"Isn't number nine a repeat of number five?"

"No, number five is a short answer, and number nine is a longer answer."

"Oh, you mean the three reas —?"

Though a stern glare would shrivel the query midsentence, some satisfied scribbles testified that the damage had been done.

Sitting strapped to one's seat amid a whole bunch of strange faces stripped one of all that. Even if you *wanted* to cheat, the logistics made it impossible. If you were figuring out geometrical proofs, you had nothing to derive from a global studies essay, albeit a brilliant one; if you were stymied by a question in *parashas Bereishis*, then *Shmuel Beis* held no clue.

The shuffling system was a form of solitary confinement. You were forced to tune out the extraneous whispers, the rustle of papers, the screeching of chairs, and turn your mind outside in. You looked around, squinted in concentration, trying to toss the question over in your mind, trying to formulate your own answer. You were there, together with everybody else, but you were on your own island.

Like I said, I've graduated the life of tests; now I'm onto the tests of life. But I'm glad for the practice. Glad I learned the techniques of independent test-taking back then in high school.

Because life never really does take us off that island. We may be in the same room, seemingly scribbling together, but it's our own test we're taking.

We may be in *shidduchim* together, in *kollel*, at work. We may be the same age, at the same stage. We may share common friends, budgets, number of children. We may face the same hardships, syndromes, diagnoses. We may live in the same communities, consult the same *rabbanim, daven* in the same *shul.* We may even be confronted with the same questions.

But it isn't the same exam we're taking.

Passing the test that our destiny hands us is not something we can do by looking at the next person's paper. We cannot copy decisions, transcribe conclusions, imitate resolutions. It's a tactic doomed to failure.

Life's multiple choice is complex. It's between home and job, family and friends, working and learning. It's between discipline and freedom, emotion and logic, creativity and restraint. It's between comfort and self-sacrifice. Sometimes it's all of the above. And then, there are challenges even tougher than multiple choice. There are those open-ended questions, those answers we don't remember having seen in our notes.

At times like those, it's ever so tempting to raise our eyes from the paper, and steal a furtive glance around the room. *What's everybody else doing?*

Everybody else, though, is a deceptive consolidation, a mistaken illusion. There *is* no everybody else. One is tackling Math, another one History. One is taking *Dikduk*, another *Yahadus*. Each one of us is on another grade level, on a separate assignment.

For one person, it might be a question of learning to accept from others; for another, developing more independence. Some people have to master techniques to help them live with their challenges; others may have to step out of their difficulties.

That person sitting in the next desk may have all the right answers.

For *his* test.

He may have the supportive family you don't have, the financial backing, the available time. She may have different physical and emotional needs, different levels of stamina and intelligence. His family may be more demanding, her job less grueling, their house more accommodating. They may have a child with special needs, a health consideration you don't know about, a *rav* or *rebbe* guiding them in a certain direction.

Copy them, and you've failed.

We have to look inward, weigh our own personal set of variables, and figure out the answers to our individual challenges. We may have to pause when others are jotting confidently; we may have to sit over a question long after the others have gone out to recess, but we've got to figure it out for ourselves.

For ourselves; fortunately, not *by* ourselves. Because The Ultimate Proctor bears no resemblance to His mortal counterparts. He shuffles the students and hands out the papers. And then He helps us get through the questions. One at a time.

He knows the ins and outs of every single test. And He has a separate answer key for each one. Because to Him, we aren't a class full of students.

Each of us is the pupil of His eye.

Shehecheyanu!

bsence makes the heart grow fonder, they say. And faint-er, if I may add. A lot fainter.

"Have you gone back to the writing?" people have been asking me, the kind of innocent question that comes after "Oh, how old is he?" and "Does he behave at night?" Good souls, they don't mean to haunt me; they don't even wait for the answer, but I am most defi-nitely daunted, if not haunted.

You see, anyone with somewhat of a short-term memory knows just when the little bundle was born, deceiving as looks may be. So though there isn't a hint of accusation in their voices, my own guilt complex seems to find a mirror in these harmless inquiries that have the irksome tendency to tag along with the standard good wishes.

Part of me groans in dread at the query, dread and annoyance at having been forcibly shoved nose to nose with reality. Most of me, though, can't resist a hearty chuckle at my own naivete that didn't foresee this reality at the outset.

Six weeks, I'd said. All summer long, as I spent night after late night riveted to the unearthly halo of light emanating from my com-puter screen, I had fingered the sweet dream, mouthed the magic words over and over again. Six weeks.

Facing sand-coated beach towels and unfinished craft projects upon my disengagement from the screen at some unsympathetic hour way past midnight, the blessed prospect of an imminent vacation stroked me like a cool hand, smoothed over my peeved overtiredness. At that point, even the inborn martyr inside me was too weary to protest.

A month and a half with my mind off the hook and the computer screen unplugged sounded like nothing but the promise of utter bliss.

Ah, the thought of it! No deadlines to meet, no ideas tickling at the edges of my consciousness as I struggled to fall asleep. No desperate fiddling with a defiant computer at 6 o'clcok in the afternoon while cranky toddlers wreaked havoc with colorful discs. Six weeks off.

Well, I ought to have known nature better. My own nature, and the nature of newborn babies, and most of all, the nature of time off. Six weeks are like a stifled yawn, a square of chocolate, a single chapter out of a captivating novel; just enough to have you notice how much more you need, how much more you crave. Six weeks lets you stretch your cramped muscles barely long enough to wake them up and get a sense of how wobbly you feel.

Oh yes, don't get me wrong. six weeks is an awfully long time.

On paper.

I had plans to walk in the evenings and sort through the pictures in the mornings. I'd see to long-neglected errands, make phone calls I barely ever got to. And it goes without saying, I'd write ahead, so that I could start working with the advantage of time on my side.

Like I said, it all makes for a good chuckle. With most of the sand in the timer down by the time baby graduated from the hospital, six weeks lost quite some of its enchanting ring of eternity. What with little high-pitched wails punctuating all hours of the day and night, and plenty of immediate concerns to tend to, it didn't take much for the rest of the particles in the hourglass to dwindle.

When had I ever found time to write? I've been trying to figure it out, trying to understand the impossibility of it, the absolutely logic-defying answer. When had I fit those articles in? Was it in the scanty morning hours between 9 and 1 o'clock, when unmade beds beckoned together with the challenge of getting a hot meal on the table and running errands before the city closed shop for its afternoon siesta? Was it in those afternoon hours, against the backdrop of homework and toys and neighbors and music, and fighting?

It had to have been the evening, oh that alluring time called evening, when phone calls and laundry and older children and tiredness all clamor for a piece of serenity. Or late evening, or predawn morning. Neither of which seem very appealing right now, from the vantage point of a prolonged six-week hiatus.

Which makes me ponder the dual quality of time, its harsh unyieldingness, and its supple elasticity. Which makes me puzzle over absolute terms like impossible and unfeasible, and wonder if they are cut of the same fabric, taut at a glance, yet pliable when need be. How had I managed the writing just a few months ago when the washing machine had rebelled, when the flu had made its rounds, when summer wardrobes had to be purchased and *Pesach* ushered in, when PTA had vied with a neighbor's Bar Mitzvah and a wedding out of town?

I had, because it had been part of the routine. Routine is the miracle of juggling more balls than one is capable of holding, should one stop for even a moment. Juggling is dynamic; it cannot be explained or demonstrated or performed in slow motion. When one tries to break it down, one is faced with the sudden impossibility of the feat, with the realization that there are more balls than hands, with the undeniable conclusion that something has got to go.

Which isn't always a very comfortable conclusion.

When you've got your familiar routine, when you've got the speed and the pitch figured out so that you can nimbly handle your load, it's unnerving to have a new ball tossed into the contest. For a moment, all your balls go rolling all over the place, and you've got to collect your act. It's O.K. It happens to each of us at some point or another, even if no one is witness to the momentary havoc.

The new baby, the new neighborhood, the beginning of a job, the first time making *Yom Tov*, or orchestrating a *simchah*. A change of yeshivah, a fluctuation in the energy level, a shift in status, social or familial. Suddenly, your old pattern doesn't work, you fall out of sync with the rhythm. It takes one short circuit to break the momentum, and the whole fluid efficiency of your magic act goes crashing.

It'll pass, you console yourself, it's just a stage, you say, as you scramble desperately for your balls and try to pick up where you left off.

Which, I'm coming to realize, is all wrong.

Indeed, most of the time, the trick of success is in the discipline of unremitting continuity. As long as you're in it, you can do it; miss a beat, and it seems impossible.

Missing a beat, though, is inherent to being human, is intrinsic to the ebb and flow of life. Sometimes it's the hand of fate that upsets our balance, sometimes the shower of blessing that spews new balls into our court; but changes and challenges will inevitably force us out of line with the rhythm, and disrupt the smooth continuity.

And the point of these phases is not for them to pass so we can arbitrarily scoop up those balls rolling closest to our ankles and make believe nothing ever happened. These glitches, these kinks in the human mechanism aren't empty time, momentary blackouts whose duration is irrelevant so long as we resume whatever has been our mode of functioning.

They are the rest stops along the highways of life, the chance to refuel and check the map. They are the rare opportunities that the regular brisk pace of juggling doesn't allow for, to reevaluate the activities that fill our time, to shift our position and swap one ball for another.

To reassess what it is exactly we are juggling, and if perhaps some old, extraneous balls have never made it to the trash heap where they belong. To recognize which obligations we are balancing for ourselves, and which we are trying to keep aloft for the sake of those around us. The idea is not to continue, but to start the sport all over again, with an updated collection of balls.

The bulk of our lives are spent juggling. There's blessing in the relentless activity, the gift of making time stretch, of transcending limits, of reaping the joy of accomplishment.

There's a boon too, though, in those shifts, in those sloppy transitions that topple our equilibrium and cause the neat trick to messily fall apart. It's the chance to stop and touch the precious stuff called time, and remake the decision of how we want to fill it.

So whether you're in the middle of a fierce round of juggling, or just picking up the art again, like me, for the next few days, we're all in this together. *Chanukah* is a communal rest stop, a *Yom Tov* that suspends routine and tosses a shot of festivity into the humdrum of winter nights. There are dancing flames and dreidel games, and children home, and latkes and family get-togethers. There are broken diets and splattered stovetops and postponed bedtimes.

Most of all though, there is the priceless opportunity to pause for a week and reflect on the laden words of *shehecheyanu*, the blessing of time, before we toss the balls in the air once again.

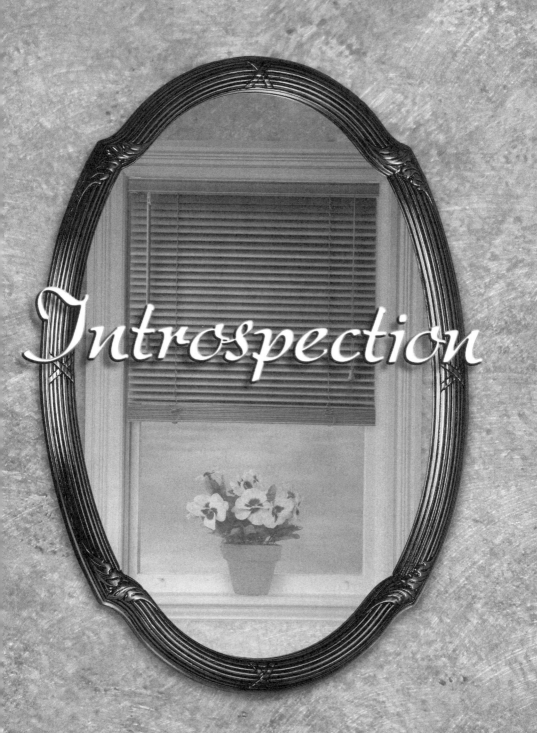

Introspection

Blind Love

"Isn't writing a lonely job?" they ask me.

Well, it depends. Writing puts you in front of an inanimate screen at any odd hour of day or night, stripped of human contact, sharing your innermost thoughts and feelings with people you've never met. Without even picking up a telephone to make the connection, you punch some keys, and presto, your private introspection is up for sale, for critique, for analysis, which you never get to listen in on.

So it's lonely, if that what they mean. But there's a gift to this solitude. It's what enables me to share my thoughts uncensored, as if someone furtively attached a little microphone to my inner mind, without me being aware of it.

Besides, writing has actually brought me into contact with people I never would have encountered; it has introduced me to individuals I would have had a slim chance of meeting otherwise.

And I sort of enjoy the intrigue of these anonymous telephone meetings. There are no impressions based on outer appearances. You don't get to see the cut of the suit, the shade of the lipstick, the jewelry or absence thereof. You don't spend your conversation pondering wrinkles, dimples, or bifocals.

It sounds paradoxical, but when you aren't distracted by all the trappings, when you relate to a person before you know anything about his age, appearance, or origin, you form a certain personal bond that the visual aspect of face-to-face encounters precludes.

So when she introduced herself as Rut Schreiber from Chaifa in a soft-spoken voice that could have passed for a little girl's, but for the subtle deliberate undertone, I assigned her an agreeable face, small, sensitive features, and about 38 years.

"*Erev tov,*" she opened pleasantly, "Is this a good time for you?" When I assured her that it was, she said she had been referred to me by a mutual acquaintance, who had worked for her in the past (Stringing pearls? Running a daycare center?) .

"Hmm," I prodded politely. When people started off like that, business oriented and speaking in Hebrew, I knew they usually had some kind of translating job in the offering.

"I'll tell you what I'm calling about."

Suddenly she sounded hesitant, a little uncomfortable, not sure how to cross the bridge from formal introduction to intimate revelation. I remained silent, trying to give her the time to collect her thoughts and her composure.

"I'll tell you," she began again, "I'm sure you do jobs like this all the time, so it's no big deal, but to me, it's like entrusting you with a piece of my heart."

Now I was really curious, but I sucked in my breath and kept very still. I could sense that she needed to feel alone for a moment, so she could take the plunge and tell me just what it was she wanted.

"My son, David, he was our prince, *bachur meyuchad*, 21 years old; I lived for him." Her sweet voice came out stilted and broken, like a clear *shofar* unexpectedly cracking on the *baal tokei'a*.

"I'm sure you heard about the tragedy in 1997; everyone heard about it, it made the news, but it was our David."

I saw her in her kitchen, hands clutching a mug of hot coffee or tea, eyes blurred by a film of tears. I had to say something, show her I was with her, but it was all I could do to cluck sadly and sigh.

"I'm sorry," she said, and I saw her dab her eyes with a tissue and square her slight shoulders. "You're probably wondering what this has to do with you."

"When David was 5, we moved to the United States for about six years. David developed very close ties with my husband's side of the family living there, and now my in-laws, who are pretty well off, want to do something meaningful to perpetuate his memory."

"Hmm." Again the dull monosyllable. Barring condolences, though, which had lost their pertinence with her swift transition to the technical aspect of her quest, I could think of nothing more appropriate with which to interject.

"They would like something really emotional written up for the dedication ceremony, and I have a text here in Hebrew, written by one of his close friends at the time of the *levayah*. Rivka told me that you are warm and perceptive and would be able to do justice to the job. Do you think I could fax the text so you could skim through it and tell me what you think?"

"I would definitely like to see it," I said, still unsure if I had conveyed enough of the warmth and perception that Rivka had attributed to me. Perhaps Rut Schreiber had wanted me to question her about the tragedy, to which she had made such an explicit, yet vague allusion.

"I hope I will be able to keep all the feelings intact in translation. I'm sure every word is significant and laden with meaning to the family."

"It is, it is," she lapsed into thoughtful silence. Then she took my fax number, thanked me, and promised to be in touch.

All evening, I pictured David, a young *bachur* with a sprouting beard, a mere little boy to his parents, a serious, beloved *chaver* to his friends. I tried to envision the fax from the perspective of his *chavrusa*; the portrayal of an earnest *masmid*, a gentle *baal middos* with a heart of gold and an inborn desire to do *chessed*.

How many *mesechtos* had he mastered? What kind of legacy had he left behind for his family to take solace in?

My thoughts were jarred by the ring of the telephone and the steady inching of a paper coming through the fax machine. I ran to scoop up the pages, the words that were wedged into Rut Schreiber's heart to stop the bleeding hole.

"David was born in Kfar Galim near Chaifa. He weighed 4.1 kilograms at birth. The doctors at Rambam Hospital took a look at his long hair and joked that he was ready to be enrolled in kindergarten.

When David was 5, his family moved to the United States, where they settled in Dallas, Texas. He was enrolled in the Solomon Schechter School in Dallas. Although he didn't know a word of the language, David was soon famous throughout the student body for his deftness at deciphering the Rubic cube; he could unscramble the entire cube in record time with his eyes closed!

When David was 11, his family moved back to Israel. David learned to play the guitar and the piano ... He loved sports, especially tennis ... He was always smiling and was constantly surrounded by a friendly ruckus of tumult and commotion. He loved the telephone, and sports and music. He loved his friends, and they loved him ...

On July 27, 1994, he took a flight course in the Artillery Corps ..."

I felt like someone had pulled a chair out from under me, and I had landed on the floor. Hard. Rut Schreiber, the soft-spoken mother, whose pride and *nachas* had been plucked from her. "Our prince, *bachur meyuchad*."

David Schreiber, the *masmid*, the *baal chessed*, the earnest young *bachur* with the serious eyes and the sprouting beard.

"... He saw his service at the artillery corps as the fulfillment of a family tradition; his grandfather had served as the commander of the battalion ... His stint as an officer was undoubtedly the best period in his life. His ever-present broad smile grew even broader when he was in the company of his fellow officers ...

... On February 4, 1997, two Sikorski helicopters took off to Machanayim Camp, en route to two IDF posts in Lebanon. At 6:58 p.m. the two helicopters collided over Shaar Yashuv, crashing into the tributary of Nachal Dan. Seventy-three soldiers were killed, our beloved David among them ...

He left behind a gaping hole that is filled with pain ... the memories are sharp and vivid ... his speech echoes in the vacuum that was left in his absence ..."

How many *mesechtos* had he mastered? What kind of legacy had he left behind for his family to take solace in?

David Schreiber. His name would be engraved on the monument outside a secular library for young college students in Tennessee. Millions of misguided dollars, thousands of misguided tears, to eternalize the aching memory of one innocent, misguided soul.

My heart hurt for the tragedy of David Schreiber, the tragedy of his death, and the tragedy of his life.

How many such tragedies did I face every day? At the bank, at the bus stop, around the corner, tens of them, thronging wildly out of the public school, polished toenails, girls and boys, shredded jeans, every single one of them Jews, every single one of them tragedies.

How many times had I met David Schreiber gibing with his friends at the bus stop, rifle slung over his khaki uniform, laughing coarsely, sticking a glob of gum on the glass panel of the bus shelter? Had I ever thought to cry?

But I had never met his mother.

I had never heard her still, small voice the way I had today, never seen her sweet face from the unbiased vantage point of my mind's eye, had never before felt her heart beat flush against mine in the clasp of two Jewish mothers.

Tonight I hadn't seen her uncovered hair, hadn't related through the barriers of hostility or prejudice. Tonight I had bonded with her first as a Jewish mother like myself. And even when the mirror I had held was abruptly shattered, Rut Schreiber and her son David remained where they had been planted, deep inside my heart.

My grieving for her didn't wane; it took on a new dimension, the throbbing intensity of a loss within a loss. The loss that she mourned, and the loss that she knew not to grieve; the pain of 21 years, and a gentle *neshamah*, and the gifts of charm and talent and youth squandered on ephemeral ideals.

He was as much an orphan as she was a bereaved mother, both of them orphans, innocent children of Tzion bearing the terrible scars of her widowhood.

Rut Schreiber was a fleeting shadow in my life. Her presence intercepted my existence and then flitted out of it, but she imbued me with a lasting gift, the reward of my lonely career. She gave me the gift of love, and the gift of pain for lost children. Children of *HaKadosh Baruch Hu* who don't even know they are lost.

Perfection

It's one of the ironies of life.
The house becomes the messiest
in the process of becoming the cleanest.
The contents of the closets
clutter the beds,
mattresses vertical
leaning on the doorframes.
You sort the clothing for the dry cleaners,
while the regular dirty laundry
stagnates,
You bleach some tiles in the hallway,
the rest of the floors
sticky with neglect,
The mess!
You bump into it,
and stumble over it,
The refrigerator moved out of its regular niche,
square in the middle of the kitchen floor.
Vacuum cleaner pipes
sprawled across the foyer.
A stranger happening in on the scene,
would be scared off,
by the disarray,
shake his head, run away,
He'd wonder in earnest,
"Where's the *balabusta*
of this home?"
Little does he know,

the cleaning's at its peak,
Just come back in another week,
All the loose ends will be tied
into a glamorous knot,
spic and span,
shining, gleaming,
sparkling clean,
testimony
to the *balabusta*.

Yes, it's one of the ironies of life,
This world's most chaotic
in the process of reaching perfection,
Daily bombings,
Shootings, stabbings,
Fear permeating the corners,
clouding the horizon.
The tragedies!
You bump into them,
and stumble over them,
They blare out of the radio
on the bus,
and greet you
as you leave your door,
And we strangers,
happening in on the scene
are scared off
by the disarray,
shake our heads, run away,
We wonder, in silence,
"Where's The *Balabus*,
of this world?"
Little do we know,
the final *tikkun* is at its peak,

Just come back in another week,
Hang on
just a trifle stronger,
Wait it out
just another bit longer,
Soon,
Very soon,
All the loose ends will be tied,
into a glamorous knot,
perfect in their harmony,
radiant in their perfection,
shining, gleaming,
sparkling clear,
bearing testimony,
to The *Balabus.*

Film Stripped

I don't know why they never mention it in the parenting
books, when they talk about the terrible twos. If there ever
was an effective tool that helped me get through some difficult moments with a toddler, it had nothing to do with empathy or positive
phrasing. In fact, it had rather little to do with psychology at all.

It was a simple black device called a camera.

Looking through the viewfinder has a way of diffusing the impact of an emotionally charged scene. Just the simple act of zooming in on a tot coating her baby brother with peanut butter, or a three-year-old rebraiding the rising *challos*, removes the photographer from the scene long enough to see the humor in it.

Perhaps it's a simple diversionary tactic. Or maybe it's the urgency of snatching the camera in time, which gives rise to an absurd sense of mission. *Keep jumping on those eggs,* you suddenly find yourself praying, *just until I snap that picture.*

I have my own theory about photography, though. Squinting through a lens the size of your eye helps you keep tabs on time. It leaves the entire periphery out of the situation, and shrinks the present into the tiny little frame it deserves. You can't record something for posterity without paying a thought, if only a fleeting one, to posterity.

And what's a batch of crumbled cookies in the scheme of eternity? What's a puddle of oil, of glue, of shampoo in the scope of a lifetime? Forget about a lifetime; all it takes is about 24 hours to put any toddler-wrought catastrophe behind you.

Or almost behind you.

If you've captured the moment on film then you're left with net nostalgia, the joy of real life with the frustration siphoned off. It's a winning number for any album. No professional portrait posed in pretty white wicker against tall tulips can compete with a candid snap of pudgy hands submerged in applesauce.

So we've been taking to the trade. With a pair of imps in cahoots, we've had ample opportunity to preserve amusement for generations to come. In the weeks since *Pesach*, we've recorded doors varnished with Vaseline, faces painted with *chrein*, cocoa-simulated sandcastles. And with the camera handy in between these destructive disasters, we've managed to arrest some startlingly beautiful expressions, the kind of bubbles that usually float away and pop before you manage to catch them.

We've gotten the gleeful gasp of the baby crawling to his reflection in the mirror, the serious musing of a 7-year-old peering up from a page of print. We've zoomed in, unawares, on the preschooler, her face wreathed in smiles and, in her brand new petticoat, curtsying to no one in particular. And we've filmed a serial strip of the spontaneous skit the kids performed one *Motza'ei Shabbos*.

Last Wednesday, when a neighbor phoned me to tell me she was leaving to America, I jumped at the chance.

"Can I send a batch of pictures with you?" I asked. "I think I have one or two shots left; I'll finish the roll, make copies, and get them to you."

I ran to fetch the camera. Smiling faintly, I glanced at the little window, the tiny triangle of yellow exposing the minuscule black double digit.

My heart fell.

The window was blank. Black. No film.

For a moment I stood there, dazed, staring at the dark, hollow cavity. My heart felt gagged, where it had fallen, all the way at the bottom. Then it slowly came up to the surface, google eyed, voiceless, blinking, like a swimmer spluttering up from the floor of the pool.

How can it be, some strangled sentiment moaned; *I took all those pictures.*

I looked at the empty glass again, just to make sure. It was as futile an effort as trying to crawl back into bed to continue a good dream. It was all I could do to hopelessly hold the shards of fantasy in my hands.

The images flashed through my mind, one at a time, in full color, like a filmstrip in reverse. I saw the pile of prints, brown eyes winking with mischief, glossy lips drooling with glee, sparklingly vivid on the matte finish. Mentally flipping the photos, I held each one in my heart for a moment before I bade it a sad farewell. It was amazing how many priceless pieces of nostalgia had been lost.

I'd never particularly favored photography fired in machine-gun succession. I like when pictures merit being taken, when they are snapped singly, or tell a story in sequence; when the collage of them gives you a multifaceted overview of the particular point in the family's life. So I had filled my quota of snapshots slowly, ever so deliberately, over a considerable span of time.

And now, like a shadow in the sun, the whole collection was no more.

I had gone through all the motions. I had focused and flashed, zoomed out and zeroed in, dropped down on all fours and stood on tiptoe. I had forgotten to check one trivial detail. To think that a little thing like film could make all the difference.

And to think that we could go through our lives without the film.

We could wake up in the morning and tidy up the house. Click. Warm up a bagel and smear butter. Click. We could drive to the office, take the car for a tune-up, pick up the shirts from the cleaners, and give in the stereo to fix. Click.

We could teach our children to count and tie their shoes. Click. Do their homework with them, and get them to bed on time. Click. We could take out a mortgage on a house, marry off the children, and renovate the basement. Click.

We could go to exercise, get a new *sheitel*, eat only protein, and lose weight. Click. We could watch our sugar intake, be careful with cholesterol, cut out salt, go for acupuncture. Click. We could paint or play the piano or write or do crossword puzzles, and encourage our children to do the same. Click.

And we could get to the end and we could notice that, hey, we never put the film in.

Never did take the time to load our inner compartments, to put thought and conviction into our hearts, to make sure our intent was in its proper place. Never did insert the stuff that turned a mundane shot into a winning picture, that transformed a passing pose into an eternal experience.

All we did was click the camera. And if we are lucky enough, all we have for the album are those few professional poses we took along the way: Torah and *tefillah*, *chessed* and *tzeddakah*, *kashrus* and *Shabbos*.

Most of our days, though, much of our days, are spent out of the professional studio, removed from the picturesque scenery and perfect props. The bulk of our waking hours are consumed with perfectly ordinary scenes.

Like every other human being, we peel and cook, eat and drink, scrub and shop. We dress and launder, read and relax, listen to music. We make weddings and go to weddings, work, carpool, take kids to the baby-sitter.

Like every other human being.

Almost.

There's a simple little thing inside that makes the difference. If we remember to put it in, that is.

Loading the camera isn't painful or painstaking. It doesn't take more time or talent. But it determines whether or not the myriad snapshots throughout our lives will become everlasting pictures.

It's a matter of looking at the very same activities through the viewfinder, with a frame on the present and an eye out for the future. It's a question of putting our pursuits into perspective, of infusing meaning into our tasks, of remembering that the most aggravating moments make the most treasured mementos.

It's eating that bowl of cereal so we'll have the energy to get through the morning, it's putting away the clean laundry so that the boys can dress in time for *minyan*. It's filling up the gas tank so we can make it to teach *Yiddishe kinderlach*, it's going to the office so we can support our families with honesty and integrity.

It's taking a nap so we can better cultivate our patience, it's administering discipline so that our children will master the right *middos*. It's dressing with modest appeal, in order to make a *kiddush Hashem*, it's losing weight so we'll be able to function as healthier, happier people.

Recording our days for posterity is not an esoteric issue. It's very much in our hands. And chiefly, in our hearts. Because if we're in this world, then we're going through the motions.

Let's not forget the *emotions.*

Day Off

$\mathcal{T}$eaching has fringe benefits. The *type* of benefits depend on where you're teaching, of course. In America, teachers are definitely candidates for the heartfelt assurance that *"HaKadosh Baruch Hu yishalem secharam* (Hashem will give them their reward)." Forget about monetary benefits. The measly salaries they receive, *if* they receive them, every month, don't nearly justify the hours upon hours of preparing, grading, counseling, and extracurricular planning that goes into the job description.

In fact, it would be a nice mandatory exercise for every parent of a child in school to sit down with a calculator and figure out the teacher's pay per hour, at the end of the day (and the night, for that matter). That way, at least we'd appreciate that our children's teachers belong to a lofty category; a realm somewhere very close to our community volunteers.

In Eretz Yisrael, it's different. Although teachers' salaries don't add up to much past the American minimum wage, there are all kinds of advantages that make teachers stick to their jobs the way a family sticks to a precious heirloom: for generations on end. There are paid maternity leaves (for no less than three months), paid vacations, bonuses and raises that work according to a hierarchical system of points, which the teachers toil long and hard to amass.

I'm not discussing those kinds of benefits either, though. I'm referring to peripheral advantages not related to money, nor to the country of one's residence. I mean something aside from the heady feeling of accomplishment, the air of mission, the joy and challenge of educating. That isn't peripheral; it's a predominant part of the job.

What I *am* talking about is the simple concept of a day off. Though any jobholder appreciates a day off, teaching is a mind-engaging task that follows one home and occupies one's evenings and nights. A 24-hour lull where one has no immediate school-related concerns to tend to is a cherished opportunity. So if you've never taught, you may have 365 nonteaching days on your calendar. But you've never experienced a day off.

A day off, for those who don't know, begins like *Yom Tov*, the night before. It actually starts the moment you exit the classroom, and leave the burden of school right there behind you. Even before you reach the car, you mentally part with your students, your colleagues, the school building, and your briefcase. The sound of fierce protest to some scheduled test, or the whining of your preschoolers waiting their turn, recedes into the blissful distance, as you walk past the office, past the bulletin board, past the thronging hallways, past, past, past. For the time being, you can switch gears and swivel into the pleasant mode of just *being*. It's something like that relief of kicking off high-heeled shoes and slipping into a pair of comfortable household slippers, of stripping those constricting layers of evening wear and getting into a loose-fitting bit of clothes.

You fade out all those nerve-grating phrases ("Is this going to be on the test?" or "Do we have to write this down?"), and you shut the hectic screen cluttered with deadlines, stencils, unfinished lessons, and promises to look things up. Then you snatch the blessed moment and savor the delightful emptiness of your mind's terrain. You know that it is empty for but one moment, that in 60 seconds, the blank screen will be flooded by a thousand urgent tasks vying for a piece of your day off. You know it all, but right then, it doesn't matter. Right then you slurp that freedom, the way a kid sucks a peppermint candy; noisily, consciously, savoring the invigorating new vitality that comes with each breath.

It takes a day off to highlight the treat of "only" having to cook, tend to laundry, pick up Shmuly from the dentist, and supervise homework. Only someone whose mind is constantly clogged with classroom cliches and unresolved educational challenges can actually savor the soothing classical music during the usually annoying wait on hold to speak to some service department or other. And for someone who never gets a glimpse of the kitchen clock during the a.m. hours (except to tell her that she's running late for work), everyday phenomena like traffic free lanes or the baby's nap at 11:30 in the morning are nothing short of bliss. That enthralling sense of liberation just doesn't come when you're a full time stay-at-home mom and housekeeper.

Much as we sometimes love to fantasize about hitting the pillow and sleeping a good, long, solid sleep, as long as it would take until we'd awake of our own free will, rosy cheeked, replenished and refreshed; much as we dream of that elusive period when time won't perpetually resemble a game of musical chairs, always one short of the tasks frantically circling; much as we'd love to believe that life without work would constitute an ongoing paradise of days off, it's a fond illusion. A day off comes only in the midst of a workweek, like a warm day in the middle of the winter, like dry weather after oppressive humidity.

And yes, I concede. A day off isn't the exclusive privilege of teachers. Which of us hasn't, at one point or another, encountered that enormous sense of emancipation that comes after any relentless struggle? Anybody who has ushered in *Pesach*, battled illness, married off a child, or done renovations knows the feeling. It isn't necessarily the aftermath of unpleasantness. It's simply the fringe benefit of having invested a powerful spurt of concentrated energy toward any single goal.

And once we've experienced that gush of relief even once, once we've tapped in on that appreciation for the tiny mundane details of just being, we can try to recapture the sentiment at some plain, mundane moment later in time. With some imagination, we can try to access that feeling as we wait for the light to turn green, as we drill the multiplication tables with our third grader, as we do something as ordinary as eating breakfast.

In a game of pretend, we can add some luster to any dull Monday or Thursday by making believe it's a day off; by simply savoring the passing particles that make up the gift of life. Why should that keen awareness of our good health, our freedom, the bounty we enjoy, only come following a hectic whirlwind of frenzied activity?

That's where the creativity comes in. It doesn't necessarily have to be a day off from school. If we can try and imagine, for instance, that we're out on parole for 24 hours, we'll be tempted to grab a piece of the big open sky, bask in our untarnished reputation, exult in the sheer delight of living in our own familiar quarters. If we pretend we've just triumphed over a bout with pneumonia, we'll appreciate every effortless breath, and rejoice in our ability to run our homes independently. If we imagine ourselves some decades hence, suddenly reimbued with the gift of youth, we'll be grateful for every bit of our stamina, hug our sanity, our long-and short-term memory; revel in the fact that we are so pivotal to the lives of those around us.

Indeed, it takes some overcast weather to appreciate our day in the sun, but those rainy days don't have to be something we've just recently experienced. They can just as well be some vivid memories of harder times, or the thought of someone else's plight. If you don't have a real storm whipping through your life right now, be thankful.

And remember, you can always make good on some old rain check for a day in the sun.

Bubble Bath

I remember reading that Chinese healers ascribe incredible therapeutic effects to leisurely warm baths. My kids seem to know this without ever having read up on the subject.

It's usually between 7 and 9 o'clock in the evening that all their latent talents and dreams come to life amid warm suds and running water. Something about the bath seems to be a potent relaxant, as whomever it is inside most often remains there undeterred, despite the insistent knocking of impatient siblings in waiting (not to mention Mom).

If anyone wants to hear the latest in *chazzanus*, or the leading lines of the most coveted role in the upcoming school play, an ear cocked to the bathroom door during these hours can be very revealing. Actually, ear cocking tends to be unnecessary; underwater singing lends itself to a substantial rise in decibel.

Theoretically, I'm all for bathtime therapy. The fact that our apartment has only one bathtub, though, to accommodate several anxious clients, necessitates abbreviated sessions. And the additional fact that that single tub isn't five yards from the younger set who are blissfully asleep makes for some very frantic interference on my part. "Please stop that drumming now!" I'll rap urgently on the door, forgetting all about therapeutic benefits, "You're waking up the baby."

The worst part is the coming out. After all that whooshing and splashing, after all the dawdling and singing and calling for someone to turn up the heat, I finally know that the little bathed fairy is about to emerge, when I hear the familiar call laced with desperation, "Ma, can I have a towel?"

Why the prince or princess predictably forgets to take one in is one of those mysteries that seems destined for Mother to solve.

It still is not as stymieing a puzzle, however, as the dialogue that invariably ensues, as he or she emerges from the steamy bathroom, hair dripping in wet strands over pitch-red ears.

"Oh good, you're out. You look like you enjoyed that bath. Did you wash up well?"

"Yeah." For some strange reason, he (it usually is he) always looks a little caught off guard, like I was asking some kind of surprising question.

"Is that ketchup on your face?"

An absentminded scrape of the cheek with a water-rippled finger is what I generally get for an answer.

"Did you wash your face?"

I ask it because it's my line in the script, though the answer is quite self-evident. The accusation cloaked in rhetoric unfailingly produces a puckered forehead, as if I was posing some memory-jarring challenge. I stand there for a moment, my disbelieving frown punctuating the silence, before a sheepish grin spreads on the freshly bathed, ketchup-smeared face.

"Oh, I forgot."

Forgot, no less. I find it incredible. I know the bath is a good place to relax, to bask in the warm comfort of soft suds and silken hair floating almost indiscernibly in a semicircle around one's consciousness. I recall the soothing pleasure of staring up at the tiled ceiling, feeling leaden, almost asleep, far, far away from the tumult on the other side of the steamed-up door. And I'm not that far removed from childhood that I don't remember the faint indulgence of absentmindedly watching my fingers turn long and curved or short and stubby as I submerged them again and again beneath the surface of the still-warm water. Yes, I do remember all these things, and I'm not about to negate the importance of fringe benefits, but come on, let's face it, what's a bath made for, if not washing up?

I shake my head in baffled annoyance, the kind of exasperated incredulity reserved for 8-year-old boys, and sigh. "Can you tell me what you were *doing* in there all this time?"

It's one of the saving graces of nature that children are as amusing as they can be annoying. Adults are somewhat less endearing. And though when it comes to washing up, most of us get right down to business, the thought of emerging from our lifelong task of soul cleansing like my 8-year-old son from his bath is a prospect that falls frighteningly short of amusing.

I think of myself, days running into one another, deadlines jostling and bumping, trying to find a comfortable spot in my crowded schedule. I think of myself, mind always on the run to catch the bus that will take me to the next stop, rarely free to contemplate the eventual effectiveness or the direction of my itinerary. And the picture that comes to mind is of a child, submerged in the water, engrossed in the water, lulled into a sense of infinity by the water, forgetting about the world on the other side of the door.

Not that I actually forget. As I go through my days, I'm constantly clutching that washcloth in one hand, mumbling *berachos*, even making *berachos*, ushering in *Shabbos*, discussing *hashkafah*. There are times I actually abandon all else and scrub feverishly, like *Erev Yom Kippur*, or in a moment of naked fear. But when I review the overall contents of my days, I seem largely carried away by the fringe benefits of lapping in the tub.

There are appetites to be satiated, and an enormous amount of variety available toward that end. There's summer and winter that bring with them the deliberations of which cottons or velvets or woolens or silks, in what combination of styles, and colors, and in what price range. That's an awful lot of mental and physical exercise to be considered fringe. And it's not even half of it.

There are all the trappings that come along with home and job, there are obligations to family and friends; there's even a bulky part of our existence expended toward the externals of *Yiddishkeit*, planning *simchos*, preparing for *Yom Tov*, presiding over parlor meetings and school dinners. None of us are sitting around, so I can hear some indignant protest rising over the relaxing-in-the-bathtub analogy.

No, it isn't a question of our bodies sitting idle. We all go through the motions, in fact, sometimes at a dizzying pace. And it's not either to say that all these vital functions are merely unnecessary distractions. After all, were we to try and do away with them, these duties would nag us incessantly in the form of whining children, unkempt surroundings, flagging spirits, and neglected routines.

Besides for which, if Hashem wanted us to cleanse ourselves in grim, pursed-lip fashion, I doubt this universe would boast colorful flowers, scented bushes, and tasteful cuisine. Looking around this world bears definite testimony to the fact that He wanted to make our task here pleasant.

No, it isn't a question of what we're occupied with; it's what we're *pre*occupied with.

Each of us as individuals face the minute to minute challenge of remembering what we're doing in the tub. As we drive our carpools, and pick up our grocery orders, as we read the news, flip through advertisements, and wait in the doctor's office, we've got to keep wiping the fog off the steamed-up mirror, and check to see whether our faces indeed look cleaner than when we've entered.

Baths don't last forever. Those knocks on the door, they're meant to remind us of the question while we're still inside, the question we don't want to face for eternity:

"Tell me, what were you *doing* in there all that time?"

The Ultimate Pitfall

I guess I was naive. Or maybe I was simply ignorant of the ins and outs of boys' seasonal games in these parts. But I fell for it.

As we filled up bags with tomatoes and cucumbers, onions and potatoes, my son suddenly spotted them. "Apricots!" he whooped in delight.

"Mommy, can we buy *mishmishim*?"

It must have been my maternal weakness for wholesome nutrition that momentarily tempted me to accede to my son's request. A minute later, my good sense took over. The sign over the display had me know that the new fruit, gingerly packed and nestled under protective red netting, was going at the ridiculously inflated price of 11.90 a kilo.

"They're *very* expensive," I mused, "I think we'll wait until they're in season."

I saw my son's face fall as he glanced longingly at the apricots, and then at me to assess if there was room for another bid.

Which, evidently, he figured there was.

"Pleeeeeeeeease Ma, only a few? This many," he cupped his hands to show me what a modest amount he had in mind.

If there's anything I dislike about shopping with children, it's the pressure of these spur of the moment decisions. With my child's eyes pinned upon me in hopeful silence, I stand there feeling helplessly cornered, wishing some concerned shopper would bail me out.

In anticipation of these scenarios, or perhaps in the wake of them, I've created a firm provision with regard to supermarket-and toy store-shopping. "Whatever isn't decided in advance cannot be purchased in the store."

This instance, however, seemed different. My son wasn't begging for toys or sweets, wasn't wearing me down about some worthless article of junk. He was showing sincere interest in something as wholesome as fruit. How could I let him down?

"You know what, O.K.," I suddenly conceded, and I could see his eyes register a flicker of thrilled surprise.

"Why?"

"Why what?"

"Why are we going to buy them even though they're *very* expensive?"

"Because they're delicious!" I smiled, swallowing my impulse to add "and healthy." For 11.90 a kilo, I wanted this binge to exude the full sweetness of an indulgence, an almost forbidden pleasure.

Apparently, it worked. With my son still gung ho about the apricots three days later, I patted myself on the back for the adroit psychological maneuver. Past experience had shown that attractions of this sort generally lost their appeal once they were inside our own refrigerator.

This time proved different. Chezky took two with him to *cheder* each morning, and had one instead of a cookie for his afternoon snack. I even heard him trying to cajole his sisters to do the same.

I was just thrilled. Until I heard about the gogos.

Gogos, I learned, were the name for the smooth round apricot pits, and constituted a coveted collector's item in the Israeli boys' lexicon. Dated years back, when apricots, I suppose, were an affordable treat, collecting gogos had become nothing short of a national summertime tradition. I don't know whoever coined the peculiar name, but that was immaterial.

The important thing was that as soon as apricots made their appearance for the season, it was as if an inaudible cue had been sounded for boys all over the country to begin feverishly hoarding gogos. The pits were cleaned, dried, counted, swapped, and used to play a dozen variations of some ancient tossing game.

You could tell a popular kid by how many gogos he'd amassed, and if someone didn't rank, he could buy himself an insurance policy with one of the hotshots by offering to hand over his own humble collection. I didn't get all the rules; I certainly didn't get the point of all of it, but there's one thing I got very straight.

My son hadn't developed a sudden affinity for summer fruit.

He'd been petitioning for the pits. And I'd been gullible enough to be moved by his entreaties.

I don't want to cast a shadow over anyone's undying trust, but I've learned to squint at some of my children's innocent requests. And in my heart of hearts, I've begun questioning some of my own motives.

I barely ever reach the *Ani Maamin* section of my *siddur*, but I don't think a day passes that I don't somehow give voice to my sentiment of "*achakeh lo b'chol yom sheyavo* (I await him [the Messiah] with each coming day)." It usually takes the form of a wistful expression following a long suffering sigh, in reaction to one of the many, many painful *tzaros* afflicting *Klal Yisrael*.

I see the daily headlines, am confronted by tragic *tzeddakah* posters imploring for help. I hear about young mothers suddenly stricken, young fathers suddenly taken, and my lips instinctively murmur the well-worn line.

"*Oy, Mashiach* has to come already."

Either I say it, or someone else does, or we both think it silently as our aching insides fervently beseech Hashem to hasten the *geulah*.

We walk along the fault lines of political insecurity, trip over the ravages of financial instability. The *malach hamashchis* seems to be playing with his whip, recklessly flinging strife and havoc, mental and emotional anguish, while we terror-crazed people scramble blindly in an effort to dodge his path.

And all the while, we clamp our sweating fists over that crumpled piece of faith, whispering over and over, like a charm to allay our panic, "That's it, *Mashiach* has *got* to be coming already."

As the heat of summer heralds the Three Weeks of mourning we begin to tell our children, even our very young ones, about the *Beis HaMikdash* and its only surviving vestige, the *Kosel HaMaaravi*.

The Nine Days hang low on the horizon, and the light mood of summer darkens, like a sunny afternoon abruptly turned gloomy by an overcast sky.

And we recount the story of Kamtza and Bar Kamtza, and we remember the cruel siege on Yerushalayim, and we describe the little children begging their mothers for water.

And then, before we can't bear the pained expressions, our eyes light up with anticipation, and we talk of the *geulah*, of *Mashiach* whose footsteps we can already hear. With words of faith and hope, we wash away the tears, our own, and our children's, and those of all our suffering sisters and brothers, as we depict a time when everything will be only good.

A time when there will be no illness and no poverty and no pain; no wheelchairs, and no IV lines and no stretchers. When all children will have healthy fathers and mothers, and all fathers and mothers will have healthy children, many of them. And food to feed the children, and money to buy the food, and the time and the energy and the mental wherewithal to take care of them.

And no, there will be no wars, and no bombs, and no threats. No sirens, and no gas masks; only peace, peace in Eretz Yisrael, and peace all over the world, and happiness forever for all of us.

And as the kids thirstily drink in our descriptions, and a little seed of yearning is planted into their tender hearts, we feel our own passions stirring for that ultimate point in time, for the golden era of *Y'mos haMashiach* that will dawn soon and set all wrongs right.

We ache to see the tears wiped off all the anguished faces and vacuumed out of the crevices of the many bereaved hearts; we pray to witness the banishment of loneliness and deprivation from our midst, poverty and illness forever extinguished.

There's got to be something more, though, tugging at our heartstrings as our voices crack with longing on the notes of *Achakeh lo*. For all our pleading, our praying, and our pining, It's got to be something a lot bigger, and a lot brighter than gogos, even adult-sized gogos.

It's the intoxicating scent of holiness, a sweetness we don't know the taste of, and the pure, cleansing, waves of intimate closeness lapping gently at our hearts as we bring a *korban*. And the clarity, the magnificent, dazzling clarity that will wipe the faintest trace of doubt and confusion off the horizon.

And the quivering relief that comes at the end of all struggling, the inebriating sense of freedom from the grips of pride and anger and envy and lust. No more the sickening illusion of fulfillment, the blinking, winking, neon bulbs of emptiness that lure tender souls into abysmal darkness.

Only the shimmering rays of *kedushah*, like the sun upon the ocean waves. And the truth and the kindness and the glory of Hashem glittering and sparkling and crackling atop them, like a million diamonds in the blinding radiance of His light.

And we, all of us, floating atop those waves, freed from the vise of poverty and anguish, stripped of the personal weights that drag us down and keep us thrashing about wildly, barely holding our heads above water.

We, cleaned and trimmed and changed, like children after a bath, our hearts and our minds and our souls fresh like newborn babies, and filled with an irresistible craving for Him, Him and nothing else.

Of course we want *Mashiach*. We desperately want *Mashiach*. We stand, like pleading children, our eyes pinned heavenward, hoping, waiting, begging for the *geulah*.

Let's try and be honest, though; do we really mean the apricots, or are we pleading for the gogos?

The Living Dead

They were sitting *shivah* in their sunny Yerushalayim apartment, two young parents for their young daughter. The signs of life were everywhere; organdy curtains edged with pink rippling in the breeze, colorful books beckoning from the shelf, and smiling dolls swinging their legs from their perch on the pretty Formica hutch.

Everything was there, but the most precious thing itself: Life. That had been snuffed out of their pink-cheeked, ponytailed first grader on her way home from school, on her way into childhood, on her way into discovering the wonderful secrets of growing up.

She had been bringing home her first report card, proud, serious, holding the document that charted her progress, that marked her budding potential with neat little letters in clean white boxes. The report card was lying now on a small plastic chair, together with some drawings.

There was a yellow sun crayoned in the corner, smiling down at a patch of grass, three tulips in different colors, and a stick figure of a little girl with a basket in her arm. Beneath that was a *mitzvah* chart she had made for her little sister, perhaps they had been playing school, with her sister's name in uneven block letters heading the page. A few of her cherished stickers had been peeled off their page in her sticker album, and placed on the chart in an act of love toward her little sister.

Lying in a stack were some freshly developed photos, edges still curled, of her *siddur* play that had taken place only the week before. Eyes glittering like jewels, wisps of brown hair escaping the gold crown on her head, like a wreath around her beaming face, she stood hugging her most prized possession — the *siddur*.

It was a picture of a little girl, a picture of joy, a picture of *Yiddishe chein*. It tugged at my heart, it stung my eyes. I wanted to flee the room, bury my head in a pillow, and cry for all the sorrow that that picture of joy evoked.

On the bus home, that's what I did. Huddled in my seat, very much alone, I watched the deep orange sun melt into a pool of gold, and in minutes I was wrapped in the cape of darkness gathering its folds around the holy city. Riding along in that comforting darkness, I sobbed quietly, thinking of the report card, of the crayoned drawings, of the sparkling photo.

Only last week, those very same items had lain strewn around the house, tacked to the refrigerator, in the drawer, on the dresser. The way they do in my home, the way they do in most homes of little first-grade girls. Unobtrusively, unceremoniously, taken for granted; the kind of everyday items that invite a fleeting smile, or an absent minded chuckle, or a tug of affection.

Today, they were like the lights strung across the velvet blackness of the night sky, luminous, brilliant, stark, outlining the beauty of a stilled landscape. Today, these jewels of light were what remained, what would be remembered, what would be treasured and missed.

Had she fought with her little sister? Had they pulled each other's hair, and called each other nasty names? Had she pouted and stamped her foot when she had been asked to clean up the toys? Had her mother heaved a long-suffering sigh when she'd come out of bed for the umpteenth time at the end of a tiring day? Probably. Surely.

Those had been passing moments, though, transitory hardships, temporary clouds. They had dotted the present and had created the natural, boisterous setting for those priceless bits of childhood, those pieces of *nachas*, those gems of innocence, and purity, and unlimited potential. The noise and normalcy of the ordinary, everyday challenges had almost obscured the radiance of the special gifts.

I looked around the bus. The seats were filled with people, ordinary people, at the end of an ordinary day. Some were reclining in their seats, heads drooping forward in exhaustion; others were involved in animated discussion. All of them had conducted some affairs in Yerushalayim today, and were returning home after a tiring trip.

They'd be greeted by their families, by their neighbors, by a clean or messy home, by a leisurely evening, or by a cacophony of loud demands. They'd be swallowed right into the familiar setting where they'd be taken pretty much for granted, as a package deal of faults and virtues.

What if they hadn't returned tonight, Heaven forbid? What if some accident had precluded them from ever returning home? Whom would their loved ones remember? What memories would their spouses and siblings, children and neighbors, friends and colleagues hold on to? What picture would the thought of each of these ordinary people conjure?

"She was a strong woman," they'd say, "she had real determination. She was never happy with just good enough."

"He had the most fantastic sense of humor," they'd recall wistfully. "He knew how to lighten any situation."

"She really knew what it meant to listen."

"He didn't know about monkey business. If it wasn't straightforward, then it wasn't for him."

Sitting here on the bus, as they were, they were simple, commonplace people. Darkness only had to set in for the shining essence of each of their personalities to emerge, powerful, resplendent, radiant.

And like the crayoned drawings, like the stickers, and the photos, little pieces of their everyday existence would suddenly take on renewed meaning, magnified proportions.

"Oh what a wonderful time we had shopping together for a jacket last week. It was so cozy, so warm, so deliciously normal, the two of us walking and chatting about everything and about nothing."

"How I'll cherish that note he scrawled on a napkin before he left the house. It was so typical of him, thoughtful and careless at the same time."

"Just fingering her *siddur* makes me feel her presence all over. I could close my eyes and picture her fervently whispering *Shema* at the kitchen table."

Sure, they may have lost tempers and credit cards. They may have criticized and gossiped, may not have held the baby or a steady job. They may have pitched in too little, or interfered too much. They may have taken advantage, taken sides, or taken offense, too easily and too often.

Because everybody has faults. Every living, breathing human being inhabiting this universe has failings and imperfections.

It's just a shame that we tend to wait for the darkness, for the stillness, to bring out those inner gems, those shining lights residing within every ordinary person we know. What a sad fact of life that we don't allow the sunshine flooding our days to pick up on those beams of extraordinary light. Instead we opt to get stuck in the shadows, in the dim crevices.

Death is sad. There is so much to learn from all those dear ones who are lost. Life is even sadder; there is so much that is lost in those dear ones we can learn from.

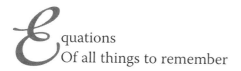

Integrated Math II

*E*quations
Of all things to remember

about algebra,
apples and oranges,
but that's what stuck.
I guess my whim for imagery
Preferred polished red apples,
flecked with green,
shiny, textured, oranges,
to somber x's and y's
devoid of character,
Though I'm not sure I could solve
an equation today,
untangle parenthesis,
dissolve a long string
of mathematical jargon,
into a neat little answer,
though I'm not certain I'd know,
exactly what to do
to one side,
and then to the other,
What's remained of algebra
for me,
is the principle behind the variables,
the analogy behind the principle:
x and y,
like apples and oranges,
don't add up.
Can't combine them.
Can't compare them.
Got to tackle each one
as a separate entity.
Like Mr. X and Mr. Y,
Like Mrs. X and Mrs. Y,
baby X and baby Y,
family X and family Y,

in the equation of life.
No two can be thrown
into the same basket,
different appearances,
tastes,
abilities,
different struggles,
inner
and outer,
different tools,
temperaments,
and needs,
different duties,
and different expectations,
different countries,
and different standards,
different siblings,
parents
spouses
children,
different pasts,
and different pastimes,
different gifts,
and different failings,
different thresholds
for pain
and frustration,
and talking of brackets,
there's the financial one
to take into account.
No amount of reckoning,
of calculating,
of questioning,
"How come *she*,

he
can,
can't,
do,
not do,
this, that
the other thing?"
No amount of figuring
will give you the answer,
because there *is* no
one answer.
If you can figure out
instead
the enigma of your own existence,
if you can break the code
of the single variable
that represents you,
without sending sidelong glances
to the a's and b's
and x's and y's
around you,
Indeed,
If you can succeed
to unravel the equation
Without equating,
you'll have solved
a problem
much tougher
than any
in the algebra book.

Tasting Time

I clearly remember the year I decided to make *holipches* for *Purim*. My mother had always made them for the *Purim seudah*, and to me, just the smell of the meat-filled cabbage simmering in tomato sauce evoked images of crowns and masks and cellophane.

Until that year, I had skipped tradition in favor of convenience. My brood was too young to appreciate the delicacy, my husband claimed he didn't need them, and I, well, I wasn't going to go through all the bother for myself.

But that year I decided the time had come to reinstate the *Purim* tradition and serve *holipches* at the *seudah*. Judging by my daughter's newfound interest in string beans, and my son's recent appetite for mushroom soup, I decided they had reached the point where they could appreciate stuffed cabbage.

I was excited as I set out to work checking the cabbage. This year it would be a *real Purim seudah*. It would smell like a *Purim seudah*, it would taste like a *Purim seudah*, and the smeared red plates would bear testimony to the fact that my efforts had been well worth their while. I basked in this sentiment as I painstakingly checked each leaf, rinsed it, and then held it up to the light.

As I served the steaming dish a few days later, I smiled, carefully checking my family's reaction. After the initial "What *is* this?" from the older ones, and "I don't want" from the younger set, I sat down to enjoy my portion. "Eat, *kinderlach*," I coaxed in between mouthfuls. "You'll see, it's delicious." My confirmation was not long in coming.

"I know, Mommy. I finished mine already. I ate the whole thing. I just left over the peels."

So much for my assessment of junior taste buds. Well that took care of my appetite for the rest of the meal, but I had plenty of food for thought as I discarded a heap of "peels" at the end of the *seudah*.

I thought of *Pesach*, next on the horizon. Like most conscientious housewives, I was well into my preparations for the holiday. I was dutifully checking my lists each morning, and triumphantly crossing off chores that had been accomplished, at the end of each day, which most often was past midnight. All I dreamed of as I hit the pillow was that gleaming set *seder* table, the symbol of freedom, of victory, of having reached the goal.

Now with *Purim* behind me, I was nearing that goal. The *sedarim* were looming closer and larger, and I felt the excitement of a toddler taking the last few steps to reach the prize dangling in front of him. And suddenly, on that *Motza'ei Purim*, thinking of all the hard work and anticipation leading up to *Pesach*, I was filled with resolve to make the most of the coming *Yom Tov*.

To stop and enjoy the crunch of the matzah, to smile with the sweet singsong of the *Mah Nishtanah*. To get out of the kitchen and push the little ones on the swings, and laugh with delight as they squealed, "Higher, Mommy!" And inside the kitchen, too, to savor the warm atmosphere, the smell of beets foaming over the top of the pot. I was seized with determination not to let the days slip through my fingers, not to let my *Chol HaMoed* become just some more days to concoct some more compote and mashed potatoes. Instead I would focus on feeling the *Yom Tov* spirit, on filling my lungs with the smell of spring and the feeling of renewal that *zman cheiruseinu* brought along with it.

My kids had highlighted for me the irony we adults live all too often, without even noticing. As I looked at those discarded "peels" that had taken so much time and effort to prepare, I couldn't help making the parallel. How often do we opt to skip over the stuff that gives life its spice and flavor?

I thought of an old neighbor of my mother's when we children were growing up. I remember being amused each year by her dramatic declaration as she greeted my mother the morning after the first *seder*.

"One down!" she'd heave wearily. "One more to go." Then she'd launch into a detailed reckoning of how many guests she had hosted, how many potatoes she had peeled, and the late hour at which she had gone to sleep. As she was talking, she would suddenly look at her watch, shake her head, and hurry back into her house, apologizing that she couldn't while away her *Yom Tov* morning schmoozing when there were so many important details to be seen to before the next meal.

With the culmination of *Pesach*, as she hauled the last of her boxes onto the upper shelves of her storage closet, her voice was hoarse with relief. "We made it!" she'd exclaim. "Eight more months until we have to start cleaning again." Though she had never really struck me as the humorous type, she did have a dramatic flair, and so I assumed her proclamation had been made in jest.

Over the years, I've met some more like her, and believe me, I've learned that it's no laughing matter. From the minute *Yom Tov* sets in, they begin their countdown. Actually the countdown starts way before *Yom Tov*, shortly after the *Elul — Tishrei* countdown ends. Somewhere way back in *Teves* or *Shevat* they've already begun crossing off the days, checking off lists, pushing time, and praying to be over with it already. One more closet done, one more week past, another room finished, another day behind. One *seder* done, first days over, we can start packing away the pots for next year.

And with the onset of *Motza'ei Yom Tov*, they're on to the next countdown toward the coming *Pesach*, or the coming *Motza'ei Pesach*, or whenever. Whenever that elusive finish line that they are perpetually working for will call a halt to all activity and usher in a magical time when there is nothing left to be done. Which just happens to be never. After all, life on this earth is about doing. And so they are perpetually out of breath, counting and waiting for the thing to be over, whatever "the thing" at the moment may be.

What a shame. A shame, because when we look back, most of the special things in life are those ordinary little pieces of our past.

Most of the beautiful times we remember with a twinge of nostalgia are those delicate crystals of time that we held up to the sun long enough to allow its light to reflect their beauty. Like the tinkling laughter of childhood, the chocolate smeared over a toddler's face, the crunch of the autumn leaves.

Like a mother jumping rope, while all her children giggle with glee, or a father excitedly pointing out a plane making its descent, as he steers the car over the bridge. Like the thrill of the tree in the front yard proudly wearing her first green buds, or the sight of the everyday kitchen suddenly transformed, outfitted in her *Pesach* attire of aluminum foil and contact paper. The shrieks of delight accompanying the pulley constructed by the neighborhood boys to haul their junk from the patio below to the porch above. The scene of red-cheeked children cowering under a flapping chicken, *shlugging kapparos*, and the picture of lanky *bachurim* towering over an old tin garbage can, enthusiastically stirring the burning *chametz*. A kaleidoscope of priceless memories made of tiny colored bits of passing time.

And if we don't stop to capture them, to cradle them in our arms, and feel their rich texture, to imbibe their aromas, and admire their vivid colors; if we don't pause to stroke those moments, to relish their flavor, and listen to their music, then we aren't really experiencing the essence of life, the juice and the zest of it.

Life is a present, a delicacy made to savor and enjoy. We've got to develop our taste buds to appreciate the flavor of those little particles that make up that present. Because sometimes, too often, we are so busy getting to the meat of the matter, we leave over the best part.

Auto Edit

Sometimes those hours between midnight and dawn are most conducive to introspection. There are no disturbances like phones and bells to disrupt one's train of thought, and no burning priorities like homework, and carpools, and sibling rivalry vying for one's attention. Sometimes those hours are just about the only time when everything is blessedly peaceful, quiet, and orderly, so that it almost seems like a shame to waste them sleeping.

The stillness of the night invites a spirit of creativity and fluid thinking, and often it's just then that I'm tempted to flick on my computer and watch an idea take root as my fingers dance over the keyboard. On the other hand, at that hour I can hardly boast of hawk's-eye vision.

So it was at 2 or 3 o'clock one such morning, when I quickly scanned the paragraphs I had written to check for errors, everything seemed all right. I made some deft corrections to those words high-lighted by the spell and grammar check and sent off the piece to a friend who serves as my critic. Then I wearily shut the computer. Stretching my muscles, I yawned noisily and began my bedtime rituals, still thinking about the piece I had just completed.

My thoughts had been inspired in a moment of conscious aware-ness and I hoped they would strike a responsive chord in the readers in the same way they had touched me. That's the last I remember thinking before I drifted off to sleep.

Well, I don't know about inspiration, but it certainly struck a responsive chord.

"Tell me," she began warily, when I picked up the phone pretty early the next morning, "did you send your article to the editor yet?"

I knew that was a thinly veiled way of telling me that something about the article hadn't found favor in her eyes.

"No, not yet. What's the matter?"

"I usually go for your sense of humor, you know that, but I think you carried it a bit too far this time."

Sense of humor? I mentally reviewed last night's article in search of the line that could have jarred her sensitivities. As far as I remembered, though, I hadn't made even the slightest attempt at amusement. The piece had been a serious essay on *tefillah,* and I couldn't imagine what my friend could have found to take issue with.

"What's this about 'pouring out our souls to our Pappa in Heaven'?" she demanded, before I had much chance to ponder.

This time it was my turn to be horrified. "*Pappa* in Heaven?" my voice took on a shrill note. "You're sure?"

"Positive," she responded. "I have it right here in front of me. Not once, but three times in the article, you refer to our 'Pappa in Heaven.' I think it's in very poor taste, if you don't mind my uncensored opinion."

There was a moment of confused silence, as I tried to make sense of her ridiculous accusation. Then, suddenly, realization dawned. I stood there with the phone in hand, as my shoulders heaved with laughter.

"It sure sounds funny," she ventured. "Would you mind enlightening me?"

"Not a bit," I gasped, calming down, "you must have really been wondering!"

"Well, yes, sort of."

"Here goes," I smiled. "A few months ago, I wrote a short story depicting a Jewish family in early America. When I reread the first draft, something sounded not quite right, and then I realized what it was.

"Originally, I had referred to the father as 'Father,' but I thought the story would have a more authentic ring if I switched it to Pappa. With a computer, everything was simple, right? So I clicked the mouse on 'edit' and in a flash, the screen politely inquired what it could do to help me. Entering the word 'Father,' I instructed my loyal editor to locate every appearance of the word and replace it with 'Pappa.' Which is exactly what my computer did. Presto. One command, and the job was done."

"I get it, I get it," she chuckled. "Somehow, your computer never canceled the command. And it's still religiously on the lookout for Fathers, obediently turning them into Pappas. 'Pappa in Heaven,' though, is really strident. I guess there are certain things computers have yet to learn," she laughed.

And people too, I thought

How many times do we reach a conclusion, implement a rule, adopt a new approach, in the hope of solving some problem. Relishing the truth of the new idea, we enthusiastically apply it to our lives. Often, though, we throw one word of caution to the wind.

Not every solution is true for every problem, not every approach will work with every child, not every schedule is appropriate for every stage of life. At some point or another, life may warrant a command to be canceled or revised. People aren't static beings, and reality is unpredictable. Much as we'd like it otherwise, human beings completely invalidate the notion of "once and for all."

Computers make decisions once, and for all. People are of a more complex design. Each and every situation justifies a separate decision; we must exercise our faculties of distinction each time anew.

Just because I've allowed my children to visit certain places in the past doesn't exempt me from reevaluating the pros and cons the next time around. In New York, certain behavior may be the norm; in Eretz Yisrael, it may not be acceptable.

While charts may have worked wonders with an older child, this one may require a different technique. And while you may have thought color war was a fabulous idea in your previous experience running a day camp, new considerations may behoove you to rethink your perspective.

Life constantly sets us down in front of the crossroads, and it's tiring. Sometimes we'd love to click on the mouse, "select" a certain decision, and put it in effect forever after. But as Jews, constantly striving for bigger and better, the only domain where ironclad rules exist is *Halachah*. In every other area, it means painstakingly holding up each decision to the light for inspection.

No matter what an advanced era we live in, decisions cannot be mass produced. Neither can they be borrowed or bought. Each judgment must be handcrafted for the particular instance, with Torah sensitivities serving as the magnifying glass. Otherwise, we may just end up with some ill-humored situations. My faux pas with the computer proved that.

For once and for all.

Decisions

Follow-Up

*I*ve spent my afternoon and evening today doing something wholly unplanned. Not that that's very unusual. I think it's part of the human condition, or at least part of the woman condition, that has us winding up in very different places than we'd ever projected ourselves.

You go to the drawer to put away that invitation, a distraction whose duration should amount to any number of seconds, and you suddenly find yourself weeding out all the unnecessary paperphernalia that's been cluttering the drawer's recesses for weeks.

Or alternately, you answer the phone quite innocently, only to be suddenly reminded of some all-but-forgotten past commitment, future deadline, or present opportunity, that whisks the mundane chores off your agenda, and has you rushing out the door to some urgent destination. All this aside from the emergencies that tend to crop up, whose only predictable property is that they always arise so very unpredictably.

So I'm used to detours. What happened tonight, though, wasn't a detour. It was a full-fledged wild-goose chase that took place right in my own kitchen. It led me around and around in circles and got me no closer to my target, which happened to be a story about some winged entities, though geese would be way off the mark. If I've piqued your interest, believe me, mine's been piqued since two weeks ago when I first heard the story. As I've said though, not one of my 20-some phone calls, local, intercity, and trans-Atlantic, have gotten me any closer to un-piqueing it.

I'm accustomed to keeping my eyes and ears open. It's a trait I sometimes suspect I was born with, though perhaps it's a habit born slowly over the years out of natural curiosity combined with a creative need to give color to everyday events. In any case, I've always found fascination in the nouns of life; the people, places, and things that create the background for the endless lists of verbs, state of being, and mostly action.

The story I'm talking about, though, was not one for which anyone would have to keep their eyes or ears open. It was the kind of astounding narrative that opened your eyes wide in shocked disbelief even if they'd been initially shut tight. It was the type of tale that reverberated in your ears, rushing like waves, haunting like whispers, ringing with a newfound clarity. It was the kind of story you wanted desperately to share with someone as soon as you heard it because your eyes and ears couldn't contain it all, the excitement, the amazement, the encouragement.

So naturally, in my own brand of sharing, I was just itching to take a pen to paper, and spill my amazement over the events that *hashgachah* had brought to my ears. The title, in perfect time for *Chanukah*, was on that paper before I could even collect my thoughts: *Bayamim Haheim, Bazman hazeh* (In Those Days, in Those Times); Modern-day *pirsumei nissa*. As I was very soon made to realize, though, collecting my thoughts, and others' thoughts, in this instance, would take a lot longer than I'd ever have surmised.

It seemed innocent enough. I'd heard the story straight from my sister-in-law, who had heard it from her neighbor, who had heard it directly from Rebbetzin Chana Weiss, a renowned speaker in Jerusalem, who, the neighbor emphatically vouched, had heard it firsthand. Fair enough. You can't expect the stories to happen to *you* all the time, though I've often been accused of it.

The procedure, I naively reckoned, should be relatively simple. Call Rebbetzin Weiss (okay, take into account that that should take two days; I was *that* realistic), get the name and number of the protagonist, and call her yourself.

That was two weeks and about 23 phone calls ago.

Since that first conversation with Rebbetzin Weiss, who surprisingly answered the phone on the second try, and was incredibly gracious about sharing the details, I've been meaning to pick up the lead she gave me, which allegedly was going to connect me to the sought-after main character in the unusually dramatic real-life fiction. The only missing factor was the woman's telephone number.

Little missing factors such as these have, in my experience, often served as catalysts to cool down determination and allow procrastination entry. Which is why, over the past ten days, I have repeatedly rewritten self-directed reminders to trace the telephone number of some Mrs. Kamirnik who apparently was not listed in the regular directory.

This afternoon, armed with the number, and equipped with ample paper to catch every nuance of Mrs. Kamirnik's account, I set out to document the story for posterity. Or so I thought.

Now, some ten hours later, I've just about relented. The cover page of my sheaf of papers is adorned with names of people I've made my first acquaintance with, doodles as I've waited for phones to be picked up and busy signals to clear, and digits comprising country codes I've never dialed before.

Like concentric ripples in an ever-widening circle, my simple quest has left the realm of my kitchen, of my city, of my country, has left me turning myself inside out, ducking under and over, in and around the tangled loops of the grapevine, with no end, indeed no beginning, in sight.

And so, though it's not nearly as startling, as powerful or incredible as the original, I've got a story to share. If like me, you've been prone to relying on popular verification, if you've come to resolutions regarding halachically implicated actions solely based on your friend's or relative's say so, if you've been toting quotes that you picked up secondhand (at a discount of time and energy), please try to trace your purchase.

The term secondhand information, I've learned, should be regarded with utmost caution. Unless the source is first and you are second, the label "secondhand information" should alert you to do what an expired date on a medicine bottle does: Search for a fresher product.

Stories invariably undergo a refining process in which artificial additives work against the natural preservatives. Characters switch ages and affiliations, an additional child or two is granted to a family, all by well-meaning perpetrators of the original tale. I've heard stories about myself after they've circulated the neighborhood without a name, with some very interesting revisions to my life.

Yet the unsuspecting consumer buys it. When a story is professionally packaged and affixed with the seal of some respected notary, it makes easy bait. Which isn't necessarily alarming in and of itself. A beautiful story has the power to inspire regardless of whether the details actually took place, and some tales are natural fiction, stories that *could* have happened, whose purpose is growth rather than accuracy.

The danger, as I see it, is when the rumors aren't some innocuous stories, but involve the intricacies of integrity and *Yiddishkeit*. When we swallow decisions, opinions, and halachic rulings, author unknown; when we conceive notions based on condemnations or approbations that we've blindly adopted as fact, or worse yet, quote these with finality, leading other people to believe that we can be relied on as the first link in a crucial chain of Torah and *Mesorah*.

We've learned to check our caller ID's in an almost instant visual sweep of the display. Like most things in today's day, verification has been made simple and quick. When it comes to the important things in life, let's not suffice with a shrug when the display flashes "out of range." Whether it's about *kashrus* or *tzeniyus, hilchos Shabbos* or *chinuch*, let's not cite flimsy proof for our actions based on evidence that would never hold water in court.

There's good reason, I've discovered, for *Chazal's* seemingly disproportionate reward of "*Mavi geulah l'olam* (being a catalyst to bring redemption to the world)" promised to anyone who repeats information in the name of the one who recounted it. Getting to the source can be time consuming, frustrating, and downright painstaking. If we want to live our lives on the books, however, we've got to go for it. Secondhand is fine for furniture and toys, even books, but who wants anything less than the original when the tale in question is the story of our lives?

Kaleidoscope

I tell you,
We can be a little mixed up.
One second we're agonizing
over atom bomb threats,
The next minute
over missing buttons.

One minute we're contemplating
the *churban,*
The next, we're making plans
for our vacation after *Tishah B'Av.*
On one line
we're sighing over real *tzaros,*
On the other,
over the choice of Formica
for the new kitchen.
Oh yes,
We can be kind of mixed up,
But that's what it's like
to be human,
A collage, a hodgepodge
Of issues big and little,
Dangers, concerns,
inconveniences, appointments
Pasted atop
Surprises, scares,
disappointments, demands,
Phone calls, invitations,
Yamim Tovim, meetings,
Haphazardly overlapping
Carpools, emergencies,
bills, obligations,
A thousand big and little matters,
Rubbing elbows,
Vying for our attention.
And life's most challenging chore,
Is sifting and sorting
Through the closet
of our day-to-day existence,
Making room
in the crowded confines

Of twenty-four hours,
For all that's got to fit in.
Junking the junk,
And organizing
The rest
of the mixed-up mess.
And though sorting
Is a pretty tedious chore,
One thing's sure,
tempting as it may seem,
When you're creating order
in the closet,
The trick is *not*
To throw away all the little things,
But to put them
In their proper place.

Tile Tale

*Y*ou won't find it listed in the Hebrew-English dictionary, and I don't remember learning it in *Ivris*, but the word certainly gets a lot of attention around here. *Balatas*.

There are very few things within the length and the breadth of this beautiful country that are quite as dull and as unremarkable as these freckled, speckled, beige and brown tiles. Yet for some reason unbeknown to me, they've succeeded in making it to the top, or the bottom, of every Israeli household.

Regardless of the size or shape of the room, its purpose, or the color of its decor, there are the predictable, stodgy *balatas* lining the floor. One size fits all. If you chance to be stepping on really high style, they might be flecked in gray and black, rather than the common beige and brown. Whatever the shade, though, you can be sure of one thing; they will nearly always be *balatas*.

Practical, I remember thinking, the first time I came across the phenomenon; why, you could spill a bag of beans and no one would know the difference.

The crying ignorance! There's nothing, I've learned, nothing, that consumes as many hours of the local homemaker's schedule, dollars out of the advertisers' pockets, and gallons out of the dwindling Kineret, as the upkeep of these lackluster stone floors.

It's an art, I've discovered, a skill that requires no less dexterity than painting or dancing, to spill the water, spread it, and scrub it into an even soapy foam, and then collect it all into the drain hole so that not a vestige remains. There are those hardy souls who venture the operation every morning. Squeaky clean, if you will. Not me.

I've got better things to spend my life on, I say, then this senseless drudgery to inanimate stone. I've got more interesting things to analyze than the extent of the sheen or the uniformity of the polish, the footprints that show up in the direct sunlight, or the water marks that glare at you in the waning light.

That's what I say. Annoyingly, however, I find myself squinting, a trifle too often, at the strip of hallway or kitchen that meets my eye when I enter or exit. Earthly matters, these scuffed, smudged, sticky tiles, and yet they insist on colliding with my line of vision, insist on calling attention to their state of being and ruffling my sense of peace and control.

Fortunately, I'm not alone in my frustration.

Oh, no, the Israelis see nothing wrong with their *balatas* or their preoccupation with them. It's the occasional appearance of a fellow American on the scene that offers me the solace of shared troubles.

"Why don't they use ceramic tiles?" my neighbor Chaya asked me the first time I came over to demonstrate the nuances of *sponga.* "Or parquet. You know, the kind of floors you can just wipe over without all this ado."

"I wish I knew," I commiserated. "They do *have* ceramic. It costs a fortune, though, to put down, and the Israelis claim the tiles crack."

"Oh." She was put out for a moment.

"Well, when I win the lottery, the first thing I intend to change are the floors."

That was some years ago. In the meantime, we're still battling *balatas*, Chaya and I. But the Israelis have come up in the world.

You definitely won't find speckled beige floor-tiles in those state-of-the-art kitchens they're advertising, or in the new offices, or the renovated apartments. "Keramika" is what they're showing; good old ceramic tiles in good old English.

So when I heard the earsplitting sounds of machinery vibrating through the stone walls all the way up from Chaya's first-floor apartment, I dared hope that she had finally won the lottery. Chaya's brood has grown, and the traffic in her small apartment has a way of unbuffing *balatas* in a fraction of the time it takes to buff them. I went down to share the moment with her.

Chaya smiled. For some reason, her smile looked a little weary. There were piles of crumbled tile in the front hall and a cloud of white dust obscured the back of the house.

"Haven't I told you that we're trying to sell our apartment?" She closed the door behind her so that I would be able to hear her over the deafening noise.

"Sell?"

My eyes must have held all the questions.

"The broker advised us to put in new floors. He said we had a much better chance of getting a higher bid that way."

My heart groaned.

So they hadn't won the lottery.

They were moving out.

And someone else would enjoy the new floors.

The door opened, and an Oriental worker sprinted past us to fetch some supplies from his truck. I stepped backward, tripping awkwardly over the yellow extension cord slithering beneath my feet. It was just as well.

My bubbling enthusiasm had died on my lips, and left me a trace disconcerted. It felt like the asynchrony of blurting a breathless "Hello" into the receiver just as the ringing stopped short.

"So you're actually putting down new floors, and you're not even staying to enjoy them."

Chaya smiled feebly, "You never know; if it looks nice enough, we may just buy the apartment!"

Good sport, she. I wished her lots of stamina and success.

"Listen to a word from the wise," Chaya called after me, as I trudged up the steps, "Don't wait until you're ready to move out; you may as well put down ceramic now."

Wise woman.

Not that we've unearthed the *balatas* or chosen new tiles. Not that we're even remotely thinking in that vein. Revolutions take time around here.

There have been other revolutions though, quiet ones, thanks to the din from downstairs. I've found myself weighing decisions with a new yardstick, Chaya's yardstick.

If you're going to change the floors anyway, do it in time to enjoy them.

If you're going to give in at the end of the argument, if you're going to decide to go to sleep before you finish the project, if you're going to end up setting limits, do it while you can still reap the benefits.

If you're going to be worn into compliance anyway, why shouldn't you have the pleasure of taking the initiative and being the benevolent benefactor? If you're going to run the errand, why not do it in the morning and spare yourself the burden of planning it all day? If you're going to have to sweep the room, wash the dishes, fold the laundry, why not get it done right away, and revel in the pleasure of tidy surroundings?

The human survival instinct is wary of giving in. There are so many reasons not to relent. We haven't got the means, we haven't got the time, we haven't got the patience or the conditions, or the skills. And then there's our inner ego that balks at the injustice: Why should *I* foot the bill?

If we can get away with it, then fine. Chances are, though, that life will eventually grab us in its tongs and fling us against that which we have postponed for so long. Most of the time, reality will catch up with us and have us digging into our pockets to find that which we thought we couldn't afford.

And by then, we've burned both ends. We've paid for ceramic, and we've lived with *balatas*.

Chaya's floors have become somewhat of a giant hourglass to me, trickling in time to my conscience. If we're going to wind up replacing the tiles, why shouldn't we do it now, while we can enjoy the advantages?

If we're going to end up overlooking our spouses' failings, why not do it with forethought and love instead of as a last-ditch effort to save the relationship? If we're going to invest time understanding our children's needs, why not do it in a fun, enriching fashion, rather than as a desperate strategy to retrieve a kid from the fringe?

Life is about bringing up the value of our estate, our *real* estate. If we don't invest early on, life may teach us some very expensive lessons.

I was lucky.

I got a floor sample.

The Million-Dollar Question

I was married two weeks,
She, two months,
an old pro.
We were discussing the financial issue,
two sages on the matter.
I said something
about newlyweds being stingy,
And she shook her head
waved her hand,
dismissed the idea.

"My husband says" —
she began importantly,
"There's no need to be stingy,
The golden rule is this:
You can buy whatever's necessary.
Just leave out the extras."
I was duly impressed
by her husband's wisdom.
Repeated the rule
to whomever was ready to listen.
I tried implementing it
in my own home,
Until I hit the catch —
The million-dollar question,

which I haven't quite figured out yet.
The rule is bliss,
It solves everything but this:
What are the necessities,
and what are the extras?

Payoff

"What do you do these days?" I asked her, sooner than I could take the question back and rephrase it. As a stay-at-home mom, inferences that equate productivity with earning a livelihood always rankle. So I was dismayed with myself, noble soul that I am, for perpetrating the same injustice in this opening line with an old acquaintance.

She, however, seemed slightly less ruffled by the question, even pleased, I'd venture, that I'd asked it.

"Me?" she chuckled, "I'm into correspondence these days."

"Correspondence!" I echoed, that annoying undertone of admiration shadowing my exclamation. Fancy myself repeating "dishes!" or "laundry!" with the same gusto I had lavished upon her professional-sounding vocation, or pursuit of one. I smiled to myself. This would make good material for mutual speculation as soon as we completed this crude, three-minute sketch of the past five years in our respective lives.

"I knew you'd go in for that!" she laughed, a mischievous twinkle playing in her eyes. "But no, I'm not into speech or psychology, or anything ambitious like that. I'm mainly busy with my blessed, not-so-routine routine, besides for an occasional substituting stint every now and then, and oh, I sell appliances in the evenings, if that's what you meant. I would hardly paste a star on my badge of honor for that, though."

There, she'd put it all together so neatly, just like that, without all the philosophizing or bush beating. I'd always enjoyed Shani's refreshing straightforwardness. I guess the dynamics hadn't changed much.

"You mentioned something about correspondence, Shani?" I nudged persistently.

"Oh, my correspondence," she chuckled again, as much to herself as to me, and I could tell she was savoring the flavor of something hearty, if not quite funny.

"It actually started with the appliances. Customers came in with damaged parts, claiming their right to a guarantee. I could have told them to contact the company directly, but somehow, I always feel personally responsible for an item I've sold. So I took to letter writing."

I nodded, knowingly. I could just see her letters. Polite, yet assertive, positive without being patronizing, and always eagerly awaiting a response.

"I discovered that writing really yields results, and so I've adopted the tack on a personal basis. You want to hear what I've gained on the deal?"

Shani took my amused smile as a cue, and launched into a list of the most recent acquisitions accrued by virtue of her new occupation.

"I've gotten a new mattress for our folding bed, after the old one tore during the first *Succos* we purchased it. I've received a pretty traveling bag when I sent in a complaint letter about a defect in my son's briefcase, and we have a brand-new toaster in place of our

eroded sandwich maker, which the company stopped manufactur-
ing in 220 voltage."

My smile was losing its verve. The folding bed sounded okay,
though I wasn't hot about the idea of a mattress disintegrating on
its first test. What purpose did a handbag serve, however, when you
needed a briefcase, or a toaster, for that matter, brand new or otherwise, when you were missing a sandwich maker?

Shani noticed my waning enthusiasm, and again I regarded my
censor too late. Voicing my indignant opinion, I expected either to
see her crisp excitement turn soggy, or else to hear a defensive tone
creep into her recital.

Neither of the two happened. Shani seemed unfazed by my
assault on her bargains.

"Of course, of course," she countered. "Look, in this country,
you're not dealing with Fisher Price or General Electric. I don't
even *expect* perfect remuneration, but they give you what they call
pitzuyim."

Pitzuyim. I scoffed inwardly. I had always frowned at the term,
at the notion of someone claiming monetary compensation for a
broken ankle due to the city municipal's negligence, or for losses
incurred by a bad-naming campaign. As if the money would assuage
the pain, cushion the emotional trauma, blot the hurt and injury out
of one's life.

Pitzuyim to me had the ring of a piece of candy dangled in front of
a 2-year-old in order to quash a mounting tantrum. It was an insult to
an adult's dignity, a foolish diversion from the matter at hand.

Shani, however, seemed unperturbed by my attitude.

"I never think of it as a replacement of the damage. Things have
got to break and tear in this world, if we want to keep our *Olam
Haba* intact. I see these things as a bonus, a kind of pleasant benefit
reaped on account of the loss."

Oh.

For a moment, I felt disoriented, kind of dizzy, as if somebody
had strung me by my shoelaces from the telephone wire, and I was

viewing the familiar landscape from that dangling position, upside down.

The next moment, I was off the wire and we were on to other topics, me wordy and pensive and listening carefully, she forthright and uncomplex and chuckling a lot, the way it had always been with the two of us.

Later, though, as I made my way home from the *Misrad HaP'nim*, a morning chalked off to bureaucracy, I couldn't help ruminating over the particular piece of our conversation. Shani had unwittingly touched a switch, turned an integral part of me inside out.

It wasn't only folding beds, briefcases, and toasters. It was the way I looked at inconveniences and difficulties, fleeting or constant. The way I reacted when I collided with unfairness or insult, with disappointment and misunderstanding.

Of course I knew there was something positive to be gained from pain. *Gam zu l'tovah* had been as central to my upbringing as nutritious breakfasts and punctual bedtime. Somehow, though, the concept had always held more of an abstract consolation, a loftier understanding of events one couldn't construe, through the belief that they had some deeper meaning in the ultimate orchestration of things.

I had never thought of *gam zu l'tovah* in terms of immediate gratification, as a concrete, shallow, right here and now kind of formula. In fact, something inside me always objected to the oversimplified if-you-missed-the-plane-it'll-probably-crash philosophy. Trying to put one's finger on the rationale behind everyday mishaps reduced Divine Providence to something very elementary.

Here, however, was a revolutionary concept, so simple I had somehow missed it. It wasn't the resigned acceptance of hardship, nor the self-righteous martyr's sigh of *gam zu l'tovah*. It wasn't an attempt at second-guessing Heaven's intentions or even a childish bid at deluding one's self that some grandiose gains were in the making.

It was the plain irrefutable logic behind Shani's correspondence: Hitches are an inescapable reality of this world; we may as well capitalize on any payoffs we can get.

We may as well maximize those small joys, those insignificant pluses that come along with the annoying, even distressful, inevitabilities. Like enjoying the relative respite from nonstop communication, forced upon us by a rebellious cordless telephone, the ease of a simpler cleanup after a disappointing turnout, the extra space in the closet accompanying the ache for another precious child sent abroad.

It's relishing time-out on a plush chair in the doctor's waiting room, the pleasantry of a cleaned refrigerator necessitated by a precariously placed pitcher, the brisk exercise afforded by a car in repair.

For some odd reason, we usually feel guilty, almost disloyal, rejoicing in any part of what should be a disturbing event. If I don't clutch the grief, we reason with a distorted kind of logic, if I don't keep a tenacious grip on my utter dissatisfaction, I'm sort of accepting the situation. Suffering is supposed to be suffered, we think somberly; where does enjoyment fit in?

Well, without even picking up a pen, I've presently begun my own correspondence course. I've lost a productive morning, and I've already gotten just returns: a complete crash training at Shani's university. It may take a while, but I'm aiming for nothing less than Master of the Art.

Upward

When I contemplated
the prospect
of making *Aliyah*
I made some inquiries,
did some research,
asked friends,
How do I go about it?
What do I need
to bring along
in order to get the process started?
I was told
I needed passports,
pictures,
proof of my Judaism,
And a letter,
a rationale,
explaining the reason
that had spurred my decision
to settle in the Holy Land.

"What do I write?"
I asked, unsure,
Oh, anything, anything at all,
Any *bubbeh maaseh*
about wanting to walk the soil
of your ancestors,
about yearning to live
in the Holy Land

to raise your kids
in an atmosphere of sanctity,
Oh, but that's not
a *bubbe maaseh*
at all.
That's the truth,
the *bubbe maaseh*
is all the bluff
and fluff,
that clouds that truth,
and so many other truths
throughout my days,
eclipsing my inner dreams,
fogging the glass
on my heart's compass,

Red tape
can do a lot of things,
Among some others,
it can make you rethink
your rationale.
Not the reason you want to live
In Israel,
But the reason you want to live
at all.
If you can pause
in your quest
to settle down comfortably,
to furnish your dwelling,
learn the local language,
get accustomed to the climate,
find a way
to earn money,
and then spend that money,

If you can find one moment
amid all that,
to sit down
with pen and paper,
and draw up the rationale
that stands behind
every one of those actions,
without concocting
bubbe maasehs,
Well,
then you can
stand on line
to make

      h

     a

    y

   i

  l

A

Priorities

Excuse Me!

The month of *Tishrei* has its own associations for each of us. Some of us think of the penetrating *shofar* blast; others automatically imagine the sun-dappled walls of the *succah* glinting with foil stars and metallic chains. For most kids, the *Yamim Noraim* are almost synonymous with snacks.

Dangling at the side of many a festively clad child, the good old traditional *pekele* plays a prominent role during this month packed with spiritual opportunities. As all of creation attempts to rectify their profiles, potato chips and pretzels (nay, sour sticks and dipsy doodles) join the rest of the universe in atoning for the damage they've done all year long, and crinkle with the promise of a few minutes of undisturbed prayer.

So it was, armed with an ample supply of the above, that I set out to *shul* on the morning of *Rosh Hashanah*, confident in the ability of nosh to keep the kids blissfully quiet while I would recite some prayers. Packed in individual bags to preclude fighting, stuffed with napkins, tissues, and pre-opened packages, I was smug that I had packed nag-proof bags to foresee all eventualities. I was pretty right on that count.

What I hadn't considered was that my barely 2½-year-old had mastered the art of swapping treats.

Standing near the *shul* window, fervently murmuring the introductory *Lamnatzeiach*, I relished the moment. There's something special about standing under the open sky, *siddur* in hand, ear cocked to listen for the *shaliach tzibbur's* lead. Standing there, unconstrained by the cramped rows of folding chairs, undistracted by holiday finery rippling under the swiveling fan, one can enjoy the combined benefits of *tefillah* in privacy and *tefillah* with a *minyan*.

It's not the kind of privacy that comes with silence, or even seclusion. Unlike the still murmuring of the inside chambers, window-sill-*davening* is performed against the noisy backdrop of giggling, squealing, chasing, and chirping. If one focuses inward, though, into the window of the *shul*, and into the window of one's soul, then all that tumult blurs into the remote distance. It creates the perfect diffuser as one stands awake and alert, free to intone the words audibly, and even to sigh with heartfelt regret, without anyone looking one's way.

The spell of the moment wasn't lost on me as I swayed softly, chanting the words along with the *minyan* inside. As spells of nostalgia tend to be for mothers, this one was very brief. The sound of violent coughing cut off my fervent whispering midword. Dropping the *machzor* on the sill, my gaze frantically swept the radius of the open lot near the *shul*. There, not three yards away from me stood my toddler, her face a deep purple, gagging on what I surmised was a hard candy she'd traded for something in her bag. If I hadn't felt *eimas hadin* up until then, I experienced it at that moment.

Anyone who has ever witnessed a medical emergency, unequipped to offer assistance, knows that during those heart-stopping seconds, time ceases to exist. I don't know how long it actually took until one of the onlookers administered the right maneuvers and dislodged the candy, but the feeling of utter panic and helplessness that washed over me, then, was beyond time. The only coherent thought I remember thinking in the grips of that blood-draining terror was a thought that continues to plague me, and echoes with my first footsteps into the new year.

Why? Why, why, why? A thousand guilt-filled times why. Why wasn't I, a young mother of mischievous tots, sufficiently conversant in first aid to act in case of an emergency like the one that had arisen? Oh sure, I had vague recollections of the ever-present sign in the school lunchroom entitled, "What to Do With a Choking Victim."

I knew enough not to stick a finger down a gagging child's throat, and I faintly remembered the basic maneuvers. Faint memories, however, though just about adequate to score a decent mark on a surprise quiz, were horribly wanting when the test was alive and every minute was of essence.

There had been so many occasions where I had heard about crash courses offering the basics of first aid and artificial respiration. Each time I had paused to seriously consider the prospect, and each time there had been excuses. I'm not talking about flimsy excuses.

I mean good, solid, plausible reasons, like a sibling's wedding, a hailstorm, a bout with the flu. Each time there had been valid considerations that had stood in the way, excuses that even the sternest teacher would have been hard pressed to turn down.

The trouble with excuses, though, is that they're very poor attorneys. They may save you from momentary indictment, but don't ever count on them to revoke your ultimate sentence. Not in real life, anyway. And in the wake of palpable *eimah*, one suddenly realizes the very futility of them. They may be true, they may be logical, they may even be convincing, but when life hangs in the balance, they are useless.

Life presents us with an infinite array of excuses, from unpredictable traffic jams, to biological mood swings. Inclement weather, bad eyesight, late paychecks, canceled baby-sitters are all specks in the vast panorama of excuses that sweep our existence. "No one ever told me," "I wasn't there," "I never got it" clinch the chorus in our litany of *terutzim* to get us off the hook.

I'm not even discussing the excuse addicts. Everyone knows that some things predictably happen to certain people time and time again. And if we happen to be one of them, we've got to check if we're leaving enough allowance in our lives for the natural mishaps that come up and have to be dealt with responsibly.

I'm talking about the *real* excuses; the kind you'd be exonerated for in a stringent school system. All my life I'd gone around thinking that if the excuse was really good, it was *machshavah k'maaseh*. Perhaps in *HaKadosh Baruch Hu's* book that holds true, and as tolerant friends trying to emulate His *middos*, we should aspire to be forgiving individuals where others are concerned.

As our own closest friends, however, let's have our best interests in mind. Though we may successfully sell our excuses to those around us, it hardly makes for a profitable living. So as we step over the threshold of a new year, carrying our brand-new resolutions of a few days old, let's remember one rule that may preclude the need for first aid. Don't swallow the excuse in the first place, and you won't choke on it later.

Liberation

I don't mean to be self-deprecating, but we women some-times have a strange insistence on clinging to our problems. It seems to be a phenomenon inherent to the makeup of our gender. Difficult as we have it juggling the myriad responsibilities in our lives, frustrating as we find it navigating the unpredictable seas mother-hood tosses us into, we have a natural tendency to kick up resistance upon the mention of anything that sounds like a solution.

"Yanky's impossible at bedtime. He just refuses to go to sleep."

"Maybe you should try a chart?"

"It'll never work. Anyway, I'm not consistent enough for charts."

"How about letting him read for half an hour or so?"

"That's all I need! He'll never fall asleep if he starts reading."

"Have you tried officially delaying his bedtime?"

"No, no, it's hard enough as it is with him in the morning. I'm just at my wit's end with him, that's all."

Perhaps it's the human need for empathy and understanding, per-haps it's our womanly way of requesting emotional feedback; what-ever the reason for our irrational rejection of practical solutions, I imagine it can be very trying for our well-meaning better halves.

For their part, they seem to have an inexhaustible repertoire of pragmatic answers to any and all of our problems. Like skipping supper. Or ordering cleaning help. Like putting away the pile of midterm papers to grade after *Pesach*.

In the most unruffled tone of voice, they'll suggest that we go to sleep, leave the dishes in the sink, let the children go to sleep with-out linen on their beds. Whatever the problem, every man has his own version of the versatile Band-Aid that would cure all ills, if only his wife was wise enough to apply it.

"Open cans," was my father's line. Even today, as I'm running late, spinning in my own tracks, futilely wishing a meal would just appear on the table without the accompanying preparation and cleanup, I can hear my father's voice reverberating with the all-time solution.

"Just open cans: tuna, corn, pineapple. Why do you have to make supper?"

You'd think that after years of receiving full course, home-cooked meals, including hot soup and dessert on every evening of the year down to the night of *bedikas chametz*, my father would have given up his notion of opening cans. No. Any time the tension was high, mood low, time tight, ends loose, my father would repeat his offer, albeit with an unmistakable wink in his eye.

In my home, it's the cleaning lady proposal. No matter if it's children to be bathed, bills to be filed, groceries waiting to be unpacked, whenever that overwhelmed look creeps into my eyes, my husband jumps in with the cleaning lady.

"Can't you get the cleaning lady to help out?"

"What cleaning lady?" I ask in exasperation.

"I don't know. Any."

Oh.

You'd imagine we had a full-time maid living on the premises. Even if we did, I've yet to meet a cleaning lady who makes *kugels*, tries on pants, or takes children to the orthodontist.

I know I'm being unreasonable on that count. If I had a cleaning girl to tend to the domestic chores, I wouldn't need one to do the rest of the tasks I've just mentioned. I guess it's an inexplicable aversion to strangers puttering about my abode that prevents me from internalizing that bit of logic.

In honor of *Erev Pesach*, though, I decided to put personal dislikes aside. I took the card out of my husband's back pocket, the one he proffers any and every time things seem to be swelling out of control, and arranged for a cleaning lady, if only to explode his myth that hired help was the magic cure-all.

Tuesday morning found me rushing around the house, frantically putting things into place, ironing and folding stray bits of laundry, organizing the papers near the computer. Can't go out, can't sit down for breakfast, can't get ahead on the computer. I've got to get the house ready for the cleaning lady. When you're allotted three hours of help, you don't want to squander them on unimportant trivia like sticky breakfast dishes or unfolded pajamas.

Tanya arrived, trim and pleasant looking, contrary to my stereotyped image of a frumpy, gray-haired matron gesticulating in incoherent Polish. This may not be so bad, I thought, cautiously laying down my skepticism long enough to smile a greeting and offer some brief instructions.

I don't know how it happened, but in the interval between 9 and 12 o'clock, I suddenly found myself absorbing many more directions than I was issuing.

"You've got to buy a longer stick, Malka. I can't work with the one you have."

"I don't like this scouring powder. I'll tell you what to buy for next week."

When it comes to cleaning, I've got my own hang-ups. I don't like abrasive cleansers, I prefer things dried immediately, and I don't appreciate riding toys piled on the beds. Tanya, though, had her routine down pat and apparently wasn't too moved by my requests.

"Don't you worry about this Formica getting scratched. This is the way I do it; you'll get used to it."

In no time, she had all the windows flung open wide, and the steam shut off.

"I can't work in this stuffy heat," she explained. So be it. I put on an extra sweater and resumed my activities. I don't know why, but I was beginning to feel like a little puppy padding after its master.

I served Tanya a hot tea and brought her the screwdriver she requested. I tried to keep the baby from crawling on the wet tiles, and dutifully scurried to flick on the hall lights so she could see better, though I thought the sunlight was more than sufficient. Panting in between her demands, I suddenly remembered that I had wanted the floors shined.

"I would like you to wax the floor," I mustered the most authoritarian voice I could manage, as I handed Tanya the bottle of floor polish and a new rag.

"Oh no," she vetoed firmly. "I don't use this junk. All it does is accumulate on the floor, and get into the corners, and then you'll have to strip it all."

You mean *you'll* have to strip it all, I wanted to amend. Instead, I took the bottle meekly, and put it away.

Getting accustomed to cleaning help, the experts said, was a matter of time and training. As far as the time was concerned, I thought I had hired help to solve my own dearth, and as for the training, it seemed I had missed something. I never did clarify who was supposed to be training whom.

And though I'm still not sure, *I've* definitely learned on the job. Cleaning ladies, I've discovered, are far from the ultimate salvation. At best, they're a self-respecting species who resent being bossed, bugged, or bothered in the middle of a job. They like doing things their own way, dislike wiping, and have a habit of stashing single socks and unpaid bills in some innovative hiding places.

At worst, they're a nuisance who keep you very busy cleaning up before and after them, cowering at their demands, and swallowing your aggravation over the chipped vase, the broken vacuum cleaner, and the scraped buffet.

Like so many other devices in this world that are supposed to be serving us. We've got a whole plethora of time-saving gadgets at our fingertips. The world's never been more rife with luxuries than it is today; the bounty is overflowing the retailers' shelves, flooding the market, inundating our households.

We've got cell phones and faxes, voice mail and e-mail, caller ID, and complicated telephone menus. We've got a solution for everything from the sweltering heat to the hassle of setting up a *kiddush*. For better or for worse most average kitchens can boast of a food processor, a microwave or two, an automated breadmaker, all this aside from the finest ready cuisine stocking the freezer.

So it figures we're all sitting on the back porch reciting *Tehillim*.

Besides, of course, for when we're baking fresh bread and microwaving J&J blintzes for some needy recipients. Or calmly watching our neighbor's children in the air-conditioned playroom. Or, you know what, forget the neighbor's children; how about our own?

Somewhere, somehow, in the midst of all this liberation and enlightenment, the tables have turned. Instead of severing the shackles subjugating us to the relentless demands of this world, instead of easing our burden so our minds and hearts could be freer to soar, we've become slaves to the bounty.

We've become thoroughly engaged in our gadgets, acquiring them, cleaning them, trading them in for the latest model. We've adopted sophisticated new lifestyles, devised updated standards, built fresh forums for rivalry and competition.

Modern slavery dons a cloak unlike the straight jacket of *galus Mitzrayim*. It's wide and plush, too wide and too plush. Let's not go for appearances, though; it's the same ancient technique. Both hold the mind captive, divert the soul, keep the feet stuck in the mud.

This time around, however, we've got to liberate *ourselves*. We've got to take stock of all our holdings, the assets we own, the tools we engage. We've got to remember who's supposed to be helping whom. So that when we sit around the *Seder* table in our finery, when we ponder the *Yom Tov* expenses, with everything they encompass, we can honestly say: It serves us right.

Cash and Carry

*I*t's an interesting phenomenon, but I've observed it on more than one occasion. Newlyweds tend to be more watchful of their expenditures than any other sector of society.

It doesn't matter that they've just been endowed with everything from beds to baking pans. It doesn't matter that for the time being, she doesn't lack for as much as a button, and he possesses more socks than he'll ever own in his lifetime. It doesn't matter that for the most part, they're being invited out for *Shabbosim*, and that much of their frozen foodstuff is coming straight out of Mom's all-encompassing freezer.

All those assets make them no less hesitant about splurging on a yogurt, or about spending on a not absolutely necessary service. And the fact that they have no diapers or formula on the budget yet makes them no less obsessive about comparing the price of crackers in all the local groceries, and then walking those extra three blocks to save the difference.

I don't know how the dynamics work, but by the time you're buying the diapers and replenishing husband's socks, the budget's too complicated to figure out on paper. Unlike those meticulous ledgers of the first few months, where the figures tally down to the last dime, the bookkeeping takes on a mysterious property. No matter how much comes in, the money all disappears. It doesn't matter much whether it's an emergency root canal, some extra hours of cleaning help, or private tutoring for one of the kids. The point is that at the end of the month, the money's gone.

Conversely, you'd think that when the cleaning girl doesn't show up, Aunt Lori sends a check in honor of the new baby, and you've undertaken some extra jobs, you'd feel some kind of bulge in your wallet. Right? Wrong again. Although that would make perfect logical sense, *Hashgachah Pratis* has its own way of playing with economics.

When you're first starting out, though, you don't know that yet. You're still trying to keep a strong hold on the cash flow, and make sure that you're earning more than you're spending, and even putting some cash into reserve each month.

It's that unrealistic thriftiness that marks fresh young consumers at the checkout counter of the supermarket. Or maybe it's just in the *Kollel* store that one gets a glimpse of it. Whatever the case, I spied one such young lady last week as I wove my way through the aisles of the store, nimbly reaching for the items I needed, and quickly filling my cart.

Four cans, no, make that six, of corn, ten tunas, three tomato sauces. I was enjoying the rhythm as the cans clack-clacked into my cart two at a time, when I saw her deep in thought at a complete standstill in front of the tuna. Would it be the Starkist, or the Dagim?

I could almost feel the suspense as the fateful decision hung in the balance. I watched her scrutinize the labels, probably checking the net weight on each, and then fretting over the price stickers. I didn't stay around long enough to see the final outcome, but I met her again in front of the freezer.

This time it was a package of frozen mixed vegetables poised in her hand, awaiting its verdict. In and out again it went, the conflict written all over her face. Not wanting to disrupt her concentration, I waited politely on the side until she emphatically returned the package, and I unceremoniously dumped four of the identical bags on top of my overfull cart.

It was at the checkout counter, however, that I really knew she belonged to the newlywed club. As she unloaded a wastebasket, a dustpan, and some multipurpose plastic baskets, I imagined the brand-new apartment she was setting up. No matter how careful you are, the first supermarket trip after moving into a bare apartment is an expensive venture, and so I watched her brow pucker in consternation as the figures on the register progressively jumped.

"That'll be 927 *shekels* (about $220), please," the cashier announced. "Bags or delivery?"

She hesitated, as she weighed the options. "How much will the delivery be?"

"Well, it's seven *shekels* for the first box, and six *shekels* for every additional box delivered."

I stood patiently as she wavered for a minute, and then said, "Make that one box, please." Then she began packing the heaviest items into the carton, weighing, maneuvering, trying to fit the full seven *shekels'* worth into the single crate. The rest, which included some bulging bags of cleaning supplies, milk products, and a few other items that I missed, would somehow accompany her home.

I looked after her worriedly, and couldn't help shaking my head in concern as she dragged herself through the automatic door, heaving her bags. What were 6 or even 12 *shekels* when one was spending 927 anyway? I imagined her homecoming, weary, exhausted, spent. And somehow I could picture her young husband disapproving.

"Listen," I could almost hear him say, "I'm glad you're mindful of the budget, but those 6 *shekels* aren't going to impoverish us. We'll pay for them the same way we'll cover the rest of the bill."

But those are things she'll learn with time. And in the meantime, she's taught me my own lesson. Sometimes, when we're still under the illusion that we pay our way in this world, we worry about this thing or that. We fret and consider, and ponder and wonder, and weigh our options and compare our possibilities, and then we worry some more.

We worry a lot, and we pray a little, scrimping on the requests we make of the One Above. We delude ourselves into thinking that we'll carry the bags by ourselves. That this solution or that will alleviate our problems, that this policy or that will bring an end to our suffering.

In our newlywed conception of things, we don't realize that the bookkeeping's out of our hands anyway, and so we might as well relinquish our grip and leave things to the One in charge of the budget. He's always come through with everything we've needed, so what's one more thing on the list?

Klal Yisrael is standing at the register, and we honestly haven't got the means with which to pay our huge debt. But if the bill's this big already, and He's brought us this far, then please, Hashem, we've really got more *pekelach* than one nation can *schlep*. So no, we won't hesitate with our final request.

"Deliver us, please."

When Opportunity Knocks

*L*iving in Eretz Yisrael is not what it used to be.

Forget about the Eretz Yisrael of half a century ago. I'm talking about the Eretz Yisrael of 10, 12 years ago, the country to which people lugged cans of tuna fish, and aluminum foil, and peanut butter, and *cholent* beans, to last until the next trip home.

It isn't all that long ago, but times have changed. Israeli peanut butter has come a long way, and for the sticklers who still haven't shed the stereotype, most *makolets* (groceries) proudly stock Gefen's or Rokeach's best. Good old American gefilte-fish rolls, also known as "vitefish" in these parts, are available in any self-respecting fish store, and "Fisher Price" and "Little Tikes" can almost be missed for Hebrew adjectives.

Like I said, things have definitely come a long way to make us Americans feel at home, sometimes to the point of aching disillusionment with our dream of leaving materialism behind for the land bathed in holiness and purity.

Not to worry, though. There's plenty of holiness and purity left. And even as far as material ease, there's more to physical comfort than peanut butter and gefilte fish, much of which still remains both deliciously and annoyingly Israeli. Like medicine, for example.

Perhaps it's all part of a deliberate scheme by the health department to keep patients active and fit, but getting medical care and the coverage for it keeps people in this country on their toes.

Taking a simple throat culture is a complicated hassle. The instant cultures haven't reached these shores yet, and the standard ones must have been the impetus behind the expression, "a pain in the neck."

The doctor will usually recommend taking antibiotics without a culture, but if you insist on having one done, you need to pick up a referral from your doctor, take it to the lab the next morning before closing at 9 (yes, *9 a.m.!*), and then pick up your results some two days later. The whole process can take about a week, and in the event that the results are positive, you've got to start all over again in order to procure antibiotics.

All this for the sake of diagnosing a plain old strep throat; forget about complicated stuff like an ear, nose, and throat specialist, or occupational therapy.

Which is what made my cousin's nonchalance so startling to me.

It was a Thursday morning, I think, on her end of the trans-Atlantic connection, Thursday afternoon for me, when the ring of her doorbell interrupted our conversation.

"Oh no," she moaned, "Don't tell me she's here." Her reluctant clucking was all I heard as she made her way down the steps to unbolt the door.

"Who's at your door?" I asked, my curiosity piqued. I could think of a few candidates who would elicit that kind of unwillingness on my part to open the door on a Thursday morning, but for all my creativity, I never would have guessed who was at her doorstep.

"It's Avromy's therapist," she answered, in the most self-evident tone.

"*Who*?" I croaked.

"Avromy's therapist; I told you he was getting early intervention to boost his speech."

"*She comes to your house?!*"

"Yeah." Her tone was as natural as mine was surprised.

"She's coming to your house, and you're not in the mood."

I said it slowly, almost dazed, pondering the possibility out loud as if it was the most novel thought I had ever encountered.

"Yeah, she was supposed to come yesterday, but then she couldn't make it. Thursday morning is not exactly my favorite time."

"*She's actually coming to your door, and you're not in the mood.*"

It was all I could do to repeat myself, just checking to see if I had gotten it right. I couldn't help remembering the bus trips I had made two summers ago to an occupational therapist in Rishon L'Tzion.

With a 3-year-old and baby in tow, I had traveled by bus, and then stood on a grassy patch in the middle of a busy intersection, trying to flag down a taxi to get us to the medical center. This, after weeks of running to various offices trying to get the consent I needed, and months of waiting for an appointment.

I suddenly recalled all the baby-sitting arrangements that had gone into those trips, all the hours on the road or sitting at the stop, waiting idly for the next bus to come. It hadn't been easy, but which 21st-century mother in good conscience would deny her child the benefits of early intervention, on account of inconvenience?

And here was this cousin of mine, balking at the proposition of a speech therapist paying her a housecall! I hated to sound so jealous, but to my Israeli, red-tape mentality, a therapist coming right to one's door seemed like a scene out of fairyland. Fancy ushering a professional into your own playroom, paraphernalia and all, while your chicken soup simmered on the stove, and you got busy tending to some laundry.

"Never thought of it quite like that," my cousin admitted. And though I didn't blame her, I secretly gloated in my finely honed sense of gratitude, born of the everyday struggles of living in this country.

My ego trip lasted just about a quarter of an hour, when it suffered an abrupt landing. It was just in the middle of suppertime when my own doorbell sounded insistently.

"Who's there?" I called, not managing to keep the exasperation out of my voice. I shot an annoyed glance at the clock. Didn't people know not to ring the bell at 20 after 6?

"It's Miri, Ma. She wants you to help her with her English assignment."

I felt the indignation rising inside me, as my 11-year-old neighbor walked into the front hall, holding her pencil case and her English notebook, looking up at me expectantly.

I knew what she wanted. This wasn't the first time Miri had come at this hour with a whole list of questions regarding her homework. And I couldn't help feeling taken advantage of. She had a mother, and older sisters. What was I, the neighborhood tutor?

I took the notebook wearily, as I gave the older ones instructions to clear the table.

And suddenly, in a painful flash of insight, I realized that I was replaying the scene of a few short minutes earlier; that I, just like my cousin, was balking at an offer right out of fairyland.

Here was my personal therapy coming straight to my door. I hadn't had to invest any time making phone calls or filling out forms. I hadn't had to get onto a bus or flag down a taxi. All I had to do was open the door and usher in the therapist for a session in the art of giving. Like a flashback, my own incredulous words came echoing back at me,

"She's actually coming to your door, and you're not in the mood?"

Yes, but it's 6:30, and this isn't the first time, and anyway, who said her English homework is more important than supervising my family's supper? That last thought hit a good self-righteous chord, and fueled my line of defense. This wasn't some indigent pauper or even a harried mother in a pinch. Who said 11-year-old Miri's homework was supposed to be my *chessed* therapy?

The One Who sent her.

Simple as that.

But who said … My thought wilted midsentence. I suddenly knew the answer. Therapy wasn't about doing or not doing the homework with my neighbor. Therapy wasn't about my neighbor at all. It was about myself.

It was an exercise in the joy of doing little unsung acts of *chessed*, fueled by the genuine *desire* to give. It was about cultivating that inner swell of eagerness, independent of whom the recipient was and what he or she needed to receive.

That was my first session. Ever since then, the therapist has been kind enough to accommodate me several times each week. I haven't had to expend a single effort to set up the appointments; she shows up at my door. Sometimes she even meets me in the supermarket, at the bus stop, or on the telephone. Each time she appears in a different guise with varying props, and slowly, she's teaching me what it means to give.

I'm learning. I'm learning that giving is not about saying yes when you wish you could say no. Sometimes it's even about saying no, when you wish, you honestly, sincerely wish, you could say yes. Giving is not as much about the actual act as it is about the readiness and happiness and *desire* to do for others.

Therapy is hard work. It trains one to ease those sinews stiffened with resentment and exercise the smile inside one's heart. It shifts the focus and puts things in a new light. The lady who pushes ahead on line, the neighbor who asks you to baby-sit her teething infant, the person on the phone imposing on your time; the student who takes up your recess break, the classmate who borrows your notes before each test, the co-worker who takes it for granted that you'll share your ideas, they're all personal therapists.

And yes, let's not skip the husband, the wife, the child, the sibling, who not only come straight to the door; they even live on the premises. Whatever it is we're doing, we aren't doing it for them; they're doing it for us. They're giving us the early intervention we need so we won't have to suffer through corrective therapy.

So next time your doorbell rings on a Thursday morning, or right in the middle of suppertime; next time someone appears unbidden into your hectic schedule, your early night, your coveted quiet time, find your most genuine smile and usher them right in.

It might not always be easy. They say life isn't a free ride. Indeed, it isn't; it's door-to-door service.

Frontlines and Backdoors

They've been talking about this war for months. They've been issuing ultimatums and setting deadlines, and around here they've been warning civilians to renew their gas masks in event of chemical warfare.

There's something about the human spirit, though, that defies these sort of warnings. There's some mechanism in there that pushes aside pragmatic thoughts of foresight and precaution where the ominous is concerned, and makes room for more cheerful concerns. I've got important things to tend to, we've got a way of twisting logic; don't badger me about life and death.

Of course there are some prudent people out there, the kind who have emergency first-aid kits in the car, who know just what to do should an earthquake erupt unpredicted, who have battery-operated lighting installed in case of power failure. I, however, do not belong to this eventuality-foreseeing group. Optimist by nature, and I'll confess, technically disinclined, I'm very much prey to the irrational "We'll deal with it when it comes" attitude.

Well, it has come. That which has been spoken about and tossed around in theory, that which has taken up pages of speculation, has actually arrived. And suddenly, with the declaration of war, with the wild run on the bottled water in the grocery, and my neighbors' accounts of their harrowing experiences during the Gulf War, I was washed over with panic by the fact that we had no gas masks in sight.

If I thought I was singly plagued by the last-minute syndrome, I took consolation in the long lines of impatient humanity snaking out of the emergency distribution center. It was the sole factor, though, that afforded solace. The place was understaffed, overworked, steaming with the fumes puffing from the irate recipients, charged with the short-tempered glowers emanating from the resentful servicemen and women trying to create some order.

"Where were all of you until now?" the frustrated distributors demanded. "We could have done this in an orderly fashion weeks ago, so don't any of you complain about the lines now."

I looked down at the floor like a contrite child, and waited my turn in placid silence. The air was dank and gloomy, heavy with the tension of war that found expression in terse remarks over the impossibly slow service.

Some of the older men, tolerant folks, bonded by the couple of wars they'd been through on this narrow strip of land, made an attempt at joining in song. It was no professional choir, I'll assure you, but the conglomeration of hoarse voices trying to take off in the stuffy, unpoetic surroundings dissolved some of the pettiness, the tension, dabbed some humor on the taut nerves.

Throughout the disconcerting wait, I kept my eyes fixed on the automated video demonstration of a family getting into their gear, with detailed instructions captioned underneath. The sight of the equipment alarmed me. Gas masks, in my mind, conjured the image of the black rubber caricature I remembered from the Gulf War. The kits they were showing on the screen though, designed for children under 8, more closely resembled state-of-the-art space suits.

Clear plastic hood and vest, replete with pipes and valves, filters and clips, they looked just like the type of apparatus to intrigue anybody's 15-year-old son, and keep me away with a 10-foot pole.

Despite my misgivings, however, I consciously fought the film of blurred obscuration that usually descends upon me at the first sight or sound of technical instructions. I willed myself to concentrate, to study the steps that I might need to carry out at the ominous onset of the siren's blare.

It was 1 o'clock in the morning when I finally got home. Haunted by the pitch blackness and the boxes I was holding, I clutched my rustling bags tight, as I heard the hum of the elevator coming down to fetch me.

There's something about those predawn hours that finds those almost imperceptible emotional bubbles floating around one's conscience, and inflates them to the size of balls, then balloons, that grow and expand and soar in spheres unencumbered by logic. There's something about the stillness, the moonlight, the eerie sounds punctuating the vast darkness that brings tears and laughter close to the surface, that sends one's unbridled imagination on a wild stampede, dragging mind and heart along with it into irrational territory.

By the time that elevator jolted to a halt, I was almost dizzy with the fear of chemical warfare. I thrust myself into the doorway, kicked off my shoes, and set the boxes right down onto the dining-room table. The even breathing of my loved ones only fueled my frenzied state. So did the note I found on the table from my husband, thanking me, and reassuring me that he'd assemble the masks in the morning. When there's a war on and you're dealing with a madman, you don't wait for the morning. You do what has to be done.

So I sat there with the myriad screws and clips, the plastic tubing, the filter and the suction tube, scrutinizing the numbered diagrams, trying to grasp, where, between the detailed instructions, the purple cap had sneaked its way onto the end of the black tube, without receiving even cursory mention.

Straightening my back, I yawned and stared ahead into the tidy kitchen, glad for something large and clean to divert my eyes from their grueling focus on plastic minutiae. Suddenly, like a robot set to perform a routine duty, I entered the kitchen distractedly, and turned a little valve, a kind of rote I'd adopted for the last couple of weeks. There'd been a definite odor trickling from the stovetop lately, and until I'd call a serviceman, I'd been taking the precaution of shutting the gas line before bedtime. The brief reprieve from laborious activity had somehow reminded me of the nightly ritual.

Suddenly, I stopped in my tracks, hit by the irony of the senseless paradox. Here I was, zealously protecting my loved ones against a far-flung eventuality of chemical poisoning, when there was real toxin seeping insidiously into our home. Here I was pummeling my fists against an elusive foe, while carelessly neglecting the infiltration of dangerous warfare in my very own kitchen.

I didn't need any statistics to juxtapose the probability of toxification from our leaking gas pipe against the likeliness of chemical warfare penetrating our home. The answer was obvious. And sobering.

How many times do we go out to battle against those fat-headed enemies, recklessly neglecting the breaches in our own fortresses?

How many times do we invest our energies to join forces with big, dramatic causes, casually dismissing the silent enemy worming its way into our walls?

We're so careful to protect ourselves against outside influences, to cement those walls insulating us from enemy warfare; we decry intermarriage and Reform divorce, we dabble in solving community problems. What about the air our families imbibe on the home front? What about the books we read, the expressions we use, the subtle insinuations we make in regard to *kavod habriyos, bitul Torah, bitachon*?

It's easy to toot the horn against Saddam Hussein, to spend hours on line in a concentrated spurt of fear-generated action to ward off the threats of a wicked despot. It's a trifle harder to conjure that same measure of alarm when the gas is trickling, slowly, but ever so surely, from something as mundane as our very own stovetop.

It's those personal conflicts though, those battles held eyeball to eyeball with our own reflection, that determine our victory in the big war. And it's those subtle influences dribbling in via unnoticed channels that pose the biggest threat to our safety. So let's remember that security measures vary from war to war; sometimes we've got to *un*mask ourselves in order to combat the gas.

Sometimes we're so busy fighting the big wars, we forget the real danger on the back burner!

Foreign Policy

Ozeret. Short of running a private practice, it's one of the most lucrative jobs in the country. No degree necessary, only the barest smattering of Hebrew, and a working knowledge of *sponga* sticks and drain holes. It's thirty *shekels* an hour, net profit, for as many hours as you can handle. That's more than you can say about the average high school teacher.

So it's no wonder they come running all the way from Moldavia, under the threat of heavy penalty, to fill the sought-after position. Industrious workers, these Tanyas and Olgas and Katies, they've worked their way into our lives. They know all about *Shabbos* and *Pesach*, *milchigs* and *fleishigs*, and of course they're going to come next week, *"b'ezrat Hashem."*

If they aren't caught before then, that is.

The Israeli police force is definitely bent on it. Why should these illegal Romanian workers be raking in all that money when so many law-abiding citizens stalk the streets, unemployed? I see their point. But when it's Tuesday morning and I'm waiting desperately for another pair of hands, it's a trifle difficult to wax idealistic.

Moreover, they're a hardworking breed, these alien cleaning hands. They pack a full day, from dawn to dusk and often beyond, heaving and hauling, scouring and scrubbing. Not a job I'd easily wish on any of my beloved ones.

They don't seem to mind, though. In fact, they don't seem to mind at all. They appear single-mindedly determined to earn money, the faster the better. Toward that end, they are willing to forgo decent housing, fashionable clothing, good food. Anything, to keep the cash flow running. They know they can be shipped back any day, and they would like to earn their keep before that time comes.

So employing them runs its risks. You get a solid worker for as long as it lasts.

With Tanya, it was a short-lived pleasure. If I had had my gripes about her last year, I learned to appreciate her. Too late.

A police officer stopped her one morning, and requested identification. When she couldn't produce any, she was carted off to headquarters in Be'er Sheva, and within three days she was back in Moldavia.

Since then, it's been tough going.

It's a lot easier, I've discovered, to get accustomed to luxuries than it is to get used to their absence. With the introduction of a cleaning lady, doing *sponga* had been deleted from my schedule and had left no hole in its wake. Trying to fit it in again was like trying to stuff a heap of crumpled napkins back into their original package.

So when Olga showed up, blonde hair pinned into a ponytail, I was honestly thrilled. After weeks of dead-end attempts trying to locate a capable cleaning woman, I welcomed her in with a genuine smile, and showed her around the house. She seemed eager to please, as she nodded conscientiously to my instructions and cooed to the baby. Her Hebrew, I discovered, was good.

I sighed with satisfaction as I watched her deftly maneuver the squeegee stick into the crevices. I had hosted enough greenhorns over the course of the last few months to appreciate experience when I saw it.

"How long have you been here?" I asked amiably as she gathered the soapy water, creating wide strokes of dry floor amid the sudsy tiles. "Fourteen months," she replied with a quick smile, spraying a fine mist over the mirror, and then rubbing it clean.

She darted about the room, nimbly sliding a dusting cloth over the surfaces, as I put some laundry away in the drawers. There was a pleasant kind of momentum permeating the silence between us; the mixed scent of Windex and clean laundry creating the backdrop for the squeak-squeak of cloth against glass panes, and the open-shut rhythm of drawers being refilled.

"She's cute," she chuckled in amusement as she brushed past my 2-year-old who had a rag slung over her shoulder. Then she paused for a fraction of a second, but it was long enough for me to notice a wistful cloud pass through her eyes. It was a look I knew, I recognized; it was the tender stirring of a mother's heart.

"I have a daughter too," she told me. I transferred two piles of laundry to the dresser, tucking them under my chin, as I freed my hand to open the drawer.

"Really?" I laid the pants out carefully and looked up at her.

"She's 2 years old. Like her," she smiled playfully, as she tousled the little one's hair.

"Oh, it's the cutest age," I gushed, "she must be adorable. What kind of arrangement do you have for her while you work?"

"Yes," she responded, still smiling, as she reached for another cloth. Apparently her Hebrew wasn't as good as I'd assessed. Then she stopped in her tracks, registering my question. "Oh, no, she isn't with me. She's in Moldavia."

In Moldavia! I tried to conceal my horror. I made a quick calculation. Two years minus 14 months. That meant Olga had last seen her baby when she'd been 10 months old. Why, I bet they wouldn't recognize each other. Poor kid. Poor mother.

"It must be hard," I said quietly.

"*Mah laasot* (What can be done)?" she shrugged, "I've got to make money. They send me pictures. And I talk to her on the phone."

"That's good," I managed. Inside, my heart gave a tremor. Pictures and the telephone; my goodness. The child was all of 2 years old.

She must have noticed my dread, close beneath the thin veneer of a tight-lipped smile. "It's okay," she chuckled, "She knows already. I ask her, '*Eifoh Ima* (Where is Mommy)?' and she answers: '*Ima osah kesef liknot shokolad*'" (*Ima's* making money so she can buy chocolate).

My pain was suddenly sucked by a wave of anger. *Ima osah kesef liknot shokolad*. What kind of crazy rationale was that for a baby to be raised by strangers, to be deprived of maternal love, to be reduced to a piece of Kodak paper in her mother's pocketbook?

What kind of mother thought that a square of chocolate, even a house of chocolate, could substitute for her kisses and hugs, for her caressing and crooning, for her patience and pride? Did she really believe it, or was it some kind of illusion, a way of keeping her conscience at bay as she slaved away for some dream house in Moldavia?

Oh, stop it, I scolded myself. For goodness sake, you can't get so carried away. She's only your cleaning lady. And she doesn't seem too perturbed, either.

For some reason, though, I was haunted all afternoon by Olga's nonchalant reasoning. I couldn't shake the image of a forlorn-looking 2-year-old staring out of some orphanage window, waiting for her mother to appear, waving a long-awaited chocolate bar.

And hard as I tried to blot out the vision, I couldn't help seeing my own 2-year-old in that miserable pose; a trick of my mind kept brutally placing my progeny, one at a time, in the window.

Stop, I pleaded. It was a plague sometimes, my fertile imagination. What did I have to do with that shallow cleaning woman of a mother, a stranger to her toddler, a slave to her salary? Nothing, nothing, nothing.

Nothing, the word echoed behind me, in front of me, rang in my ears, as I tried to polish silver later in the week. Nothing, as I rubbed feverishly, vaguely aware of the incessant whining in the background. Nothing! It fairly shouted, as I stood atop a ladder, buffing the glass door of the breakfront, desperately wishing supper would make and serve itself.

I viewed piles of little screws waiting to go back into the toolbox, curtains waiting to be hung. I heard children, cranky, overtired, bickering, a clock that said it was past their bedtimes.

Nothing, nothing at all.

I was making *Pesach*. I was working hard. For us, for the family, yes, for the children. *Pesach* was their time, their *Yom Tov*. Was that a note of derision I detected in my own defense? Who did my conscience think I was doing all of this for, myself?

Well, I was kind enough to myself to elegantly sidestep that one. It either was or it wasn't myself. But it surely wasn't the children. They needed gleaming furniture like Olga's baby needed chocolate. Or less.

What they needed was a mother, and yes, they needed *Pesach*, a *Seder* staged especially for them, calm smiles, patient explanations. They needed songs and happiness, love and togetherness. They needed to know that Hashem took us out of *Mitzrayim*, and that He makes every big and little miracle happen, and that the *chametz* we were trying to eradicate was anger and jealousy and pride.

What good was all of it if we weren't there, if we were living somewhere in a zone of lists and deadlines where children didn't exist? Who needed clean mattresses, organized files, waxed floors if it meant neglected faces looking dejectedly out of some figurative window, waiting for Mother to return?

Ima osah kesef.

We are busy. We are tired. We are working. *Erev Pesach*, and all the time. What are we doing it for? Whom are we doing it for?

The answer is simple. And it wasn't meant to be bittersweet.

Present Speculations

*C*hanukah brings back many warm memories. One of the fondest ones is of my grandmother. If I only close my eyes, I can feel the draft coming in from outside as I accompany her up the steps into our dining room; the soft caress of her fur coat brushing my arm, as we carefully avoid the lit *menorah* standing on a stool by the front door.

I can feel the chill of her flushed cheek on my lips as I kiss her, the warmth of her beaming countenance radiating from within, reminiscent of the contrast between the freezing outdoors and the cozy scene inside.

Having *Bubby* over for supper on *Chanukah* evening was a treat we children anticipated with glee. Always lavish with her praise, my grandmother exuded a combination of happiness and pride as we each shared our latest tidbits with her. The boys repeated their rendition of *Maoz Tzur*, replete with a round of dancing, as *Bubby* reveled in the performance, her face glowing with *nachas*.

Praise wasn't the only thing *Bubby* was lavish with. As soon as we had finished eating, she would ask one of the children to hand her her pocketbook, so she could distribute the customary *Chanukah gelt*. It was a tradition created precisely for her.

One could see, as she handed out those bills, that the activity provided her with the most immense sense of pleasure. And for us children, who barely ever received cash, the annual distribution was an event about which we could say the same.

For the couple of ensuing weeks, even months, there were endless discussions revolving around the hot topic of where and how to spend our *Chanukah gelt*. Should we pool it and invest in something really expensive that everyone could enjoy (what was that, pray tell?) or should we each do our own research and spend it accordingly?

In any case, every time we were ready to go to the store and cash in on the gift, we experienced the flutter of finality, and invariably had a change of heart. Usually our money landed up in a *gemach* account for lack of the ability to decide where to channel the cash.

I must admit, it's a difficulty I haven't yet outgrown. Though the days where my grandmother plied us with 5-, 10-, and 20-dollar bills are relegated to the trove of most cherished memories, we still receive largess from our parents every now and then, particularly in honor of *Chanukah*. And I still can't ever seem to decide what to do with it.

Not for a dearth of ideas, but for a proliferation of them.

There's a distinct difference between money you toiled for, and money received as a present. It's an interesting paradox inherent to the human condition that has us stubbornly insisting on independently earning a livelihood, and yet delights in the prospect of receiving an occasional gift.

I suppose there is a certain sweetness in not being beholden to any particular human benefactor for one's bread and butter. Once in a while, however, a gift is an indulgence that most human beings, at least those who are not past craving luxury, enjoy.

Heavenly assistance stretches hard-earned cash to pay anyone from the mechanic to the dentist, when urgency dictates that their services be used. Frills, however, are to the budget what extraneous text is to the computer's printer, "out of the margins."

That's where gifts come in. What they lack in terms of being hard earned, they compensate with the joy of being so easily spent. A gift is something you put into an envelope and relish for the next few weeks as you mentally spend it on anything you set your eyes and heart on. That $25 or $36 or $200 goes a merry long way, as the ideas for your prospective purchase fluctuate each time you come up with yet an even more appealing candidate.

The order isn't of consequence, but by the time a few weeks have elapsed since the initial endowment, you've mentally acquired with that earmarked cash a set of encyclopedias, an artificial plant, a state-of-the-art microwave, and a new set of linen. Just about anything that winks at you from the showcase, and doesn't justify squandering hard-earned cash on, brings to mind the envelope with the money.

The danger, the very real risk you are gambling by playing this stalling game of imaginary affluence is the jeopardy of turning your gift into a temporary living fund. It never happens on purpose, but it inevitably happens nevertheless.

One Wednesday afternoon when you just can't find any cash handy, and the guy from the cleaners is tapping his foot impatiently as you frantically turn pockets inside out searching for some forgotten change. Or one Monday morning when you make a spur-of-the-moment decision to take advantage of some final sale opportunities, and you can't find much more than a few nickels and dimes in your purse.

It's then you suddenly remember that you've got an intact fortune sitting inside your drawer, waiting patiently to be redeemed. You feel some pangs of guilt, almost as if you were committing sacrilege, as you open that envelope allocated for extras, and take the booty to the door. You proffer the crisp bills to the bewildered delivery boy, as if you've known you had them stashed away all along, but deliberately put him through the wait so he could enjoy some comic relief on the job.

And while he shrugs and sprints down the stairs, in your heart of hearts you know that you have just bid farewell to your gift. Anyone with some experience realizes that cash funneled into the ocean of living expenses is about as hard to recover as a marble flushed down the toilet.

And I don't know if it's a loss worth mourning, but I always do. Because I know that if I hadn't had the alternative of going to the bureau and pulling the cash out of the envelope, a liberty I usually live without, I'd have arrived at some other resourceful solution without squandering my precious pool of frivolous funding. I know that somehow, at the end of the month, we'd have managed (or not managed) to cover our basic expenditures in much the same manner, with or without the aid of the envelope.

And besides, it's a pleasure I think I owe the gift giver to say, "Oh how we're enjoying the new set of crystal glasses," or "the gorgeous matching sweaters," or "the dainty centerpiece," or whatever the gift could have bought. "Thank you so much; I never would have indulged and bought that for myself." I feel sort of accountable to report on the new acquisition enhancing our household thanks to the thoughtful generosity of a parent or aunt.

A gift spent on milk and crackers, on masking tape and phone bills, is, in my opinion, an unjustified gift. It is an insult, and a waste, and a downright shame. And it's a good way of forfeiting your privilege of getting the gift the next time around.

And though we may not all receive *Chanukah gelt*, we are each the recipients of bountiful gifts, individually wrapped and lovingly bequeathed. They don't come in envelopes, and sometimes they are hard to discern, mingled as they are among the abundance of givens we receive from our Creator, all of them free of charge.

Aside from the universal gifts bestowed upon all of humanity — the gift of life, of air, of nourishment, of water — aside from the grants Hashem gives us the illusion of earning — like our livelihoods, our reputation, the homes we build and maintain — every person, if he executes a frank reckoning of his assets, will come across personalized gifts that he or she, as an individual, has been imbued with to a remarkable extent.

A good many individuals are obviously endowed. They don't have to dig too deep to hit the treasure, the chest containing material beneficence, exceptional genius, charismatic appeal, or striking musical ability. *Those* aren't the sole properties, however, that fit the bill.

Anything, anything at all, that enhances one's life, and one hasn't invested effort to acquire, constitutes a gift. It may be a loving, supportive family, exceptional stamina, inborn patience, or a naturally happy disposition. It may be unusual leadership qualities, a strong physical constitution, uncanny intuition, aesthetic talent, or incredible organizational skills.

Whatever it is, it's supposed to get you further than just the grocery and the butcher. Not that I'm underestimating the enormous pool of resources everyday living consumes. Just to go about our daily responsibilities, including breadwinning, learning, and child-rearing takes an unusual amount of aptitude.

Still and all, I think we owe it to the Gift Giver, to conduct a thorough search and find those envelopes within us. To set our sights on some extras, things we may never have been able to afford on our own, so at the end of it all, we'll have something to point to and say, "Thank You, Hashem. *This* is what I've done with Your gift."

Of Doughnuts and Doing

It was the second evening of *Chanukah*, and I was feeling very sorry for myself. Although the two flames were dancing merrily atop the gleaming *menorah*, neither their warmth nor their enthusiasm seemed capable of igniting my spirits. My first *Chanukah* abroad, separated from my family by a vast ocean, seven hours, and culture shock, I felt very much in the mood of crying.

Early in the evening, as soon as three stars had been apparent, my husband had lit the *menorah* with a quiver of excitement. Then he had lingered on the home front, trying his hardest to infuse our humble abode with the *Chanukah* spirit. He had sung with all the fervor he could muster, and even did a solo dance around our barely furnished dining room. I must say, he did an impressive job.

But I was a sore loser. I wanted to be back home (that was back then, when the sentimentally laden word still tugged at my loyalties, and more often than not, evoked images of the family abroad). I wanted to hear the lilt in my little brother's voice as he chanted the *berachah* in close imitation of my father's tune, his face wreathed in a halo of golden light. I longed to hear the boys erupting in song, half a dozen voices blending in alto and soprano, chorusing the timeless *Maoz Tzur*. I yearned to feel the dining-room floor vibrate as they stepped in rhythm to the uplifting tune, pajama-clad toddlers atop the older ones' shoulders, one big circle of joyous celebration. And I ached to smell my mother's famous doughnuts, sizzling in the hot oil; puffy, fluffy, golden-brown doughnuts draining on a bed of paper towels, waiting to be sprinkled with sugar.

So though my husband made some very valiant efforts at placating me, the subdued scene in my home was a pale replica of the vividly colored nostalgia that crowded my heart and mind.

Actually the memories seemed lodged right inside my throat, a growing lump that threatened to engulf me in tears. I willed them to stay inside, as I smiled wanly, and thanked my husband who cheerfully wished me a happy *Chanukah* as he left the house to learn with a study partner.

For a moment I sat there, staring at the front door, before it melted into a blur of brown, distorted by my tears. Not bothering to reach for a tissue, I cried silently, letting the tears course freely down my face.

I don't know if it was a minute, or ten, but after a while of sitting there, I decided to share my misery with someone. My first impulse to dial home was instantly canceled, as a quick glance at the clock revealed that there was probably no one at home. I didn't even risk trying. I was in too sensitive a mood to handle the rejection of an indifferent telephone ringing incessantly into my ear.

My next few ideas were similarly vetoed. And then I thought of Shiffy. Just the thought of Shiffy made me get up and square my shoulders. She would understand. She would empathize. And she would know just what to say, and what not to say, to lift my flagging spirits.

Shiffy, an upbeat mother of two, had been living in Eretz Yisrael for five years, and was my sort of mentor when it came to the difficulties of adjusting. She would surely remember her first *Chanukah* abroad, and perhaps just airing my feelings would do something to dispel my dismal mood.

So I dialed, and waited for Shiffy to answer. After three rings, she picked up, and I heard her 7-month-old gurgling in the background.

"Oh, it's you! It took me a minute to recognize your voice. A *freilichen Chanukah*! How are you doing?"

"Great," I attempted, sorry to dampen her cheerful state. Then I dropped all pretenses.

"Shiffy," I blurted, the tears coming again, "it doesn't feel like *Chanukah*! The house is so quiet. I have a whole long evening ahead with no plans to fill it.

"It doesn't feel festive or anything," I sniffled, groping for the words to convey what I was feeling, what I was missing. "It doesn't even *smell* like *Chanukah* around here. I wish … I wish I had some doughnuts!"

"Well, how about making them?"

I was too stunned to answer. I don't know if it was the hurt, the disappointment or the shock that rocked me like a wave, but I felt as if I had been stabbed. How could she toss such a flippant response when I was feeling so lonely, so miserable, so low? Didn't she realize that I hadn't meant the doughnuts per se, that they had only been a symbolic expression of my longing for home, for family, for warmth and togetherness?

I wistfully remembered those warm cozy *Chanukah* evenings, munching fresh doughnuts, as we watched my mother pack up all the extras into several round tins, tightly pinching the aluminum foil around the rims.

"Whom can we take some warm doughnuts to?" she'd ask us, and we'd readily come up with a list to match the number of care packages on the counter.

There was Aliza, the mother of a broken family battling with so many odds, whose children would delight in the indulgence, and there was Susan, an earnest young *baalas teshuvah* who would be warmed by the thoughtful gesture. Then there was Mrs. Finkelstein, whose two married sons lived out of town, and who surely hadn't bothered to fry doughnuts …

I had wanted to share these pieces of home with Shiffy, but now, suddenly, I felt the warmth of the memory evaporate, as I fumbled to decline her unexpected suggestion. The doughnuts hadn't been the point at all, and if she didn't have it within her to empathize, well then, I guess I would hang up.

And then, I don't know what triggered it, perhaps it was Shiffy's respectful silence as she waited patiently for me to sort through my tumultuous thoughts, or perhaps it was her well-meaning intent in the first place, but whatever it was, I suddenly experienced a change of heart.

Shiffy had understood. She had felt my misery, and had perceived as well as I that the doughnuts had only been an alibi, an expression for my longing on that *Chanukah* evening.

And still, and although, and *because* she so deeply cared, she was inviting me to share her own secret of survival, the secret she had discovered on some dreary winter nights, and on some quiet, lonely, homesick summer days.

You want doughnuts?

How about making them?

Stop stewing in self-pity. Stop expending all your efforts on paddling your rowboat in circles around yourself. Stash away all those legitimate reasons justifying the fact that you could and *should* be wallowing in distress, and do something to help yourself.

You want a nicer neighborhood? Do something to make it nice. You wish there were some stimulating classes available? Do something to arrange them! Wouldn't it be lovely to enjoy a leisurely shmooze on the telephone? Be the one to pick up the receiver and initiate the connection!

It isn't the slightest bit easy, and sometimes, usually, it's the last thing you want to hear, especially if, like me, you're a lot more comfortable balking, blaming, and feeling helpless than getting up to heat the oil.

But once you do, once you wrench yourself free of that glum pessimism gluing you to your misery, you feel liberated. You feel invigorated. And while the tears may still escape the corners of your eyes now and then, you feel different. You feel your rowboat finally beginning to sail forward.

I guess you could say it's the difference between seeing the doughnut and seeing the hole.

Playing With Fire

A little knowledge, they say, is dangerous. Better to remain unequivocally ignorant than to dabble, when it comes to matters of consequence. Like treating infection.

Or repairing appliances.

The way we did.

It started when our heating system failed. Our air-conditioning unit, which doubles as a hot-air system in the winter, has given us its fair share of trouble. We've had the thermostat break, and the motor stall. This winter, for variety, the fuse kept blowing after twenty minutes or so of the system running.

I jotted an urgent note to seek out a competent repairman. In the interim, I tried my hand at some impromptu doctoring. I turned the motor off, flicked the popped fuse back up, and restarted the motor. All was well; the simple trick got the machine to work again.

Until the next incident, that is, whereupon we repeated the strategy. Even the kids learned the maneuver. I don't know if it was resourcefulness sparked by indolence, or indolence sparked by resourcefulness, but as soon as I'd figured out some way, albeit a cumbrous one, around the hitch, I became somewhat less ardent about getting to the core of the problem.

Until we got a guest home from yeshivah.

"What are you doing there?" he asked, his thrill for tinkering aroused, as he watched me efficiently execute the switch-pop-ignite feat.

"Just getting the heating back on," I replied complacently, as if fiddling around with a fuse was the standard procedure used to get the unit started. Then, as an afterthought, in response to his raised eyebrows, I added, "For some reason, this thing insists on being disciplined from time to time."

Like most teenage yeshivah *bachurim*, this one in particular doesn't sit very well with complacency. In a minute, he had a chair pulled into position against the fuse box, and a screwdriver in hand.

Up, down, open, shut; after he'd ineffectively toyed with the fuse box, he industriously stationed the chair in front of the switchboard on the wall.

"Tell me when the motor turns on outside," he instructed from his position, hunched over the crisscross of wires. He tapped and tinkered, and then, on impulse, unscrewed a metal piece. Then he replaced the plastic cover, and flicked on the operating switch. Magic. A shudder and cough from the motor outside, and warm air was flowing in through the vents.

He got off the chair, face glowing.

"See?" he said, holding the offending plate like some hard-won piece of booty. "This was causing all the trouble!"

I was skeptical.

"Just wait," I predicted pessimistically, "it'll quit again soon."

It didn't though. The machine worked like a faithful horse. In fact, it ran almost nonstop for three days, without incident. My amateur repairman left back for yeshivah, beaming. And then we started smelling smoke.

This time I didn't try any shortcuts. I called a licensed electrician post-haste. And from his demeanor, I can tell you, it was a very close call.

"Who played around with this thing?" the electrician demanded irately, the minute he peeked inside the switchboard. I was glad the culprit wasn't around to suffer the anticlimax of his success.

"There's a piece missing here," he said pointedly. I nodded solemnly, hoping he wouldn't probe any further.

"The fuse kept blowing on you, didn't it?"

I kept quiet, sensing a tirade in the brewing.

"Well, there was a reason for that!" he seethed as he emphatically shut the power off, and withdrew a screwdriver from his belt.

I stood back like a chastised child as he deftly snipped some wires inside the box, and extricated a new plate from his assortment of screws and tools. He must have sensed my contrition, because his tone softened, as he turned to me.

"I'm saying this out of concern for your safety, *Giveret*. Never, ever, take anything out of an electrical device without consulting an authorized electrician."

I tried to convey my remorse, but he seemed insistent on having me understand the full gravity of my mistake.

"When the fuse blows, *Giveret*, it means the system's overheated. Whoever tinkered around here trying to fix things took out an important safety feature. That piece was installed to shut the system down in the event that too much heat was being generated."

"Look at this," he showed me a blackened piece of metal with exposed wires protruding. "The whole wiring inside here was burned out; another few hours, and your house could have gone up in flames."

I paid him his due, and hung to the side as he packed up his tools, unsure of how to end the unpleasant scene. I thanked him, and he dismissed my praise.

"I just hope you people learned your lesson," he muttered as he left the house.

And believe me, we did. We've learned more lessons than one.

For starters, we've abolished the notion of do-it-yourself repairs. We've come to see the danger in a smattering of knowledge, and we've developed newfound appreciation for blown fuses.

And their conceptual counterparts.

I remember marveling over the clever design of circuit breakers when we first learned about them in the introduction to the basics of electricity. The workings of electrons and neurons were beyond me, but they opened a new window of understanding.

A blown fuse was not some kind of breakdown; a hindrance, a pain in the neck. It was a built-in mechanism, a safety device deliberately installed to prevent a major conflagration!

Somehow, electrical intrigue had eluded me when the fuse had blown in real life. When I needed that unit to work, all I wanted was to circumvent the nuisance and carry on with the smooth running of things.

Well, I learned. Sometimes, in the process of elimination, we put our lives on the line.

Air conditioners aside, somewhere, sometime, the fuse is bound to blow. In the house, or outside of it, but I'd venture to guess that everyone has encountered some sort of short circuit today. Every day.

Sometimes they're nonworking heating systems. Other times, they're the checkbook left at home, the navy sock in the white load, the irretrievable pictures on a roll of exposed film. Sometimes, they're the painstaking hours of work lost on the computer, the giggling soloist who botched the perfectly synchronized choir, the contractor who never came through.

No one likes to have the system blow in his face. Oh sure, we mumble something about *kapparos*, but please, not *now*! Not when the final rehearsal is tomorrow, when the kids were supposed to be sleeping two hours ago, when business is already so rotten as it is. We'll have *kapparos* some other time. Now let's just get the system working again.

And so we do the switch-pop-ignite feat, in the hope of fixing up. We make some desperate phone calls, try to pull strings with the higher-ups, fiddle around this way and that, all the while earnestly pleading. *Please, Hashem, let this work out.* Who hasn't done some of his most earnest praying in the face of minor crises like these?

Not that anything is wrong with praying. Or even with taking the normal measures to treat problems or prevent slipups in the future. We most definitely should make the effort to leave on time, to back up our computer files, to exercise caution with breakables.

The fallacy is in our speculation that life would be ideal if it ran smoothly, all day, all year. If it were up to us, we'd cancel burned cookies, burst pipes, broken telephones. Okay, not *really*, but while they're happening, would we ever!

We'd do away with gained weight, lost credit cards, failed tests. We'd omit the sprained ankle, the stolen bike, the business blunder.

And we'd be headed for disaster.

We'd be tampering with the safety feature built in to protect our ultimate well-being. We'd be letting our insides smolder beneath the calm, burning away at our inner wires until they were charred to destruction.

Aggravations aren't mistakes. They aren't imperfections or flaws in the design. They are the shut-off system that diffuses the heat when the friction inside our soul starts sending sparks. They are the circuit breakers that cool off smoldering decrees before they can become full-scale explosions.

So let us try to humbly embrace those little blown fuses, those obstacles and disappointments built into our existence. Let us try to swallow the impulse to agonize over minor mishaps, even when they really rankle, and try to appreciate the magnificence of the design.

Because in the long run, what's a short circuit?

Behind Every Gadol

"Imagine," I remember my father marveling, when we spoke of one *gadol* or another. "He was only 28 when he wrote his responsa on *Shas*." Or alternately, "He was only 32 when he became appointed as the *Rav* of the entire town."

Only? My 8-year-old perception of age was slightly thrown, but I knew better than to question a bunch of adults so obviously in awe of something I couldn't grasp. I remained respectfully silent, but inside, the contradiction puzzled me. Had they said *only* in reference to numbers like 28 and 32? Or perhaps I hadn't heard right. According to my calculations, my own father was probably about that age, and to me he personified the apex of wisdom garnered with age.

And that wasn't the only time that the adults seemed to have a diminished sense of the value of age.

It was on *Shavuos* afternoon, I distinctly remember, and we kids sat on redwood benches on the back porch, relishing the reappearance of watermelon. My mother sat nearby, misty eyed, with a book in hand, occasionally looking up to smile at us. "Who wants to hear a story?" she suddenly invited, and we all jumped at the offer. To tell the truth, I had been watching my mother kind of curiously, and had been wondering what kind of stories she was reading that had prompted her to smile and cry at once.

My mother thumbed through the book, and when she found the story she wanted, she began reading with feeling, looking up intently to gauge our reactions. But I was disappointed. I didn't really know what was supposed to make me smile, and surely had no clue as to what about the story could elicit tears.

"*Kinderlach,* did you understand why R' Meir Shapiro's mother cried on the day that her son's private tutor couldn't come?"

Yes, I had understood. Reading comprehension had always been my domain, and at 9 years old I was surprised my mother was testing such elementary understanding.

"Such a short story, Mommy. Please read us another one." Maybe the next one would prove to be a little more dramatic, revolutionary. My mother indulgently leafed through the book, looking for something a little longer. But they were all short. Short stories of inspiration about women's *mesiras nefesh* for Torah.

And I, at 9, was surprised that the book was making such an issue over anecdotes that seemed to make perfect sense to me. These were grown women the book was depicting, great big mothers. Of course they baked refreshments for their Torah-learning sons with their last drop of flour and sugar. And wasn't it obvious that they would give up their dream of buying fabric for a new dress in favor of purchasing a set of cherished *sefarim*?

I would act much the same in so many years to come, wouldn't I? I was convinced I would. Somehow, however, seeing the soft glow in my mother's eyes made the sentiment die in my throat. Perhaps there was something I actually *was* missing, something I didn't quite grasp about these stories of greatness that seemed so ordinary to me, so plainly understood.

I don't know where the years disappeared, simply don't know. Somehow, when I wasn't looking, a whole long ribbon of time was swallowed up, like the cord of the vacuum cleaner slithering into the storage hole. Suddenly, here I am, so much past 9 that it scares me. Scares me to think that just a blink ago, and a lifetime back, I was so absolutely positive that at the age I can boast of today, I would be easy material for any one of those short stories of inspiration.

Today I feel much the same as I did at 9, eons younger and smaller than those legendary heroines, only my smug confidence of that bygone *Shavuos* has evaporated with the years, and I am more than a trifle unsure that I will ever reach those deceivingly simple heights.

Sitting and crunching watermelon on *Shavuos* afternoon, there had been nothing more natural sounding than devoted Jewish mothers, whose first and foremost burning desire was to see their husbands and sons develop into Torah giants.

For some reason, rushing home from work, lowering a flame, and tossing pajamas into the dryer in a frantic race to fetch my son from school, the zeal seems a little more remote from my daily life.

Sure, when I watch all those pure little *yingelach* heading to *cheder* each morning, or when I bring my precious charge a few minutes late and the sweet music of little voices singing *"vehaarev na"* greets us at the doorway, my heart swells with such incomprehensible joy and pride that I find it hard to suppress the tears. Then I momentarily join the chain of Jewish mothers whose single most fervent wish was that they be granted the privilege to fuel the torch of Torah.

During those transient moments, I feel the weight and urgency of all my daily pressures lift, and give rise to an exalted song of mission and ecstasy. In those fleeting seconds before my *cheder yingel* slips his little hand out of mine, and says, "Have a good day, Mommy," I truly feel that there is no task in the world, no job on my never-ending list of errands, that I would exchange for this one.

But there are so many other moments in the day. Moments when I feel overwhelmed by the many responsibilities of mothering and working; moments when a glance at the clock makes me wish that some cheery little school bus would fetch my little boy for me and spare me the twenty minute-spree to and from the school. There are moments when serving supper in three different shifts seems like a hassle instead of the lofty job of feeding budding *talmidei chachamim.* Or when the prospect of having my husband baby-sit is so tempting, it almost makes me forget that his nightly learning *seder* is as crucial as a million-dollar transaction.

The glistening threads of idealism are delicately embroidered on my heart; they make me surge with pride, and bring me to tears. Somehow, though, they aren't intermeshed and interwoven into my day-to-day chores. They aren't, solely, what comprise the actual weave of my existence. Very often, my personal need for order, for respite, for comfort or convenience takes precedence over my eternal goal.

It is then that I am reminded of those stories. Stories of women, my age, younger, and older, whose sheer love of Torah charged their every waking moment. Women, whose needs for aesthetic beauty, for space, for a stocked pantry, and a predictable routine, were tempered by their unquenchable desire to support Torah, to ignite Torah, to nurse the tiny flickering flames of Torah. And if at 9, I lacked the life experience to appreciate their transcendence of natural womanly inclinations, today standing a few rungs higher on the chronological ladder, I am overawed.

My child's perception of aging has drastically altered along with the process of it. At 9 I was sure that self-improvement was intrinsic to the process of growing older, that idealism was automatically cemented with the passing of years. Now, some decades later, I am forced to confront the blunt reality of life.

The numbers of age advance like the digits on a stopwatch, independent of any personal effort. Unless the person donning the number's cloak makes a serious effort to climb upward, to combat difficulties, and keep redirecting his inner focus, he may remain perpetually 9 years old, dreaming about the future and waiting for growth to happen.

So I sigh as I realize that, no, I haven't done enough spiritual exercising to have reached the planes that some of those ordinary, extraordinary mothers of Torah have. But while I have somewhat relinquished my childhood vision of myself as a lofty heroine in my more mature understanding of growth and aspiration, something within me wants to hold on to that childish dream.

Something inside me wants to be 9 years old, eating watermelon on that *Shavuos* afternoon, brimming with trust and eagerness and belief that, "That's the way it should be. That's the way I *will* be someday."

Sorry, Try Again!

"Ma?"

She charged through the door, flinging her sweating, enthusiastic, shirttailed figure into the front hall. "Can you teach me how to jump rope?"

Like bubbles rising feverishly in an unplugged seltzer bottle, an old sensation flooded me, frothing and foaming over the sides of my subconscious, where it had been safely submerged under years of success.

Jump rope. The dreaded cloud that had hovered over happy recess breaks and threatened my carefree childhood summers suddenly settled over my kitchen, mocked the clean countertops, sneered at the computer standing proudly to a side. After all these years of building an impressive mountain of achievement beneath which jump rope, I thought, was eternally laid to rest, my little first-grade daughter sailed through the front door like a summer breeze and toppled the edifice with a single innocent request.

All at once I was 7, 8, and 9 years old again, when just the sight of a jump rope evoked quick palpitations, a speeding, garbled succession of longing, determination, fear, dread, despair, and a rush of relief.

Somehow, "One a Big Girl" had never worked with me. I'd stood there bravely, just the way I'd seen the others do, the rope rhythmically hitting my calf, my fists clenched, ear cocked, temples throbbing with the intense readiness to pounce at the sound of "go." I guess I wasn't supposed to pounce. Bounce, they prodded, gently, double jump, like this.

But I never got it. I always landed up clumsily tangled in the rope, trying to gracefully extricate my shoelaces and my self-esteem from the mess. Nobody laughed. They were really nice. "Everybody learns how to jump rope," they coaxed. "Just keep trying; you'll get there."

And I did. Try, I mean. Even as I watched my cousins and classmates effortlessly bounce under and over the whirling wire like magicians, I took comfort in the reassurances and painstakingly tried again and again in the staunch hope that it was all a matter of practice.

In the privacy of my own backyard, I took that jump rope in hand and fantasized myself adroitly skipping an ever-growing amount of beats until someone would cry, "Enough, enough, you'll never be out; just give someone else a turn."

Actually, I did quite well in my solo efforts, with the two ends securely in my control, turning in time to my own pace. It was diving into the center that scared me, like the vulnerable sensation of jumping into a freezing-cold shower.

I would cower, then duck into the middle, hands flung in front of me in self-defense, eyes shut against the onslaught of the whipping arc of twine. Hopelessly out of sync, I would then let the tension die as the rope flogged my calf, and, relieved to be over with the ordeal, slunk off to take the end.

There was a limit, though, to the amount of times I was willing to subject myself to this humiliation. By the time I was 10 and 11, I'd become a resigned fixture, faithfully serving as the steady ender, watching my friends nimbly weave in and under and around in dynamic formation.

Eventually, I left the arena entirely. As girls enthusiastically clustered to form a game, I'd feign indifference. Who needs jump rope? I'd scoff. I'd much rather curl up with a book, or take a long walk with a good friend around the ball field, plucking the weeds along the beaten trail.

I invested my interests in other things, the things I was good at, like drawing and writing, behaving like the classical teacher's dream, and serving as the moderator between the convergent parties in my eighth-grade class. All of which were gratifying. No sweat, no embarrassment, no repeated failure. Only sweet success, a great deal of it, respect and recognition — gentle and familiar and non-threatening.

I'd almost forgotten it, that flush of shame, that frustrating defeat, until my first grader accosted me, hands on hips, eyes wide with disbelief, sizing me up as if for the very first time.

"What? Mommy! You *still* don't know how to jump rope?"

I smiled abashedly, averting my gaze, suddenly preoccupied with tucking in her blouse, and smoothing the stray bits of hair that had escaped her ponytail. There was no way to get around it, though.

"Would you believe it? At my age I still haven't learned how to jump rope!"

"But why, Mommy? It's so easy." And then again, as if she just couldn't conceive the possibility, she squinted at me, looking straight into my eyes to gauge my frankness.

"Really, Ma, you *really* can't jump rope?"

Talk about probing a sore point. I felt myself flush under her scrutiny, in the face of her stubborn unwillingness to believe I was incapable of so elementary a feat.

"Look, I'm good at other things," I felt ridiculously compelled to prove my competence.

"Right," she conceded generously, "you know how to write, and work the computer, and bake and clean and tell stories."

She was skipping out of the kitchen already, searching for a more eligible teacher, and I breathed a sigh of relief. That had been a close call, my self-esteem at the hands of a 7-year-old. Glad to be off the hook, I laughed heartily, my equilibrium safely restored.

Not for long, though. Something about the whole encounter had unsettled me. And it wasn't only the sour taste of failure coming up on me. I'd grown old enough to recognize that my inaptitude at jump rope wasn't the most glaring of my flaws. Not by a far stretch.

It was the other ropes, ropes I'd never quite mastered, and had given up in favor of the ones I was naturally adept at. It was the unresolved challenges I'd abandoned for the immediate gratification afforded by doing what came without that extra measure of effort.

The sudden resurgence of jump rope in my life had confronted me with the harsh fact that I could so easily appear to be a successful, accomplished individual when I had, in reality, some seriously undeveloped skills buried beneath my tower of grandeur.

All that was perfectly fine in the realm of physical ability. Not everybody was destined to be the world's athlete or intellectual or artist. The point was to get around one's handicaps and succeed in other domains.

What scared me was the unnerving truth that someone could go through life, presumably excelling, and remain close to the bottom of the spiritual ladder.

If you took the course I did, shunning obstacles and circumventing difficulty, blazing a trail out of the stepping-stones of easy victory, you could one day find your path has gotten nowhere. Nowhere other than the aggrandized station from which you initially departed.

You could be an accomplished individual, and nobody would ever guess that you've never cultivated those personal patches that have doomed you to failure. Our inner struggles are a private affair. That which is so ordinary to one person may require extraordinary effort on the next one's part. And it is so simple and tempting and soothing to switch lanes to the track we know best, so that we can speed ahead, instead of inching forward with laborious effort.

Effort is a word we don't usually wax enthusiastic about. No matter how often we mothers and teachers claim that it isn't the mark that counts, in an ironic quirk of our educational system, our students somehow learn that effort has become an accolade reserved for those who are somewhat less astute. "I can see you tried hard," is a thinly veiled way of saying, "I can see you didn't succeed."

Up there, there's a different award system in effect. The classic report card primarily assesses ability, and grades effort as an afterthought; on our ultimate rating sheet, it's solely effort that determines our grade.

We weren't put on the road to eternity in order to put our foot on the accelerator, and let the wind sail through our windows. It's those personal potholes, the ones under our vehicles, that no one even sees, that we were set down to smooth.

For some it's generosity, for some it's faith, for others it's happiness or discipline or tolerance; we each know where those potholes lie, what we have to invest serious effort and ongoing practice to master. Our chief accomplishments are not the flags we've stuck into the mountaintops; they lie low in the valley, in the place that leaves us feeling exhausted and discouraged, the climb that flings us to the bottom over and over again.

So next time you feel disheartened, ashamed that you're still getting tangled and stuck and may just never achieve mastery, remember: It isn't championship that's lauded above; all He asks is that we take it to the end of the rope.

Job Opportunities

There's a new word I've been learning to use lately, not in context, in actuality. The word's delegating. I know it seems like a simple-enough concept to those people who are natural delegators, but I've got a feeling that there are plenty of nondelegators out there who, like me, have a hard time putting the idea into practice. From coordinating a simple supper to planning a full-scale fund-raising dinner, there are inordinately enough jobs in this world to go around.

We nondelegators, though, tend to live with the undying premise that no one else can do the job, whatever the job may be, or at least not the way we can. "Oh no, that's something I've got to do myself," is the sentiment regarding the nitty-gritty and not so nitty-gritty details of making anything happen. We just seem to have trouble relinquishing work and compromising on perfection, or our very subjective idea of it.

And so we fish up some extraneous tasks, anything really, to keep the others around us busy while we tend to the important items, the ones for which we just can't fathom accepting help. We're not trying to be martyrs or anything, but really, how could we trust someone else to do the job? It's got to be done so carefully/ tactfully/ quickly — not something we can trust just anybody to do.

And then there's the "It's just not worth it" piece of logic. "It's just not worth it to train someone else to put away the laundry/ make those phone calls/ run the errands." All that time spent recruiting a volunteer and explaining the instructions just doesn't justify the bit of alleviation from the burden those tasks present.

That's assuming that the job will be properly executed, and we won't be finding telltale traces for the next couple of days. Forget about the fact that most probably some details of the chore will be forgotten, or that it won't be properly cleaned away afterward. So time and time again, we give in to that irresistible urge to do things ourselves, our own way. In the teacher's room, in the office, during family meetings, we land up biting off chunks of work, and insist on doing the chewing by ourselves.

Lately, though, I've been changing. I don't know if it's a sign of progress or deterioration, but I've begun to learn the virtues of cashing in on the potential around me. Instead of doing every-thing myself, from extending the invitation to peeling the last cucumber, from writing every narration to bringing in every prop, I've begun to discover that there are plenty of competent people around who are more than willing to share the brunt of almost any project.

Instead of "undertake," I've learned to "oversee." And the results, I hate to admit, have been downright impressive. How can I compare a performance by my one-man band, however skilled I'd like to believe it is, to a symphony comprised of the finest instruments?

The secret, I've discovered, for successful delegating, is in the matchmaking process. Give the people the jobs they like to do and are good at. Find the areas people have experience with and that go along with their nature. There's always someone who's good at coming up with the brainstorm, and someone else who's adept at drawing up the lists.

There's bound to be someone who likes making phone calls, and someone who's efficient when it comes to the shopping. There are the talented artists, and then there are those who prefer baby-sitting. When everyone contributes his or her specialty, the outcome far outshines anything one person can accomplish.

So ever since my first stint with delegating, born of necessity, which emphatically dispelled my firmly entrenched notion that I was indispensable, I've been practicing the skill. I've divided household chores among the members of my family, started a rotation system for the shared duties in my apartment building, and gotten friends to help a family in the neighborhood.

Putting others in charge saves me hours of time, and gives me a certain sense of satisfaction that I am doing things the way they were meant to be done. In a small way, I've got the feeling that I'm imitating the Master Delegator, Who "created (this world) to do," Who set up a factory with all the raw materials and appointed us workers to refine and process them.

In a very small way, though. I haven't had much chance to bask in the glory of this grandiose analogy. Because, under closer scrutiny, I've noticed a striking difference, a distinct contrast between my own version of appointing other people to the way *HaKadosh Baruch Hu* hands out jobs.

As I've said, my own success was contingent on the matchmaking component. Finding the most capable person for the task at hand was definitely my primary criterion for the prospective candidate for any job. I sought drivers to take care of errands, artists for the graphics, and mathematical minds for any project that entailed calculations. Logic dictated that I do so.

And yet, in this complex world of ours, destiny seems to defy this inescapable bit of logic. Doesn't the "neat-as-a-pin" prototype usually marry the spontaneous "throw-it-together" personality? The boisterous, easygoing family will inevitably share walls (or worse yet, a floor/ceiling) with the no-nonsense, peace-and-quiet seekers. The generous folks usually don't have the means; the ones with the ideas don't have the connections.

Young people who dreamed of setting up homes in Eretz Yisrael land up a block away from Mom, and those who so desperately want and need familiar surroundings are whisked off to foreign shores. Boys with the potential to become *geonim* are so often engulfed by waves of financial difficulties; those that are cushioned by affluence struggle to find joy in a *blatt Gemara*.

The Master Planner delegated chores, plenty of them. Sometimes, though, it seems to us that if we'd had our hands on the lists, we'd have organized things differently.

But that's because we're overlooking one integral difference.

We, in our limited capacity, want to do it all by ourselves to prove our potency. Delegating is a necessary skill we have to learn in order to preserve our strength. Hashem, in His all-encompassing might, can do it perfectly well by Himself. Delegating jobs is a kindness He performs with us to strengthen our weaknesses.

When Hashem assigned the jobs, He wasn't looking for the most efficient way to get the job done. He wasn't looking for experience or ease. For that, He could have managed very well without us. When He delegated tasks, Hashem was handcrafting the personalized challenges we each needed in order to chisel and polish our souls. He was looking for weak points, not strong points, and then

He allotted the appropriate tasks to fortify them. He gave us jobs that would make us sweat. Not because He needed us to do the sweating for Him. *We* needed it.

So although irony is instrumental to a good piece of literature, it doesn't really exist in this world. Those marriages, those situations, those twists of fate; they aren't really ironies, only opportunities; countless opportunities to tap the iron deposits that lie within each of us, just waiting to be mined.

The Good News and The Bad News

Last Monday, it just wasn't there. The rolled-up paper that's been in the mailbox each morning as predictably as the bakery truck lumbers into the grocery's parking lot at the crack of dawn, as surely as the clusters of freshly groomed little girls in light blue and navy converge at 10 to 8, just didn't make its daily appearance. When, upon my return from the morning rounds, I absent-mindedly stuck my hand out to the slot to withdraw the daily scoop, all I felt was the hard metal lip of the empty cavity.

We'd been getting the paper every day now for some time, and it has become part of the morning ritual; somewhat of a prize to be redeemed upon culminating the hassled routine of brushing hair and finding shoes and scribbling signatures. (What ever happened to "I'm not signing anything if it isn't given to me the night before"?)

As I wave goodbye to the last of the troopers and walk back up the path to face the morning wreckage, I feel my body go into slow motion, as the adrenaline, I suppose, makes its way back to wherever it's come from. It is then that I pause to pick up the morning paper for a moment of leisure, for a moment of idle placidity, during which the headlines hold my eyes hostage long enough for my mind to ponder any number of uncensored, impractical, and, most significantly, noncompelling thoughts.

Last Monday, however, it just wasn't there. Disappointed, I let my hand slide down slowly and heaved a resigned sigh, as I headed for the stairwell. The steps were another, if not as lazy, way of putting the urgent on hold so I could savor a few moments with myself before my inner taskmaster stepped in.

Indeed! I mentally smacked myself on the forehead, as remembrance flickered. A blurred vision tickled my mind, the kind of memory that flashes like lightning and has long disappeared by the time you reach the window. I grabbed at the last thread of its disappearing tail. Promotion.

As if I had pressed the code word, it suddenly came back to me. In a moment of distraction, some months ago, my husband had mentioned something about a promotional offer, something about receiving a free subscription to a popular daily for a trial three-month period.

And in my recollection of the incident, I had nodded; I had most likely been in the middle of explaining something, or listening to someone, or both. And it was about then, come to think of it, that the paper had begun making its daily appearance.

I had presumably greeted the first arrival mildly pleased, in the kind of vaguely satisfied way one acknowledges the presence of something good. I'd scooped up the paper without paying much thought, either to the reason it had begun coming, or to the fact that it would end.

Now, however, that it was suddenly missing, I found myself pondering the issue. I liked the paper. I looked forward to it just as I enjoyed savoring the minibreak it afforded me. And ironically, I balked, just when I'd become accustomed to it, almost addicted, it had ceased making its appearance.

Suddenly, I chuckled in amusement at my sense of indignity.

That's just it, honey, exactly what they had in mind. Now that you're hooked, they want you to pay for it!

And just as suddenly, as if the blunt termination of the daily paper had jarred my awareness, I was face-to-face with the more subtle disappearance of part of myself.

Call it erosion, call it resignation, or if you find these too brutal, then perhaps name it realism; I'm talking about the curious disparity between the me of 17 and 18 and 19 years old, glowing, bursting, thirsting for growth, and the muted, matted adult whose company I share these days.

Sometimes I recall those impassioned conversations conducted between midnight and dawn, those soul talks held between friends bound by their spiritual stirrings, and I don't know whether to laugh or to cry. I remember the demands we set for ourselves, the aspirations we painted in vivid colors, the surety and conviction in our minds that threw notions like compromise so far out the window we couldn't even see them.

Beauty in those days consisted of a breathtaking *shiur*, a stunning *Ohr HaChaim* or a glorious *Klei Yakar*. Which of us would ever be drawn by the appeal of a new kitchen, a comfortable couch, elegant curtains? A bunch of Rachels we were, certain of our firm commitment, privately proud of the noble lifestyles we had adopted in theory, only the slightest trifle perturbed by the unsettling thought that our ideals hadn't yet been put to the winds.

Who would ever be lured by the temptation to ask Rabbi Akiva to be late for night *seder* so that a bunch of youngsters could be dealt a disciplining hand at bedtime? Twenty-four years, admittedly, sounded daunting, but that a spouse be absent for morning and evening rituals, that he mull over a late supper with a *Rashba* in hand, that seemed trivial. We only strove to eliminate those traces of pride; Rachels like us aspired for untarnished motives.

Occasionally, I've come upon the documented evidence of those lofty years in the form of lists and resolutions, and probing questions yet waiting for answers. Impressive notes, those folded squares of myself from times bygone, brimming with *emunah* and *bitachon*, saturated with the keen awareness of Torah's eternal supremacy, and the absolute negation of any secondary interests that might fling a shadow over its gentle radiance. Commitments to recite *Asher Yatzar* from a *siddur*, of eating only sitting at a table, of never speaking above a slight whisper.

Whatever did happen, I think at times like these, to that exalted soul who gave expression to those convictions in my very own penmanship? Was I that self-deluded, that out of touch with my inner world, that I actually thought myself beyond day-to-day struggles?

What of all those *tefillos* recited consistently and fervently, those *halachos* followed with scrupulous care? How could I have shed all that in the disregardful way one removes an extra sweater in a warm room, unconscious to the point of oblivion? Had all the piety been a cheap plating, impressive at the outset, yet miserably failing the test of time?

I fold those papers quickly, almost ashamed that the young lady look down from those lofty spheres and see me this way, so preoccupied with practical issues, so inconsistent with *tefillah*, ideals trimmed to an unrecognizable skeleton.

I'd love to heed the voice telling me that it's my present state that's the charade, that the stresses of living, the urgency of the immediate, are spreading a smoke screen over my genuine self, my true desires and deepest hopes.

I'd love to believe that my real ID card still rests safely in the pocket of my outgrown idealistic attire, but I'm hardly convinced. I'm hardly convinced that principles unable to withstand the abrasion of ordinary living can have been true at their core.

And so, unable to endure my own scrutiny, I shift my gaze. I look around to gain some solace, and if comfort lies in numbers, then yes, perhaps I can sneak out of this tunnel of despair fairly easily, if not honorably.

Shopping in the shoe store, chatting at a PTA function, snatching little fragments of passing conversation, it seems I am not alone. Watching the furrowed brows reflecting grimly on the sliding economy, I am instantly jolted back to all those discussions on *hishtadlus* and *bitachon*, discussions that, apparently, have gathered dust in more than one mental attic. How many girls, or *bachurim* for that matter, are still soaring in the spiritual space shuttle of their late teen years?

Usually, somewhere in this tiring inner dialogue, wavering between harsh reprimand, amusing recollections, and shallow comfort, I end up heaving a long sigh of resignation, though the pain is never absent. This morning, trudging up the stairs empty handed, lightning struck.

It hadn't been a pretense, all that intensity and idealism, nor was the degeneration an indication of my true self. Those years back then, they were nothing to sneer at, no cheap plating, no naive facade. They were Hashem's promotional offer, a free subscription to the richness of spiritual living for a limited amount of time.

I'd taken them in much the same way I'd greeted the paper, only too happy for the effortless acquisition, quite disbelieving that the grant would ever end. And just when I'd begun reaping the fruits of realizing spiritual goals, just when I'd begun to savor the taste of growth and commitment, the subscription suddenly became encumbered with a price.

Obstacles rose up in front of me, cravings and weaknesses I'd thought I'd conquered, challenged my convictions, shook my resolutions. Realism reared its all-knowing head, scornfully dismissing the flushed enthusiasm of youth, disregarding my feeble insistence that "Oh, but why? Can't realism and idealism live together?"

The impediments, I now knew, were only Hashem's way of collecting His dues, our opportunity to pay for continuously living by Torah headlines. We weren't meant to relinquish our subscription; we were meant to be fueled by the initial freebie, to be inspired into making the difficult payments that membership now entailed.

No, it's not like sitting in the classroom, or even like standing in front of it. It's like climbing and falling and sliding and sweating. It's getting to know yourself all over again, now that you're footing your own bill, learning all the weak points and sore spots already glossed over once. Oh no, it's not about a cup of coffee over the morning news, this proposition.

But it'll pay for the subscription of a lifetime.

Motherhood

Booster Shot

There aren't too many phenomena that elicit a predictable reaction the way a newborn baby does. Or perhaps it's only in this emotionally charged country.

Wherever you take the tiny, cuddly bundle, you can expect a uniform response, one I've learned to anticipate: a wistful expression, edged with a flicker of fondness and longing. "How old is s/he?" and then as an afterthought, like a wisp of nostalgia not necessarily meant for anyone to hear, "Oh, I just love that stage."

The mere sight of a newborn seems to awaken the tender stirrings within the human soul. That tiny, warm, wriggling miniature of a person, swathed in blankets, squinting and yawning under the light; the velvety mottled skin, the soft, even, hazel-gray eyes that haven't quite decided what color they'd like to remain, and that small head craning for food, hungrily gulping air; all these things make that weightless armload crawl straight into the most unimpassioned heart.

It's got to be more than that, though. The same collection of females who will differ sharply over whether chicken tastes better broiled or baked, whether jackets are nicer tailored or casual, whether brown or mauve complement the decor, what makes them all share this sentiment about newborn babies? Don't tell me about maternal instinct; I have yet to see 20 eyes glaze over with affection at the sight of a toddler kicking up a tantrum, or a 10-year-old whining for earrings.

The thing with newborns is that they're so totally helpless, so completely submissive, and so flawlessly perfect (for as long as perfection is defined solely by charm). Ever heard a newborn answer back, tell you he didn't like your supper, or that no other mother forces kids to go to bed on time? Ever saw a newborn slam a door, tease a sibling, rip up homework?

Not to say that newborns aren't demanding. They snatch your time and your sleep, wreck your routine, sap your energy. And they cost you plenty in the way of money. The difference between them and the grown-up child is that the former make you feel kind and generous. Newborns give you the feeling of being selfless and patient and indispensable. Caring for a tiny baby is an act of nobility and love.

If the truth be said, the tugging sense of endearment really *is* motherly instinct; it's motherly instinct at its best. It's the same wave of affection that surges within us when we gaze at an older child asleep, dreams flitting over his or her brows, hair sprawled over the pillow. It's the pure spring of parental love, unpolluted by personal feelings of failure and resentment, disentangled momentarily from frustration and shame and worry. The newborn is the gift of life, the gift of motherly love, brand new, untainted, given again.

Which is, I think, the reason I find it so dreadfully difficult to visit the clinic with my 6-week-old infant for routine vaccination shots. Holding my featherweight treasure in the crook of my arm,

I feel an inexplicable need to be fiercely protective, to revel in his unsuspecting trust, in our intimate bond not yet strained by conflict and pressure.

All the while, as we wait our turn, as I croon to him, and he delights me with a hint of a smile, there's this sense of uneasiness clutching my chest. And then, as the nurse putters around, readying the needle along with some gauze on a sterile tray, I feel a cold sense of panic grip my heart.

This is cruel; I'm supposed to be his caregiver, his guardian, and he has given me the gift of his trust. I avert my gaze, I cannot see his calm navy eyes, following the nurse's fingers, smiling at the rattle I dangle, presumably to distract him, most likely to distract myself, from the looming ordeal. The nurse tells me to hold his legs down, to keep his hands fastened under my grip. I look at her plaintively; she must be talking to somebody else. And all the while he gurgles trustingly at me, trying to engage my interest, oblivious to the imminent assault about to take place on his security and comfort.

I feel a prick of pain pierce my heart, as she thrusts the needle into his flesh, and I, his mother, mercilessly pin him down so she can continue to stab him. His calm demeanor of a moment ago erupts into hysterical protest, shocked, breathless shrieks of pain, as he looks to me for help, and struggles to wriggle out of my iron vise. All I see, before that congealed lump inside me dissolves, blurring my vision, is an expression of stunned betrayal on his pained features.

Each time the nurse asks me if it's the first time, and I say yes. The first time for this child, for this love, for this trust. It never gets easier. And it doesn't help when she patiently reminds me of the importance of inoculations. I know all that; that's why I came in the first place, why I agreed to this cold-blooded task of holding my child down so she could repeatedly jab him.

She looks at me, the nurse, unnerved, and rips off another piece of cotton so I can dab my tears dry. I don't bother to explain, or to apologize. I scoop my little infant into my arms, into my warm, reassuring embrace, as if to shield him from the trauma he's been through. Brushing aside thoughts of future vaccinations, I let his tearstained cheek touch mine so he can feel my pain.

He looks at me, and his waning cries escalate again. He's too young, too little to make sense of the contradiction between my apparent indifference of the moment before, and the tears of compassion on my face. "Why did you allow this to happen to me, Mommy?" he seems to accuse me, and I am powerless to defend my maternal love, the love that has brought me here, the love that has brought me to tears.

I cannot explain it to him. I can try to soothe the stinging, to administer Tylenol and apply compresses, but no, I cannot explain why, if I am so terribly sorry for him, I will allow the same nurse to inflict the same pain several weeks hence.

And so I pick up a newspaper from the low table in the center, to help pass the requisite half-hour wait following the shots, and I smooth it in front of me. I catch a glimpse of three black and white snapshots, three faces, adorned by *peyos* and glowing with *Yiddishe chein*. I glance distractedly at the caption. Winners of a *mishnayos* contest, perhaps?

Avishai, Neria, and Tzvika Shabo, *Hashem yinakem damam.*

Hashem — what?

Again the tight constriction, the choking lump, the hot tears, as the words describing their tragic murder swim before my eyes. No! No! I can't. Innocent children, bright with life. *Ribono Shel Olam,* Why?

I squeeze my eyes shut, futilely dabbing the piece of soaked cotton to my cheeks. Neria has braces like my neighbor's son, the thought dizzily passes my mind, as I unabashedly wipe my wet face on my sleeve. I look into Avishai's big brown eyes, two pools in his skinny face. He looks about 5, yes he must be 5, and I think of my Chezky, and a tender wave of maternal love cramps my heart so hard, I cannot breathe.

It's those squeezing spasms of pain, and the gush of tears again, and the recurring waves of dizziness, and I feel like my baby is about to fall out of my arms. Tzvika's soft smile haunts me; I see a hand lovingly resting on his shoulder, the rest of the pose is cut off.

And suddenly, an absurd thought, almost a hallucination, takes shape in front of my tear-streaked focus. I see my baby's sweet, trusting smile merge with Tzvika's, and that hand on his shoulder, strangely, it's an extension of my own, my own arm as I lovingly hold my babe and brace myself for the pain I know he will have to endure.

I blink away the tears, and I gaze at Tzvika again, a picture of trust, a picture of innocence and love. A picture of a child smiling in his mother's arms, about to receive a stunning stab. Suddenly, I see the invisible face behind the hand on his shoulder, the hand of the *Shechinah*, trembling with pain, pulsing with *rachmanus*, torn with anguish.

And at once I know, I feel, that the human mother's passion for her newborn baby is but a tiny spark of Hashem's inexhaustible love for every *Yid*. That well of tenderness, those waves of affection, they are the faintest ripples extending from the central core of His embrace.

He held Tzvika in his arms, He held his two brothers, and their mother too, as the cold steel pierced their flesh. Each child was a separate agony, a fresh gash of unbearable pain. Like infants, we cannot conceive the justice behind the anguish. We can only imagine that the maternal love He imbued us with is a trifle of His.

My newborn son sleeps peacefully. He's received a booster shot, and so have I. I fold the sodden paper, and head toward the heavy swinging wooden door. Blinded by the sudden arc of sunlight, I carefully maneuver the carriage down the steps and pass the newsstand where new faces take the place of Tzvika's gentle smile.

Instinctively, I squint up at the tranquil expanse of deep blue sky, belying the turbulence of the world below, and for a moment, for a warm, fleeting moment, I feel His hand resting on my shoulder.

Full Circle

I used to get frustrated,
by the impossibility of it,
How was I
to fit it
all
Into twenty-four hours?
Counselor, cleaner,
cook, volunteer,
Secretary, tutor,
shopper, nurse,
Bread baker
and breadwinner
Maintaining the liveliness
And the livelihood,
If I could do without sleep,
Then perhaps,
But I couldn't.
I asked around,
There must be some trick,
Dozens of Jewish women,
For dozens of generations,
Have been juggling these
Dozens
Of duties.

"You've got to
cut corners,"
they told me,

simpler meals,
less ironing,
quit washing the woodwork,
making dessert,
polishing all the shoes
every evening.

Well,
I did,
I cut corners,
Plenty of corners
And I don't mean things
Like woodwork
And polishing shoes.
I'm still cutting,
Believe me,
I can hardly recognize
Myself,
Stripped
Of all my corners,
And my pride.
All I have left
Of either
is a teensy-weensy orb,
My badge of honor.
Testimony
that I've come
full circle.
Who ever said
Motherhood
Wasn't
a well-rounded
Job?

Of Ponies and Prayers

Vacation is a highly subjective term. For some, it means a weekend in a posh hotel room, cushioned by lavish elegance; for others, it's the smell of charcoal in one's nostrils mingling with the sweet scent of pine, and sleeping bags under the stars. For the less adventuresome, it's paper goods and fast food in the comfort of one's own kitchen, a picnic in the local park, an engaging novel on the back porch. For me, right now, however, vacation is none of the above.

Vacation shall begin tomorrow morning, when children in starched uniform blouses and polished shoes shall step over the doorstep at 10 past 8, and turn around to wave, "Goodbye, Mommy; have a great day!" And their mother, who is me, will feel her eyes fill as they do every year at this auspicious moment.

And as if she hasn't spent every waking moment of the past month and a half with these youngsters, as if she hasn't begged and cajoled that they go down on their own for just a little while, she will insist on accompanying them all the way down the steps, on this very first morning of their new year.

Yes, vacation shall begin some 20 hours hence, when that mother will walk back up the path, her heart laden with the choking fullness of gratitude and anxiety and prayer, and swing open the front door to the serene silence of early morning.

When she will disregard the soggy cornflakes swimming in pools of milk on the kitchen table, and the cucumber peels on the counter; when she will chuckle at the abandoned jumble of pajamas and discarded tights on the floor. When she will eye her bed and the telephone and the refrigerator in fleeting succession, and then shake her head to all of those beckoning temptations. When, instead, she will slowly retrieve a *siddur* from the first shelf of the dining-room bookcase, and settle down with the precious volume and her swelling emotions.

That's when vacation shall begin.

Not that these past few weeks haven't been a blessing to that mother, who is me. Not that I, given the liberty, would ever abolish summer vacation, or that I haven't imbibed some very restorative energy from watching my children exchange secrets and giggles against the backdrop of a rickety train bumping through open farmland.

I have. But now that it's drawing to an end, I feel the excitement of a descending plane passenger suddenly deciphering the familiar outline of rooftops and infrastructure bursting through ever-thinning wisps of cloud. Now that the tantalizing routine is only hours away, I feel the thrill and relief of having completed something wonderful but weary, the quivering ripple of touching down. And I'm glad to be able to stow away the luggage, to snap the table into its upright position and watch the receding backs of expectant youngsters as I cradle that *siddur* and pray for their success.

There is something about that prayer, coming right on the heels of the arduous stint called summer vacation, that lends itself to humility and sincere submission. Something undefined and fuzzy that makes my mind flash with the memory of a recent trip, that brings up the image of those pony rides on the rural *moshav* we visited just last week.

It was a brush with nature, just the way the advertisement had described, there on the *moshav*, amid the sprawling beds of green, and the bales of hay, and the mixed smell of goat's milk and cow manure. Somehow, though, I hadn't reckoned that a brush with nature would mean literally grazing against the fleece of romping sheep, and bumping into braying donkeys.

When the sign at the entrance had announced pony rides as one of the attractions included in the admission fee, I had envisioned an organized line behind the gate of a large fenced-in area, where some friendly farmhand would graciously lead proud children on horseback for two or three turns around a hay-strewn radius. I should have known better.

The ponies were indeed free, in every sense of the word. Three of them, to be exact, were nibbling at heads of cabbage and whole eggplants nestled in the grass, and nonchalantly waiting to be of service. Forget about a fence. And forget the farmhand. This was a do-it-yourself affair.

The kids hung at our sides, eagerness and hesitation flickering in their eyes as they waited expectantly for their gallant mothers to take the reins.

"How do we go about this?" my sister-in-law, practical soul, was the first to find her voice.

"Just put Yossi on," I replied, trying to sound casual, as I took a step back and watched her advance toward the animal zone with her eldest in tow.

My son unlatched his grip from mine. "I want to ride the pony together with Yossi," he declared, confidently following his cousin. My heart skipped a beat. I retreated yet further back as the two kids hovered excitedly near the older one's mother, waiting to be lifted.

"Should I?" asked my sister-in-law, turning around for reassurance, as she haltingly approached the saddled animal. "You don't think she'll kick?"

"Of course not," I answered sweetly from my safe perch a few yards away. "Ponies don't kick; just put the kids on gently; no, from the other side, uh, good, just like that!"

I took a deep breath as she gingerly lifted her son. He mounted the pony, smiling tentatively, and then my son followed suit. I almost exhaled with relief, when the beast suddenly shook her mane, and emitted a loud sneeze. The boys started wailing in fright. My sister-in-law backed off, instinctively dropping the leash.

I was quick to the rescue. Verbally, of course. "It's nothing, Chani, only a sneeze," I prodded. "Just take the reins and start walking. She'll follow you."

Sure, sure, coward; how about entering the rink and trying it yourself?

A crowd of onlookers had gathered to watch the scene. The pony, though, seemed to have her own ideas about being taken for a ride. She wouldn't budge.

"See that red loop near her ear?" ventured a helpful woman from the sidelines. "You've gotta tug that firmly, and she'll get the idea. Just start walking."

"Don't wait for her to move," I interjected, echoing the woman's sage advice. "You just tug the loop and start walking."

That was the cue for a barrage of directives, all safely aimed from an agreeable distance.

"They say you have to talk to them softly."

"Try tickling her ear."

"Pull harder; she couldn't have felt such a meek tug."

A bunch of experts, we stood around offering our guidance in self-evident tones, edged with exasperation. For some strange reason, no one volunteered to take over.

We were busy, you see, flashing snapshots and flinging bits of constructive suggestions.

Not that the scene needed much recording. Looking at the shots now, a week later, they strike me as the picture of a chronically unfolding drama, a reality continuously being replayed.

The same reality that begins on the first day of school each year, as we entrust our tender souls into the hands of our valiant *mechanchim,* daring to hope that they will somehow take the reins, and figure out everything we haven't managed to. The reality that continues as we step back, retreat to a safe distance, and wait in tense anticipation, to see our child riding aloft, embodying cooperation.

And, oh yes, we've got lots of criticism to toss until that happens. Or advice, the way we like to call it.

"They just don't teach the kids to *think*. Why can't the children do anything but spit back exactly what they've been taught?"

"If his *rebbe* only had more patience to wait until he figured out the *Rashi*, Baruch would develop the confidence he's missing."

"Why don't they concentrate more on *halachah*? Isn't that the crux of *chinuch*?"

We have pearls of wisdom to offer the teacher, the principal, the G.O. director. We know why the rules are ridiculous, when the workload is too demanding, how the curriculum should be switched. We know that the kids are acting up because they aren't being challenged, and because the classrooms are too small, and because there is not enough exercise incorporated into the system. We know what should be done, what could be done, and what is not being done to make the pony budge.

So who wants to volunteer to take the reins?

I finger the shots again. The 20 hours until vacation begins have dwindled, and only the shortest stretch of time lies now between fond memories of pony rides, and my eager dream of a quiet morning. Only the littlest sliver of night is left before my offspring will awaken to don their brand-new uniforms, and sling stiff bookbags filled with freshly covered books over their shoulders.

Then they'll leave, eyes shining with the gleam of renewal, to the unfenced area where some courageous teacher will try to lift them aloft and teach them the art of skillfully riding the unbridled pony within them.

And I, who have tried my hand at the training process all summer, who have struggled with the odds of jealousy and laziness and unhappiness and rivalry, will humbly retreat, with only gratitude and admiration in my heart for these devoted messengers, these courageous volunteers. I will look on and I will swallow my impulse to toss unbidden opinions from the comfortable confines of my dining room.

And I will take my *siddur* into hand, and fervently pray.

Someone Special

"**W**hy is the faucet dripping?" I ask of no one in particular, twisting the loose knob closed a trifle too emphatically. I sense a shadow hovering close behind me, expectant eyes hanging in crucial suspense, the fragile flutter of a heart hungry for something from this solid frame of a mother, this practical, fast-moving adult whose opinion means everything.

Too late. I see the hurt and disappointment clouding my daughter's face, I see that bright gloss of anticipation turn watery with tears, and I know a delicate flower of good will has been slashed by my merciless shears.

She's too young to clean the kitchen properly, my flower, too little to scour pots and stack them neatly so that they fit into the cabinet just the way I like them, and scrub the counter and dump the gook gathered in the sink drain. Too young to remember to sweep the floor, or to sweep it properly even if she did remember, to think of pushing in the kitchen chairs, and shining the faucet, and refolding the towel.

But she did try to clean the kitchen. Fueled by a burst of sudden consideration, she cleared the table strewn with leftover salad, open cheese containers, smeared spoons, knocked-over cups, and soiled paperware.

A mess like that could have daunted any able-bodied mother, but she'd been determined. Of her own initiative, she found the right covers for the tubs of cheese, discarded the plates, and washed the spoons under a thin stream of lukewarm water. And she left the faucet dripping.

Which is what I noticed.

Rushing about the house after the first bedtime shift, I'd been spurred on by the brisk wind of annoyance, sparked by the irritating presence of wet towels and tangled tights, open briefcases and smashed crayon stubs. It's the time of day when my patience is dangerously dwindling, the peace of evening so elusively close, and yet so tauntingly far away.

Thus I entered the kitchen, on the last gust of my peeved storm-wind, and purposefully shut the drip-dripping faucet. I also, unwittingly, trampled the shadow behind me, flicked out the light in those expectant eyes, smothered the delicate petals of hope and pride fluttering within that fragile heart.

Backing into her, my tight rubber band of a mood suddenly snapped, and my heart took the course of a deflating balloon: flying, flapping, circling madly as the air rushed out, and then landing noiselessly, a flimsy piece of collapsed membrane, flattened on the floor.

I had done it again. Borne down so heavily with my rake and hoe, that I had squished a dainty little bud on its tender green shoots. Glared so hard with my eagle's eye that I had pierced right through the translucent beauty of tentative efforts, of pristine intentions.

I scooped my shriveled little raisin of an ego off the floor, and made every attempt to salvage the situation. Reentered the kitchen, the way I'd request of a stomping youngster, and opened my eyes with amazement, as if I was seeing it all for the first time. It wasn't feigned. I *was* seeing it for the first time, at least from this perspective.

Thank G-d little girls are more resilient than withered roses; my daughter's fallen face came alive. As I admired each detail of her spectacular cleanup and commended her for the lovely thought, I saw the shine return to her eyes, and I was suddenly inspired to unearth an old trove of letters, letters I'd received from my grandmother, so that I could share something very near and dear with her. And so that I could infuse its essence into my own being yet again.

Dearest Malky,
Your dear letter brought much joy and happiness into my day. You write so nicely and describe the children's costumes so well that I

can just imagine how outstanding they look. I remember how lovely they looked last year, but this year, it sounds like they are especially outstanding. And you prepared them by yourself! I am sure you can be very proud and happy with the outcome.

Purim here was lively and simcha'dig, lebedig in the house, and listig on the street. Chaya Sorah and Yisrael Yitzchak came over with the darling children; everyone is someone special to me. They will soon be leaving for the States for Pesach. I am so happy for all of you. I am sure you are enjoying Chana Rivka'la and her sweet little sisters; I have their picture hanging on my wall, so that each time I pass it, I have to stop and kiss it.

Hashem should bless the entire Jewish people with peace in Eretz Yisrael and our enemies should have no power to wage war against us.

I treasure your letter very dearly. I sincerely hope and fervently pray that you my dear write again soon.

Kindest personal regards and best wishes for the best of everything,

Love,
Babi

Kiss the darling yingelach from me. I am sending chocolates for everybody.

I smooth the letter, exuding love, by the soft glow of the night-light, and tousle my daughter's freshly washed, silken hair. She asks me why I am reading so slowly, and I laugh, "Am I?" and I tell her that it's an effort for me to translate the English as I go. I don't think she'll understand that it's a precarious maneuver, trying to tilt my heart like a pinball game, so that every precious pearl will roll inside.

She smiles wisely, and says through slits of eyes, "She was a big *tzaddekes*, this *Babi*," and I say yes, oh yes, and cover her gently and try to plant a whisper of my grandmother's kiss onto her soft cheek.

What was that line? I try and recall the sentence that had startled me, not because of its surprising content, but because it had jumped out at me as such a simple, shockingly lucid reflection of the song that was my grandmother. *Everyone is someone special to me.*

Yes, every*one*, and every*thing*, and every *place*. Every child, and every adult, and every teenager. Every *gadol* and every *Yid*. Every *mitzvah* and every *minhag*. Everything, indeed, every big and little piece of life was dear and cherished to her.

She didn't wait for the joy or the *nachas* to come raining down on her rooftop with pomp and fanfare. She knew how to reap pleasure from the smallest of things. And people. "Look at that *seichel*," she'd marvel at the baby who stood on his tiptoes to dismantle the stack of books on her table. "Such precision," she'd admire as the *mechutanim* hurried everyone out of the reception hall into the *chupah* area.

The eggs were so white, the fruit was packed so beautifully, the *challah* tasted just like cake. Hers, yours, and everybody's. The apartment was so sunny, the visit so enjoyable, the view from the window so fascinating.

It was as if she'd remained eternally imbued with a child's view; forever enthusiastic, forever excited, forever drinking in the rich experiences simple living had to offer. She lived her life, a thrilling climb, an ongoing *Sefiras HaOmer*, always counting that which *was*, not that which remained to be.

And when she reached the summit, she was *niftar* on *Shavuos*, reaping her harvest, a true *eim hamalchus*.

I think of myself, ashamed. Ashamed for the exercise I so often indulge in, in the name of enlightened sophistication, as I scrutinize things, analyze people, gripe over circumstances. Sometimes I seem to be going through life like a kid filling in the list on the activity page: Find 10 things wrong with this picture.

The way I'd done this evening in my kitchen. Passed right by the beautiful designs, the artful details, the pleasing decor and picked on the one negligible eyesore. *Babi* would have failed to see it. She looked at life as a fun page, indeed; she savored every morsel of it, and when the going got tough, she picked up her pencil, determined to meet the challenge.

I look at the letter, and fondly reread the beautiful lines in her light penmanship. I can see her slight build, her serene smile, I can hear her warm praise in English softened by an endearing European accent.

I turn out the night-light in my daughter's room, though the soft glow still remains. Tripping over a pair of muddy sandals, I swallow my impulse to censure, and place them lovingly on the dresser. I feel *Babi* smiling in approval. They may be dirty, and they may have been left strewn in the way, but they belong to someone special.

Maximum Wage

There are some things you really regret later on in life. Like misbehaving in the sixth grade. Don't think there aren't bigger mistakes clouding the pane of my mind's rearview mirror, when I look back. Believe me, there are plenty. There's something so senseless, however, so utterly selfish and unthinking about those ridiculous antics I was party to at the age of 10 and 11 and 12, that I cringe when I think of them.

Perhaps my horror's been reinforced by the razor edge of cruelty hidden inside some innocuous spitballs tossed my own way.

Whatever the reason, I've since come to recognize that little sixth-grade tyrants can wreak earnest havoc with a stable adult ego.

Back then, though, all we considered was fun. And what could be a surer harbinger of it than peeking out of the classroom door to catch sight of a new face atop an unfamiliar figure heading toward our classroom?

"Mrs. Gross isn't coming today! There's a substitute!" The tidings would shoot up and down the rows like milk speeding through a spiral straw, and in less than a minute, the neat formation of obedient students standing beside their respective desks became a messy tangle of rowdy conspirators.

Over the years, we had ample opportunity to pull an impressive array of mischievous pranks on a wide variety of unsuspecting substitutes. We planned coughing chains, played deaf and dumb, hid behind the coats. And like most kids, we found these feats highly entertaining, though in retrospect, I'm hard pressed to recapture the thrilling sense of amusement. I guess we assumed that substitutes belonged to a different breed apart from ourselves, our mothers, or any human being capable of nursing an insult.

Our substitutes were as varied as the pranks we pulled. We got some young eager girls straight out of seminary, some professionals' wives looking for a challenge; we even landed a classmate's grandmother! And though each came optimistically toting her own brand of discipline, when things got really out of hand, there were certain lines to which almost all of them predictably resorted. After the hackneyed "I'm waiting" and book banging, the most popular one by far, was the "I'm getting paid anyway" bit.

"Look, girls, if you're happy this way, then so am I. I'm getting paid in any case, you know, whether or not you girls do well on your spelling test."

We never took the bait. If the comment was supposed to daunt us, it most certainly didn't. Our substitute's attempt at feigning indifference was a porous veil thrown over near breaking-point frustration, and we kids certainly weren't taken in.

Yet despite our open ridicule of the phrase, despite its proven inefficacy, somewhere in the back of my mind, I guess I've registered the expression. Like a long-forgotten article suddenly surfacing after years, the declaration unexpectedly floated to the top of my mind the other day.

Perhaps it was the thorough helplessness of the moment, that miserable ineffective feeling I was experiencing, that put me into mental cahoots with those substitutes of times bygone.

Whatever inspired it, I suddenly abandoned my despair, and got into a perfect imitation of that folded arms' pose, a rebellious smirk lighting my face, "You know what, everyone? If you're happy this way, then so am I. I'm getting paid in any case, whether or not you kids get to sleep."

Wonder of wonders, it worked. Oh no, it didn't get the kids into bed, or the decibel down, or the bedroom straightened up. I'm not even sure if anybody heard me.

But I did. And I guess if I don't remember anything else any substitute ever taught me, it was worth their misery for that one flash of pedagogical insight they unwittingly imparted. That one line, born of sheer discouragement, had hibernated silently all these years in my mind, and suddenly emerged one day as a butterfly of encouragement.

Our job isn't about long-term success or finished products. It's a by-the-hour engagement, provided one is in the classroom and trying to man the fort.

I'm talking about the job of living as a Jewish daughter or son, spouse, friend, neighbor or sibling. Chiefly, though, I'm talking about the task of educating the next generation to do the same.

I don't know about other parents. I, for one, am often stymied to know what happened to my baby-sitting prowess, to my natural tendency to commiserate with children, to tolerate their annoying hangups and habits with a grain of salt, or at least with a grain of humor.

What is it about the apple cores in my daughter's briefcase, or the sleeve-wiping habit of my son, that have the ability to evoke such intense reactions in a fairly even-keeled adult? Why does the constant bickering or the shirking of household responsibilities or the preference to ride a bike over reviewing the day's *mishnayos* invite such a disproportionate wave of aggravation on an otherwise calm coast?

It's especially mystifying since I'm familiar with most of the advice. Don't lecture; don't blame; empathize rather than criticize. I can pinpoint all my mistakes when the children are asleep, and do admirably well in my own dreams.

When that chronic pouter mopes about a chipped ice-cream cone, though, at the end of a perfectly successful outing, or the two older ones swipe snide remarks as if they were practicing emotional boxing, my imagination seems to gallop off like a runaway horse leaving my intellect hopelessly behind.

This child is never happy, never! How is she going to deal with life if she can't deal with a cracked cone?

Boy, this kid is going to need a really selfless wife; I hope whoever's raising her is doing a better job than I am.

Most of us can be very courteous sales people, patient tutors, tolerant aunts and uncles. As business colleagues, we have the grace to swallow a barb with good humor; as dentists or landscaping professionals or financial consultants, we know how to overlook reckless neglect and dwell on constructive repairs.

When it comes to our own charges, though, these latent abilities seem to lapse. Our eyes are always darting off into the future, our minds feverishly calculating the phenomenal interest that can accrue on an innocent breach left undisciplined over two decades or so. No, so he won't be twisting his brother's glasses in 10 years, he'll be arguing with his boss, his neighbors, his in-laws.

We each have aspirations of raising children who are at least as successful as we are, usually infinitely more so. We want them to be honest, happy, responsible, loyal individuals. We want them to be *masmidim* and *lamdanim* and *yirei Shamayim*. No, we want them to be *thin, smart, respected, masmidim* and *lamdanim* and *yirei Shamayim*.

And when somewhere along the line we notice that as tightly as we yank the strings, the little puppets just don't perform the way we wrote the script, it takes some very supreme efforts to keep our cool. It takes all our conscious energy to remember that we never *were* in charge of the script writing.

It's He Who stages the ultimate finale; we're only mortal substitutes. And yes, if the kids are happy, happy to be around us, and happy to be Jews, then so can we be. As long as we're in that classroom trying, we get paid for our pains, whether or not our children make the grade.

And just as an added bonus, they are twice as liable to make the grade if that isn't our goal.

The blessing of time's finite nature is that it puts a frame over each individual minute. No matter how daunting our overall mission seems, no matter how many weighty repercussions loom outside that narrow frame, we get paid for successfully zooming in on the challenge of the single particular moment.

Like I said, I know all the advice. I'm not nearly as good at putting it into practice, especially when the door to my classroom is slightly ajar and some stranger or two gets a glimpse of my less-than-perfect discipline.

Still, I'm trying.

And if that's the case, then I'm getting paid.

Midnight Chat

In the middle of the night,
Or perhaps it was morning,
She opened her eyes,
A flicker of blue skies,
"Mommy?"
A smile,
My fingers dancing
All the while,
Stringing sentences
Across the screen.
Mommy?
Hoarse voice,
Loose hair,
Rosy cheeks,
You're still up?
Yup.
Since last night?
When I went to sleep?
Yup,
Mommy?
I have a boo-boo
On my knee,
Yaeli pushed me,
You want to see?
Sure,
Cluck cluck,
Boo-boo unseen
Eyes intent on the screen,

Yawn,
It's almost dawn.
Mommy?
You can lay with me,
I'll make room,
Here,
You can share
My blanket,
A stretch, a tug,
There.
A cozy hug.
Ohhhhhhhhhh ...,
To let go.
Mommy's tired.
So go to sleep.
I can't, honey,
I've got to work.
So go work.
Sweet smile
Delicious dimple,
If only life were so simple.

Kids Will Be Kids

hat's it. I've officially joined the ranks of mothers the world over. I've actually begun citing the phrase I thought I'd never hear myself say, never mind shout.

"Nobody listens to me unless I scream; it's the only thing that works!"

All the books say that actions speak louder than words, but I guess it all depends on how loud the words speak. In my house, as of late, nothing seems to move my unimpassioned progeny. I've tried speaking quietly, using one-word directives, taking the child's hand and looking into his or her eyes. Usually all these efforts to retain my self-control yield an uncommitted, "What?" Which is when I feel the decibel rising.

"What do you mean, 'What'? Please *listen* when I talk."

"I didn't hear that you were talking."

"I know! That's just the problem. Why do I have to scream to get a response?"

I've heard of selective hearing, but it just beats me why any child would *select* to hear an exasperated shout over a polite request accompanied by a smile. Why would any kid knowingly invite an angry outburst if he can easily have a pleasant mother addressing him in a nice calm tone of voice?

But the kids claim they didn't know. They didn't know, and they didn't hear, and, "What did you say?"

Who can blame them either? They're a very busy populace, this species called children. Busy collecting junk, and comparing projects, and checking the freezer to see whether the ices are frozen. Busy trading stickers, and cutting the P.C. symbols off the cereal boxes, and mimicking the substitute's accent.

They're too busy arguing and drumming and rewinding the tape to their favorite part, to hear a mundane old thing like a mother talking in the background. They don't mean to be indifferent, they really don't. It's just that being a child is like living inside a big balloon: light, colorful, and, at times, impenetrable. Which is, I guess, the reason I'm here.

So I try hinting, pointing, and gently reminding. All of that, though, does little in the way of prompting action. It's the last resort that does the trick.

So it was, during one of those evenings last week, that I found myself winding up a tirade with the famous line:

"Nobody listens unless I scream; it's the only thing that works!"

It had been a pleasant afternoon together. I had gone out of my way to give each of the children the right dose of attention, fun, and love. I'd let the little ones take out the play-doh even though I honestly detest the aftermath of soft bits of colored dough squishing under everyone's shoes. I had sat with the third grader, scouting through catalogues and coloring books in search of pictures for her *berachos* scrapbook.

I had quelled my urge to get some laundry under way, and had instead watched my son master the art of juggling three balls. "One more time, Ma," he had said, his eyes shining, "this time the balls won't fall even once." So I'd stood there with my eyes fixed on the balls "one more time" for nearly half an hour. I'd done all that, and it had been wonderful. Now, however, my patience was beginning to falter. Couldn't it end just like that, for once, on a nice soft note?

But it didn't.

So I dropped my sweet steady tone, and began to, well, not quite yell, but talk louder than I'd like most respectable people to hear me. That did the job. Yitzy dropped the toothbrush he was trying to balance, Dina slammed the book she was reading. It actually seemed as if things were beginning to calm down.

And then the phone rang. It was Bracha. I'm used to Bracha talking in subdued tones at this hour. She usually calls me as soon as she has her two little ones tucked in for the night, and tries to keep her conversations to a whisper. This time, however, her hello sounded tremulous.

"Is everything okay, Bracha?"

"No, not really."

I panicked. "What happened?"

"There was a bomb, another bomb. It was on the street of my dentist's office. I was there just yesterday afternoon."

I was silent. Numbed. For a long moment there didn't seem to be anything to say. I clutched the receiver tightly, her grim tidings reverberating in my ears. A bomb, another bomb.

Ask her, an inner voice prodded me, *ask her how many people were hurt, if anyone was killed.* Something inside me rebelled, however. I didn't want to know. I didn't want to hear. I didn't want to listen to the gory details of a mother who crumpled to the ground with her newborn infant, or a son who ran with his ebbing strength to alert help for his father.

In what way would my knowledge ease the pain of the families who were plunged into abysmal darkness; what difference would my inquiries make to those lives that had been so brutally severed?

For a moment, the impact of her words washed over me in waves, knocked me over into the nearest chair. I sat there dizzy, forgetting Bracha on the other line, forgetting the day behind me, the night ahead. My entire being shuddered with that one ominous phrase. *A bomb, another bomb.* I didn't ask for the gruesome details. She didn't offer any. It was a moment that felt like an eternity. Then, like a contrite child, I whispered,

"Bracha, I lost my temper tonight."

"And I slipped with *shemiras halashon,*" she confessed. "Why do we wait for these tragedies to shake us out of our complacency?"

"Just like the kids." I sighed, "Too involved with our own things to listen for Hashem's voice. We have so much goodness abounding, and yet we insist on waiting for calamity to stop us in our tracks. If only we'd learn to respond before He's forced to shout His message."

"Chaval!" she echoed. A word defying translation, a term laden with sadness and regret, and keen anguish.

We each sat silently on the line, reflecting the truth of what we'd just said. Hashem is talking every waking minute of every day. He whispers to us through the perfect features of a newborn baby, and smiles to us through the cloudless blue sky, the rain we need so badly, the myriad acts of *Hashgachah Pratis* we are *zoche* to each day. Why aren't we prompted to action by these soft tones?

Somewhere in a haze of pain, we parted somberly with wishes for better tidings and for *Mashiach* to come soon.

I looked around, surveying my kitchen in a kind of detached state. I saw Dina's jacket draped over the chair, and Yitzy's ball lodged in a corner beneath the cabinets. A flutter of tenderness crept into my heart, dissolving the day's frustrations. I thought of Dina, of Yitzy, of the rest of them, and smiled. Then my lips quivered, and I felt the sting of tears on my eyelids.

Ribono Shel Olam, we're kids, only kids. And yes, we wait until You scream, as kids tend to do. But please, listen to us before we scream. Listen to us while we're smiling and happy, and trying.

Because after all, we're only kids.

Change

Shifting the Weight

Where do you keep your bathroom scale? If you own one, that is. I don't. Not in the bathroom, and not anywhere else in the house. A scale is one of those household items, I find, like a tweezers to remove splinters, a battery tester, and a plunger, that a house is just supposed to have, though I don't know exactly when you acquire them.

Usually, these items are bought either in an emergency, or following one. The difference with the scale is that the crisis builds up slowly, and by the time it's an emergency, you don't need the scale to tell you.

Which is, I guess, why I don't have one. I'm not one of those people who do things they aren't compelled to do, especially if the chore causes any amount of discomfort. So I keep the scale safely in the doctor's office, where I obligingly weigh myself during my periodic visits there.

In between, when I catch sight of the ominous thing, in the pharmacy, or at the local baby clinic, I waver between curiosity and dread, depending on the present state of my eating patterns. Then, I either step up with cautious excitement, or make a beeline for the exit. Once I'm aware of my numerical value for the time being, I know I can breathe free until my next encounter with a scale.

Recently, I was confronted by one rather unexpectedly. Visiting a friend in the *Beit Hachlamah*, I accompanied her to the dining room, enjoying the quiet, relaxed reprieve from my normal hectic, albeit blessed schedule. We chatted lightheartedly like two girls enjoying their recess break, when suddenly I stiffened. If I had felt like a schoolgirl during recess, now I felt as if I had strolled straight into the principal, totally unawares. There was a doctor's scale standing reproachfully in our way, demanding its rightful respect.

"I tell you, they know how to ruin your appetite around here," I joked, as we circumvented the thing and entered the dining room. A buzzing conglomeration of women from every walk of life was clustered around a tastefully set buffet, where steaming tureens of soup beckoned to the hungry guests alongside heaping platters of liver and chicken, vegetables, and a variety of attractive side dishes. There was the clatter of china and cutlery, and the engulfing racket of lively conversation as the little tables slowly filled up with twosomes and threesomes, the kind of makeshift friendships that served the sole and temporary purpose of enhancing mealtimes during the short stay at the resort.

We chose an untouched island, my friend and I, a table whose appealing decor was still intact, and sat down to enjoy the meal together. I looked at the table set to perfection, drinking glasses, pretty napkins, even *bentchers* in the center. When was the last time I'd been treated to a private lunch with a friend?

No sooner had the thought passed my mind when a robust-looking Yerushalmi woman pulled out the chair next to mine with her elbow, and set down a plate piled high with stuffed peppers, fried chicken nuggets, pasta with cabbage, and roasted potatoes nested on a bed of string beans and stir-fried vegetables.

"I'll be back in a minute," she smiled, "I just have to fetch my entree." Within moments, she was back at the table, joined by a friend, maneuvering a piping hot bowl of vegetable soup, and a smaller plate laden with liver and rice. Unlike the hesitant expression characterizing most new faces joining an inhabited table, the twosome seemed completely at ease, with us, with each other, with their portions.

"Won't you touch the salads?" the first turned to us good-naturedly, as much in an effort to make small talk, as to understand the two Americans who weren't taking full advantage of the elaborate spread. I smiled politely, as did my friend, and soon they were joined by a third enthusiastic acquaintance, which they took as a cue to leave us to our own devices and enjoy each other's company.

Our hushed tones, however, over poised spoonfuls, were no match for their heated gusto, as they heartily attacked the savory food, prodding one another to eat. Before we knew it, we had unconsciously lapsed into fascinated silence, as we unabashedly observed the threesome exchanging their impressions in zesty Yerushalmi *Yiddish.*

They were comparing postpartum experiences, and predictably, the topic turned to weight, the babies' and their own. There was some indignant balking by the second two women over the fact that the scale on the premises had registered significant gains since their arrival several days before. The first one, whose opinion was obviously esteemed by her friends, gestured with her hands as she gulped down the last of her potatoes, apparently in a rush to respond.

"*Her tzu* (listen)," she declared, her authoritative tone leaving no margin for dispute, "*Der vag iz tzubrachen* (the scale is broken). Look, it just can't be. Two kilo in one week? *S'iz pashut az der vag iz tzubrachen* (it's obvious, the scale is broken)."

I tried to hide my smirk, as the two friends vigorously echoed her conclusion, turning the tempting speculation into incontestable fact.

"Avade, yeder veist az der vag da iz nit punkt. Abisel arif, abissel arup, veist dach (Sure, everybody knows that the scale here isn't accurate. A little up, a little down, you know how it goes)."

They seemed not the slightest bit perturbed that the erratic scale never seemed to tip *"abissel arup"* where they were concerned. One way or another, it didn't really matter, as long as the scale was broken, they were free to shuffle their chairs and get up to choose their desserts.

I smiled in amusement. My friend got up to stretch and then collapsed her taut posture in a fit of laughter, as the women's proclamation suddenly hit her funny bone.

"Didn't seem to ruin *their* appetite," she quipped, referring to my earlier comment, as we passed the imposing scale on our way out.

No, it didn't, I chuckled. This was a novel approach to dieting. Instead of counting calories, getting on the treadmill, forgoing cake and ice cream, you just wrote off the scale as nonfunctional. You just piled your plate high with delectables, and in between mouthfuls you emphatically denounced the unreliable scale. I don't know about effectiveness, but anyone who's ever experienced the struggles of watching their weight can tell you. It's an awful lot easier.

Let's not kid ourselves either. We all do it. If not to lose weight, then to gain self-respect, to regain our inner peace, to muffle the cognitive dissonance that threatens our equilibrium. We do it to keep our conscience at bay, to quiet the whispers of the still, small voice inside, shrug off any implication that we may have to change.

It can't be me, we say. It's the educational system, the generation gap, the chemistry, the weather. If things aren't looking good, it isn't my fault. It's the *shadchanim*, the *dayanim*, the *askanim*. No, no, we insist, don't give me advice; you don't know my child /spouse/ neighbor/ partner, the rules don't apply to him. I've tried everything, nothing works.

There's a problem, sure, the scale says as much, but we've got an easy way to solve the discrepancy. *Der vag iz tzubrachen.* If I don't measure up, the standards must be too stringent, if I'm repeatedly met with refusal, the people must be self-absorbed.

Like the diet, it's certainly the easier method of confronting crisis. More comfortable, more enjoyable, more palatable. If you're interested in scaling heights, though, I can tell you as an onlooker; besides for weight, you've got nothing to gain.

Sugar and Spice

Eavesdropping has become quite an effortless pastime these days. With cell phones beeping, bleating, and singing just about wherever you step foot, it's become next to impossible *not* to hear what the person standing near you has eaten for lunch, where he plans to spend his vacation, and what she thinks of the prospective secretary she interviewed yesterday.

But there still is nothing like the real thing, listening in on an honest to goodness, face-to-face conversation, to gain some insight into human relations. So though I've usually got much more important things to do with my time, standing on line in the supermarket affords me a good opportunity to absorb some of the exchange that characterizes people at their best.

While I make a mental check of the errands I have yet to run, pieces of conversation buzz around me, circling until they pierce my consciousness and interrupt my train of thought. It's then that I catch myself party to the goings-on in other people's lives.

Just last week, as I was trying to figure out how much money I had saved by buying the jumbo box of Cheerios, a woman from the adjacent line swerved her cart onto my line as she spotted the blonde woman standing behind me.

They definitely didn't look like sisters, but they could have been sisters-in-law, or just plain friends for that matter. Whatever their relationship, they seemed pleased enough to meet each other. Subconsciously, I inched my own cart forward ever so slightly, so the two women would have ample space to carry on their conversation.

"Thanks for having Shaya over yesterday," the first one began, as she stooped to pick up a roll of aluminum foil that had fallen from her cart. "That grilled cheese sandwhich he came home with smelled delicious, like real pizza. What's the secret?"

"Oh, come on," the blonde woman laughed, making light of the compliment, "the usual. It's not exactly one of my gourmet recipes."

"I know, I also make grilled cheese, but Shaya finished yours with such gusto. Tell me how you do it. What do you put in? Maybe I'll even make it as a quick-fix dinner tonight." She checked her watch, and instinctively I did the same. *Her grilled cheese idea may just be serving another family tonight,* I thought, as I counted three people on line ahead of me. I cocked my head to listen for the exact instructions.

"Well, I make a mixture of tomato sauce —"

"Tomato sauce? Na, my kids like ketchup. I guess it's the same idea."

"The tomato sauce gives it that authentic flavor, but, yeah, I guess you can use ketchup too. Anyway, I mix that with some sugar —"

"*Sugar?* In pizza? I'll skip that. What else?"

"Some oregano, a drop of garlic powder."

"Oh, I can't stand the smell of garlic powder. I don't even have it in the house. Won't it be good without the garlic?"

"Well, if you don't have it in the house, then try it without the garlic powder."

"And that's the whole thing? You're sure?"

"More or less. I just smear the mixture on the bread, and grate some cheese over it."

"Can I use the sliced American cheese? That's what I have in the fridge."

"You can use whatever you like. I told you, it's not an exact recipe."

"It sounds easy enough. You're sure it'll come out like yours?" she asked enthusiastically.

I'm sure it won't, I thought wryly, as their conversation turned to other vistas. *Why did she even bother asking in the first place if she intended to stick to her own version?* I smiled in amusement, wondering if I ever sounded like that myself.

We humans are a funny breed; forever looking to improve, to change, to discover the secret to other people's success.

She's so easygoing with the children, we'll think to ourselves admiringly, and, *"How does he manage to get to bed on time if we both conduct the same learning sedarim?"* "I wish I could learn the trick that enables him to have such a close rapport with his students," we'll remark with undisguised envy, or "When does she find time to do all that *chessed* what with a job and all?"

We'll take note of someone's orderly kitchen, or fitness routine, or commitment to *davening* or *shemiras halashon*, and we'll ask them for their recipe. And usually, after their initial denial of our claim, most people will be happy to share their tips with us.

They'll tell us about shortcuts they've learned to take, schedules they've begun to make; they'll tell us about different modes of communication, or creative alternatives to the tried-and-not-so-true methods. When we start hearing the formulas, though, we tend to become a little dubious. "That won't work for me. Never in a million years." Or worse yet, we'll overlook the subtle nuances, and wonder, "Oh, is that all there is to it? I do pretty much the same thing."

"Pretty much," however, just isn't the same thing. It obviously hasn't been yielding the same results, or else we'd never have been prompted to ask for the recipe to begin with. We tend to forget that when we listen to the other person. *If* we listen, that is. Most of the time, we're too busy interjecting our own variation of the recipe, backed by our rationale for the way we do it.

We want to improve; we honestly do. We want to expand our horizons, enrich our understanding, develop our raw potential. That's why we ask for advice in the first place. Improvement, though, suggests change, and change requires courage. When it comes down to it, how many of us are willing to actually drop something we've been doing all along and welcome a revision into our firmly entrenched lifestyle? Like an old pair of shoes, habit may be unattractive, outdated, and even detrimental to the feat we're seeking to accomplish, but it still feels most comfortable.

So though we may have the recipe basically right, we might be missing out on some of the really special flavors in life. You never know who may have that secret ingredient to enhance your life at its present stage; who may have the solution you are searching for, or an idea that has eluded you although you've tried virtually everything. So start doing some eavesdropping. And don't hesitate to integrate other people's ideas.

Contrary to old folk wisdom, it's often one stubborn cook (and not the proverbial too many) who spoils the broth!

Weight Watchers

I don't know when it happens, but somewhere along the way, numbers take on a very personal property. The simple, "How old are you?" is no longer a friendly inquiry inviting a proud response, but a laden question answered in whispered tones, following a furtive glance around the doctor's waiting room.

"How much do you weigh?" usually next in succession, merits an equally anxious sweep of the horizon. The answer is mouthed as unobtrusively as possible, and quietly jotted onto the paper, eyes never meeting. No longer innocent facts of life, to be duly recorded on the front cover of a second-grade autobiography, these numbers.

It's a pretty funny thing, this privacy regarding our weight. We can be in full sight of friends or family, tugging at that skimpy jacket, and keenly uncomfortable, yet somehow we like to savor the illusion that that fateful number is a sacred secret, a cleverly concealed fact.

Irony notwithstanding, we members of the diet club respect each other's delusive attempts to keep the facts under lock and key. Judging by the nonstop chatter as we pound the treadmill, pedal the stationary bikes, heave up artificial steps, it seems we'll disclose almost anything about ourselves, save the obstinate digits that sum us up. As long as it remains a riddle, the unspoken reasoning goes, there's some standing chance that someone may underestimate our numerical value.

So there is no talk of numbers, per se. "Up or down?" has become the cautious approach, as the member in question steps off the scale trying to wear a stoic expression. There's usually some giveaway trace, though, residing in the corners of the dieter's eyes, either of triumphant glee, or else of drooping discouragement, sometimes even a shiny film of tears.

All of this, however, is only speculation. The most tried-and-true method of confirming suspicions is to follow that dieter home. Just watch her as she walks into her front hall, and you'll have an instant barometer to go by. If she begins attacking her chores with gusto, sets a package of broccoli out on the counter, and firmly shuts the freezer door, then mark my words, the scale has had some good news for her. Chances are, she'll eat a hearty vegetable salad for lunch, no dressing, thank you, and will be thus sustained until dinner.

If by contrast, your woman has encountered dismal tidings, she'll head straight for her kitchen with a single-minded expression on her face. Then, disregarding every bit of discipline, she'll open her freezer door, quickly, as if some imaginary mother was due home any minute, and grab for the nearest edible. Anything will do. Anything, that is, but the bag of broccoli. An ice-cream pop, some chocolate-chip cookies, the two-layer cake from last week's birthday party.

And it won't be one slice either. Trust me; I've been there. No, not snooping behind some anonymous door, trying to track someone's progress. I've been in that kitchen chair, mind tossed safely out of sight, conscience momentarily unplugged, trying to cram as many cookies as I could before my sensibilities returned.

Which they invariably did, grim and pessimistic, harsh and reproachful, as they viewed the forlorn pile of cake crumbs on the tabletop.

"Why in the world did you do this to yourself?" they'd demand. "Why, why, why?"

Indeed, why?

Believe me, I don't know. Never did come up with a plausible answer. Why do we human beings indulge in such logic-defying, self-destructive behavior? Why, if the numbers were on the rise, wouldn't we garner every bit of self-restraint to keep them from swelling out of proportion? Didn't the pedagogues say something about natural consequences being the best teacher?

I don't know, but I can tell you, it's an incontestable fact of life; the fat get fatter.

And the clumsy get clumsier, the messy get messier, the lazy get lazier. I hate to sound like such a prophet of doom, but it's true. I've yet to see someone bounce off that bleak scale, glowing with inspiration, driven to action.

"This is not funny," is the closest to motivation I've ever heard, or felt, in those thoroughly disheartening circumstances.

And funny it isn't. Or fun. Who likes to look failure straight in the eye?

Not to imply that people at a disadvantage are permanently stuck there. In fact, I'm not talking to the people at the disadvantage. I'm talking to the scales among us; the teachers, the parents, the older sisters, in-laws, spouses, bosses.

I'm talking about the ones among us who walk into a disaster area of a home every evening, who find the prescription unfilled day after day, who encounter perpetual white lies, black collars, gray attitudes. I'm talking to the ones who have to contend with the unbalanced checkbook, the provocative disobedience, the unnerving habits.

It's pretty easy to respond to these bungled expectations with any level of anger from fret to fume. Let's assume though, that we know about the debilitating effects of anger, on ourselves and on those at whom we lash out. Let's assume we know that fury is like fire; that it spreads quickly and burns bridges, and leaves nothing but a trail of smoke in its wake. Let's assume that even if we occasionally do lose it, few of us will lose our temper as a conscious tool to foster improvement.

In our more controlled moments, however, sometimes we're tempted to react like a scale: frank and forthright. *This kid has to know how mean he's being; how will he ever know if no one points it out to him?*

Maybe if I'll tell her how inconsiderate she is, how ungrateful, disorganized, irresponsible, she'll finally *realize*. What's the sense of beating around the bush? You can't argue with facts, can you?

Well, maybe you can't argue, but you can certainly concede. You can accept the assessment and claim defeat. You can decide it's not worth bothering, and that you'd never change even if you did, and forget it, you may as well go back and get the most of your deviant behavior.

At least if they all think I'm lazy, let me enjoy it. If I'm constantly scolded for instigating fights, why go the extra mile for peace and harmony?

It doesn't matter whether you are a paid worker or a top executive, a kindergarten student or a high school principal. Having failure flung in anyone's face makes them feel like quitting. And seeing success in the mirror, even the tiniest bit of it, makes them reach for more, even if they have to get on tiptoes to reach it.

Just watch any dieter lose five pounds. One pound. Even a half. You may not notice the lost ounces, but you'll notice an instant metamorphosis.

"Hey, I might even fit into that dress for the wedding. Half a pound a week for eight weeks; sounds feasible."

One half a pound off, and you have four more pounds in the offing. A shadow of an egg, and you've already got a chicken roasting. One half a success, and there's a smile, a vision, a surge of adrenaline.

It's incredible to witness. And to experience. And it's a universal fact of life. I haven't yet met anybody who has outgrown the rule.

So let's take the next 24 hours to listen carefully to ourselves, to record our reactions, to censor our comments. We may know, in that pocket where old truths lie, that success breeds success. The erosion of everyday frustrations, though, has a way of wearing knowledge thin. It may take a day of honest evaluation to realize that, no, we haven't been saying it all that sweetly.

Never mind; let us not allow that to hamper our verbal downscaling. From here on in, our words carry a lot of weight. Especially the affirmative ones. Because an ounce of encouragement is worth a pound of criticism.

Finish Line

The frustrating part
Of all this cleaning
Is the feeling
Of never arriving at the finish line,
by the time the last
of the cupboards are gleaming
the first have lost
their freshly groomed appearance,
by the time the drawers are neatened
closets organized,
papers sorted,
curtains washed
bedspreads laundered,
fixtures shined,
headboards polished,

it's time to neaten the drawers again,
isn't that the way it is?
The way life is?
Working at it
Again
And again
And again and again
And yet again,
A million times over?
If we only realized
We aren't really doing
Anything *again.*

Each time, it's a new loop
In the design of our destiny
If we only saw
the spirograph of time
Shifting the paper of our life
Ever so slightly clockwise,
Overlapping those infinite spirals
In an ultimate scheme of perfection
We wouldn't find it so frustrating
Wouldn't wish
So hard
To see the circle
Complete,
because when we finish
With the unending cycles,
When we finally close
The gap,
And stop,
Our time in the spirograph
is up.

Turnabout

"*M*a, where's my umbrella?"

Some questions have dynamite inside.

"Where's *your* umbrella? I don't know. Where'd you put it the last time you used it?"

" I didn't put it anywhere. I think (a point for *derech eretz*) you put it in the bathtub to dry."

Of course I put it in the bathtub to dry. As he said, *he* didn't put it anywhere, which means he left it, dripping wet, on top of his rubbers in the front hall. And now he can't find it. The blame, for which, of course, is exclusively Mommy's. The same way I'm held accountable for the missing pencil case, the wet art pad, the torn *Chumash* test.

I'm glad my progeny are growing up in a normal, functioning household, where their needs are usually met. Yes, I'm truly thankful they can anticipate meals on the table, clothing that fits, new heels on their worn-out shoes.

When the kids begin to shift responsibility for their personal belongings to my domain, however, the thankfulness takes on a frustrated edge. Especially when these accusations are tossed my way against the backdrop of the morning rush, as the child is frantically searching for the items he or she should have prepared the night before.

This time, however, the article in question was an umbrella, whose necessity could not have been foreseen, and the timing was late afternoon. What provoked me more than the insinuated charge was the nonchalant manner in which my son was planning an excursion in the miserable downpour raging outdoors.

"Where are you going, Binyomin?" I asked pointedly, curtailing further discussion of the misplaced umbrella.

"To the stores. Oh, you need anything?"

Kids have a way of sounding too casual when they are in the midst of doing something they suspect their mother won't approve of. "The stores" are a considerable walk in decent weather, and to get Binyomin to undertake the trip generally takes a significant amount of perseverance on my part.

The last time I needed a couple of housewares, it was a tiring effort trying to coax him to part with the book he was reading. Not that I blamed him. I was just wondering what had him diving headlong into the rain now, as if it was the most natural thing in the world.

A few days have elapsed, and I'll tell you. Nothing can raise my eyebrows anymore. I've witnessed a complete turnabout in the child. He's shown newfound alacrity, even latent talent.

Without a word of prompting from me, he's cleared the shed downstairs, a chore I've been nagging him to attend to since last summer when he cluttered it with the paraphernalia for his club. He's braved the trek to the stores at least half a dozen times, two of them in nastily inclement conditions. He's even shown interest in learning how to thread a needle, a skill I consider primarily feminine.

They say training sometimes has startling effects, but I was kind of dubious. These things usually don't happen overnight, not to me, anyway. When Binyomin mentioned that he'd been elected the head of the *Purim shpiel* committee, I smiled broadly. It all suddenly made sense.

Kids, I thought to myself, and boys in particular, are incredible. Ask them, beg them, bribe them, to clean the shed, and you might get a half a shelf cleared before they've disappeared into the backyard with some friends. Tell them to get the leaves raked and bagged, and you'll have a whole apparatus set up, vacuum cleaner, extension cord and all, enabling them to blow the leaves for an initial enthusiastic spurt. Don't count on the bags getting to the front, though.

It's remarkable to see what these unmotivated youngsters can accomplish, down to the most tedious detail, when something really sparks their interest. And I'll admit, it's not only the youngsters; the oldsters are only slightly less surprising.

Most of us derive some self-righteous satisfaction from telling the kids how many chores we see to despite our keen dislike for them. I won't take that away from us.

How many people have you met who enjoy sticking a snake down a slimy clogged drain, keeping dentist appointments, picking dirty socks up off the floor? How many adults really relish running a bunch of dead-end errands, taking down the garbage, mending torn pants? And then there are all the personal hang-ups every individual is entitled to.

Still, we do all this in the interest of our families, our health, our environment. Without a mother over our shoulder, we wipe the counters, and sweep the floors, return defective purchases to the store, and wash out the garbage can. We do.

And if we want to be really candid, there's a lot we don't do. A lot of important things we don't have time or energy for. Phone calls we postpone, visits we push off. Projects that pass our minds, but get brushed aside for lack of funding or wherewithal. Requests we turn away, ideas we forgo, plans we scrap.

Even within the realm of that which we do, there's a marked difference in the way we execute different tasks. We all have that which we consistently end up getting to, even in our busiest times. For some it's that daily workout, for others it's a few *pirkei Tehillim*, or work-related obligations. It's all a matter of that which is truly close to our hearts.

Think of the way we pursue an item, a phone number, a recipe we desperately need. Think of the unreasonable things we're willing to overlook and overcome in order to get somewhere we really want to get.

We've only got to observe the children to see; impossible is a relative term. When there's willpower fueling the venture, most undertakings are humanly feasible. When there's personal pleasure and a sense of immediacy inspiring the assignment, the most tedious drudgery can become a labor of love.

Purim may be just behind us, but the joy of *chodesh Adar* is still up for grabs. Let's take the gaiety, the excitement, the quality of transformation inherent to *Purim*, and try to infuse those chores we've got to do anyway, we want to do anyway. Let's take the energy, the laughter, the creativity and dress up those bland duties that comprise so much of our existence.

We each have it in us to perform. *Purim's* over, but the *shpiel* is only beginning.

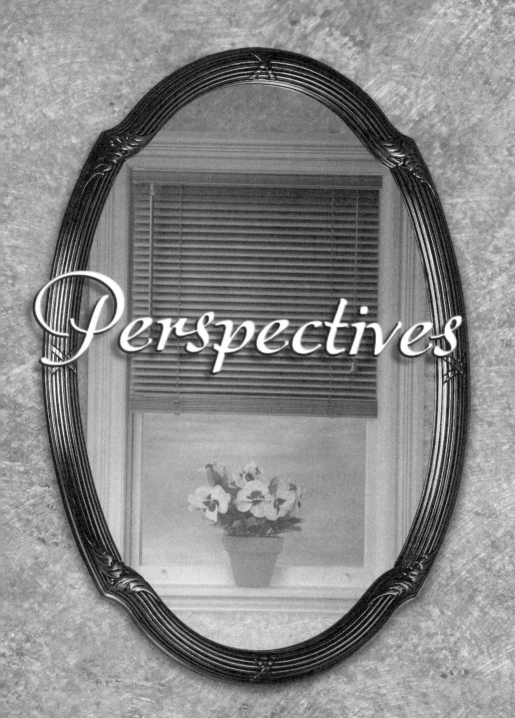

Perspectives

Gauges and Ages

"*H*ow old is he?"

A simple-enough question. It's the answer that tends to get a little longwinded. If anyone waits around to hear it, that is.

Most of the time the question is posed in a tone very close to rhetoric, by strangers temporarily sharing close quarters. We're either waiting for an elevator, or for a doctor's appointment, when I look at my watch and then distractedly meet the baby's eye and smile. Which serves as the perfect social cue in a boring waiting room, a polite invitation for a rejoinder.

This time was no different.

"*Chamud*," the graying man chuckled as he cluck-clucked some kind of baby gibberish toward my little son. *"Ben kamah hu?"*

"He's five months old," I answered, fixing the blanket that had fallen, and then lapsed into a friendly, smiling silence.

"Five months?" the woman right behind him echoed in disbelief. She frowned, a fleeting line of disapproval. "Small for his age, isn't he?"

She turned to the man. "Natalia's Anna must be at least double his size."

Oh, that's funny, I mused; they're a couple. I'd never have thought so.

Oblivious to my analysis, the woman cocked her head to the side and tried dangling her keys in front of the baby. I don't know why, but I felt myself getting defensive, as if she was putting my infant through some kind of developmental test. For all you knew, Natalia's Anna, whoever she was, might be rocking on all fours already.

"He's a preemie." The words were out before I thought to say them. I felt somehow compelled to justify my miniature 5-month-old.

"Oh," she said, looking nonplussed, as she quickly put her keys back into her pocketbook.

The man seemed unfazed.

"How early was he born?" he asked.

This conversation had definitely crossed over the line of accepted courtesy between strangers. I didn't care, though. I'd been in this country long enough to know that where social conduct was concerned, international conventions did not apply.

Besides, there was something nice about this fellow, his stocky build, his graying hair, his genuine interest in the baby, that made me drop my guard. Not like the pink-lipsticked woman, whose tone made me uncomfortable, apologetic almost.

"About eight weeks," I replied, fussing with the blanket again. Grandmothers knew what they were talking about when they said it was always good to take an extra blanket along.

"That makes him just about 3 months old!" the man concluded jovially, directing the comment straight at the baby. In perfect synchrony, the baby giggled.

"Why, he's even ahead for 3 months. Look at him giggling like that, alert and cooing."

"Yes, that's the way they count it in the neonatal unit," I said, feeling a childish urge to lend authority to his verdict. It was foolish, this, I knew, my self-worth plummeting and rocketing in time to two strangers' unbidden assessment of my infant. As if his weight and development had anything to do with me. Still, I was glad to have had the matter cleared. It felt better thinking of my son as an advanced 3-month-old than a delayed 5-month-old.

Back then, in the neonatal unit, it had been a technical bit of information, part of the detailed list that Claudia, the nurse, had reviewed with us prior to discharge.

"The baby's physician will refer to the infant's revised age," I faintly remembered her expounding. "That means that as far as his weight and development are concerned, you start counting his age from the time he would have been born full term."

She must have caught my blank expression. "It's simple, just subtract the amount of weeks your baby was early, from his real age."

"Just subtract the amount of weeks," I had echoed in an effort to show I was following. I was too lightheaded, though, at the moment, too intoxicated by the heady sense of anticipation of our imminent release from the neonatal unit, to internalize anything she was saying.

Now, her words came back to me, soothing and authoritative. "Revised age" wasn't a congenial man's resourceful way of placating an emotional mother. It wasn't a subtle turn of phraseology to cleverly camouflage a discrepancy. It was a real, medically affirmed meter, an authentic gauge determined to measure a baby's progress.

All the way home, as I clutched my son's *bituach l'umi* forms, I savored the words like a rich piece of chocolate. An advanced 3-month-old. It tasted good.

I considered taking a bus, and then thought better of it. I flagged down a taxi. The driver watched me fumble with the carriage for some time before he considered getting out to help me. I felt myself growing peeved. There he was, sitting comfortably, watching me struggle with one free arm, while the taximeter ran. And then, suddenly, an amusing thought flashed in my mind.

Perhaps he was also a preemie, this driver.

Perhaps he'd been born less considerate than most, perhaps his upbringing had made him that way. Perhaps the sight of newborn babies and carriages hit an emotional black-and-blue mark; perhaps he was less mentally agile at responding to sensory cues.

And all that notwithstanding, he was getting out now to help me. He was actually getting out of the comfortable seat inside his cab, and offering to give me a hand.

I watched him put the carriage into the trunk, and mentally saluted him. He was a late bloomer, and he had challenged inertia. No, not delayed, he, but an advanced 3-month-old. I felt a certain sense of kinship. We belonged to the same club.

As, I've come to realize in the ensuing days, we all do.

Every single one of us, diverse members of humanity, are preemies in some sense of the term. Every one of us, down to the most competent, talented individual, was born premature in some way. Some of us have a hard time with order, others with punctuality. Some people naturally resist discipline, others are born compulsive. Some individuals have a low threshold for pain, others for frustration.

Think of the people you know, yourself, your spouse, your colleagues, your children. Everyone was born with some underdeveloped aspect. Some have an innately fragile ego, other's an inborn temper. Some are predisposed to jealousy, others to despondency. Some find it difficult to follow practical instructions, others to perceive abstract ideas.

That's as far as personality goes. And then there's a whole set of external functions that are no less vital to a person's development.

There's the family he was born into, his parents and siblings, their physical and mental health. There's the upbringing he received, the level of observance, the degree of tolerance and support. There's the country he hails from, its attitudes and its policies. There's the physical resources he was allotted, the money, the energy, the appearance. There's the schooling he received, the influence of his classmates, the competence of his teachers. There's destiny and fate, the punches life has dealt him, the trials and challenges and disappointments.

Nobody has access to anybody else's personal chart. We don't see a history; we see a person in action. We've got to use more than mathematics to figure out that person's revised age. It takes imagination and sensitivity. It takes perception and patience and tact. Qualities that we may just be struggling to master ourselves.

Because we are all struggling.

It's so easy to look around at all those precocious, roly-poly infants around us and give up. It's so easy to watch all those perpetually organized, patient, slim, smiling, ambitious adults sailing ahead full speed, and feel ourselves grind to a discouraged halt.

It's during crises like these that we've got to remember the first fundamental rule of the neonatal unit. Preemies are charted on a graph of their own. It's where we're coming from, not where we *are*. It's how much we've struggled and how much we've grown. It's how much we've battled and how much we've learned. Not how high we're soaring, but how many miles we've scaled.

So welcome to the preemie club. Whether you're on a diet, or working to control your anger, whether you are toiling to maintain a consistent schedule, or are struggling to overcome anxiety, take a pen and paper, and figure out your revised age. It's certainly a good way to stay young.

And happy.

Relatively Speaking

$\mathcal{I}$ first heard the term *landsleit* from my grandmother, and though I've long forgotten in what context the word came up, I do remember the flush of nostalgia it evoked.

"Ah, *landsleit*," she sighed with fond yearning, and though I knew enough to understand that the word meant fellow townspeople, I failed to grasp the emotional significance of the term.

I had always had a soft spot for old friends, for classmates and neighbors of years gone by. There is a certain sense of acceptance, of familiarity and mutual understanding that lends these deeply rooted relationships special appeal, even after years of being unused. There is something comfortable and comforting about being called by your childhood nickname, about reminiscing with someone who remembers your mother's *mandelbroit*, or your older brother's run-in with his math teacher.

People who are considered *landsleit*, however, simply by virtue of them sharing the zip code of one's youth, never tugged at my sentiment. Never, at least, until that fateful day in Charles de Gaulle airport.

It's been a good many years, but I can still remember the helpless feeling of traveling alone, saddled with a bundled newborn and a bulging handbag, sandwiched between a crowd of passengers trying to deplane a Tower Air 747 for a stopover in Paris.

I remember milling about the orange couches snaking around the airport lounging area, floating amid an indecipherable muddle of Hebrew and French. There was no dearth of people; clusters of unfamiliar faces bobbed all around me, secular teenagers and laughing couples, crunching on snacks, posing for pictures, sitting cross-legged with a copy of the daily news.

Shuffling along with my handbag between my feet, however, and baby in the crook of my arm, I felt like the eternal *galus Yid*, so markedly alone. I scanned the jostling crowds for the familiar sight of a yeshivah *bachur*, a *sheitel*, anything that would indicate the comforting presence of a *frum* Jew in those thoroughly alien surroundings.

There were none in sight. I tried to silence my growing sense of disquiet, and searched for an unobtrusive corner where I could block out the hullabaloo and recite some *Tehillim*. I had just about settled into my pose when the baby began to fuss. Oh no, I groaned, glancing at my watch; where was I going to procure hot water for her bottle?

I got up and headed for the cafe area, the baby's cries growing steadily more persistent against the fading backdrop of announcements in lilting French, followed by stilted English.

Distractedly watching a courteous waiter pump green slush into a tall paper cup for the young man ahead of me at the counter, I tried to formulate my request for hot water. I don't know when it happened; preoccupied as I was patting the baby and thinking of how to approach the bartender, but suddenly I sensed an eerie silence behind me. Turning around instinctively, I noticed with alarm that all my fellow passengers had left the lounging area and had joined either one of two lines.

I remember that rush of panic, that sensation of feeling utterly abandoned. Had I missed a crucial announcement? The subdued hum suddenly presiding over the bustling hall of a minute ago made me feel like the last underwater straggler emerging from the pool, dripping and startled, bewildered by the sudden stillness of the water and the hush following the lifeguard's whistle. Was it time for departure?

The lines were moving forward at a constant pace. I felt my temples throbbing. Should I wait for the hot water, or was it imperative that I get on line immediately? I couldn't think. In my arms, the baby was flailing her little fists and shrieking; in the background that unnerving silence. In the desperation of the moment, I asked the man behind the counter if he could help me. He shrugged indifferently. *This isn't the land of Israel, lady, where a screaming infant gets anyone to do anything.*

And then suddenly I spotted her at the far end of the line. An unmistakably *frum* woman, middle aged, scanning the fluorescent green letters on the digital display.

Landsleit. I had never before experienced such an overwhelming gush of relief at the sight of an absolute stranger. Heaving my handbag over my shoulder, I all but skidded down the length of the hall to the line to where the woman stood.

Dropping my natural inhibition, I blurted out my predicament without preamble, and asked the woman if she thought I had time to procure some hot water.

"This isn't departure yet," she reassured me in English, "Just some preliminary form to fill out. Give me the baby; you go make the bottle and I'll keep your place."

A surge of warmth coursed through me, and I felt the tingling joy of recovering my senses after the numbness of emotional frostbite. My panic dissolved, my aloneness dissipated, I suddenly felt firmly anchored in this unfamiliar island; there was someone I knew, someone I could cling to and depend on: *landsleit.*

Later on, and many times since, I've had occasion to ponder that strange relationship of a few hours, the transience of it and the intensity of it. Studying my newfound companion, it struck me that my chances of my pairing up with her under any other circumstances were close to nil.

If attire said anything about an individual, then our lifestyles were miles apart, and so was our personal idea of tasteful apparel. She was at least double my age, and our ensuing bits of conversation revealed that neither her background, nor her family setup, nor her profession, would have ever fused any bonds between us.

And yet, on that alien soil, we were drawn to each other like natural soulmates. Against the bold contrast of those stridently foreign surroundings, the two of us represented the same thing, hailed from one source, respected identical ideals. I didn't flinch for a shadow of a second before entrusting her with my little infant and my personal belongings; she didn't hesitate a moment before offering to watch them.

It was the combination, I suppose, of having no one else to fall back on, and of feeling so vulnerable and helpless, that lent our alliance that sense of kinship, stronger than any I've ever felt with an ordinary friend on just any day.

And now, as often when I'm feeling a little low, that encounter in Charles de Gaulle airport brings me a measure of solace. *Tishah B'Av* is officially behind us, and though we've washed the laundry, and soiled it again since, and turned on the music, and flung right into our plans for the rest of the summer, there's this sense of unrest beneath it all.

We've been hit by bombshells hard and strong during these days of mourning, so it feels a little phony stashing away the tears the way we put away the *Purim* costumes after *Purim* and the *menorahs* after *Chanukah*. *Mashiach* hasn't come yet, and if I can give voice to that unthinkable thought that I keep trying to swat away before it dares step foot into my consciousness: What in the world is going to make him come?

If the giants of previous generations haven't brought him, if the pure faith and *mesiras nefesh* and *deveikus* of the common *Yidden* of times bygone haven't heralded the *geulah*, how can we even hope to do it? What can possibly lend the kind of power we need to our little mundane acts of *chessed*, our fragmented *tefillos*, our shallow sacrifices?

There may be dissenters, I know, who will think it's a cop-out for a lazy generation, but my spirit is restored when I look around at the world we live in. Clutching the barest hand luggage after two millennia of traveling alone, we are wandering around alien soil in the coarsest company, bombarded by immorality, by the brazen mockery of anything pure and holy.

Far away from home, disconnected from our stronghold, wallowing in the influence of a generation warped by indecency and corruption, our profile still resonates with the notes of *v'hivdilanu min hato'im* (separated us from those who have gone astray). We may look very different from the Jews of previous generations, but we are trying, valiantly trying to preserve our image as the only *frum* Jews on the flight.

Shuffling through the crowds, assaulted by the luring announcements promoting physical pleasure in forms and amounts that have never been known to humanity, we learn and support Torah, adhere to the laws of *kashrus* and *tzeniyus*, observe *Shabbos*, engage in *tzeddakah* and *chessed*.

In an age where discipline and education have totally disintegrated, young 13-year-old boys wake up fastidiously for *minyan* every morning, young men of 16, 17, and 18 spend the bulk of their vacation inside the *beis medrash*, over ancient tomes.

In these days, when literature and entertainment have to be splattered with the basest filth to deem them marketable, unadorned posters announcing *divrei chizuk* and *mussar* bring in standing room only crowds for men and women thirsty to improve.

Like my companion in that French airport, all this may not have merited much attention in ordinary times. In this chaotic airport of the 21st century, however, every drop of *yashrus*, every morsel of faith and modesty and selflessness stands out starkly. When the *Shechinah*, stranded as we are in these alien surroundings, combs through the crowds for someone who speaks His language, someone He can undoubtedly count on, we are His sole *landsleit*.

And *landsleit* on foreign soil, as I've come to learn, are a priceless relation. No matter how vast the gaping disparity, that single common link, that one precious familiar face, so distinct against the strange surrounding, melts the stringent criteria of normal circumstances and sparks an unnaturally fierce sense of devotion.

Nachamu, nachamu, ami. Take solace, My nation, My *landsleit.* Hang in there; we're on the last leg of this harrowing journey, and you're the only one I have. Very soon we'll be reunited. Just make sure I can pick you out of the crowd.

Mere Tools

When it comes to education, I'm a firm believer of giving children tools. In real life, I can hardly say the same. In fact, I take quite a vehement stand against children handling tools. My ardent opposition does little, though, to deter my son from lugging out his father's toolbox and helping himself to a wrench or a screwdriver. I've tried storing the box in the most far-flung spots around the house, but my 5½ year-old budding repairman seems to have a built in tool-detector.

"Buy him his own set," well-meaning friends have tried to advise me. I guess they just don't appreciate the difference between the genuine article and its simulated counterpart. But my son does.

He owns a plethora of plastic wrenches, hammers, screwdrivers, and even a battery-operated drill. All those do little to still his itchy fingers from stealthily inching their way into the real collection and choosing from among the assortment of apparatuses. Because, as he says, a real repairman needs real tools.

Explanations are in vain. Although he's done a lot more damage than repair in his short career, my little handyman is smug with the belief that nothing is beyond his deft hands. He's partially right. Nothing in this house *is* beyond his deft hands; it's simply a matter of whether or not the item will survive his screwdriver picking.

Although I'm constantly confiscating his paraphernalia, I always find the little guy back at his stance, hard at work, with something or other in his hands and an intense look of concentration on his face.

So I'm sort of resigned to the fact that my alarm clock is almost perpetually devoid of its batteries, and that most things that should have screws are usually missing several. *I'm* resigned, but my son isn't even considering the prospect. Not after the success he's tasted this summer.

It was one of those hectic summer mornings, with mounds of wet towels and bathing suits from the most recent expedition to the pool waiting to be laundered. Between the ices, watermelon, and the hot, sticky weather, vacation time always seems to double the volume of soiled stuff. So I wasn't very pleased to find my washing machine in nonworking order. Although the motor emitted a low droning hum, the ensuing sound of water filling the drum failed to follow.

As I stood hunched over the machine, fiddling with the knobs, I suddenly sensed an onlooker standing behind me. "It's broken, Ma?" asked my junior repairman. His eyes were glittering with the challenge.

That was at 10 o'clock in the morning, as my son was on his way to day camp. Nodding in response to his query, I quickly saddled him with his knapsack, gave him a parting kiss, and wished him a great day. Then I thumbed through my personal phonebook and left an urgent message for my repairman to come down as soon as he could.

To his credit, I must say he did. One half-hour and 200 *shekels* later, the repairman stretched his cramped legs and informed me that the new gasket around the door was installed. He slammed the machine door shut, turned the knob, and had me listen to the reassuring sound of water rushing into the drum. I smiled with relief as I paid him his due and saw him to the door.

With all the activity going on, I probably would have forgotten the entire incident by the time the afternoon rolled around. In the way of the world, working items aren't given too much thought, and other than a fleeting swell of gratitude as I folded a load of clean towels, my mind was on to other things.

Someone else, however, apparently hadn't forgotten. As soon as my son entered the door, sweaty and smiling, he flung his knapsack off his back, and sprinted out of sight. When he reentered the kitchen, brandishing a screwdriver, he was sporting the most triumphant smile I'd ever seen on his face.

"It's fixed, Ma," he informed me, trying to sound casual. The gleam in his eyes, though, betrayed his sheer ecstasy and disbelief. Seeing that recognition hadn't dawned, he quickly added, "The washing machine."

Oh, so that's where he had disappeared. "Yes, I know," I was about to say, but something about his radiant face made the words die on my tongue.

"I fixed it," he continued, cheeks flushed with pride, chest puffed out importantly. "I stuck the screwdriver into the hole — look, Ma," he all but towed me to the site of the repair, as he demonstrated exactly which maneuvers had fixed the machine. "Then I turned the knob with my wrench, not too hard, like this." He proceeded to twist the knob, all the while wearing that glowing smile of accomplishment. "And then the light went on, and the machine made a noise, and it started working. I fixed it!"

I've got a weak point when it comes to bursting kids' bubbles, so I went right along with his charade. "You fixed the washing machine!" I exclaimed, hiding every verbal trace of the morning repairman, of the two hundred *shekels*, of the brand new gasket. Not a very astute move on my part, I concede. If he had ever harbored any doubts regarding his fixing ability, now he was convinced.

Over and over he recounted his feat, to anybody who was willing to listen. "All day in day camp I thought about how I could fix the machine," he repeated tirelessly, "and then I decided that maybe the orange screwdriver could fit into the hole. And it did. And I fixed the machine."

I let him gloat in his illusion, while I chuckled at the thought that he'd been spending his day contemplating my broken washing machine, when it had long been repaired. But I kept quiet. If it made him happy to think that his dabbling had cured the problem, then so be it.

What about us though, I thought? Don't we tinker with those tools too, convinced that if not for our timely interference, some crisis or other would never have been averted? Don't we often assume that the hours we've spent thinking, discussing, and researching, have brought about the ultimate solutions to some of life's knotty issues?

Like little children living under the delusion of personal grandeur, we pucker our brows and putter busily with that screwdriver, oblivious to the fact that the Repairman has already done the job. We pull and push and heave importantly, trying to take control of things that have long been resolved. And when our efforts bear the desired results, that little boy inside us beams with pride and waits for the cheering committee.

Silly kids, the machine's been fixed already. And if it hasn't yet, then no amount of tinkering with any orange screwdriver is going to do the trick.

Hashem humors us, though. He does His repairs ever so unobtrusively, and then He lets us step in and make a lot of noise and pat ourselves on the back when we suddenly realize that something's worked out. He let's us exult in our achievement without ever saying, "Just for your information, Yanke'le, while you were so busy wondering and worrying, there was a Repairman down. Yup, if you had only dropped your screw driver for a moment, and just tried the knob, you'd have known that simple truth."

He doesn't say that to us because He wants us to grapple with our *emunah* and *bitachon* on our own. Most often, though, we're glad to remain the oblivious little boy who thinks he's in charge.

MERE TOOLS / 343

Actually, we're not always that *glad*. Sometimes we're sad and mad. Sometimes we're worried and fearful and tense and anxious, because we believe it depends on our best efforts. We toss and turn over *parnassah* and *shidduchim*, over our health and over our job. We spend our day pondering and planning something that's long been decided. And then we try this device or that, sure that if we haven't yet met with success. It's because we haven't been smart enough, or industrious enough, or efficient enough. What a ridiculous pain to go through for an illusory game of repairman.

So the next time the machine doesn't start, let's do ourselves a favor and spare ourselves the pain. Let's relinquish the screwdriver, and call straight for the Repairman.

Optical Allusion

Nowadays
Even *mitzvos*
are state of the art,
s'*chach*,
simple *s'chach*,
isn't all that simple
anymore,
it comes in mats,
of select bamboo

bound by machines,
graded
according to
varying degrees
of quality,
You've got to be a *meivin*
to tell the difference,
and I'm no *meivin*,
but still,
I miss
the optical illusion
that came along
with the old *s'chach*,
separate canes
of simple bamboo,
sparsely spread
over the beams
of our wooden *succah*.
During the daytime
They seemed so
far above
And scantly spread,
All the sunlight
Filtered in
Through the gaping spaces
between the canes,
big wide stripes
of bright blue sky
sailed like streamers
overhead,
you barely saw
those bamboo canes,
But come the night,
as if some magic hand

had pushed those rods
all together,
squeezed them close
and lowered them
so that they hovered
just above
our heads,
come the night,
and you felt that covering
but good,
cozy and dense,
blocking out the inky blackness
outside.
Funny,
how the same protection
could seem so porous
when all
was bright and light,
you almost missed its presence,
and then
when night fell,
so dense
and so much closer down too,
making you aware,
just how dependent you were
on its comforting
cover,
Funny,
I never ceased
to be amazed
by the wonder
of this optical illusion.
Nowadays,
As I said

S'chach isn't that simple,
But then
It never was,
It was always special,
State of the heart.

Missing the Mark

I know some of you may vehemently oppose the terminology, but I've been doing some *Pesach* cleaning as of late. "It's called spring cleaning," my husband reminds me every year as I revel in the order reigning in my closets, the organized photo albums, the labeled negatives, the vanished stack of tapes to return.

He's got a point. Among the many self-made woes plaguing society in our day is the mistaken notion that the prohibition against *chametz* behooves the Jewish homemaker (and family) to undergo weeks or months of harrowing slavery to some socially accepted, halachically rejected, norms. Scrutinize as you wish, you won't find one stanza in the *Shulchan Aruch* (Code of Laws) that mentions mattress beating, carpet shampooing, paper sorting, or appliance dissecting.

It's all a matter of perspective. Still, if I've got the energy, and the time to pace myself properly, I insist on referring to these annual chores as *Pesach* cleaning. If I'm planning to go through all the bother, though admittedly there's a sense of profound accomplishment that accompanies the completion of these tasks waiting to be tended to since last winter, then I may as well be getting some Heavenly compensation. Besides which, I do occasionally find a pretzel hiding in some crevice behind the picture books.

Or some other reminder of the despicable enemy, looming innocently in the most unsuspecting places.

As I said, sometimes *Pesach* is the reason, and sometimes it's the excuse. Where my teaching files are concerned, the latter is definitely the case. If not for that once-a-year evacuation of the attic, when would I ever get a chance to sit crosslegged on a precious morning, and while away those scarce hours of quiet, in fond remembrance of *Chumash* lessons and *dikduk* sheets?

Though I often engage in serious conflict, as I stand atop a ladder, hand outstretched to retrieve some item from the loft, I firmly harness my impulse to drag down the files and melt away in nostalgic reverie. Just wait until *Erev Pesach*, I placate myself; then I'll sit in justified indulgence with those files for as long as I'd like.

Which is exactly what I did last Monday. Sitting in a pool of papers, surrounded by the disarray of cardboard boxes, piles of outgrown clothing, and a basin of lukewarm water to afford the illusion that there was actually some cleaning underway, I sat completely engrossed, my fingers inky blue from the smudgy backs of old stencils.

There were looseleafs, and folders, letters and songs, games and scripts. There were photocopies and quotations, highlighted *Rashi's*, excerpts from the *midrash*, scrawled memos, frayed roll books, copies of school bulletins, raw drafts of report card comments.

In one moment, as if I had touched down on the scrolling button of my memory's screen, the solid entirety of my present, all those years and months and weeks, all the commas and question marks and exclamation points dotting the pages and pages of the last decade of my life, zipped backward at a dizzying speed, dancing, flashing, disappearing past me: marriage, Eretz Yisrael, the children, swallowed up in a second by the hypnotic reality of those tangible memories.

I could almost smell the aroma of turkey nuggets in a peppery sauce, school lunch in the brewing, following me all the way up the high school steps on a Wednesday morning, as I mentally reviewed the differences between *ma'aseh marivah* and *mei marah*. I could see the pale yellow tiles in the hallway, scuffed by scores of shoes, navy, brown, black, loafers, ties, pumps. I could feel the sunlight coming through the big windows at the back of the cramped classroom, looking out at the bare post-autumn branches against the gray blue sky.

Assaulted by these sensual associations, I thumbed through the pockets of my file, eyes catching each heading: *Chumash, Yahadus, Ivris, Dikduk*, tests, reports, review sheets, extracurricular, miscellaneous.

There, in that cavity carved to catch that which didn't quite deserve a permanent dwelling, lay a sheaf of *dikduk* quizzes, about fifty of them, waiting obligingly to be returned to their owners. *Tisbakshu, shva na, hi; pual; asid, nitzalten, acharei shva nach.* Numbered 1 to 5, these terms, or their mistaken alternatives, were written vertically beneath the headings on 50 papers, in as many different handwritings.

Some were etched deliberately in blue ink, pressed down hard, almost embossed. Some were scribbled in pencils that needed to be sharpened, others were penned in pink pen over glossy patches of Wite-Out.

Universal to all, was the confident presence of my own markings, checks and x's penned lightly in fine red marker alongside each answer. Five out of five, three out of five, four out of five, two out of five, with an occasional excellent or good splashed across the top.

I checked the names on the upper right-hand side of each paper, and couldn't help smiling. Pessy, Devorah, Esther Kaila, Dina, Tirtzah, Brochy. As I held each one for a moment in my mind, I saw a fleeting image, a smile, a puckered forehead, an indignant frown, images arrested in still life, frozen on sophomore faces, in the last pose I'd captured them.

I knew I'd be openmouthed to see them today, active, accomplished adults, wives, mothers, teachers in their own rights. And I knew too, that wherever they were, one thing was certain: They couldn't give a hoot about these *dikduk* papers lying in my possession.

That five out of five wasn't going to redeem anyone from a sticky interpersonal mess at work, that *dagesh* inserted correctly for the right considerations wasn't going to help any mother get an obnoxious toddler dressed.

And I was willing to bet that some of those unfortunate beholders of one, or two out of five, were blossoming adults now, responsible, loving caregivers; creative, caring, contributing individuals.

Those checks and x's that had evoked so many heated reactions in their time, that had ignited or extinguished the triumphant sparkle in dozens of anxious eyes, were like void checks now, worthless, irrelevant, reduced to a bunch of scrap to be unceremoniously dumped into a flimsy trash bag, and carted out to the garbage.

Not that I'm denigrating the importance of *dikduk*, or of all academic achievement, for that matter. Not that I'm making light of Sunday morning quizzes, of punctilious reviews opening *Chumash* or *Navi* lessons, even history or math classes. What that impertinent heap of quizzes confronted me with, more than the irony of scholastic excellence, was the shocking reality true of all too many of us, students of life.

How many of us invest our most prime time, expend our most fertile energies, pin the entire question of our self-worth, on our excellence, our achievement, our attainment of passing grades? How often do we become wrapped up to the point of complete absorption in subjects that may be of trivial, if any, import, 10, 20 years down the line?

Perhaps it's the red ink that diverts us. True inner development doesn't receive any public exclamations; self-control, unshakable honesty, cultivated patience, the tranquil acceptance of life's punches, those aren't feats that merit honors in this social university of transitory success.

People laud professional degrees, efficient housekeeping, creative thinking, slim figures. The good marks come in for chic taste, for business acumen, for impressive performances, intellectual prowess.

It's sobering to think that the grades we receive for the tasteful wedding invitations, the original *mishloach manos* theme, the fancy dessert, will mean so little to us after the wedding is over, the children grown, our physical strength sapped. What enjoyment will we reap from that five out five, sitting in a forgotten pile, in the miscellaneous pocket of someone's old, extraneous memories?

If it's the real leavening we're after, we've got to drop our pursuits of perfect order, exclusive attire, temporary esteem; we've got to relax our efforts toward external excellence. Let's shift the concentration in our degree program. Because when the schooling is over, there's only one set of *dikduk* marks we'll be concerned with: *dikduk b'mitzvos*, and *dikduk chaveirim.*

Smoke Detectors — Burning Issues

Even before I turned the key in the keyhole, I was able to discern the acrid odor. I groaned. I had completely forgotten about the stew. I had left the chicken and potatoes simmering on a low flame, sure that I'd be back in time to shut it. So much for estimation. Somehow, the alleged 10-minute sprint to the hardware store had turned into a 55-minute excursion. And now I was smelling the consequences.

I know, in the scheme of things, burned stew is a pretty minor aggravation, but when it's 6 p.m. and you should have been home an hour ago, the thought of supper having gone to pot can loom rather large.

I knew I could expect a delayed bedtime, some grumbling over an improvised menu, and a badly burned pot to salvage. What I *didn't* expect was to find was my two daughters complacently shmoozing in the kitchen, not two yards away from the offending pot.

The look on my face as I dashed into the kitchen told them something was amiss, but they didn't seem to have a clue as to what that something could be. I really hate to greet my loved ones with criticism, especially after I've been out and they've been holding the fort, but this time I just couldn't contain myself.

"Didn't you *smell* the potatoes burning?" I asked in disbelief. "You kids are right here in the kitchen! I smelled it all the way out on the front steps."

The younger one stopped talking and dropped her stationery album, while the older one turned instinctively to the stove, a look of sincere contrition spreading over her features. She spoke for both of them.

"I'm so sorry, Ma, I really am. I didn't realize that there was a flame that had to be shut."

"Didn't realize? Didn't you *smell*?"

Shaking my head in frustration, I muttered something about the irony of supper burning under your nose, as I lifted the lid to assess the damage. A flood of smoke escaped, nearly choking me.

"Please open the window," I said flatly. Both of them jumped at the request, relieved to be able to do something tangible to make amends. "And take out some pizza. Rochel, you can cut a salad." I tried to keep my voice calm and constructive, but it took iron discipline not to keep repeating the rhetorical reproof: "You were right here in the kitchen! Didn't you smell the potatoes burning?"

Seeing my daughters' miserable, apologetic faces, I realized I was being far too somber about so trivial a mishap. So I told them it was all right, and it wasn't their fault, and let's forget the whole incident. Which we would have done happily, if not for the annoying fact that whoever entered the doorway considered it his personal duty to bring the smell to our attention.

"Hi, Ma, something's burning, you know?"

"Hi, Yitzy. Yes I know, it *was* supper, and it's over with. How was your day?"

"Heeeello! Hey, what smells? I think something's burning."

"You'd think something burned in the front hall," I joked. Inside the kitchen, our noses seemed to be providing us with automatic shut off service, a service we all appreciated. It's one of those tiny but awesome wonders of creation that any odor, no matter how unpleasant, becomes bearable, even unnoticeable, after a few minutes of exposure. It usually takes a stranger coming in from the outside to point out that the house smells of fried fish, or that someone must have been using a permanent marker.

And that's fine.

But if the human power of distinction is the nose of the mind, then that shut-off mechanism scares me. It frightens me to think that no matter how discerning and how intelligent we might be, when something is burning in our own kitchen, we may remain oblivious to the fact. Not in *spite* of our close proximity to the problem, but *because* of it.

We may be able to dispense the most sensitive and sensible advice on child-rearing, on time or money management, on tips for an effective relationship. We may know all the virtues of seeing things from the other person's point of view, of not being judgmental, and not getting on the defensive.

But when the stew begins scorching on our home front, in our community, in our family, or our school, we fail to smell the smoke. We're either so emotionally entangled, or else so accustomed to the situation, that our hearts and minds become desensitized to the odor calling for our attention.

How many times have I caught my heart lurching with pity for a 10-year-old boy being publicly chastised for having left his brand-new jacket in yeshivah? Somehow, when that 10-year-old is mine, I fail to see the tenderness of the situation.

And the same holds true for teenagers, spouses, students, and in-laws. The same is true of our lifestyle, our dress code, our speech, and our habits.

We humans were endowed with the lofty ability to distinguish right from wrong, discord from harmony, admirable from disdainful. Our moral sense of smell is what guides and directs us, helping us to exercise our power of *bechirah*. It is also what tells us when something is amiss. But we've got to be tuned in, or our mechanism will shut off. And we've got to install spiritual smoke detectors in the form of nightly, weekly, and yearly *cheshbon hanefesh*.

Aside, though, from our own periodic introspection, it's important to listen to those who are coming in from the outside. As annoying as it is to have our flaws pointed out, an objective opinion, especially one infused with Torah wisdom, can sometimes salvage a precarious situation just in the knick of time.

So from time to time, whatever you are in the middle of doing, step back and look around. There may be a pot smoking. And it may just be your supper inside.

Wishful Thinking

I remember waking up early *Erev Rosh Hashanah* to the hushed tones of my mother on the phone, wishing someone or other a *kesivah v'chasimah tovah* and a *Gut gebentcht yuhr.* While I got dressed and opened my *siddur* to *daven,* I'd hear my mother puttering in the kitchen, repeating her heartfelt wishes over and over to the many relatives and friends on her list near the telephone.

It was a warm, reassuring feeling, hearing those early morning phone calls against the backdrop of tinkling silverware and running water, the wishes wafting into my room together with the smell of simmering chicken soup, and carrots stewing in brown sugar.

Years later, I've adopted my mother's tradition of making those calls early in the day, as my own children wipe the wisps of sleep off their eyelids. There are some phone calls, though, that I like to make yet earlier. There are certain people for whom I need more than just a few minutes to wish the customary blessings for a happy and healthy new year, usually those acquaintances who are most in need of the happiness and the health.

So it was, that a few spare minutes one *Motza'ei Shabbos* in *Elul,* found me leafing through my personal phonebook, trying to find the page where I had jotted down the number of a friend who for some time now had been in the hospital with her young son.

Spending time in the hospital near a sickbed is never a picnic. Spending *Shabbos* there is always worse. So when I picked up the receiver, I was expecting to find her in low spirits. Her downhearted hello confirmed my prediction.

After the preliminaries, I fished around for the right thing to say. "I've been thinking of you, Yocheved. How was your *Shabbos*?"

"Better don't ask," she sighed wearily. "You should never have to see what I witnessed here over *Shabbos*."

Images of stretchers, bandaged heads, and IV lines rushed to my mind. Walking the corridors of any ward in any hospital leaves a person sobered for a while. Visiting a pediatric ward, however, is like encountering a disturbing distortion of a beautiful picture.

To watch little children who should be skipping and climbing and getting into trouble, lying limply under sterile covers, can make any heart ache. To see cheeks that should be flushed with excitement and enthusiasm, pale and hollow; to meet eyes that should be sparkling with spunk and curiosity, worried and pained; to hear lips that are supposed to be chattering and laughing, ponder existential questions, all that can dishearten even the most spirited soul.

There was silence for a moment, as these grave thoughts charged our connection. I waited for her to go on and describe some of the heartrending sights she had witnessed, half wishing she wouldn't tell me.

"It just isn't funny. How can *Klal Yisrael* go on like this?" she asked, and her words rent my soul. It's not that her question was a new one. With the political tension so taut these days, it was a question that hovered close to everyone's lips; lingered in the air, weighed heavily on every *Yid*'s heart. It was a question that echoed a million times behind the daily headlines, a question that punctuated our greetings to one another and our entreaties to the One Above.

Still, the words had a different meaning when I could almost touch the pain that had prompted them. The question had a different ring when I knew they were coming from the depths of an anguished mother's heart.

"The *chillul Shabbos*," she continued, oblivious to my train of thought. "You cannot fathom the blatant desecration that went on here over *Shabbos*!"

Oh, so that's what she was talking about. The tears stinging my eyelids suddenly abated, and an immense gush of relief washed over my heart. My grip on the receiver loosened, and I felt the intense emotion of one minute earlier subside, as I listened to her pained description.

"You nearly forget there's a *tzelem Elokim* inside when you see the long bleached hair, the tight jeans, the strident slogans splashed across the cheap T-shirts. You almost don't feel the aura of *Shabbos* when you hear the coarse laughter over the crass humor emanating from the screen. The cell phones beep and sing and drown out any vestige of holiness, as they pick up and exchange slang as if it were a day like no other. These are Hashem's children, and they don't even know it!"

There was real hurt in her voice, genuine anguish. And if my heart had been flooded with pain and compassion one minute earlier, now I was gripped by a different sense of sorrow.

Why had the thoughts of illness and suffering evoked such a strong surge of sadness within me, while the reality of the *Shechinah* languishing inside these hostage souls almost made me sigh with relief? Why did the piercing question about the length of this *galus* take on such relevance when physical suffering was under discussion, but somehow recede into the intellectual realm when it was spiritual pain in question?

Perhaps these questions were appendages to the first, original, penetrating question: "How can *Klal Yisrael* go on like this?" If thoughts of *galus HaShechinah* could assuage my pain over our own ailments, that was a sign that the *Shechinah* was, indeed, hiding deep, deep within the folds of this exile.

It was a quiet, thought-provoking phone call, in quite a different way than I had expected it would be. Long after I had returned the receiver to its cradle, I sat scribbling a question mark in the margin of my list. Over and over, I traced that question mark, eclipsing all the personal wishes for health and happiness that I had doodled all over the notepad. It was a question and a request and a searing plea for the *Shechinah* to shine forth in all Its glory so that Its resplendent rays would reach even the darkest crevices of every Jew's heart.

It was a real *Rosh Hashanah* wish, not for ourselves, and not for our children, not for our health, and not for our happiness. Not even for *nachas*. It was a plea reverberating with the greatness of a simple Jewish mother, and resonating with the sweet melody of the *chazzan* on the first day of the brand new year.

V'yeda kol pa'ul ki atah pealto, v'yavin kol yitzur ki atah yitzarto, v'yomar kol asher neshamah b'apo: Hashem Elokei Yisrael Melech umalchuso bakol mashala.

Half Full

I violated the law today. In fact, I violate the law dozens of times each day, and nobody bats an eyelash. Business resumes, and the law remains firmly entrenched in humanity's mind.

I don't know who Murphy was, and I don't care to know, but I do know that Murphy's law dictates that anything that can go wrong, invariably will. Buttered toast will inevitably fall on the buttered side, as surely as the traffic light will turn red just as one is racing to avoid traffic. So much for the law.

And I, in simple defiance of it, have proven Murphy wrong time and time again. From the moment I utter the words of *Modeh Ani* in the morning, thanking Hashem for the priceless gift of yet another day of life, until late in the evening when I entrust my soul to my Creator, my day is one long rebuttal of that bleak, dismal assessment of life.

The very first blow to the validity of this pessimistic prediction is the simple (?) fact that I wake up at all. Someone unfamiliar with the notion of sleep who had seen me sprawled on my bed, mute, immobile, and virtually lifeless would stare in open-mouthed wonder at my scurrying silhouette, wrapping lunches, firing orders, simultaneously feeding, dressing, signing tests, and tying shoes.

My life, which had been temporarily suspended while slumber held my body hostage, has been handed back to me anew. I've been imbued again with the gift of vitality, with the strength and vigor to face a new day. Upon my awakening, all my organs immediately began actively working. And the moment my eyelids fluttered open, my memory automatically resumed its function, enabling me to pick up the threads of yesterday with effortless ease.

Incredibly, this whole miracle of resuscitation took place with little pomp and ceremony other than a noisy yawn and a quickly mumbled *Modeh Ani.* And if that weren't enough to dispel the myth that things tend not to work out, a glorious sun was smiling down at the world, streaming into my window, and stroking my arms as I hurriedly washed my hands.

Wonder of wonders, the blouse I had chosen to wear was washed and ironed, the hem on the skirt blessedly intact. To add to the list, my husband was home from *Shacharis* in time, there were enough Cheerios to go around, and the milk in the fridge wasn't sour. There was a pen in the drawer to sign Chezky's *mishnayos* test, and it wasn't leaking. All five kids found both shoes, Shayna agreed that her stomach ache would wait until I came home from work, my car keys were just where I had left them last night, and I even remembered where that was!

It's amazing how many things can go right in one short morning. It's even more amazing how we humans insist on highlighting the exception to the rule. No matter how many wonderful things transpire in the course of a day, we somehow pass up on them in favor of griping over some mishap or other.

The funny thing is, we almost don't *notice* that things are running smoothly until there is a kink in the mechanism and something goes awry. Who takes note of a working boiler, an unclogged drain, or a toenail that isn't ingrown? Who raves over made beds, the absence of lines in the supermarket, or the fact that the blinds we've ordered have arrived in the right color?

Ask any teacher, carpenter, shopkeeper, caterer, or author. Just ask them when's the last time anyone called especially to thank them. To tell the teacher that the way she rearranged the seats was so perfect and must have taken hours of thought, to let the carpenter know that the hinges were just the right size, and thank him so much for making the special order; or to express appreciation for the fact that the grocery store was so well stocked so soon after *Pesach*.

We humans seem to take special pleasure in making a pet out of our peeves. Annoyance, disapproval, and frustration find their way into the written and spoken word a lot more often and a lot more emphatically than gratitude and satisfaction.

Of course that's wrong, but then let's remember. Not everything that *can* go wrong will, and not everything that *does* go wrong must. With a little awareness and a lot of willpower, we can instate a new law. Most things that can go right, do.

All we've got to do is take out a pen and paper and jot down everything that has happened in the last hour. We'll suddenly be made to see that the bank could have been closed, that important folder could have been accidentally left at home, and the baby could have swallowed the button on the floor.

No matter how many things have gone wrong, there are bound to be a million more that could have, but didn't. That is all the evidence we need to abolish Murphy's law. Let's try it. We'll be the most sought after lawbreakers around.

Positively so.

Kaleidoscope II

Life is a bubble,
Effervescent,
Iridescent,
full,
of clattering pots,
And whining tots,
shopping lists,
last-minute twists,
Renovations
Preparations,
Invitations,
Obligations,
Full
of ringing phones,
and sprained bones,
watering plants,
hemming pants,
exterminating ants,
Life is hectic,
Busy,
juggling
home and work,
homework and housework,
the three pages of math,
the principal's wrath,
A pot of boiling soup,
Recurring croup
And a whistling kettle,

bickering to settle,
A million choices
And a half a dozen voices,
Life is busy struggling
with leaking pipes,
and teenage gripes
loose knobs
and undone jobs,
pouting lips
and canceled trips
tactless remarks,
and unfair marks.

And then amid the frantic flurry,
The hasty hurry,
Amid the hectic pace.
The perpetual panting race,
the pendulum of routine
is frozen midscene,
The bubble of life
Is deflated,
slashed,
By the sledgehammer
Of tragedy,
the cold knife,
Of strife,
Leaving nothing of the bubble
But a mound of rubble,
And the pure
Invincible core,
Making me squint at
Petty problems
Like burned eggs
Or aching legs,

Like missing boots,
Or stained suits,
And wonder
How they ever loomed
So LARGE,
Knocking me awake!
Making me shake
With the sudden dread
Of how very dead
One can become
With the trivialities of
Life

And how very alive
One can be kicked
With the whispering of
Death.

I watch my whirlwind,
My tension,
Dissension,
recede into the background,
I watch monumental
OBSTACLES
Shrink and shrivel
And become specks
On a horizon,
Too LARGE
And too AWESOME
To conceive
I feel the tingling
Of a numbed soul
Waking up
I taste the mingling

Of tears
Of pain and gratitude and awareness,
I suddenly feel
Like I have shrunken,
And become
Very
Very
Small,
And all at once,
The gift
of life
seems so very,
very,
ENORMOUS.

Discovery

Castles in the Ear

*I*t was on the way home from the post office that we first noticed it was missing. Waiting together for the light to change, she had squinted up and commented on the perfect blue sky. In response, I had fondly tucked her hair behind her ear the way I like it, the way her pretty tanned face looks best, when I noticed her ear was earringless.

Before I could think, I checked her other ear. No luck. The other pearl was securely in place, glowing against her complexion. This wasn't simply an erratic case of responsibility, where Gitty had uncharacteristically decided to remove her earrings after *Shabbos*. I would have guessed as much.

Like her mother's, Gitty's jewelry habits follow a pretty predictable pattern. If the earrings are on for *Shabbos*, you can expect that they won't see the jewelry box for the next couple of weeks. So the single earring boded no good.

Noticing my horror-stricken gaze, she instinctively put a finger to her ear. "Huh!" she gasped, "It's gone!"

"Do you remember feeling it on your way home from school?" I tried to keep my tone even.

Gitty furrowed her forehead in concentration as she mentally reconstructed her walk home from school.

"I remember turning it during *Navi*," she said slowly, her forehead still puckered, hoping to come up with some more-recent clue.

"Good," I said, encouraged. "That means you lost it today, some time between *Navi* and now. At least we won't have to go through the dumpster."

"Yeah, but it could be anywhere outside. Maybe I should ask Shevi if she would walk back to school with me."

Which she did. Only after we first walked back to the post office, eyes combing the sidewalk inch by inch, the way you drag a finger along a floor, feeling for a lost button.

Had they been a pair of ordinary studs, I probably would have called a halt to the search right then and there. Trying to salvage spilled milk, I've found, is oftentimes as unproductive as crying over it. Anything reasonably replaceable should, in my opinion, be replaced before enough time and energy are squandered to turn the loss into an irretrievable one.

In this case, though, my philosophy took exception. These were not just any simple earrings, this pair of twin pearls. They were a gift from my grandmother, Gitty's great-grandmother, given with love, worn with affection. They were nice, perfectly matching, round pearls with a sheen quite unlike any I'd ever seen before. She was a *meivin*, my grandmother, and she'd chosen them with care.

"Pearls are always nice," she'd said at the time. "They aren't dated, and they're always age appropriate. Wear them *gezunterheit*."

Which Gitty did, amazingly, for about a year and a half, until that fateful moment at the crossing when we noticed one of them was missing.

We diligently searched. Through streets and sidewalks, pockets and papers. Got down on hands and knees and groped around on tiptoe, swept the crevices, moved the beds.

The earring eluded us.

Finally, in resignation, I went into a jewelry store with the mateless pearl. The sentimental value, I knew, couldn't be recovered. The pearl, though, I'd reckoned, shouldn't be too hard to replace.

I guess I'd never tried to find a precise match.

There wasn't a single match in the showcase. There were salmon-colored pearls and yellowish-tinted ones, larger ones, smaller ones, grayer and greener. Who had ever dreamed there were so many hues to the universal cream-colored stereotype?

I took the lone pearl home and carefully slipped it into a little white bag in my top drawer. Whenever I'd go anywhere that was in the radius of a jewelry store, I'd stash the parcel into my pocketbook in hopeful anticipation. I'd go into the store, unobtrusively take out my paper bag and carefully compare my pearl to the ones under the glass. Then I'd politely decline the saleswoman's offer for help and slink out of the shop, shaking my head.

If I could only have the original back. I'd never, even in passing, thought to appreciate the perfection of the match. I had never studied the luster, analyzed the exact shade, measured the circumference. I had thought they came like that, a perfect pair, equally lustrous, symmetrically round. Like so many things in life that we become painfully aware of only after they are gone.

I considered getting her a new pair of pearls. There were plenty of sets in the showcase. But they weren't quite as round, or quite as dainty, or quite as iridescent as the ones she'd had before. I'm usually not the frivolous type, but in this instance, some indefinable stubborn streak refused to compromise. These earrings had to live up to my grandmother's standards. Not because she'd ever know. Because *I* would know.

Life has some very unexpected surprises hiding behind the corners. So does cleaning for *Pesach*.

Last week, as I stuck my hand into a space I'd created by pulling out the bottom drawer in the bedroom wall-unit, my hand hit something round and shiny, like a popcorn kernel, only slightly larger. I pressed my finger down on it and dragged it along the floor tile, my heart jumping up and down like an excited little child.

I knew what it was before I saw it, but still, I closed my eyes for a moment of delicious anticipation, before I opened them to the long-lost pearl.

What do you know, here it is, I thought wryly, smiling down at the grand find. Some pun about rags to riches flitted through my mind as I let go of the damp, dirty cloth that had unearthed the pearl.

I picked up the earring.

Unexpected endings often happen like that, so much plainer and quieter and less dramatic than one would have imagined them.

I ran to fetch my pocketbook. I wouldn't say a word. I would bring the other pearl, pin them both back into place on their original black velvet background, and present them to Gitty.

Well. It would have made for a nice ending, but it didn't go like that. As I set the precious pearl alongside its pair, I felt a slight twinge of shock.

The two were not identical.

One was noticeably larger and pinker than the other. They were definitely a pair, but not the way I had remembered them. Not in that perfect, flawless way I had recalled them all along.

I was stunned and, in the strangest way, disappointed. I had found the original, and it was a very ordinary, albeit beautiful, pearl. Fingering its solid presence, I felt as if I had lost some kind of dream, some kind of vision, a romantic mirage of perfection that didn't really exist.

As I said, I don't believe in agonizing. If I was a tinge disillusioned, I didn't let on. We screwed the earrings into place, and celebrated the merry occasion. With a beautiful smiling face like Gitty's in between them, no one would ever dream the pearls weren't a perfect pair.

Unless, of course, that person's ever lost an earring and tried to match it up. Or a dream.

It's a curious part of the human psyche, this thing called nostalgia, the elusive ingredient that sweetens stolen waters. It's the distinct finality of locked doors that makes the contents behind them beckon with torturous appeal. It's the apparition of time or distance or loss that plays tricks with the mind's photography; fades out imperfections and bathes dreams in shades of glowing utopia.

We all experience it at some point or another. We all fondle private hopes and desires, wishes and memories, cravings and ambitions, lockets whose keys, for some reason or another, lie at the bottom of the ocean.

We go around with that locket on our hearts, hopelessly hunting for the key. We hold on to that pearl in our purse, and carry around the graven image of its pair, in the hope of finding its spitting reflection. We know what perfection is, we think; we just need to find it.

And when we find it, we are shocked. If we find it, that is.

Sometimes we are too busy looking for something else, some nostalgic vision, some far-off, larger-than-life pearl, to recognize the genuine article when we see it. Sometimes we are so busy looking for the yeshivah of our dreams, the *chavrusa,* the *shidduch,* the job, the house, that we don't even find the pearl when we see it.

This isn't it, we cluck as we veto the samples in the showcase of our everyday lives. *I know what I'm looking for. I once had it. I once saw it. It was perfect.*

We don't realize that the ones we have in mind weren't perfect either. There *are* no perfect pearls. Or perfect pairs. The secret lies in taking them as a gift, as a given, as a fixed pair. When they come together, they grow on you. And anyway, almost any two on either side of a smiling face will look dazzling.

Elokai

*J*ust the other day,
I heard a lady say,
"I'm not getting on a bus, no way,"
('twas I, no less,
I'll confess).
Countered a man,
They've got to ban
These bombers and their trusses,
From boarding civilian buses,
Give their entire nation
Separate transportation.
Declared a boy,
I'm staying put,
Not setting foot,
Onto a boat, a mountain, a plane,
I'll fill my summer with things mundane.

Why,
thought I,
we'd make,
the perfect 21st-century rendition
of Pharaoh's advisory coalition,
same old conclusion,
same old illusion,
havah nischakmah,
the age-old delusion.

After all those

heavy blows,
men healthy as oxen,
clear of a single toxin,
felled on an ordinary day
by nature at play,
people on the safest soil,
free of political roil,
plucked one bright morning,
with no hint of warning.

After all that,
we still chat,
of skirting danger,
outsmarting fate,
by coming early, leaving late,
by better inspecting,
detecting,
rejecting,
by using the past,
as a guide for correcting.

We forget,
Haven't learned yet,
Human man,
May sit and plan,
Devise,
Revise,
Improvise,
stay off buses,
Avoid fusses.

It isn't the Arabs, the illness, the tree,
It isn't the place one happens to be
'Tis Him on land and Him at sea,

'Tis all He, only He.

Neshamah shenasata bi,
Atah meshamerah b'kirbi,
And at the instant You decree
asid l'tlah mimeni.

'Tis all He, only He,
and nothing we can oversee,
but *kol z'man shehaneshamah b'kirbi,*
Elokai,
Modeh Ani!

Forgiven and Forgotten?

I know we're supposed to keep our gaze ever upward, looking toward our elders for guidance and advice. Sometimes, though, it turns out to be our children who spark our greatest moments of inspiration. There's something about the fresh clean lens of childhood, unscathed by the harshness of reality, not yet clouded by the passing of time, that captures the startling image of things just the way they are. And sometimes, for a special, fleeting moment, we are granted the privilege of crouching momentarily beside a young child, and getting a glimpse of life through that lens.

I experienced one of those flashes of illumination last year as I was sorting through a box of winter clothing and nodding in response to Yitzy's ongoing chatter.

One minute he was enlightening me on the difference between tricycles, bicycles, and training wheels, and the next minute, even before I grasped that the conversation had taken a turn, Yitzy was looking at me plaintively, waiting for a response to some request he had made.

"Okay, Mommy?" he looked into my eyes, his eyebrows slightly knit, pleading for an affirmative answer.

"What'd you ask, Yitzy?" I asked absently, a polo shirt tucked under my chin. I was trying to assess which of the shirts and pants in the box would fit the boys for the new school year.

"You'll let me go to *Selichos* with *Tatty*? O.K.?"

I was about to blurt a distracted O.K., as I measured his pants against a new pair. Then suddenly, his question penetrated my consciousness, and I dropped the pants.

"*Selichos*, Yitzy? Oh no, *Tzaddik*. *Selichos* is very early in the morning, when it's still dark outside. Little boys don't go to *Selichos*."

"But my *rebbi* said everybody has to say *Selichos*. We have to ask Hashem to forgive us for all our *aveiros*." His endearing smile of a minute ago was completely gone, and his face puckered in disappointment and indignation. I sensed a storm in the brewing.

"My *rebbi* said," he was plainly wailing, "*everybody* has to say *Selichos*!"

There was no arguing. His new *rebbi* was the last word in authority.

"Yitzy," I cupped his tearstained face in my hand, "ask your *rebbi* if 6-year-old *yingelach* go to *Selichos*. You can say *Selichos* at home if you want, or maybe your *rebbi* will say something with the class in *cheder*. And you know what?" I added brightly, trying to capitalize on his subsiding cries, "Maybe next year I'll let you go to *Selichos* with *Tatty* one morning!"

Yitzy's wailing stopped abruptly as he looked at me in utter astonishment. I was surprised myself. I hadn't expected to trigger such an instant turnabout.

"Next year?" he hiccuped, bewilderment all over his face, "My *rebbi* said every *Yid* has to do *teshuvah* and promise never, ever to do *aveiros* any more. How come we're gonna be saying *Selichos* again?"

How come? How come indeed? He looked at me waiting for an answer, and I hung my head in shame. How could I dash his little 6-year old perception of *teshuvah* as a dramatic one-time operation that effected everlasting results?

I must have offered some sort of evasive response that placated Yitzy for the time being. But I was left with his question reverberating in my soul. Oh sure, I was old enough to know all the answers. That with all our good will, and all our resolutions, *Teshuvah* was an ongoing, painstaking process for which we humans were allotted 120 years in this world. That refinement of the soul wasn't a job like repairing the refrigerator or exterminating roaches that came with a lifetime, or even a one-year, warranty.

Teshuvah was a dynamic process that occurred over days, nights, months, and years; a state of being whose goals shifted and changed ever so slightly from one *Rosh Hashanah* to the next. *Teshuvah* was not about never succumbing, but about washing our souls with true regret, and then hanging them in the sunshine of the *Ribono Shel Olam's* abounding *rachamim*. *Teshuvah* was about taking that new soul off the line, and yearning with every fiber of our being to retain its state of pristine perfection.

Still, the question he had so plainly posed had hit a sensitive spot. The fact that I was old enough to know the answer wasn't what bothered me. What hurt was the painful realization that I had lost the sincerity to have been able to consider the question; that the badge I so proudly sported as life experience had eroded my very basic belief in the power of *teshuvah*.

Teshuvah was an opportunity, and *teshuvah* was a commitment. *Teshuvah* meant believing that you could really change, and become a different person than you've ever been before. Even if you've tried unsuccessfully in the past. Even if you've made so many failed attempts to break away from that decadent behavior before. *Teshuvah* meant saying *Selichos* from within your heart, not your *siddur*. My son knew what *teshuvah* was about.

What about me? Did I really perceive the gravity of the pledge, or at least the burning desire, "never ever to do any *aveiros* any more"? Was I tossing in bed formulating my apologies, dreaming of the clean bill of spiritual health I'd soon be granted? Did I even have a clear idea of what it was I was planning to ask forgiveness for, exactly what kind of commitments I'd be promising in exchange for a *kesivah v'chasimah tovah*?

Or had I been standing like a passive observer in front of the conveyor belt of time, watching the *y'mei Selichos* come around the bend sandwiched in between the Three Weeks and *Yamim Noraim*, just as they'd appeared and vanished last year and the year before?

My son was a first-time voyager. He was simply awestruck by the idea of the early rising, the description of the subdued mood, the heartfelt apologies, and Hashem's gift of true forgiveness. Like a passenger in the baggage claims' terminal, he'd been waiting in suspense, squinting in anticipation for the trunk of *Selichos* to come his way. And when he'd spotted that promising speck advancing toward him, all his senses had become taut with anticipation to haul the treasure off the belt before it passed him by.

Simplicity. What a deceiving word.

And so I stand before the *y'mei Selichos* once more, and I can still see my son's big, questioning eyes before me, piercing my conscience, knocking my soul awake. My shiny resolutions of 12 months ago have become dented and faded; the perfect penmanship of those first crisp pages of 5762 have turned into a hurried, uneven scrawl. I am as in need of *selichah* and *mechilah* as I've ever been in the past.

And in my quest to grow older and wiser and better, I find myself praying to be imbued with a child's vision; to be granted the ability to shrink my horizons so that the past and future fade and I can view these priceless days of *teshuvah*, these cherished *yimei selichah u'mechilah* for what they are: a powerful and potent present.

Evening Espionage

"Are you looking for *Zutchka*?"

"Yes, yes," I replied hastily, instinctively retreating. I felt like a spy who'd been caught in the act, snooping as I'd been around the brush near a dilapidated little building on a side street in B'nei Brak. They had told me it would be the third building from the corner, on the left-hand side of the street, yet there was no clue; no sign above the entrance, no parking lot, no people.

I had warily approached the side steps, uneven, worn, stone steps that led to a small closed-in porch behind some untrimmed bushes. As I cranked open the old door, I knew I was in the right place; there were folding chairs leaning against one wall, and a table with some *siddurim* against the other. There was a *pushka* on the windowsill, and a sign tacked to the wall with the timetable for the upcoming *tefillos* during the *Yamim Noraim*. And there was the smell, that indefinable mixture of *sefarim* and wood and tea bags and damp towels.

I peeked through the sliding windows, looking in on the interior of the *shul*. It looked like a typical side-street *shtibel*. *Sefarim*-lined shelves, tables strewn with *siddurim*, a faded *paroches,* and a simple *bimah*. There was not a soul in sight.

I waited around in the fading daylight filtering in through the porch windows, feeling rather like an intruder. Shifting my weight from one foot to another, I scanned the notices on the bulletin board, trying to find some indication of what time *Maariv* was to begin.

Perhaps they didn't hold a *minyan* in the weekdays, the thought crossed my mind. The place seemed eerily silent, a million miles away from the center of the hectic metropolis just around the corner.

I wished I had been wearing a watch. Having just arrived from the hospital to the *Beit Hachlamah*, I had suddenly realized that I hadn't yet heard *Barchu*, (the prerequisite *tefillah* heard by a mother after birth before leaving her home). Remembering that I had to leave for the hospital again early the next morning, I had snatched my *siddur* and dashed out of the building, sure I was going to be late.

"I think there's a *minyan* at *Zutchka*," the receptionist had kindly called after me. "It's on the next street, third building to the left. You should be able to catch *Maariv* there."

So I had zipped down the street, and had arrived breathless, certain that I would be following a steady stream of *mispallelim* into the *shul*. It wasn't quite that way.

Here I was, the single congregant, waiting for someone, anyone, to appear. The initial relief of having made it in time was wearing off, giving way to definite unrest.

Perhaps she'd been mistaken, I thought, as I made my way down the steps and wavered near the bushes. I paused in my tracks, and rubbed my chin with my forefinger, trying to decide whether or not to hang around. That's just when the elderly man walked up the path and spotted me.

"You're looking for *Zutchka*?" he assessed.

And then, without waiting for an answer, he instructed, "Just wait there on the little porch. *Maariv* is about to begin."

I sighed with relief. Waiting is a funny thing. As long as you're unsure of your whereabouts, or that your timing is right, it can be one of the most anxiety-fraught activities. The minute you know you're stationed in the right place at the right time, it can be pleasurably relaxing. You turn your emotional motor off, and calmly observe the scenery, thrilled to be absolved from doing anything else in the world.

I opened a folding chair and found a perch near the window, where I could watch the goings-on in the main *shul*. The elderly man was sitting and humming over his open *siddur*. Some muffled conversation from the entrance heralded the arrival of the next few congregants. One of them took out his cell phone and switched it off. Two of the others took a *sefer* off the shelf, and entered into an animated discussion near another table.

A few more *mispallelim* trickled in, some in short jackets, some in long frocks, a small group of 11 or 12 people, fusing for a special event.

A *klap* on the *bimah*, and *Maariv* was underway.

I opened my *siddur*. The *shaliach tzibbur*, a slight, middle-aged man with a thin graying beard, intoned the words, slowly, pleasantly, his face flushed with warm enthusiasm.

"*Baruch Atah Hashem ...*
Asher bidvaro maariv aravim.
Bichachmah poseiach she'arim.
U'visvunah meshaneh itim.
Umachalif es hazmanim (Opening blessing of the *Maariv* prayers)."

He uttered each phrase separately, deliberately, as if he was composing the *tefillah* right then and there, as if he was practicing in private for a very personal speech he was going to deliver.

"Ahavas olam, Ay, ay, ay, ahavas olam!"

The *mispallelim* swayed along with the rendition, totally absorbed in every word. I sat huddled on the dark porch, eyes riveted to the men's section where a handful of men had converged on a very ordinary summer evening to pay homage to their Creator.

It was as if they'd staged the *davening* for me; as if they'd known someone was coming to eavesdrop, to look in from the window on their *Maariv* prayer. It was as if they were making a special effort to give it their all.

Shema.

Kaddish.

The scuffing of chairs against jaded tiles. Silence. A delicate, almost inaudible, filigree of whispers flitting over the slight rustle of frocks and jackets flapping to and fro. An eternity.

I tried to concentrate on every word. When was the last time I'd been afforded the leisure of standing by myself on a little porch in B'nei Brak at 6:30 in the evening, and *davening Maariv* along with a *minyan*?

I finished *Shemoneh Esrei*, and waited patiently. My eyes swiveled back to the window, to the light. One, two, three *mispallelim* stepped back. There was no impatient tapping, no hint of fidgeting; only the swish-swish of the rest of the congregants swaying interminably.

Time seemed to have been suspended in this little *Zutchka shtibel*. It was as if this *Maariv Amidah* was taking place in a vacuum, as if the *mispallelim* had not been coming from anywhere, and weren't headed anywhere.

I groped around my mind for the image to describe what I was feeling; for the metaphor to pin down the elusive brush of fragile sublimity that stroked my soul.

It was like trying to touch the transient beauty of iridescent soap bubbles.

This *minyan* seemed so far removed from anywhere I had ever been at 6:30 in the evening. It was far, far away from suppertime and bathwater. Far away from traffic lights and honking horns. Far away from closing stores and neon signs and the smell of falafel. It was the like *Shabbos*, like *Ne'ilah*, like the *siyum HaShas*.

But it wasn't Shabbos, and it wasn't *Ne'ilah*, and it wasn't the *siyum HaShas*. It was a plain old Monday evening in a plain old *Zutchka shtibel*, on a plain old street in B'nei Brak. It was no crowd to rave about, no roaring *Amen* to shake anyone out of his sleep. It was the sweet simplicity of it, the peaceful pace of it, the natural ordinariness, that made it so remarkable.

These men hadn't run out to *"chap a minyan."* They weren't ripping through the *tefillah* to get over with it, to get back onto their cell phones, to hurry home before their suppers grew cold. They had gone out to *daven* the way people go out to eat; with anticipation and appetite. No matter that they'd done it hundreds of times in the past. They were savoring the words of the *tefillah*, relishing each morsel, licking their plates clean.

The way they'd done yesterday. And the day before. Tomorrow they would be here again. *I* wouldn't be here, but they would. They'd be hungry, these men in the little *Zutchka shtibel*.

I was glad now, that I hadn't brought my watch. It would have spoiled the experience, tampered with the otherworldly aura pervading the dark porch on this Monday evening in *Elul*. Six remaining men swayed timelessly to the worn words of the *Maariv Shemoneh Esrei*. The clock would wait. These men had to finish their portions.

Next week this little porch would be suffused with light, packed with women coming to hear the *shofar*, coming to listen to the words of *U'nesaneh Tokef*. They would weep. They would sway. They would hear the *chazzan* and feel the tremor and watch a sea of men clad in white.

But they wouldn't see what I had seen, alone, on an ordinary Monday night.

They wouldn't hear the echoes that followed me home, that reverberate in my heart, forever.

Yisgadal V'Yiskadash Shmei Rabba.

Life Without the Bones

"I wouldn't mind doing *sponga*,"
said 12-year-old Dina
to me one day,
"if I didn't have
all the bothersome stuff
to handle,
the chairs to pick up
the plant to slide aside,
slippers on the floor
doll carriages in the way."
Yeah, I know,
me too,
I wouldn't mind cleaning
for *Pesach*,
I wouldn't mind a bit,
if I didn't have to stop
and serve lunch
and fold laundry,
and wash the table
from supper,
in between.

I wouldn't mind
holding the baby
until 4 o'clock

in the morning
if I didn't need my wits
the next day,
to write *mitzvah* notes,
and find hair clips,
wake up Dovy for *minyan*
and keep the smile
on my face,
and in my heart
when he pouts,
or shouts,
"It's all because
Mommy
woke me up
10 minutes late."

Oh no,
I wouldn't mind
doing all the big things
in life,
if someone
got all those little things,
out of the way.
Believe me,
I'd learn *mussar* all day,
engage in *kiruv*,
embark on missions
of truth
and kindness,
If somebody
got the little stuff out of the way,

But no one ever volunteered.

Who wants to do
the little things,
when there are big things
to be accomplished?
Who wants to be busy
with what's in the way,
when they can
just as well
be getting places?
So I wink at Dina,
And say,
"Oh yes,
Wouldn't that be just great?"

"Hmm."
"Except,"
she adds
thoughtfully,
"in a home
without
chairs,
and plants,
and slippers,
and toys,
I guess
you wouldn't have to
wash the floor."
Yeah,
I'll second that,
In a life
without,
interruptions,
and sleep deprivation,
and messes to mess with,

and tempers to temper,
I guess
you wouldn't have to
learn *mussar.*

$\mathcal{F}$ollow up | |

It happened in South Africa, to an ordinary woman, or perhaps not so ordinary. If the things that happen to people are
any indication of their inner composition, then I suppose extraordinary would describe our protagonist well.

Walking the streets of South Africa after twilight unaccompanied
is like putting one's life on sale in the front page of the paper. Not that
daylight is much of a deterrent for the bloodthirsty ruffians roaming
the neighborhood. During the daytime, however, life must go on, and
people dart through their daily routine with one eye over their shoulder,
breathing an audible sigh of relief when they arrive home unharmed.

Nighttime is quite another story. The blazing pool of color streak-
ing the sky at dusk seems to blow the whistle for all the hooligans
to come out of their cracks and mingle with the ebony darkness
enveloping the streets and alleys. Hardly anyone steps foot out of
doors after nightfall of his or her own volition. And when it is absolutely unavoidable, a nighttime venture is carried out with no small
amount of trepidation.

The heroine of our story had an important errand to run one evening, a *mitzvah* that could not be delayed. Defying the terrifying blackness and the heaviness in her heart, she donned her coat, kissed the *mezuzah*, and set out on her way. Her sense of mission propelled her forward despite the overwhelming magnet of fear drawing her back to the safe confines of her home. As she turned out of the street where she lived, she tried to still her pounding heart, to focus inward and block out the raucous sounds reverberating in the distance.

One more step, she willed herself, the way she would coax a toddler stalling on the sidewalk, one more step. Then she changed the chorus. I'm on my way to take care of a *dvar mitzvah*. A *mitzvah*, a *mitzvah*, the words seemed to echo with her brisk step, reverberating in her mind, slowly prying open her brain's petrified grip on the all-consuming dread.

And then she saw him. A two-legged savage charging in her direction. There was no mistaking the bloodshed in his eyes, the murderous intent in his menacing swagger. Her heart stopped. Her blood ran cold, as her mind searched crazily for some cue. All it could muster, like a computer program gone berserk, was a garbled blur of indecipherable thoughts that kept growing alarmingly more garbled and alarmingly more indecipherable. Like a postoperative patient battling with the effects of anesthesia, she felt her mind floating somewhere outside of her body, in a kind of detached numbness brought on by the paralyzing terror.

And then, at once, she felt the blood rush to her head, as if someone had untied the tourniquet stanching the flow of coherent thought between her heart and mind. Like a tape recorder after a blackout, her mind resumed just where it had left off: a *dvar mitzvah*, a *dvar mitzvah*. You're on your way to take care of a *dvar mitzvah*. On their own, her lips began feverishly whispering, "*Miyemini Michael, mismoli Gavriel, u'milfanai Uriel, u'me'achorai Refael, v'al roshi Shechinas Keil.*"

Ribono Shel Olam, her heart pleaded as she donned a mask of fearlessness and forced her feet forward, "You know I never would have ventured out into this lion's den were it not for my desire to fulfill Your will. Nothing is beyond You; please spare me from a horrible end." She fixed her eyes on a spot in the distant horizon, and kept repeating the *pasuk* that had sprung to her lips, "*Miyemini Michael* ...."

A shadow flitted over her, as the monster in flesh passed right by her, almost brushing against her sleeve. Her blood froze again, as the heavy sound of his breathing vied with the wild hammering of her heart, and then she almost collapsed with sheer relief. He was gone, past her, his hefty footsteps receding into the infinity behind her back. She could wake up from the nightmare and stretch her taut muscles.

Or so she thought. Not three minutes had passed when she heard bloodcurdling screams rip the night air. At first she thought it was her traumatized mind playing tricks, but from the shrill cries reaching a crescendo, and then fading into the night, she knew that an attack had taken place not very far behind her. She didn't dare turn her head, but kept moving her legs mechanically, desperate to be out of the radius of the heinous scene.

When she saw the notice in the paper a few days later, she knew she had been spared from certain death. "Anybody with any leads attached to the murder that took place on Tuesday, November 3, on ... Street, at 8:57 in the evening, is requested to appear at the local precinct for questioning."

Her body gave an involuntary shudder. She had brushed right past a murderer, wriggled right out of death's clamp. She had witnessed a miracle. She would report.

At the station, two burly officers listened carefully to the description of her encounter, sizing up the woman in front of them. "Can you point to the assailant?" they asked her, presenting her with a poster of a dozen or so faces, all of them obvious portraits of brutes.

Without a moment's hesitation, she pointed to the face that had loomed a few yards from her on that fateful night. The officers nodded silently. From her demeanor, they had surmised this woman's tale was credible.

"You had a real miracle, ma'am."

No other word would do.

The following week, she appeared in court at the trial. When she was done with her testimony, it was her turn to pose a question; a thought that had begun to nag at her as she had related the narrative in the courtroom. Why had the murderer gone right past her if murder had been his obvious intent? What had made him swoop down on the next object of human prey, when she had so conspicuously intercepted his path? A miracle was her only viable explanation; how would the murderer explain it?

"That woman?" the convict asked, incredulous, when the judge posed her question, "You've got to be kidding. She was flanked by two armed fellows; I wasn't gonna start up with *her*."

Thus the story circulated in Yerushalayim, the echoes from Cape Town reverberating in the holy city and then bouncing as far as Beit Shemesh, Kiryat Sefer, B'nei Brak, Tel Aviv, and Ashdod. Its drama has charged many a *shiur* like an electric current, inducing goose bumps and shudders, sparking smiles of amazement and pride. But I'm sorry to tell you, and I *truly* am, it seems to be a fable.

I can almost hear the collective groan playing back my own cry of disappointed protest when phone call after expectant phone call left me dangling the end of the rope. It was all I could do to blink in disbelief at the dissolution of so promising a matter.

This was the second time I had lost my breath over the story; the first had been upon hearing it at all, and now, on account of hearing that it probably hadn't been at all.

Oh sure, there had been a woman who had nearly been assaulted, and yes, she'd been miraculously spared as she fervently recited *"miyemini Michael …,"* perhaps some suspicious report of a murder could even be ambiguously linked to that incident, but the whole fanciful part, the part that raised people's eyebrows (either in awe or skepticism,) and took one's breath away, had apparently been frills fashioned by some creative mind. For as hard as I tried to pursue the source of these remarkable details, it eluded me like a magnet being chased by another.

And then the thought dawned on me. I could still skip, solo, in the rope, even if no one was holding the other end to turn it into that sensational game. What was wrong with the story undergoing a metamorphosis and becoming a fable, a legend, a piece of fiction that wasn't really any bit stranger than the unadorned truth?

Why was it of such dire consequence to me to *know* whether that thug saw the accompanying angels, when I allegedly knew since kindergarten that, *"ki malachav yitzaveh lach lishmarcha b'chol d'rachecha"*? What had been the earth-shattering *chiddush*, the incredulous element of chilling surprise, when all I had heard was the belief I carry around with me, mirrored in actual reality?

Evidently it was the mirror that had startled me, though I preferred to think that it was the glimpse of His image that I had seen in its reflection. Didn't I remind my children several times each day that the seemingly simple *mitzvos* they performed were creating *malachim*, guardian angels?

Had I been paying lip service to a fundamental tenet of *Yiddishkeit*, unwittingly relegating angels to the esoteric realm, something apart from down-to-earth, everyday existence? I'd been reminding my progeny, but I guess I wasn't beyond needing a reminder myself.

So now that I've given up on my wild-goose chase, now that I've left the last discouraging lead in Cape Town, and resumed living on my own continent, I've decided it doesn't really matter. I've been splashed with the cold water, shaken out of my humdrum performance of *mitzvos*, confronted with the very tangible awareness that each time we act as emissaries of The One Above, we merit celestial protection.

A good story provides new inspiration for an old aspiration, and if this fantasy has been the catalyst to bring a forgotten truth to life, well then, fable or fabrication, I think it's justified its existence.

Generation Gap

It hits me every time I arrive home in America. Actually a lot of things hit me. There's nothing like reentering an environment you've been stranger to long enough for people to raise their eyebrows when you say "home," to render you more keenly cognizant of subtle changes that have taken place over time. Sometimes those subtle changes are within one's self, sometimes they're manifest in the surroundings, but always there are the changes, for better or for worse.

It might be the six-family complex that has suddenly arisen, where my memory sees a pastel green Colonial encircled by untrimmed rhododendron bushes, or the newest glosses to "Bais Yaakov's Revised Edition of Teenage English." Whatever it is, visiting my hometown, following a considerable absence, always spawns substantial material for small talk and broad speculation.

What I'm particularly pondering in this instance is something more self-contained; something that has less to do with the economy and the infrastructure and the local fads, and more to do with my personal upbringing. Upon stepping over the threshold of the home where I grew up, I am overtaken by the vague sentiment of beholding a somewhat distorted reflection of my memories, as if my home has turned into one of those entertaining mirrors that casts back an image one recognizes, quite dramatically altered.

After the initial perusal of the house and some enthusiastic remarks over the new bedspread in the "boys room," and the blinds that my mother has finally seen fit to replace after 20-some years of living in the home where they were originally part of the package deal, it always begins.

"Ma, *what* in the world is Dovid eating?"

"Oh, don't ask. It's the latest *shtick* in nosh. It's called a paintbrush, and Dovid chose it as a prize for his learning tickets."

"Huh?"

Now don't get me wrong. It's not that I don't know what a paintbrush is. You can accuse Eretz Yisrael of not being up to par with dress or with nutrition, of being too crowded, or warm blooded. One thing the "Land flowing with milk and honey" is not to be charged with, however, is lack of the latter in its incarnated version. The baby's bottles are a colorful array of red, orange or brown (cola, not tea), and the kids' sandwiches are piled with a thick layer of chocolate spread, *halvah* for the real health minded. So I know what a paintbrush is.

What I'm gawking at is its appearance within the fortified walls of my parents' home on an ordinary Monday afternoon. Back when I grew up, and of course Dovid is out of earshot sooner than these words can create any cognitive dissonance for him, nary a potato chip was available for consumption once *Havdalah* had been recited. Forget about lollies, caramel bars, and the rest of that sticky junk. It was potato chips, popcorn, and wafers for *Shabbos*, and on occasion, for *Shabbos Chol HaMoed* or something, there were M&M's (Shufra's probably, but the name stuck), sesame candies, or something really far out, like jelly rings or bar-b-q corn chips.

Of course there was always plenty of good old delicious home-made cake, which there still is. Some things, fortunately, don't change. But again, it was strictly relegated for *Shabbos*, or a *siyum* or a birthday. With the exception of chocolate chip-cookies and marble cake that accompanied our apple a day and carefully wrapped sandwich replete with cut-up vegetables.

Which reminds me of the brown bags. "Ma," I call from the kitchen, "I'll fix the kids' snacks. Just tell me where you keep the used brown bags these days."

I hear the chuckle all the way up from the laundry room. It's a good sound track for the bewildered look in Dovid's pupils, as he eyes his married sister from Eretz Yisrael with her outmoded ideas.

"Never mind," dismisses my mother, over the steady sound of the scrub brush attacking white collars with gusto. As I said, some things don't change. "We don't do that anymore. Just take a new bag, and let him '*tzureiss gezunteheit*' (tear it in good health)."

No problem. It's just that recycling brown bags was such an integral part of our growing up. You took the bag with your goodies to school, and at the end of the day, you brought it home carefully folded, because it was, after all, a good brown bag. There was always the debate if the individually packed snacks should or shouldn't be labeled for easy identification, given the fact that labels later greatly encumbered the recycling system. But the bags always came back, and if they didn't, their absence elicited a slight shadow of disappointment, quickly eclipsed by a smiling reminder to "Please remember tomorrow."

It isn't only the snack bags, inside or out, which jar me out of the nostalgic cloud of *deja vu* that has comfortably settled over me. It's the ease with which Dovid wriggles free of taking out the garbage, or the noticeably thinned list of chores expected from Chany on *Erev Shabbos*, both of these observations true despite the vacuum left by the transfer of the more able bodied troops to their own homes abroad.

Forget about my father's newly acquired knowledge of Lego building systems, or my mother's informed opinion of Hi Beary stationery and stickers. I still didn't quite catch on to the points system, or what did Dovid call it, tickets? All I know is that the cash they accrue on a pretty constant basis surpasses, by a considerable amount, the sum of our joint *Chanukah gelt* account of times bygone. (The money, however, is still kept in an envelope in my mother's top drawer for safekeeping, and can be withdrawn only after careful consideration, which makes for a surge of that fond sense of familiarity.)

I'm not alone in my sentiment. Friends of mine share my amusement at their parents' mellowed stand, at the tardy bedtimes enjoyed by their younger siblings, or the filed-down table manners; at the doting packages to the *bachur* in yeshivah or the unlimited spending money for the seminary student, depending on the age and gender of the lucky youngest.

When I remark to either of my parents, in feigned indignation, that at Chany's age I was expected to walk the distance to day camp in the sweltering heat, or that at Dovid's stage, the older boys did the weekly grocery shopping, and returned on foot (without protest) if an item had to be exchanged, they smile in a mixture of resignation, indulgence, and wisdom that, I suppose, comes with age.

"What do you expect?" they chide, laughingly. "There are changes only a *ben zekunim* can affect. Times have changed, children have changed, *we've* changed, and like Dovid says, "You should see what the *other* kids have in their snacks!'"

I chuckle, and secretly, I feel condoned for the lenient attitude I wield, where discipline with my own charges is concerned. More than that, though, I feel exonerated on a deeper level. I feel a surge of relief wash over me with the realization that we, as a collective *ben zekunim*, have a case to present in *Shamayim* these days.

In these times, when I, in my little cocoon, innocently wrap avocados in newspaper, and am rudely reminded that we are living atop a volcanic mountain; when I gaily greet my troopers piling in from school, and am informed that "Ma, there was an air-raid drill, and we had to go single file through the window into the *miklat*"; in this choking era, when the smoke of *milchemes* (war of) *Gog uMagog* assails us as we do the most ordinary things a person could be doing, there is a line of defense in our favor.

No, we are not nearly as righteous as the generations preceding us. We fall hopelessly short where our spiritual callings are concerned, and are smothered with material bounty. We can only imagine what our "siblings" from some centuries back would offer as commentary were they allowed entry unto this earth; what they would think of our alleged *histapkus b'muat*, and our *yiras Shamayim*, and our *chavivus hamitzvos*.

And sometimes we, in the privacy of our hearts, despair. If our ancestors, with their inconceivable suffering and their pure prayers and their zealous learning untainted by personal motives, if *they* haven't gotten us out of this *galus*, how can we, so miserably wanting, ever hope to affect a response?

But our *Tatte* looks at us differently. He is "*meshaneh es ha'itim u'machalif es hazmanim*," so He knows more than we do, that times have changed, and along with them, so have the children. And He knows something else. He sees what the rest of the world is toting in their snack bags.

So, as the threads of history are being twisted and turned in preparation for the final knot, let's not underestimate the impact of our *tefillos* and *maasim tovim*, pitiful as they appear in contrast to those of *Yidden* in times bygone. There's a different rating chart, a tender spot, reserved for the *ben zekunim*, and as any parent (and older sibling) can testify, it's not to be made light of.

Sole Searching

Packing for Eretz Yisrael,
"These will be for Yom Kippur,"
I had said,
gingerly stuffing
the snow-white canvas sneakers.
But that was before I knew about
sponga.

In Eretz Yisrael —
"All you need is a good pair of *sponga* shoes."
She had said,
Consciously eyeing
The snow-white
Canvas sneakers.

I swallowed my resolution.
Yom Kippur was so far away.
I'll worry then —
About later.
I donned the shoes
With just a twinge
Of fleeting regret,
And before I knew it —
The white canvas
Was sloshing in pools
Of dirty water,
Sopping the brown suds off my floor.
Once.

Twice.
Three times.
I ought to wash them,
I thought,
More than once,
As I watched my snow-white sneakers
Turn light brown.

Sivan.
Tammuz.
Av.
Elul!
A far-away memory
Flickered in my mind,
About brand-new
Snow-white
Shoes for *Yom Kippur.*
But with *Erev Yom Tov*
And all that extra grime,
My sneakers barely had
a telltale trace of white —
on the inside.
"Who ever said *sponga* shoes
can't be *Yom Kippur* shoes?"
I had said,
But that was before I tried washing them.
Now it was
Erev Yom Kippur.

I tosssed them
Into the washing machine.
Easy — I thought,
In and out.
Just like that.

Automatic.
But it wasn't quite that way.
They came out
Not actually black —
But faded brown wasn't quite
What I'd had in mind for *Yom Kippur*
Either.
Out came the bleach,
The wool whitener,
The "Easy off"
Anything that smelled of a promise
To make white
White again.
But no magic
Would make my sneakers look new
One night before *Yom Kippur,*
When they'd been wading in mud
For half a year's time.

Time's elapsed,
And I haven't come
Such a long way
Since,
But I've bought a new pair
Of sneakers,
And I've learned a thing or two
About "soles."

Playing Cat and Mouse

*M*y computer and I enjoy a nice civil relationship. We try to live in peace with each other, without getting too intimate for comfort.

Like a polite neighbor, I care to know only as much about it as our direct working relationship requires. And so, I am perfectly comfortable with my typing ability, and my usage of the mouse to get me in and out of the program I need. Other than that, I am in blissful oblivion to the rest of the workings of the computer's brilliant mind.

"Come on, why don't you enroll for a course on the basics of word processing?" friends have cajoled me once and again. "What can you lose? You'll learn the basics. You don't have to become a programmer, but you've got to know the basics."

All their attempts, however, went over my head, or under my motivation level. Like I said, I was very complacent with things just the way they were. I've always had a sort of mental block when it came to technical instructions, and it made me feel constricted just to imagine all those codes and directives to follow.

I was the type of person who'd get lost, and then get even more lost trying to follow the directions I was given. I usually preferred to ask for directions at each red light. Then I'd look back in embarrassment, hoping my previous benefactor hadn't been close enough behind to have seen my window roll down again.

So when it came to computers, I was going to do it my way, the easy way, the hard way, however you wanted to put it. As long as it was the unfettered, spontaneous way that didn't dictate a whole set of ominous rules for me to stick to.

And it worked pretty well for pretty long. That is, until my devoted mouse died on me. Over and out. There was no reviving it. I tried clicking, rolling, shaking, and even talking to the mouse. It was an effort in futility. The screen stared at me, waiting for my next directive. I had none. I only wanted out. Let me just shut this thing until I get hold of a new mouse.

Even the simple step of closing the computer, though, was fraught with fear of the unknown with my loyal mouse out of working order. Reminded of the fable in my second-grade reader, I felt very much like the humbled lion, suddenly made aware of how dependent on, beholden to, completely vulnerable I was, without the little creature.

My hands darted over the buttons of the cordless phone beside me. Chany knew the control buttons well enough to direct me out of this mess. All I wanted was to get out of the program and shut the computer. That shouldn't take too much time.

If you knew how to proceed, that was. But I didn't. And Chany wasn't answering. And Yocheved wasn't home. I even gambled and called Brochy overseas, but her cheery recording knew nothing of mouseless computers.

There I was, at 11:30 at night, staring bleary eyed at the unblinking screen. I was tempted to wish it a good night and leave it to its own devices. If not for my toddler's affinity for the computer, and his curiosity of how the keyboard operated, I would definitely have done just that.

But my little one started his workday at 6 o'clock, was out of the crib and going strong at 6:10, and was bound to have some very serious damage done by about 6:12.

This is going to be fun, I thought, as I willed myself to think logically.

There's no way to think logically, though, when you don't know the logic. My friend's prodding reverberated in my ears as I tried to recall what she had once said about precisely such a situation.

No, one minute, here was a key dubbed, "End". That sounded right. Tap, tap, tap, BANG! My frustration mounted. Alt plus Shift. Shift plus Enter. Alt F3. Shift, Alt, F2. Bleep. The screen blinked something in recognition of my efforts. I was glad to see a change, any change, and my eyes quickly scanned the toolbar. "Help". That definitely sounded like something I needed. Desperately.

How did I *get* the help, though? This daunting world of technology! Help was on the horizon, I could touch it with my index finger, and yet with a broken mouse, I had no way of reaching it. Some more guesses. Another couple of tries. Back to the cordless. Chany, Yocheved, Brochy. Eleven fifty eight. Desperation.

Had I wanted to learn by trial and error, the, the- what had I called it? The unfettered spontaneous way? Well, right now, if there was no other word for it, I felt utterly fettered. I knew there was a way out of this maze, a laughably simple formula that probably took two seconds to execute, and here I was, sweating in my seat, eyes stinging from tiredness, in the name of spontaneity.

I don't even know what worked in the end. It was some last ditch effort at hitting a combination of keys I thought I had already tried. In an instant, my friendly computer charmingly blinked the familiar choice of "Open," "Close," "Reenter."

"Oh, so that's what you wanted?" the screen seemed to chuckle, "Why didn't you say so?" And I, almost crying with relief, got the thing to retire for the night.

It was only later in bed, wrapped in that semi-conscious blanket of blurred reality, that I found my mind toying with a memory I had almost forgotten.

I had just completed a correspondence course, and policy required me to come down in person to receive my term paper from the professor who had graded my work. I was sitting opposite the professor's desk, as he reread something he had jotted on the top of my paper. Then he handed the sheaf to me, complimented me on my well-researched writing, and pointed to the third page, where I had cited something from *Tanach*.

"I don't believe in that stuff."

"Oh?" I raised an eyebrow in response.

"Da ma l'hashiv l'apikores", had always been somewhat of a philosophical issue in my education. I had never thought of *Chazal's* dictum in actual, practical terms. But here I was, face-to-face with an honest-to-goodness specimen.

"I once saw a two word bumper sticker," he pronounced smugly, "that encapsulates my approach to life." And before I had a chance to back off, to retreat, to politely end the conversation, the professor boomed his two-word philosophy, his life's charter: "Challenge authority!"

"Try out all the options. Don't take any rule as a given. You're a free man. Why live under the constraints of all those rules and regulations, stifling your freedom, when you can have your rights, your options ..."

Not knowing what *Yiddishkeit* demanded of me at that point, I tried to play it safe. Displaying blatant disagreement, I tactfully steered the conversation to an end.

Something about my experience with the computer had jarred the distant memory out of my psyche. I suddenly saw the entire world scheme shrink into the size and shape of a computer screen, and somehow my own figure in front of it turned into a silhouette of that skeptical professor, in a frantic attempt to man his life freely, unconstrained, with all the options open.

Freedom, trial and error, enlightenment. It all sounded tantalizing in a lecture, on paper, as a logo chanted by a mob in the name of democracy. Not when one came to realize that one's life was an all encompassing computer, whose every directive had been preprogrammed by its Creator.

Having every option open essentially meant having none. It meant wasting a life, playing a frustrating guessing game, when the simple instructions that empowered the universe were clear and accessible for all those who cared enough to follow.

There were 613 codes to world processing, and those who were too enlightened to take heed of them were reduced to living life on a toddler's level of keyboard banging in an effort to elicit some progress, some meaning, on the screen.

I had experienced the effects of this kind of "liberation" for a few moments. Believe me, it had been difficult enough to shut down that way. To begin, to live, to grow would be utterly inconceivable.

Active Listening

veryone has his own associations of *Purim*. To some, it's stage makeup and fuzzy beards, canes and glasses, earrings and capes. To others, it's cellophane and ribbons, *hamantashen*, chocolates and pineapples. To almost everyone, it's the traditional *Purim* tunes blaring loudly from passing cars, that unique admixture of merriment and sanctity, of chaos and joy.

Purim, for me, has another dimension, a dimension intertwined with the image of my grandmother. Each year, as I label wine bottles and curl ribbons, sew some last touches onto a costume, and sweep up little bits of cellophane, I feel a sense of nostalgia creeping up on me.

I can almost smell *Taanis Esther* in my parents' home, the meat roasting for the *Purim seudah*, the pastries set out festively in the dining room, silver or iridescent bags lined up in neat rows on the dinette table. I can vividly recapture the mounting sense of anticipation, can hear my mother call from somewhere, presumably the guest room downstairs, "I think I hear Mr. Roth!"

That would be a cue for all of us to go scrambling outside, down the wooden steps, onto the driveway, where Mr. Roth's van would be pulled up, back doors flung open. There stood my grandmother, elegantly tall as always, *sheitel* untouched from the journey, blue eyes sparkling with exuberance, as she smiled her hello, and warmly thanked Mr. Roth for the ride. Within moments, Babi's baggage would be whisked out of the back compartment and the doors slammed shut.

We would each receive a kiss, not a peck-on-the-cheek formality, but a zestful exclamation of her love that came along with a passionate squeeze and a giggle of glee. As if the scene had been rehearsed, Babi would lift the tall tin can holding her *hamantashen*, and a procession of proud followers trailed after her, carrying her *sheitel* box and pocketbook and the rest of her personal items.

I can almost feel the cool shiny touch of the navy nylon garment bag draped over my arm as I mounted the steps in delicious wordlessness, stepping in time to the reassuring click-click of my grandmother's polished shoes. It was a quiet kind of excitement that hugged us together then as we welcomed my grandmother in a ceremony of reverence and love.

The first thing she would unpack were her reading glasses, set out on the buffet together with her *Megillas Esther*. There was an excitement that accompanied this little act, a quiver of delight reminiscent of our own barely restrained anticipation as we rearranged our costumes on the dresser near our beds.

Then there would be the arrangements, the decisions of who would stay home to baby-sit, and who would accompany Babi to *Megillah leining*. There was the flurry of last-minute activity, pulling out *megillos* from the shelves in the boys' room closet, the closing of lights, lowering of flames.

And then I'd be alone with Babi, walking alongside her in the crisp evening air, my hand encircled in her firm clasp. I kept my eyes on her quick, long strides swallowing up the gray pavement of the steep incline, as I panted to keep up with her brisk pace. It was an invigorating experience, half walking, half running under the starry sky, reveling in my grandmother's secure presence as we brushed past the swishing satin of an occasional proud *kallah* on her way to *shul*.

I can almost hear the creaking of the flimsy gold folding chairs, with their graying off-white vinyl upholstery, scraping against the worn parquet floor as the last latecomers wove their way to their seats. I can feel the hush that swept the packed little room, can hear the shifting and rustling and then the emphatic clap introducing the *berachos*.

Eleven years old again, I am listening to the sweet melodious voice of the *baal koreh*, my eyes sneaking out of the small print to study the fascinating ensembles around me.

And suddenly, there would be a lull in the rendition, a pause that was quickly filled with hurried whispers as women and girls traditionally intoned the next few words ahead of the *baal koreh*. All, that is, but one. My grandmother was apparently in no rush; neither did she seem to perceive the unspoken convention that the words be recited inaudibly.

"Ish Yehudi hayah beShushan habirah, u'shemo Mordechai ben Yair ben Shimi, ben Kish, ish Yemini!"

She read the words loudly, dramatically, giving character to each syllable, as befit the first piece of foreshadowing in a spectacular story. All eyes turned, or so I felt, in my flush of embarrassment to be the center of attraction in the packed room. I glanced quickly at my grandmother, to check her reaction.

She seemed completely unfazed, unaware even, of the diversion she had created in the small women's section. Her eyes were riveted to the text, index finger carefully following each word, clearly entranced by the unfolding drama.

I would barely manage to regain my composure, when *Haman* would make his grand entrance. There was some imperceptible rapping on the tables and floor by the women, and the deafening cacophony of whooping and clicking from the junior division. It took a while for the *gabbai* to reinstate order. I was glad.

Only the people sitting in my immediate vicinity were witness to the passionate vengeance that fueled my grandmother's vehement stamping at the mention of the cursed Amalekite. Hers wasn't your ladylike tapping, a formal curtsey to tradition. Hers was a spontaneous venting of fury, a deep personal expression of hatred for *Haman*, for *Amalek* and all his henchmen throughout history.

I was too young back then, to appreciate, even to realize this. All I remember was feeling positively awkward, desperately hoping that my friends hadn't seen us coming into *shul* together. Couldn't my grandmother just keep it low key like all the staid adults crowding the room?

My grandmother, though, oblivious to my self-conscious blushing, oblivious actually, to anything around her, didn't harbor a thought of keeping it low key. Why, this was high drama! She persisted with her zealous stomping each time *Haman's* name was mentioned, and was fairly aglow as she exclaimed a fiery *"LaYehudim hoysah orah v'simchah v'sasson v'ykor!"*

Squirming in my seat, all I wanted was to disappear.

Time has a way of editing emotions. Sometimes it's the objectivity created by distance, but more often it's the unfolding of the little pleats of life that spin a more flexible fabric, a richer and deeper tapestry of feeling. Looking back at the annual *megillah* experience under the spotlight of adulthood, I am overawed by the magnificence of it, the simple, startling beauty of it.

My grandmother wasn't part of our anesthetized society. She wasn't numbed against pain, or hardship. And she wasn't desensitized to beauty. Her *megillah leining* was the microcosm of her *Yiddishkeit;* alive and vibrant, completely independent of sidelong glances and thoughts of conforming to socially set norms. She had a way of preserving her enthusiasm, of breathing life into her actions, into her words, the words she uttered and the words she listened to.

She was never one to march along to the beat of some anonymous trumpet blower, to hop aboard the bandwagon of accepted practice. She retained a fresh outlook on life, kept the fire burning to keep it piping hot, and if need be, threw a few towels over her to keep the cold air out. She lived life the way she listened to the *megillah*, always looking inside; never looking around.

The way I do. The way we do. The way, judging by the pages and pages of full-color advertisements for *Purim*, many of us do. *Purim* has become a contest of themes and styles, a synonym for elaborate arrangements and expensive gifts. We've almost forgotten the *Hamantashen*. Never mind *Haman*.

Purim, the way we celebrate it today, has become a member of the masquerade. I think my grandmother would be hard put to recognize it. We are so busy outdoing and overdoing, who has time to do? We are so preoccupied thinking of themes; who has any head left to ponder the theme of *Purim*?

Pictures change colors over time. So do memories. Holding that photograph in my mind, a little girl of 10 or 11 sitting near her grandmother, I can feel myself flushing with shame once again. This time though, it is for the woman that has become of the little girl, a woman who just barely keeps her eyes open to the fine print of the *megillah*, a woman who looks around more than she would like to.

A woman who gives a halfhearted rattle to the sound of *Haman*, and just barely stops to mumble, *"Ish Yehudi hayah beShushan habirah ..."* She's tired, you've got to understand. She's been busy with *Purim*.

No condemnations here; they say ours is a weak generation. It is. So let's preserve our energy. Let's stop expending so much of our physical and mental resources looking over our shoulder. Perhaps if we won't be so preoccupied trying to come up with an original idea, we won't lose sight of the original idea.

Business Bargain

"Hein gaalti eschem acharis k'reishis l'hiyos lachem l'Elokim"

When I first came
    to these shores,
    young,
    idealistic,
    naive, if you will,
    I looked for the closets,
    They laughed,
    Closets!
    They don't *come*,
    Nothing comes,
    You've got to order them,
    So I did.

    I ordered a wardrobe,
    to fit inside my room,
    seven doors,
    pearly-white finish,
    plenty of hanging space,
    And oh, yes,
    how much will that be?

    Good little girl,
    I counted out
    every last penny,
    4200 *shekels*.
    Wondered why the carpenter

and his apprentice,
looked at each other,
funny,
as I handed them the money.

American greenhorn,
newlywed optimist,
trusting baby,
never dreamed
of withholding the cash
until I saw that closet
safely through my door.

Well,
they had a heyday,
of a payday,
and I had a shock
when my closet
finally
arrived,
badly scratched
Formica mismatched,
wrong hinges on the doors,
shelves
where I'd ordered drawers,
but honey,
they had their money,
they had it all,
I could have spoken
to the wall.

Life
made me wiser
turned me into

a hardened miser,
I've learned to
insist,
hold a tight fist,
Show me my order,
I say,
and I'll pay
every last penny,
bring me those knobs,
the hinges,
the shelf
and I'll see to release the bills.
myself.

If there's one rule,
In business,
It's goods before gold,
product before payment.
No one,
NO ONE,
pays
in full,
up front.

No one,
but One.
He did it once,
took us out of the depths,
across the sea,
A whole nation
of impoverished paupers,
not a penny in advance
did He receive,
only our word,

our promise,
did He go by,
blindly believe.

No businessman
would have done
what He did,
Cold Cash,
He counted out.
Ten plagues,
fifty each,
on land,
two hundred and fifty,
at sea,
A blind loan,
Not even a bank account
did we own.

Newlywed optimists,
we defied all the skeptics,
Made good
on our promise,
Came through
with our word,
Believe me,
He got goods,
Some goods!
Sturdy, steadfast,
Waterproof,
Fireproof,
Bulletproof,
More than He ever
bargained for.

And now
Those goods have dwindled,
We sit
like kings,
at our *Seder* tables,
but He knows,
We've been through rough times,
We're at rock bottom,
cleaned out,
the way we were
when we first struck the deal,
Nothing but our word,
Nothing but our plea.

Hein gaalti,
You've delivered us once,
Bailed us out,
A nation on the verge
Of bankruptcy,
You've delivered us once,
Haven't You found
It was a profitable business
The last time around?

You split the sea,
but we jumped right in,
Followed You
through thick and thin.

That was years ago,
and we're still holding on,
Still rejoicing
Still relating
Your kindness,

Floundering,
But still afloat.

That was years ago,
but we're still holding on,
Groping,
Grabbing,
Grasping,
Our sole standing chance,
One final endowment,
Of cash in advance.

No Strings Attached

*L*ately, we're into *gevurah* around this house.

It comes in phases and stages, the sudden impetus to apply more than just a stopgap Band-Aid onto any one of the chronic ailments afflicting my household. There can be bickering going on for weeks, or whining, or dawdling, and I sort of ride the offending wave, vaguely unhappy about its annoying presence, yet not focused enough to row back to shore and take stock.

It can take days of this ineffective surfing, during which I go about my daily duties and alternate between dispensing disapproval and trying a toss at bribery, before I wake up to the futility of my half-hearted protests.

My perfunctory efforts, I realize in a flash of sudden inspiration (or desperation, whichever hits first), are about as productive as trying to ward off a burglar with a fly swatter and then pulling the blanket over one's head so one can dissolve into the rosy oblivion of a disappearing dream. Something has got to be *done*, the awareness dawns. And it's during moments like these that things like our *gevurah* bulletin are born.

Our *gevurah* bulletin is an unsophisticated rectangle of corrugated white plastic the size of the kitchen door, with a dry erasable marker attached. Yes, I concede, a commercial memo board would have been slightly more aesthetic, and perhaps easier to wipe clean, too. The makeshift materials are simply testimony to the spur of the moment nature of my decision to salute heroism in our own private chambers.

"Guess what?" I had challenged, late one afternoon, when the bickering had escalated enough to shake me out of my complacency. "We're going to post a *gevurah* bulletin."

And for the sheer inaptitude of any simple English word I know to potently translate the term, I'll use the original word that even my toddler has learned to pronounce: The bulletin is there to applaud anyone who has found the strength to be *misgaber*.

To be *misgaber* means eating the red pepper you vehemently dislike, or walking away when your brother flicks your ear for no apparent reason. It means swallowing the impulse to sprint out of the kitchen with a piece of freshly baked cake, or owning up to the crime if you didn't manage to be *misgaber* on the first round.

For the senior members of the household it means dealing with all of the above in a dignified and loving fashion, plus a good many other things, most of them too private to put into print. The common factor is the incredible amount of inner fortitude these acts require. And the *gevurah* bulletin is the place where these personal victories are lauded in washable marker until new acts of heroism claim their place.

I don't know if the number of those acts is actually on the rise, or it's just our heightened awareness of the delicious thrill of self-mastery, but the white board is growing ever messier with the scribbles and scrawls of triumphs in a rainbow of shapes and sizes.

"Does it work?" my neighbor asked me yesterday, her eyes scanning the unconventional headlines as she waited for the two cucumbers she had come to borrow. Her tone conveyed amusement not absent of admiration and hopeful suspense.

The two little ones were entangled on the floor in a brawl over a light blue balloon on a stick, the sole survivor of our recent trip to the shoe store. I couldn't resist the temptation.

"Who wants to be *misgaber*?" I beckoned, brandishing the magic erasable marker. "Let's see, who's going to give up that balloon and have her name posted on the *gevurah* bulletin?"

My neighbor watched in fascinated incredulity as the older one got off the floor and bravely handed the balloon to her younger sister. With a gallant flourish, an unrehearsed grace that I haven't seen many adults demonstrate, she held the stick between her thumb and forefinger, and daintily proffered the balloon to the younger one.

"What a *giborah*!" I exclaimed, my face suffused with unconcealed pride in my little heroine, and admittedly, in my own ability to have empowered her with the awareness of self-conquest.

The joy of *chinuch*, I exulted, as I took the marker and recorded the act, dramatically exclaiming each word as it hit the bulletin.

Gitty smiled her tiny, shy smile as I rewarded her with an exuberant hug. She giggled a little bashful, self-satisfied giggle, and then, right before my neighbor closed the door on the storybook scene, turned to me in the most angelic little voice.

"Can I have a balloon now?"

So much for illusions of courage.

So much for bulletins and washable markers and pride. My children's and my own.

Gevurah is marked by an uphill climb, a sweating battle, a long and arduous inner struggle. *Gevurah* is the inner strength to recognize the bittersweet beauty of leaving a dream behind in pursuit of something better, loftier, longer lasting. *Gevurah* is not the act, nor the nobility of it. It's the courage to pay a price out of one's own pocket.

Out of one's own pocket, and out of one's own ego, and out of one's own need for perfection and convenience and recognition. *Gevurah* means twisting off a piece of one's self so close to the core, it almost feels like one's essence, and offering it in exchange for refinement of one's spirit.

It means prying open one's vise, and slowly letting go, and watching that piece of self sail off like a balloon, vanishing into a tiny invisible speck. And it isn't easy. Never.

Most of us are pretty solid where our ambitions are concerned. We want to be upright, caring, modest, Torah Jews. We want to be faithful spouses, devoted parents, selfless neighbors. We want to *daven* and learn, and do *chessed*.

And we want the balloon. Yes, please, after all that *gevurah*, we want the balloon.

We want nice, furnished homes, fashionable clothing, time to cultivate our own little interests. We want the right car, the right house, the right schedule. We want to be sweet-natured, well-rested wives and mothers, and yet we want to putter around until way past midnight reveling in our pursuit of domestic perfection.

We want to be legendary *masmidim*. And yet we want to snuggle under a warm quilt and sleep. We want to be agreeable neighbors, in-laws, colleagues, but please, let us do things our own way. We want to be self-effacing. And we want recognition for it. We want to be there for our families. And we want to be community activists.

Being a hero in theory doesn't take much. It isn't all that strenuous to fill a cart with lofty ideals off the shelves of yeshivah education and teenage euphoria, and tote it around the supermarket.

Everyone, however, reaches the cash register at some point. It's the time when we actually have to dole out that cash, when no Visa or Mastercard will do. It's when we have to make the conscious choice to step both of our feet into either one of two worlds if we don't want to stay rooted to the spot. In plays, it's that moment heavy with the drama, punctuated by conflicting voices offstage, and clashing images cloaked in black and white.

In real life as we live it, it most often is a very mundane moment on a very ordinary day, or many mundane moments on many ordinary days. It's those times when we've got to be brutally honest and leave go of something we want for something we *really* want. It is giving up that extra cake, that prestigious job, that ideal working partner. It's forgoing an evening of privacy, an hour of pleasure, a lifetime of ease or affluence.

It's parting with our own personal balloon forever. And ever. Because eternity just doesn't sit very well with a bunch of hot air.

Homespun Tales

My bedtime stories for the little ones have usually been of the makeshift variety, where some Shevi learns to do the right thing even when no one is looking, or some Yanky or Zevi discovers how to speak instead of resorting to hands. Lately, I've decided, the kids are ready for the next size.

A bedtime tale, I think, like a new pair of shoes, has to more than just fit; it should leave the children with plenty of room to grow. So I've started investing some more time doing research, and we've begun recounting tales of *tzaddikim*. There's something about telling the kids about *R' Chanina ben Dosa* and *R' Yochanan* and *Reish Lakish* instead of just any old homespun tale about Rivky or Dovy.

Just recently, though, I've hit on an untapped resource of tales that bridge the territory between the two: tales from the lives of our grandparents. And as I watch my children's drooping eyelids slowly flutter shut, I've discovered that the same stories that can put youngsters to sleep can arouse their parents.

The kids got this story, peeled, pared and cored. They've heard of the war only in the most ambiguous terms and I wanted to keep it that way. For you, I serve it undistilled, the way I heard it myself.

My grandmother emerged from the Holocaust, a towering spirit within a broken body, all of 20 years old. In the Displaced Persons Camp, she and her older married sister were just that; two displaced persons ruthlessly torn from the richest soil of an illustrious family, their roots ragged and exposed, their dainty flower heads bespeaking nobility, even in their wilted state.

They clutched each other's hands and inched their way forward, mustering all they had not to stumble over the shards of their own broken hearts. The two sisters both bore scars that told tales of their own; how they had smuggled potatoes for an ailing friend right under the glare of the watchtower, how they had risked their lives to light the *Shabbos* candles, to fast on *Tishah B'Av*. Right then, though, they wanted only to swathe their lacerated, bleeding souls in dressings of hope and faith, and to leave the past behind.

The horrors they had been through left both sisters wiser than their years. Bluma, however, was in actuality still a young girl with a future ahead of her. And though her older sister had lost a baby in the *churban*, she turned her own bitterness into sweet, gentle, motherly caring for her younger sister.

It's difficult to dress oozing, ulcerated, emotional wounds, but Rivka was perceptive. She was sure that if Bluma would have something pretty to clothe her body in, her spirit of youth would be partially restored. Crushing sadness can silence the most basic human desires, and Rivka knew it would be like a balm to her sister to reawaken that dormant instinct within every young girl; the simple joy of having something nice to wear.

A talented dressmaker even before the war, Rivka had fashioned some beautiful garments in the past. Now however, she was determined to outdo herself, to sew Bluma an outfit that would bring the color back to her pinched cheeks. There was only one problem; where to get the fabric and how to procure a machine. Ever resourceful, the two sisters spent a day foraging the quiet villages around the DP camp.

There, in one of the more industrial sections, they found a textile factory, whose owner took pity on the two lone girls and seemed eager to help.

"How about this combination?" she asked brightly as she pulled out two bolts of contrasting materials from the tightly packed shelf. Rivka fingered the fine weave of beige and held it against the bolt of rich brown. She looked at Bluma, saw the soft shine in her eyes, and nodded contently.

Thus the two girls made their way back to the camp, their purchase folded beneath their arms, a seed of giving in one heart planting a tender shoot of joy in another.

Without a machine at her disposal, Rivka had only her determination and her expertise with which to fashion the dress. Late into the nights she worked, her fingers tediously weaving the needle in and out of the delicate fabrics.

Tiptoeing into the room where Bluma was sleeping, she'd drape the unfinished garment near her sister's bed and smile, envisioning the genuine happiness that would wreathe Bluma's face as she donned her first new, real outfit since the outbreak of the war. Only then did Rivka stretch her cramped fingers and fall into a satisfied sleep for the few remaining hours until dawn.

After two weeks, the dress was ready, a masterpiece of perfection. The chic cut, the tiny even stitches, the professional finishing touches, all paid testimony to Rivka's work of devotion. As she steamed the garment one final time, Bluma gave her sister a silent hug. There were no words between them, only a fountain of pure, unstinting, love.

Friday night had Bluma tossing and turning with excitement. They had both agreed that *Shabbos* would be the perfect opportunity to don the outfit for the first time. Her anticipation wasn't like that of any young girl excited to wear something new.

After the harrowing years she'd been through, clothed in haphazard shreds, she'd really be putting on a tailored outfit, like the kind she had owned before the war, so many centuries ago. It was more than just the dress. It was a sign that life mattered, that there was still a place for beauty and renewal in the world.

And then suddenly she sat upright in her bed, struck by a strange idea. *What if the dress was shaatnez?* She had no idea where the absurd notion had sprung up from, but once the possibility had entered her mind, it just wouldn't relinquish its grip on her conscience.

Suddenly wide awake, she put on her slippers, and groped around in the darkness with faltering steps. The more she fingered the cherished outfit hanging in the darkened room, the more her uneasiness grew. No, she wouldn't wear that dress tomorrow. Not until she ascertained that her reservations were baseless. Parting with her dream for the next day, she gave the dress one more fleeting thought, before she staunchly hung it back in the makeshift closet.

Shabbos morning, she shared her fears with her sister. Rivka was stunned for a moment. *Shaatnez.* The thought hadn't crossed her mind. The hours hunched over the garment, the image of a smiling, well-dressed Bluma rose in her mind. Then she looked into her sister's eyes. They had waited until then. They would wait until after *Shabbos*.

When the two sisters came before Rav Meisels, gingerly holding a hand-sewn garment, and asking if there was someone familiar with *shaatnez* testing on the premises, he puckered his brow. "Yes," he nodded slowly and directed them to an earnest-looking scholar nearby. The *Rav*, part of the temporary *beis din* set up in the DP camp, had directed a *shaatnez* laboratory, and was an expert at discerning the composition of the fibers in a weave. As he carefully inspected the two materials so painstakingly sewn together in a labor of love, his eyes filled with tears.

"I'm sorry, *kinder*," he said softly, and his eyes told the rest.

Rivka and Bluma didn't shed any tears. They weren't consumed by regret and self-pity and aggravation. "I know you put your heart and soul into that dress," whispered Bluma, "Believe me, I appreciate every stitch."

They didn't hang the dress away into the recesses of the closet. Rivka took her sewing shears and mercilessly slashed the garment into tiny shreds. There were too many young girls who wouldn't have the strength of spirit to resist the enormous temptation if they came across the dress.

Bluma stood by, unflinchingly, as she watched the snippings of her personal offering softly swirl to the ground. She had offered so many sacrifices in her young life. She would offer one more. With love.

And that is the story of my grandmother's dress. The dress she treasured more than any other in her life; the dress she never wore. The beauty of most garments is in wearing them. Sometimes there is beauty, unsurpassed, shining radiance, in a garment that is never worn.

Days on

Receiving the report card,
I scanned the white sheet,
Crisply folded in half,
Neat boxes,
Little letters,
My eyes darted
Straight to the squares
I cared about
most.
Subjects I liked,
I'd worked for,
My mother's eyes
skimmed the report,
checked my teacher's assessment.
of my effort,
derech eretz.
Friends asked me about my marks
In this subject
or that.
One slot
I never once bothered to inspect
or correct,
Was "absences."
It was either three,
or one,
or seven,
Pretty irrelevant
in any case.

Didn't matter much.
Those were the simple days.
Today we don't receive
report cards.
We've got to draw them up by ourselves
at year's end,
And it's a pretty personal affair.
No one's looking
over our shoulder
asking us what mark we've scored
in *tefillah*
or *hilchos Shabbos*,
If we've done satisfactory
or below,
in *shemiras halashon*
and *tzenius*
and *chessed.*
Nobody's going to check
our level of *bitachon,*
or our *hachna'ah,*
It's something we've got to chart
all by ourselves,
check the grades,
and compare them to last term.
And unlike those report cards
filled out by teachers
over the years
of my schooling,
I find myself pausing,
pen poised in hand,
over what used to be
the simplest square:
"Absences."
How many absences

have I accrued,
over the term?
How many hours,
days,
weeks,
was I simply not there?
Hands, feet, mouth
going through the motions,
yet my heart, somehow
absent?
How many entire days had I passed over,
serving breakfast,
lunch,
supper,
doing everything
I was supposed to do,
while my mind played hooky,
not once pondering
the sense of mission,
of privilege?
How many *berachos*,
How many prayers,
My lips
and mind
a thousand miles apart?
How many lessons
had I missed
sitting right there
In my seat?

Too many.
Too many to count, really.
Too many
to sit benignly

in any neat little white square
without affecting the entire card.

So much for last year,
For the coming year
I have a new prayer
a somewhat-altered aspiration
from my resolutions
of the past,
I cannot dream to excel
at every subject,
I cannot hope to pass,
every single test,
I know
certain grades
will be wanting,
But one thing
I can try to aspire for,
to achieve one day
at a time,
minute by
minute,
One thing I can hope to score
on my next report card,
is perfect attendance.
Limnos yameinu
kein hodah.

Finger Tips

here is something to be said for winter. Something about the brisk air, and cold, harsh rain, something about the chapped, rosy cheeks and the kids dressed like overstuffed teddy bears, that turns the simple notion of coming home into a tantalizing experience. There is something about the sunless gray sky and the short afternoons, the warm aroma of vegetable soup and the vapor on the windows, that can make the most undomesticated fellow sentimental about having a roof over his head.

Summer has its own qualities, but I never relish the optical illusion of a bright noon sky at 7 o'clock in the evening. Try and get a bunch of youngsters to bed when it sounds like a squawking carnival outside, when sunny skies peep out of the drawn shades making bedtime rituals seems like the most unnatural thing to do.

So though winter brings its fair share of inconveniences, I welcome the cozy evenings, so perfectly staged for bedtime. Nature draws the curtains right in time for baths and dinner, and spares me the unrewarding hassle of calling kids' names in a repeated futile effort to get them upstairs. And there's nothing like kids in pastel-colored sleepers burying their heads in fluffy quilts to set the tone for a good, heartwarming bedtime story.

So it was, on one of these delicious winter evenings, that we sat together on the bed and shared the inspiring story of a little Russian boy named Yuri. After some initial "Yuri?" "Maybe it's like Uri?" and "Stop it, you're ruining the story," the kids settled into the quilt and gave me the go-ahead to continue.

Yuri's parents were irreligious Russian immigrants who sent their son to a Shuvu school in the neighborhood. There, Yuri learned all about *Shabbos* and was enchanted by what he heard. The problems began when his parents, who were slightly less enchanted, attempted to force Yuri to do his homework assignment on *Shabbos*. Little Yuri was horrified. He cried. He explained. He pouted. He moped. All of which made his mother a lot more furious than she had started out.

"You'll do that homework this minute!" she fumed, shoving a pen into his hand. By now, she had probably lost sight of the original reason for the argument. All she knew was that Yuri was being petulant, impossible, and disrespectful. She'd get him to listen.

But Yuri wasn't trying to be impossible or disrespectful. He simply loved *Shabbos*, and his teacher had said that writing on *Shabbos* was forbidden.

I paused as I internalized this conflict, this mother and this child, this child and his sincerity. His love for his mother and his love of *Shabbos*.

The kids intercepted my pensive pause.

"It isn't considered an *aveirah* if Yuri doesn't listen to his mother." That was a statement, not a question. "Because she wants him to do another *aveirah*."

"Hmm."

And so Yuri suddenly ran to the front door. His mother stood watching him, her hands limply sliding off her hips, wondering if he was going to run away. So was I.

But Yuri didn't leave his house. He opened the door and placed his hand into the space between the open door and the door frame. Then he slammed the door shut with all his might, right on his fingers.

"Because he didn't want to write on *Shabbos*!" a chorus of three voices chimed, as if it was the most natural ending to the story.

It was a good thing they lent the final sentence, because the rest of the text swam in front of my eyes as I tried to regain my composure. Imagine an 11-year-old boy having the courage and the conviction to smash his own fingers rather than desecrate the *Shabbos*! I tried to convey some of my awe and admiration for this hero of *Yiddishkeit*.

"Rivky, remember how hard it hurt when your finger got stuck under the lid of the toy box last week?"

Rivky nodded solemnly, subdued. The others looked reflective. I could see their eyes doing a memory search for some incident that would help them relate to this incredible act of *mesiras nefesh*.

Suddenly, I noticed a flash of fire in the oldest one's eyes. "What should we do?" she asked, indignant. "It isn't our fault; our parents are *frum!*"

Oh.

This was the same little angel who'd stomped at the mention of braving the cold to go to the grocery, who had encountered slight difficulty waiting the prescribed six hours until she could have her chocolate milk. And now she was peeved that her parents were *frum* and had thus robbed her of the opportunity to crush her fingers in a show of devotion to *Shabbos*.

I wanted to laugh, but I quickly thought better of it. My children are very sensitive to anyone making light of their introspection. Especially their mother. So I said, "You would love to be able to show *mesiras nefesh* just like Yuri, but your parents are *frum*." She nodded earnestly. I was glad she hadn't caught the slight tremor of amusement right beneath my grave tone.

She slithered off the bed, as I closed the book.

"So would I," I added, "But guess what? My parents are *frum* too."

I wasn't joking now. I was dead serious. I was talking for myself and I was talking for much of our generation. We, who haven't gone through the Holocaust and whose parents haven't gone through the Holocaust. We, who *have* parents, and whose parents are *frum*.

And neighbors and cousins and in-laws and friends who are *frum* too. And a kosher butcher shop around the corner, and *chalav Yisrael* ice cream in every flavor. We, who have a choice of the finest yeshivos and schools to send our children to, and nursery rhymes about Yanky and Yehudis, and central heating, and freedom of speech, and the irrevocable right to the pursuit of our happiness.

We, who sometimes hear accounts that touch the most tender spot within our souls, that make us gasp for their sheer magnitude; accounts of great people and ordinary people, glimpses of Jews, old and young, whose souls prevailed over their bodies.

We hear of starving children sharing their last crust of bread, of wealthy businessmen who gave it all up for a *blatt Gemara*. We read of mothers, fathers, young boys, and young girls who transcended their human impulses, who illuminated the murkiest darkness with their towering spirits.

And which of us, during some moment of private contemplation, hasn't wondered how he would have done, had he been put to test. Which of us hasn't pasted himself there and then forced himself with brutal discipline to stare at the nightmarish imagery and answer the unaskable question: Would I, in that position, have shown that kind of astounding strength?

Most of us cannot let it linger too long, that horrific picture, that penetrating analysis. Most of us prefer to shudder and turn the page, to dismiss the grave thoughts with a terse and passionate; "May we never, ever be tested."

Indeed, may we never, ever be tested. But we funny, mortal beings skip a very basic fact. In our longing to reach the spiritual heights we can barely touch on tiptoes, we delude ourselves into thinking that circumstances preclude us from achieving that kind of sacrifice; *it isn't our fault,* we were never given the challenge, *our parents are frum.*

In our attempt to be frank with our inner selves, we forget that we don't need the litmus paper of fabricated eventualities to tell us where we are standing. There is a lot more immediate, though less dramatic way to put our finger on our pulse.

Tests come in all kinds of packages. There are big parcels and small ones, soft ones and hard ones. There is the test of *Purim* and the test of *Chanukah*, the test of dearth and the test of plenty. There is the test of the drought and the test of the flood.

And we are awash in the flood. We, with our *frum* parents, and *frum* communities, we with our very pampered pasts and passive presents, are being washed away by the cascading torrents, *merov kol*, an overabundance of everything.

No one is asking us to give up our last, or even our first, ration of soup, no one is hovering over us with a truncheon for the crime of lighting a flame on *Chanukah*.

And indeed, no one is asking us to inflict that kind of suffering upon ourselves, to imitate that brand of self-sacrifice. Our dilemmas aren't catalogued by the infamous motto coined at the gateway to Auschwitz, "*arbeit macht* frei." Our tribulations, as we stand at the entrance to the 21st century, are the direct transposition of that phrase, as sinister and as difficult: "*Frei macht arbeit.*" Freedom breeds work. Spiritual work. We haven't been spared.

We have doughnuts and Danishes, freedom and furniture, but we also have new spiritual crematoria where *Yiddishe neshamos* go up in smoke. We have computers, and we have videos and we have the internet. We may not have to crush our fingers to keep *Shabbos*, but believe me, we have plenty of Yuris, big and little, whose itchy fingers dance along the dangerous precipice of a black abyss. No one may ever know to write their story, but the courage it takes for Yuris like these to slam the door on their fingers and retreat from the electronic underworld at the touch of the keyboard is superhuman.

Just one generation ago, Jews stripped of their bodies, naked, starved, and beaten, stood testimony to the immortality of the Jewish spirit. Right in this generation, remarkable individuals, devoid of support and encouragement, have risen above their secular backgrounds and their natural inclinations to heed their soul's calling. Could we do the same?

We don't have to. Our parents are *frum*.

We have to do other things. We want our children to be *frum*.

This article was inspired by one of the gems in the soul-stirring book, "Touched by a Story," by Rabbi Yechiel Spero.

Angels in Color

Staring at the four walls is supposed to be the ultimate description of monotony. In Eretz Yisrael, though, nothing is boring, and the walls are not about to be left out.

Staring at the whitewashed surfaces around my abode is an activity that affords an interesting view of some of the sights of raising children within limited space. Our kitchen walls provide a background of ketchup splatters, grease stains, and finger marks; the hall and bedrooms are a collage of faint crayon markings, scotch tape residue, shoe prints, and ink marks.

Which, make no mistake, I do not usually stare at in amused complacence. As much as I dream of gleaming white walls, however, Israeli whitewash just isn't the equivalent of semigloss latex paint. Despite my valiant efforts to scrub them down consistently, or perhaps because of them, the walls in our home are reminiscent of an old, peeling monument.

Lately, even my blind love for the place just hasn't managed to obscure the multicolored patches that have been decorating the interior of our home. And so this summer, we decided that the time had come to take action and call a painter.

Action, however, is usually easier spoken about than done. When I had said I wanted to go ahead with the painting job, I simply hadn't imagined the amount of hours that would go into comparing estimates, covering the furniture, waiting for the crew to reappear after each lunch break, and scraping all that residue off the stone tiles.

By the time the job was over, I knew why we hadn't done it in years. And I was ready to take any precaution to ensure that the venture would not have to be repeated anywhere in the near future.

Upon seeing the stark white walls, unblemished by scrapes and scuffs and the traces of little hands, my first impulse was to confiscate the crayons and markers. In quick succession went the clay, the rubber stamps, and the pencils. The kids eyed me somewhat worriedly when I moved the table away from the wall at mealtime, and insisted that cream cheese made a tastier sandwich than peanut butter. I found myself nervously surveying the walls every time my toddler pointed to his riding toy, and mentally measuring the borders when my husband casually moved his chair back. Preserving the walls was fast becoming an obsession.

So it was that my husband delivered his final ultimatum one day after a particularly tense lunch hour. "Listen," he said, with a twinkle in his eye, "I think we've got to make a decision. It's either the walls or us."

I conceded. Preserving the walls was important, but our sanity definitely took precedence. So I closed my eyes, and admittedly, I breathed a great big sigh of relief as our lives returned to their normal, boisterous state. As for the state of the walls, well, I guess we've resigned ourselves to the homey murals.

And somehow, each time I speculate the compromise of those splotched white walls, I am again filled with amazement and awe at the wonderful paradox of the Jewish calendar, at the incredible antilogy that keeps a *Yid's* soul bound to life.

If any of us had to come up with a suitable activity with which to occupy our freshly whitewashed souls on the evening following *Yom Kippur*, chances are, we'd keep it safe and somber.

In an effort to retain the perfect state of stain-free existence, we'd opt for something purely spiritual. You can't go wrong if you circumvent anything likely to make a mess, and stick to clean neat activities like learning and *davening*. You can't go wrong if you confiscate all the adult-size crayons that make life fun and colorful and enjoyable, can you?

Oh yes, you can. You can go very, very wrong. And that's why, just hours after the final blast of the *shofar* has split the aura of shimmering holiness; just hours after *Yidden* have stood in hushed reverence intoning the words of the sacred *Yom Kippur* prayers; they are up in the attic, down in the garage, out in the yard, sawing, hammering, bustling, and singing.

That's why the streets of Yerushalayim, that only hours earlier had been heavy with the silent sanctity of the day, are suddenly teeming with Jews, awake with music, alive with the joy of festive preparations. And wonder of wonders, though the streets are anything but still, they are no less laden with holiness than they'd been earlier on, during the fast.

Unlike my peace treaty with the flecked walls, physical activity is not a compromise born of an inevitable fact or an inescapable reality. It's the active translation of the holiness that we've experienced in shul as we've bowed down to the *Melech Malchei Hamelochim*; it's the function of the electricity generated by our heartfelt *tefillos* and sincere *teshuvah* of the past six weeks.

And so as soon as we close that *Yom Kippur machzor*, we women go headlong into our culinary preparations for *Yom Tov*, as the menfolk approach the beloved *succah* boards with gusto. Not because we have put *Yom Kippur* behind us, but because the vision of next *Yom Kippur* stands in front of us. Because we want to infuse our days with the sparks of *kedushah* that have risen from the holy *y'mei ratzon*, and we know that the murals of living *Yiddishkeit* are the prettiest embellishment for our freshly whitewashed souls.

The days between *Rosh Chodesh Elul* and *Yom Kippur* comprise a long and arduous painting job. The month of *Tishrei*, however, isn't complete without *Succos*. Perhaps for the angels, abstinence is maintenance. For us *Yidden*, keeping our souls white is a colorful affair.

And when *halachah* dictates that we begin constructing the walls of our *succah* while the aura of *Yom Kippur* still lingers in the air, I like to think it's the *Aibeshter*'s way of saying, "*Kinderlach*, in my home, it isn't either you or the walls; it's the harmony you create between both."

Notes on Note Taking

"How do you work it, the writing?" people ask me, curiosity tweezing their slightly arched eyebrows.

Sitting at *simchos*, on buses, waiting on line in the bank or post office, people I vaguely know, but who feel comfortable enough to open conversation, question me about the art of putting pen to paper, or punching out thoughts on a keyboard.

"It's a lot of *siyata d'Shmaya*," I sigh, not because I want to sound modest, but because that's what it is, a lot of *siyata d'Shmaya*. Like any art, and perhaps more evidently so, writing is solely given to Heavenly assistance. Apparently, though, that's not what these interviewers want to hear, because they press insistently, almost disappointed by my response.

"Do you have a special pad, or a looseleaf, or a notebook, where you collect all your ideas for easy reference?" they ask, their voices betraying the eagerness of a child begging for an affirmative answer. "Do you have a file or a drawer where you store your papers?"

I hate to take the thrill out of the encounter, so I'm almost tempted to go along with their notion of the professional notebook-and-file method. *I really ought to buy myself a notebook,* I chastise myself, as I have on the many similar occasions preceding this one.

But I know the truth. I know that I already own notebooks and pads and files, enough of them to keep me going for a few years, were I to decide that this, indeed, were the preferred means of recording inspiration for posterity. And I know, too, that they just won't do.

What I rely on, instead, to act as a dependable extension of my crowded brain, where thoughts dip and surface unpredictably like bits of debris in the ocean waves, are the oddest scraps of disposable material; virtually anything other than clean pages bound together in an orderly fashion.

And contrary to my questioners' vivid imagery of some highly sophisticated filing system, you'll find these scraps all over my house. In my pocketbook, under my pillow, atop a mound of clean laundry, tucked between the bills waiting to be paid, you'll find these tissues and index cards and advertisements turned over.

Folded in the recipe box, under the phonebook, inside my wallet, you'll catch sight of these frayed bus tickets, remainders of arts and crafts, torn envelopes, old invitations. In thick pencil, purple crayon, yellow pen, the kind the teachers dispense as prizes and you wonder who ever writes with them, these lines are scrawled, fragments of light, incoherent pieces of thoughts.

"You must be very disciplined to work at home"; this a continuation, usually, of the notebook-and-file conversation. Discipline! I resist the inclination to scoff aloud. My insides do a round of hearty laughter, as I look squarely into my companion's eyes, suddenly possessed by an urge to seem like the controlled person she thinks I am.

If I'm lucky, the remark is left suspended in hanging rhetoric. If my questioner persists, though, well, then I'm subject to brutal candor, which is somewhat less than flattering. You want to know when I write? You *really* want to know when?

Well the last time I grabbed a pen, it was right in the middle of peeling potatoes for *cholent*. Right then and there, like a wayward child abandoning her task for a beckoning novel or a bike spree outside, I dropped the peeler, and ran to the drawer where the pens belong. (Yes, the pens *do* have a place, surprisingly enough, in this otherwise scattered seeming disarray.)

In a kind of urgency, the way you would frantically shove a saucer under a container of fish sauce dripping on your freshly washed floor, I grabbed the nearest scrap, which happened to be a friendly reminder from the dentist's office, and began scribbling furiously.

And the time before that, I was sitting on a bus, winding its way up to Yerushalayim, toddler perched on one knee. Listening in on other people's candid chitchat, especially the younger half of the population, always makes for a window into human understanding. So while pointing out the scenic view to my restless tot with one arm, my free hand fumbled for a pen, and quickly jotted a germ of an idea onto the corner of my "To do" list.

It would be nice, idyllic really, to draw up some kind of Sunday, Monday, and Wednesday plan, from 10 o'clock until 1 strictly in front of the computer. That would leave the rest of the week unclogged, and the evenings too, and allow me to live the lifestyle that promotes health, wealth, and wisdom.

Too bad that inspiration doesn't come on order.

Too bad, indeed. Perhaps though, this shortcoming, this lack of wherewithal to predict lightning in the spiritual spheres, constitutes part of the deliberate design programmed by the Creator into the human condition. A design that carries over, of course, into the more general realm of living.

No one likes to ponder the final reality of our existence in this world, which is that it ultimately comes to an end, but somewhere in the distant crevices of our mind, each of us harbors a vague picture of what we would like the finished article to look like. Each of us, or at least so I fancy, has an ideal vision of him or herself, a few decades hence, the weaknesses somehow neutralized, the flaws admirably corrected.

We live with the fantasy of a very improved version of our personalities at some unmarked future point in time, a self whose image reflects the many *takanos* and *kabbalos* we dream of perfecting each time we experience a spiritual awakening. None of us *plan* to remain eternally lacking; we're just waiting for the right time.

A quiet Sunday or a Tuesday or a Wednesday, from 10 until 1, when we can sit down with a notebook and earnestly take stock.

Not *now* when we are 10 minutes late for work and the car won't start, or when a teenager is answering back impudently, hitting our most vulnerable spot.

Not *now*, when we've got to make a quick choice between dashing on one more errand or being there in time to greet the kids, or when we're so overtired we can't think straight. Not this week, not this month, perhaps after *Pesach*, after summer vacation, after the wedding, when things calm down.

With the contemporary profusion of courses and lectures on self-improvement and self-awareness, we sometimes get the idea that chiseling one's personality is an isolated activity, a parcel of concentrated time and energy, earmarked: *avodah.* In reality, inspiration hits like lightning, and whenever it strikes we must be prepared to grab that scrap of time, that fragment of circumstance, and record the flash for posterity.

With all due respect for order, and I *do* hold it in high regard, if you're going to wait for the notepad, you may miss some of the grandest opportunities to translate inspiration into the stuff that lasts for eternity. If you're going to wait around for a leather-bound personal ledger, you may never get your soul's desires published.

For actualizing aspirations is about stopping to catch the raindrops, or the teardrops, or the ear drops; whichever happens to be infiltrating your life at the present moment. Writing the manuscript of one's personal biography is not something one sits down to do at the age of 70 or 80; it's the thing we're consciously or unconsciously doing during our every waking moment on earth.

Let's choose to do it consciously. Let's skip the search for notepaper, and do what I do in moments of illumination: Grab those proverbial tissues and create some of life's most inspirational issues.

Beyond the Stars

One o'clock is the hour when I offer a heartfelt prayer to The One Above. It's late then for *Shacharis*, and early yet for *Minchah*, but the hour is too crucial to pass by without requesting assistance from Above. So I formulate my own entreaties that each child come home in an agreeable mood, that the food I've prepared find favor in everybody's eyes, that there be no terrible squabbling around the kitchen table as we partake in the meal and in one another's tales. As of late, I've been adding another silent prayer. Please help that there be no charts.

This last addendum was added in not such loving memory of last year's cleaning bonanza, though it all started happily enough. I love enthusiasm, and when my first grader burst through the door waving a fluorescent pink paper, I was all for it.

"It's a chart, Mommy," she explained breathlessly. "Every time we help for *Pesach*," here she tucked the chart under her chin to free her hands, and rummaged through her briefcase to find the sheet of metallic stars, "you put one of these stars on the right square. Whoever brings the finished chart back to school gets a prize from *Morah*."

"Oh wow! It sounds like I'm going to be getting an awful lot of help just when I need it so badly."

I wasn't being sarcastic. I meant every word of it. With *Pesach* looming so close, my own two hands were inadequate for the amount of work to be tackled. There was only one catch. My own and my daughter's perception of helping differed ever so slightly.

Before I could collect my thoughts, Gitty was in the bathroom, letting in the bathwater. Something inside me tightened as I threw a sidelong glance at the pink chart adorning the refrigerator.

"Gitty, why is the bathwater running like that?"

It took a minute for the response to come. My daughter was too busy lugging two buckets of Lego and a basket of Waffle Blocks to reply.

"It's for the toys, Mommy. Remember, we gave all the toys a bath for *Pesach* last year?"

Did I remember? I sure did. Which is exactly why I didn't want a repeat this year, definitely not at the peak of a hectic afternoon.

"Not now, Gitty," I said, trying to remain patient despite the tension mounting inside me. "Maybe —"

"But you said you needed me to help for *Pesach*." The wailing was on.

I stood there for a moment, wavering, alternately gazing at the clock and at Gitty's crestfallen expression. Gitty didn't miss that. I saw a renewed flicker of hope in her eyes, as her whining picked up. I steadied my gaze, and tried to restore my firm grip on the situation. I knew I would regret it later if I faltered now.

"You wanted to help so badly, but it's not the right time now. How about if we plan it for tomorrow?"

My tone attempted to convey understanding; my eyes pleaded for hers. Gitty, though, was too far gone to be listening for the inferences in my tone, or looking into my eyes. She was determined to be a partner to the pandemonium, splashing in water, dripping with suds.

"Tomorrow I have to help you do other things. Rivky is cleaning all the kitchen chairs for her mother. *That's* what I want to do tomorrow."

I closed my eyes and swallowed hard. Who was up to kitchen chairs?

"O.K.," I heard myself relent. I don't know if it was the sounds of the escalating fight coming from the kids' room, or the baby banging his spoon on the highchair for more food, but my steadfastness gave.

"O.K.," but don't get the bathroom floor all wet."

Whoever heard of a 7-year-old scrubbing a bathtub full of Lego and keeping the water localized to the tub? I guess I put in that appendage to preserve whatever was left of my status as the one in charge. And I'll tell you, not much was left.

Over the next few days I had my agenda mapped out by my offspring. Binyomin, completely infected by Gitty's's pre-*Pesach* fervor, had us know that Baruch's family was eating in the *machsan* and that he was willing to personally supervise our own family's transfer to those dining quarters.

No amount of explaining could convince him that we just weren't up to eating in the *machsan*, and even if we were, *I* wasn't up to it. He and his two assistants, namely, the first grader and her 5-year-old brother, had the pantry packed into boxes in record time. What was *I* doing, you want to know? Trying to keep the toddler out of their way. Because, "Mommy, we can't work when Yanky spills the cornflakes all over everything." I tried to cooperate, though it took some real restraint.

I hate to sound like a spoilsport, but when the last sticker was pasted on that chart, I heaved a great big sigh of relief. Now that the helping was over for the time being, perhaps my gang would go out to play. I was almost afraid to believe my good fortune as I watched the kids tumble out the door with their bikes.

As I closed the door behind them, I stopped to revel in the peace and quiet that had descended upon the pre-*Pesach* chaos, if only for a moment. The frustration of the last few days gave way to a wan smile, as I eyed the pile of soaking wet rags lying in a mound beside an empty bottle of cleanser. "The wetter, the better," seemed to be the kids' yardstick for measuring cleaning efficacy.

Not to mention the inordinate amounts of soap, clatter, and disarray that had to accompany the job to deem it worthy of being considered an accomplishment. All these were imperative to working up a good self-righteous fever so crucial to the stars on the chart, and even more, to the feeling that they were helping, *really* helping. And it set me thinking.

Weren't we all, in our own way, really a bunch of grown-up kids? More sophisticated, more subtle, yet harboring that same burning desire to do something really big, to splash around in the soapy water and help, capital H.

Didn't we each really have our own idea of doing, of accomplishing and attaining, that didn't necessarily fit in with the daily duties and obligations calling for our attention? Didn't we each cradle a dream of making a mark with our contribution, somewhere in the privacy of our hearts?

Giving is a tricky business. It's so much easier to dole out prepared gift boxes, wrapped in pretty paper and ribbon, made up to our personal taste. It's so gratifying to accompany a project from its inception, to bring a dream to fruition, to blaze a trail up a steep mountain and stick our marker in at the top.

Why, just last night, as I had been trying to pull the loose ends together at the end of the day, I'd come up with a brainstorm, an ingenious way to help others. I'd open an *Erev Pesach gemach*. There'd be window cleaner, oven cleaner, paint thinner, carpet shampoo, and nail-polish remover. There'd be toothpicks, brushes, rags, mops, and even laminated shopping lists for the first time *Pesach* maker. Anyone who'd get stuck at any hour of the day or night could come by to replenish the depleted item. I had gone to sleep dreaming of the infinite possibilities, and gloating in the warm feeling of giving.

Somehow, when my neighbor's children knocked at 8 o'clock in the morning to borrow our can opener, my spirit of generosity had dissipated. It's not that I minded lending our opener. It's just that the can opener had been in their house more than it had been in ours lately, and I'd been left stuck without it more than once. If they needed the can opener so often, couldn't they just purchase one?

There I was, with a *gemach* virtually knocking on my door, and I was pouting at the offer. I was looking to Help, not just lend some measly kitchen utensil.

Well, aside from improving my prayers, the pink chart taught me a thing or two. Some of the greatest things can be accomplished with a damp rag and little or no suds. Those simple unsung acts may not taste of glory and fame, but they cleanse the spirit. Our souls are of a delicate weave. Dry-clean only.

Spirit of the Laws

It was frightening, entering the lobby of the building. I knew it would be sad, oppressively sad, and very still. I anticipated the pensive silence, the uneasy heaviness, the silent shifting in chairs, and the whir of the fan rotating mechanically to and fro, trying in vain to alleviate the choking sorrow.

I hadn't expected the fear.

As soon as I entered the building, an eerie spider of dread began creeping up my arms and legs; then some invisible arm tied a bandanna tightly around my throat. I'd been here before. I knew the terrarium of tropical plants backed by beveled mirrors, and the polished tiles, and the wide elevator. I recognized the flyers advertising robes from America and exercise classes forming soon, and Morah Ruti's *gan*.

It was the stark notice of mourning, printed in heavy black letters, and the arrows in red marker, that suddenly set this building a million miles apart from all the others, this visit a million years away.

The elevator doors glided open, and two women emerged wordlessly, heads bowed. I entered, my heart hammering inside me as the door slithered shut, leaving me alone with the ominous sign posted onto the mirror. Up, up, up, to the third floor, to a door that had never known exceptional traffic, only occasional friendly visitors and *tzeddakah* solicitors and smiling grandparents. Up, up, up, to a private, peaceful, happy little home suddenly turned into a chaotic beehive.

A split second and an eternity. That's how long it took for the elevator to climb the three stories and spew me out into the narrow hallway. Did I knock? It seemed so crass, so intrusive, to enter without being ushered in. I stood there, faltering. Three men shuffled out in single file. I heard the scraping of chairs. The ring of a telephone. I entered.

For some reason, my eyes caught the mud-tracked floors. Perhaps it was the way they stood out in odd contrast to the tastefully decorated abode. Perhaps it was my mind's diversionary tactic as I stood in the corridor, pressed to a wall to allow a huddle of women to pass. Unconsciously, I swept the pleasant surroundings, jolted again by the unaesthetic "men" and "women" signs taped crudely onto the cream-colored walls.

Someone was puttering in the kitchen, arranging parcels of food on the counter, opening and closing the refrigerator. *Why was I concentrating on these impertinent details?* I turned my gaze. But my eyes swiveled back insistently to watch the flitting shadow through the opaque glass window of the door to the kitchen. I felt lightheaded. This was some kind of hallucination. She, veteran *balabusta*, immaculate housekeeper, culinary queen, exiled from her kitchen. What was a stranger doing in there?

I tiptoed into the small room. It was crowded with chairs, desk pushed to a side to make room for more, people sitting squashed together on the rumpled bed linens. You almost couldn't tell that the room served as an airy guest room on any other day of the year. No one seemed too preoccupied with that. Most of the eyes were downcast or glossy with unshed tears; some were riveted to the bereaved young mother sitting on a low stool.

I thought it would seem incongruous, she, the perpetually well-groomed, chic dresser, slumped in a low plastic chair. Well, it *was* incongruous. The whole thing was incongruous. Little children go together with life, not death. Toddlers may be daring and endearing, challenging and rewarding, active, independent, curious; any or all of them. But they are the absolute stuff of the present; they *are*.

You don't talk about them in the past tense. Certainly not with a snag in your voice and tears clouding your vision. And not to a sniffling conglomeration of friends and acquaintances, neighbors and family, stuffed somberly into your spare bedroom.

Of all the absurdities, though, the sight of her appearance didn't strike a discordant note. Her pale, streaked complexion, casual houseclothes, feet swathed in slippers were in perfect consonance with the grief clotting the air. The loss filled every corner; there was simply no more room for anything else.

Like an anesthetic needle, the keen edge of crushing pain had pierced right through her heart and numbed all other concerns, concern over her appearance, or the appearance of her floors, or what was being prepared in her kitchen. The disheveled linens, the disarray, the unmarked parcels cluttering her counter, all that had become blurred background: dim, indistinct, unimportant, behind the sharp, stabbing pain.

She spoke quietly; I listened. Some women got up to leave. I pulled my chair up closer to her so I could share what I'd wanted to tell her. A young woman entered and sat down next to her. She took care to nod to me before turning to the newcomer. I said the customary *haMakom yenachem*, and walked slowly out of the room. Staggered out of the apartment, out of the building, out of the suffocating sadness.

The sadness tagged right after me, though. I turned the key in my keyhole, and surveyed my quiet surroundings like an outsider just landed from space. Oh, the supper dishes. They had to be washed.

And the laundry. Yes. I threw in a load of laundry in slow motion and sluggishly soaped up the dishes. The grief wouldn't leave go.

We've met since, on happier occasions. And yes, courageous girl, she was made up and carefully dressed, smiling and vivacious. She was, though it must have taken a supreme effort. She's called me to check a recipe, and I'm willing to wager that her floors are perfectly shined, and her linens washed, corners pulled tautly over the edges of the mattresses.

They are, because life has got to go on. Mourning has got to be somehow contained, if we want to preserve our sanity.

As the Nine Days settle over us though, a week of national *shivah* for all of *Klal Yisrael*, I cannot help but see her, on that low chair, eyes fixed inwardly on her crushing loss. I cannot help but remember that mud-tracked floor, the unkempt linens, the chaos in the kitchen.

And suddenly, it seems so plain, so perfectly comprehensible why these days of mourning should preclude us from being preoccupied with any aspect of grooming ourselves or our households. It seems to make all the sense in the world that we should be drained of the gusto, of the interest, of the motivation, to want anything at all to be in order when the most cherished thing of all is missing.

It seems obvious that no one would have the head or the appetite to prepare full-course dinners. With all of *Klal Yisrael* on the mourner's chair, though, there's nobody available take over in the kitchen. So we have no choice but to get up for long enough to put together the minimum fare: simple, ungarnished, filling meals.

Ask the people who have been there. Ask them if they've cleaned in a frenzy to "prepare" the house for mourning, if they've made sure every sock was in the right drawer before they left for the funeral. Ask them if they tried to find loopholes, if they sat and discussed the menu or reveled in the delicacies that friends sent over. Ask them how much time they spent getting dressed in the morning, what with the flood of visitors coming in, and if they made sure their slippers were trendy, and if they agonized over the mismatched outfits their children sported for lack of clean laundry.

Aveilus is inner anguish, emotional pain, meant to be experienced, not observed. The *halachos* governing the Nine Days and *Tishah B'Av* should mirror our innermost feelings, our decreased appeal in these everyday activities dictated by our lagging spirits.

The pain of *galus* permeates the entire calendar. There isn't a *tefillah* we recite, or even a *berachah acharonah*, that is devoid of an expression for our yearning that the *Beis HaMikdash* be rebuilt. Yet we go on and get dressed, and cook meals, and iron shirts, and dance to music and laugh. We do that, not because we've completely forgotten, but because life has got to go on. Mourning has got to be somehow contained if we want to preserve our sanity.

And it is. It is contained in the Nine Days and in *Tishah B'Av*. It is then that our loss, our all-encompassing loss, our crushing pain, spiritual and physical, takes center stage in our hearts and souls, and flings everything else far, far back into the hazy, meaningless distance.

Tishah B'Av after *chatzos* is like getting up from *shivah*. Yes, you can make the beds, you can stretch your cramped muscles and sit on a chair. You can tend to whatever needs immediate tending, you can, but come on now, do you know anybody who got up from *shivah* and ran to bake a cake?

We've got to break our fasts, because we can't go on fasting, but if nothing's changed by the time we make that coffee at the end of *Tishah B'Av*, what's the cause for celebration over fresh pastries?

I don't want to ruffle anyone's sense of tradition, and no, it isn't the cake, per se. There's no need to consult any guidebooks. We each know how we react when we're wallowing in deep distress.

So let's temper the heightened activity preceding the Nine Days, let's drop our gourmet-supper plans, and forget about our floors. Let's try to sit down and feel a deep surge of acute, personal pain. It is those who languish in that chair, after all, who will be there when the *Shechinah* comes to tell all the mourners, *"HaMakom yenachem eschem b'soch she'ar aveilei Tzion v'Yerushalayim."*

Focus

Shabbos

*I*t's a good thing *Shabbos* isn't optional. If it were, I'm not sure how often we'd get the taste of it.

I don't know about anyone else, but Thursday very often catches me by surprise. *What? You mean to tell me it's Thursday again? Wasn't it just Thursday yesterday?* Well, no, not yesterday, I'm forced to face the facts. It was last week. Exactly one week ago.

And now it's here again. And yes, I'd better order my fish, pick up my fruits and vegetables, and get my laundry moving. I've got to put up *challah* dough, check my stock of chickens, peel potatoes, and tackle the ironing.

Yes, I know, once upon a time my second-grade teacher taught me a song in which "Sunday, Miriam washes her clothes, Monday, Miriam irons and sews, Tuesday, Miriam shops and cooks, Wednesday, Miriam cleans the nooks …"

I'm hard pressed to recall what Miriam did on Thursdays and Fridays, but judging by the beginning of the lyrics, it sounds like by the time *Erev Shabbos* rolled around, she had virtually nothing left to do.

Well, most of the time I can't say the same for myself.

Don't get me wrong, I'm very organized — on paper. I know what I'm supposed to be doing, and when I'm supposed to do it. I'm a great list writer, and I always have little pink and yellow memo squares dotting the refrigerator, telling me just what I've got to buy, cook, mend, return, bake, pick up, and drop off.

And yet somehow, it's those things that aren't the stuff of the lists that always manage to elbow their way into the week, and make a mockery of those neat little squares waiting ambitiously to be checked off. Things like red spots that look like chicken pox and call for the doctor's opinion. Things like lost lenses, blown fuses, fifth grader's history reports, and no-show cleaning ladies. Things like *shidduch* inquiries, snow days, and making good on some old forgotten promise to bake, shop, or help set up for some affair.

And so, if it were at all voluntary, many weeks I'd simply shake my head in sincere regret and say that I just couldn't swing *Shabbos* this week. Perhaps next week would be less hectic. Perhaps after the Bar Mitzvah, when the school term ended, when the baby started sleeping through the night, I'd go back to my routine of making *Shabbos*.

Because, after all, there just *was* nothing like it. But in the meantime, with everything going on, and my energy level on low, it just didn't seem feasible. Not this week. I couldn't spare a minute, never mind a whole day, out of my schedule, and two days preparing for it. Forget it, out of the question. *Shabbos* was a luxury I couldn't afford.

It's one of the miracles of creation that Hashem knew better than to leave such a crucial matter in our hands. Instead, through thick and thin, through heat and sleet, be it *Erev Pesach, Motza'ei Succos*, you name it, *Shabbos* arrives each week at sundown of the sixth day ushering every Jew into her dominion.

With or without the extra *kugel* or salad, despite and albeit a hectic week, ready or not, *Shabbos* descends upon every Jewish home and wraps her velvet serenity around its members. And with every week that *Shabbos* spends with us, shares with us, imparts to us, my thanks to the *Ribono Shel Olam* for this priceless gift is magnified a thousandfold.

I thank Hashem for the chicken soup simmering on the *blech*, and the flames dancing atop the pristine silver arms of the candelabra. For the ability to savor a hot glass of tea and a *sefer* on the *parashah*, reveling in the warmth of both. For the children in their rich velvets or starched cottons, showing off the new nuggets of *Yiddishkeit* they've mined over the course of the week.

All these are dimensions of *Shabbos*, and yet *Shabbos*, in her dazzling totality, is so much more.

Shabbos is reality.

Every other day of the week, we are swept by the illusion that we are in control, that the world wouldn't run without *us* running. From early Sunday morning until late Friday afternoon, we almost believe that our health, wealth, and everything in between has a lot to do with how much, how fast, and how diligently we accomplish.

The ingredients have got to be bought, the food must be peeled, cooked, fried or baked, the clients must be called, the test papers marked, the laundry washed, folded, and ironed. The appointments have got to be made, remembered, and kept, the disappointments have got to be tackled and solved. And all this has got to be done at top speed.

On *Shabbos* all of that changes. For one day, we abandon our charade, and let The Master of the Universe run things without pretending to need our assistance. For one day, we puppets leave our act, and actually finger the strings that attach us to our Source.

For 25 hours, we step backward, upward, inward, closer to heaven, farther from earth. For a precious sliver of the week we get to sever our bonds from the slavery of this world, from our subordination to our obligations and duties. We get to watch the curtains part, and we are privileged to glimpse a higher existence, where human effort is worth only what it effects in terms of refinement of the soul.

Indeed, *Shabbos* is a crack in the opaque shutters that block off *Gan Eden* from the human eye; a crack big enough to let in a whiff of *Olam Haba*, a taste of the *manna*, and a stream of Heavenly light.

So bogged down as we are in the muddle of the other six days, busy as we are blowing the illusory bubbles of life in this world, it's a good thing nobody ever asks us whether or not we feel like making *Shabbos*.

Because sometimes, in our frenetic rush to keep this world running, we'd forget the simple truth. Hashem runs this world. And we don't make *Shabbos*. It's *Shabbos* that makes us.

The Magic Formula

Scanning the 20-some mischievous faces smirking beside their seats, my heart fluttered. Every one of those third graders sizing up my presence at the doorway seemed capable of making any substitute regret having undertaken the stint. And *I* was the substitute. The American substitute at that. How had I ever acceded to this job?

I had known that Israeli brazenness far outdid the American brand, and I'd seen enough innocent-looking third graders in action to know that they weren't as innocuous as they appeared. When she had called me with the offer the week before, I had been tempted to flatly refuse. After some deliberation on my part, however, and some coaxing on her part, I had reconsidered. In a city where ten people pounced on a job even before it was available, one didn't turn down an offer just like that.

So here I was, entering an Israeli third-grade classroom, feeling nothing short of queasy. I walked to the front of the room trying to assume a confident posture, and pulled a large, attractive doll out of my bag. With that, I began my lesson.

To my pleasant surprise, the kids were excited about the doll, and for the moment they even seemed to forget that I was a substitute whom they were supposed to harass. They followed my explanations with interest and repeated after me enthusiastically. Arms, legs, knees, elbows, fingers, toes, eyes, ears, mouth, and nose. That lasted for a while.

Then the novelty began to wear off, and I started to sense an undercurrent in the classroom. I knew it was time for the next thing.

"Everybody line up against the wall," I called, and 27 boisterous third graders scrambled out of their seats.

"I've brought you a guest," I announced, pulling out a cap which I perched on my head. "Simple Simon is here all the way from America!"

That was all it took. The word "America" brought the escalating murmur to a grinding halt, and I took advantage of the lull to quickly explain the rules of the game.

"Simple Simon says: Hands on knees."

Twenty-seven pairs of hands flew to their respective knees.

"Touch your nose."

"Close your eyes."

All was going very well. It was a great review of the words we had learned, and the kids were having a good time. I stole a glance at my wristwatch. Only 15 minutes left. I allowed myself an inaudible sigh of relief; we were over the top of the hill.

Just then, there was a barrage of uneven knocking on the class-room door. Everyone's attention, including mine, swiveled to the peephole. Judging by the sound of the giggling on the other side of the door, and the exchange of smirks inside, it seemed to be a prearranged prank.

Uh oh, I thought, my stomach churning tensely, *I'm about to lose it.* The girls, who had been enchanted by the game, dropped their poses and started noisily for the door. I stood there, twisting my pen helplessly, watching the discipline dissolve. And then I had a brainstorm.

"Simple Simon says: Everyone run to the door!"

Twenty-seven scurrying youngsters were happy to oblige. Simple Simon then instructed them to open the door, to shout, "Come later!" and to scramble back to the wall.

That was almost ten years ago.

Simple Simon, though, is still at it.

When things are not going the way I'd like them to, when I see my plans crumbling before my eyes, when people around me aren't exactly cooperative, I switch gears and become Simple Simon. Then I order thing to be just the way they are. And wonder of wonders, things and people alike always obey. I've never yet been disappointed by the magic of it.

When one of the kids is about to miss his bus in the morning, Simple Simon says, "Today the day shall start at 10 o'clock," and when the summer plans for a minivacation don't seem to be working out, Simple Simon says, "Vacation begins at home."

It may sound like a trick, an illusion, a childish attempt to delude oneself. But it works. It keeps me in control. It turns my failures into successes, my anger into joy.

We all make schedules and draw up lists. We enter appointments and occasions into our personal calendars, and plan chores and errands for certain times. All of this, on the premise that things will work out more or less the way we'd like. It's usually less. Life has a way of playing havoc with plans.

We each harbor private dreams. As children, we anticipate our teenage years, and as teenagers we draw a picture of our spouses and our future. Then as young adults embarking on the journey of life, we envision our families.

We imagine our children, with a preconceived idea of how many they will be, and just what we would like them to turn out like. Eager to set out on the route we've drawn up, we take the reins into our hands. There is Someone else, though, holding those reins, and destiny often tugs in the opposite direction.

It's when reality deviates from our own predetermined design and threatens to shake our equilibrium that Simple Simon saves the day. He tells us we haven't failed, and that life hasn't failed us. He shows us the learning experience in every disappointment, and the promising possibilities on every new horizon. And if nothing else, he helps us sprinkle our frustration with some humor (as in, "Simple Simon says: *Nobody* go to bed tonight!").

Whether it's a minor inconvenience or a detour of more major proportions, we can put on that cap and make a valiant attempt to will things to be the way they are in actuality.

It's not easy. Playing Simple Simon is anything but simple. And in the beginning, it may feel like a game. It isn't, though. It's a conscious choice, an earnest effort to rise above our natural instincts and go along with the *Ratzon HaBorei*. Because at the end of it all, no one has the power to control his own life, but we each have the power to remain in control.

Prickly Peers

"**D**o me a favor and keep the envelope, will you?" she chided, as I handed her two crisp 50 *shekel* bills tucked into a clean white envelope. "I'm your next-door neighbor; what's the point of the envelope?"

It was my first time paying the monthly maintenance dues for our building, and I looked at my new Israeli neighbor, slightly perplexed.

"This isn't America, just cut out the formality. If you want, I'll send my Srulik up each *Rosh Chodesh* and you'll give him the money. Save the envelope for your letters home."

To tell the truth, I had never before paid a thought to an envelope. It was only ShopRite's best, I thought amused, and even with ShopRite far out of reach, it hadn't dawned on me to conserve the paper pockets.

"*Zeh b'seder?*" I blushed, as she went into her kitchen to shut a flame. Not having been formally dismissed, I stood at the door awkwardly, trying to think of a polite way to end off.

"*Tikansi,*" she called out to me from her stance, puttering over the stovetop. "Come in, why are you standing there? *Targishi b'noach*! (Feel at ease.)"

That was my introduction to Israeli etiquette where neighborly relations were concerned. Actually, the protocol, or lack thereof, extended to all and any human relations. Leave the envelopes out; they were a plain hindrance, an unnecessary barrier intercepting the direct forthrightness with which Israelis preferred to deal with each other.

There was an unwritten convention, it seemed, that read something like, "Come into my kitchen at any time, I'll come into yours;

and if your door is shut, yes that's me shouting, trying to get your attention at the window."

In the beginning I was, well, taken aback, to say the least. I wasn't your most reserved specimen, but I'd grown up in the United States of America where proper social breeding was an important value. "Please" and "thank you" and "excuse me" had always constituted a very basic part of my vocabulary. Here, they seemed to be regarded in one category with the envelopes, extraneous, indulgent, and ridiculously pretentious.

It wasn't only neighbors and friends, I soon came to learn. Esteemed doctors wore jeans and were addressed on first-name basis, taxi drivers shared their life stories without any prodding, and if you wanted to know about the general populace, all you had to do was get onto a bus with a screaming infant and accidentally drop the baby's pacifier. The way I did.

In a moment, as if there'd been an air-raid drill, the entire conglomeration of passengers had dropped down on all fours. Graying men, plump women, high school students, little pipsqueaks barely weaned off their own pacifiers. Virtually everybody, besides for the driver, who queried, "*Giveret,* where do you have to go? I think there's a drugstore on my route where you can pick up a new one."

"Nonsense," countered a high-pitched voice from the recesses of under the front seat, "You think money grows on trees? We're going to find it."

While I stood there, mortified at the spectacle I was creating, two dozen passengers, or so, scrambled underfoot, kneeling and feeling and repeatedly questioning me about the pacifier's identifying features, as if it were some priceless heirloom at stake. The rest were either offering to hold the baby, or else their unsolicited tips on how to calm her down.

As I stood there, vacillating between prayers that the baby keep crying, so I would have something to fuss over, and that she stop, so that I could tell everybody to get back into their seats and abandon the hunt, I felt a warm surge of pride and tenderness come over me. It was one of those moments, moments I've experienced many times over since, that made my entire being marvel, "Where else but in the land of Eretz Yisrael?"

It was then and there that I shed my disdain for the crude standards characterizing the social interaction in this country. Perhaps they had something to learn about tact, but there was real blood flowing through the arteries of this little land, thick and strong with caring and love. The genuine thing, not the artificial brand that was pasted on like a pretty sticker, and peeled right off when you really needed it.

There was a passion, a fierce commitment, a real pulsing sense of loyalty and kinship beneath the tough veneer that attached all the members of this very diverse family. Indeed, sometimes you heard someone addressing a stranger the way you would your younger brother, but then I guess they were not strangers. They were brothers.

And when you're living here long enough, it starts rubbing off on you. For better and for worse. "They" becomes "you," and you start harboring some deep sentiments toward the woman standing behind you on line in the grocery, even though you don't know her.

And when she starts asking for the unsliced bread because it's cheaper, and you see her putting back yogurts, because she thinks better of spending 10 *shekels* on supper, you want to dig right into your purse, and say, "Just buy your kids supper, and forget about it. You don't have to pay me back."

That's what you feel like doing, but you don't. You look the other way and you make a show of scrutinizing the notice on the wall, which turns out to be a final ultimatum to all customers that as of June 15, there will be no more credit extended. Without any exceptions whatsoever, underlined very unceremoniously in black permanent marker. The shopkeeper's also got to buy bread and yogurt, you know.

And when you pick up the phone to share your feelings, and you hear your American friend react in that laid-back tone you've almost forgotten the sound of, "Oh, the cutbacks in Israel? Oh, yes, I've read about them," you just want to export some of the good hot-blooded devotion you've come to love and admire.

You want to tell everybody about your afternoon baby-sitter, a middle-aged, weather-beaten Sephardic mother, who admonishes you, "Malka, it's hot outside, the kids need drinks." And while she puts on the baby's fallen sock and you prepare some fruit and drinks in a shopping bag, you ask her if she'd consider coming over tomorrow evening.

"Tuesday evening, Malka? I'd love to, but that's when I clean the Talmud Torah."

This, after a day of teaching nursery all morning, and doing two shifts of baby-sitting in the mid-afternoon sweltering heat. This from a mother who cooks and cleans and cares for her family, and hosts her married children almost every *Shabbos* so they won't have to deal with the extra expense that preparing for *Shabbos* entails.

And when she shows up an hour late one afternoon, and you tell her the kids have been so cranky and you were wondering where she was, she apologizes profusely and tells you her two girls are going on a trip tomorrow and she'd been busy trying to procure some money from one of her employers.

And you want to tell them about the regular people, your neighbors and acquaintances, full-time teachers and jobholders, who have begun walking to the *shuk* for their produce because it's that much more affordable, and have taken on extra tutoring jobs, and have decided to save the air conditioning for *Shabbos*, though it's in the searing high 90's outside.

And you'd like to say that you're embarrassed to send grapes to school with your little son, because who buys such luxuries here in the middle of the week?

You want to describe the gathering that took place here a few weeks ago, a gathering of *tinokos shel beis rabban* crowding the two sides of the street, rows of *yingelach* led by their *rebbis*, busloads of Bais Yaakov girls and their teachers. Boys wearing denim shorts alongside those with corkscrew *peyos*, short *peyos*, *peyos* tucked under *kaplach*; girls on the other side from first grade until seminary, sporting every school uniform in town.

"*Shir hamaalos*," the loudspeaker cried out, and an explosion of soprano voices chorused plaintively after it in a symphony of dialects, "*Shir hamaalos*." More than an hour of *Tehillim* in the scorching sun, beads of sweat from the intense heat and the rousing fervor of the desperate entreaties.

"*Abba*," the little voices chimed, in their own language, in words they could understand only too well, "*Anu tzrichim lechem* (we need bread)!"

The sweat turned to tears.

Lechem. Not vacations and luxurious cottages, not renovations and interior decorating, not designer clothing and matching T-shirts. *Lechem*.

You want to tell everybody all this, you want to tell it to them just the way you see it, you feel it, but you're afraid they'll think you've gotten carried away with emotion, that you've become Israeli.

Which is true. You *are* Israeli.

But so are all of us.

Treasure Hunt

*L*ately, I've acquired a newfound appreciation for the members of the Sanitation Department.

There's nothing like a round of hands-on experience to sharpen one's awareness of the tasks that others do for us, especially the more demeaning among them. So after the grueling hours I spent head over heels in the foul-smelling dumpster, I can sincerely take my hat off to the dedicated crew who does it several times weekly.

If you're wondering what I was doing there, you probably belong to that sector of prudent individuals who personify every mother's advice to "put things immediately where they belong." Bills go straight into the file, little screws right into a labeled sandwich bag at the top of the toolbox. And pockets are there to serve an exclusively esthetic purpose, nothing to do with the temporary placing of buttons, dice, change, and any of the other trivia strewn about on an average day.

Mine play a significant secondary role. Perhaps it's even the primary capacity of my pockets to serve as miniature foster homes for any of the myriad items out of their permanent dwelling. At day's end, the distinct rattle jingling in step with me insistently reminds me to tackle the day's accumulation.

So it was, during one of these sorting ceremonies, that I noted with a slight measure of alarm that my rings, the most prominent regulars, were absent. Dropping the mangled assortment of pony holders, *gedolim* cards, safety pins, and crayons, I went straight for yesterday's pockets. No sign of the rings. Where could I have put them, I asked aloud rather anxiously, as I deftly riffled through my closet, hope escalating and plummeting each time I turned a pocket inside out.

My palms sweating, I tried to keep my cool. *Look in the jewelry drawer; perhaps you're more organized than you give yourself credit for.* Frankly, I knew I didn't stand a chance. I couldn't remember the last time I'd opened the black leather box. But in the funny way human minds work, I left the drawer unexplored and filed it away as a remote possibility; in the event that my search elsewhere proved unproductive, I'd have a last-ditch idea to hang onto.

Trying not to get sucked into a desperate frenzy, I went about the house calmly, almost detachedly, and did a thorough check, kneeling to feel under the beds, opening and closing drawers, shaking out the linens.

There are few things as disconcerting as misplacing something. You tap around the house or office, jiggle your memory for a clue, go round and round in circles, futilely moving aside items and repeatedly muttering, "Oh come on, where could it be?" It's the case with a pair of glasses, a piece of paper, a key chain, or a needle. The sense of futility is magnified a thousandfold when that elusive item has intrinsic value, when the article in hiding is an irreplaceable document, a signed check, an envelope with cash. Or a diamond ring.

When I found myself rummaging through the refrigerator, I knew my search had ended. Fruitlessly. It was time to check the jewelry box. Which really meant, it was time to go through the garbage.

I'll try and spare you the gory details, but it was sparse fun, standing stooped over the dumpster at the crack of dawn, perusing through empty sardine cans and chicken bones, straining for the redeeming glint of a lost diamond. First came the arduous task of eliminating the nonpotential bags; Mr. and Mrs. Friedman on a stained envelope, can't be ours; yellow tissues, must be Spira's litter; turkey franks, haven't served that in a while, another one down. Interesting, I found myself musing, though the conditions were scantly suited for introspection, how revealing something as peripheral as garbage can be about a family's lifestyle.

Here and there, men with *tallis* bags under their arms threw a scrutinizing glance my way; these days, characters snooping in the garbage can arouse considerable suspicion, but I stuck to my task with admirable single-mindedness. They had to be in here, my rings, and I was determined to rise above the passing discomfort of slimy peels and disparaging looks.

So I stood there like a common prowler, disregarding the awful stench, overlooking the unpleasantness, almost unmindful of the repugnant remains going through my fingers. All my mind's eye saw was the glittering jewel set in gold, the wedding band somehow lost in these mounds of trash, and my fingers, spurred by that vision, determinedly felt for the shiny hard treasures.

Wise were our grandmothers when they admonished, "A minute lost is an hour earned." Believe me, I did some honest breast-beating for the neglected minute that cost me way over an hour of grabbling through three days' worth of decomposing leftovers.

But I did strike gold.

Wrapped in a soggy envelope of newspaper ensconced apple cores pressed in a nest of spiraling peels, lay the two rings, blissfully unaware of the trouble I'd just gone through to unveil their presence.

For a moment, I simply stood there and smiled at them, a pose of weary triumph, the kind of calm satisfaction that spreads over one's being at the end of an arduous but successful search. Then, I unceremoniously removed the booty, as if I'd known all along I'd find them right there, and dropped them into a little bag which I'd brought down with me for the particular purpose.

By the time the early risers stirred, my hands were scrubbed, rings disinfected, garbage shoveled right back into the dumpster, so that no trace remained of my early-morning rendezvous. No trace, other than the heightened sense of appreciation I've mentioned at the outset. For my rings. For the dedicated trash collectors. But mostly, for the lost diamonds buried beneath the rubbish in the people all around us.

I've always gone around thinking that giving people the benefit of the doubt was somewhat of an exercise in creativity. Why couldn't your neighbor lend you his drill when you knew beyond a shadow of a doubt that he owned one? If you wanted to be small minded about it, you chalked his refusal up to plain unkind stinginess.

And if you wanted to give him the benefit of the doubt, you could brainstorm and come up with innumerable viable options. Either the drill was broken, or perhaps he'd lent it to someone. If you didn't mind tossing a really far fling, there were endless alternatives that could go. In any case, the objective was to concoct some kind of hypothesis to resolve your doubt.

When you were in the mood of harnessing your imagination, it could be rather fun. Like when you were sitting in the classroom, trying to second-guess your teacher, or predicting the surprise twist in an anecdote entitled *limud z'chus.*

In actuality, when the scenario proved slightly less dramatic, and you were quite certain of the next person's intentions, you sort of lost your inventive flair. *Don't tell me he couldn't take his plate off the table; I saw him walk out for a game of scatter.*

Judging other's actions favorably, I've discovered, is not about doubt, not even the benefit thereof. It is rooted in certainty, in the underlying premise that the missing diamond has got to be *somewhere* amid the rubbish. The sole question is: Where is it, and how long will it take to find it?

When you lose something as valuable as a diamond, you don't search because it's the virtuous thing to do. You search because you want to find it, have *got* to find it, and you don't stop until you do. You're even ready to go through the trash.

And there's plenty of trash. People are full of flaws, full of rough spots and weak points. Judging others favorably doesn't necessarily imply that the next person's behavior will be justified.

Nor is it always an optical illusion in the play. The next person may indeed act crabby, careless, inconsiderate. But if we truly value every Jew, if we feel desperate enough to find those lost jewels, our search takes on a single objective.

As we rummage through the junk, as we cringe at the injustice, as we listen to a close one's heated rendition of the story, let's remember what we're scavenging for. We wouldn't be caught snooping in the garbage for junk. So let's keep our sights firmly fixed on finding that gem; the rest is only peels.

Singled Out

Imagine if you were shopping
  in a gigantic mall,
And suddenly you heard
your name
Called out over the loudspeaker,
You'd instinctively
check your bags,
your wallet,
Look around
Startled, alarmed, off guard
You'd think hard,
"What could I have done?"
in that one stunned moment
you'd admit,
to crimes no one could have seen you
commit.

Imagine if you were
on a plane
strolling down a lane,
in a crowded *shul*,
or *lehavdil*,
in a packed pool,
and suddenly you heard
your name,
thundering over a microphone,
you'd stop in your tracks,
quiver with fright,
blush with shame,
just from simply
hearing your name.

Well then,
listen dear,
One of these days,
They'll be calling your name
up there.
Loud and clear,
Thundering, booming,
All consuming,
And if you'd only hear,
you'd shiver and shake,
and quake
With fear
down here.

Frosty Frills

Extravagance doesn't usually move me. In fact, very often, it doesn't even register with me. "What color were the table-cloths?" my sister will animatedly ask, as I describe some elegant affair I've attended, and I'll be forced to admit, albeit abashedly, that I honestly don't remember.

Not that I don't appreciate beauty. I love the slender grace of pearly white lilies set off by dark green ferns in tall crystal. I can stare in fascinated enchantment at the breathtaking landscape of deep red strawberries and striking kiwis piled on mountains of melons and grapes. And I definitely enjoy the ambience of classy china and fine cutlery on starched linens.

I guess I like beauty in its natural context, when it is in such perfect harmony, it is almost unnoticeable. I like when elegance permeates the atmosphere like a pleasant scent, like a delicate spice, unmistakably enhancing, yet subtle enough to remain in the background.

Somehow, when the frills of an affair move into center stage, I feel as if the props have replaced the drama. When the dressing is served as the main dish, flaunted and aggrandized, I find it jarring. *Turn down the volume*, I feel like saying; *I can't hear the music.*

So it's interesting, almost out of character, that I reap particular satisfaction from this kind of lavish extravagance at a *hachnasas sefer Torah*. On that occasion, I almost wait for the pomp and fanfare, for the torches and banners and lights, for the rich velvet *chupah* and the sterling-silver crown, I am almost disappointed when the detail are downplayed.

At a *hachnasas sefer Torah*, a display of grandiosity does something to me. It makes my chest tighten and my heart pull; it makes my eyes sting with tears and a little butterfly inside me soar. And if I try to catch that butterfly, if I try to grasp its elusive transience and hold it up to the light, I find the flutter of ecstasy mingled with pride, an exuberant sense of alliance with the uninhibited expression of love and reverence manifest in the décor of the day. Where in the universe can you find a celebration like this one, a perfect synthesis of extravagance and eternity?

I usually keep this quivering joy to myself. As I walk along with the procession, reflecting on the remarkable blend of modest restraint and fiery ebullience, I usually don't give voice to the sensation swelling inside me, the invisible match striking the side of my soul and setting my passions on fire.

The last time around, however, as we moved forward, craning our heads, to catch a glimpse of the beloved *Torah* almost smothered by the entourage, the intensity of my private moment was interrupted by a charming little woman whom I'd never met before.

"Posh, isn't it?" she commented lightly in an endearing British accent.

I nodded a smile in response.

"Nice, the way people spend their money, don't you think?" she went on, and again, I smiled at her assessment. Nice, yes, nice the way people spend their money. I guess that expressed the crux of my soaring sentiment in seven words.

I liked her, this simple little English woman who had so effortlessly zoomed right in on my roiling emotions, and tied my thoughts of extravagance and eternity into a plain, neat bow.

We walked along in comfortable silence, she pumping her toddler's hand to the rhythm of the lively clapping, and I right behind her, taking it all in.

We watched the *sefer Torah* as she was welcomed and embraced by the older *sefarim* that had come out of the *aron kodesh* to greet the new bride. Again, the tide rose, and my heart surged with an engulfing wave of happiness.

Then as we got closer to the *shul*, in whose adjoining hall a sumptuous meal was awaiting the guests, my eyes caught sight of a tangle of little boys and girls clad in festive attire scrambling toward the entrance, clamoring to reach the dozen or so cartons of ice pops that were stacked near the door.

"Wow!" My acquaintance of the hour was visibly moved. I wasn't sure if it was the culmination of the dancing outside that had prompted her exclamation, or the impressive sight of the festively set tables. It was neither.

"Look at all those ice lollies!" she gasped, pointing to the scores of kids savoring the frozen treats that had been provided in honor of the occasion. "I don't know who sponsored this, but he must be really rich. Imagine what this cost him, all these ice lollies!"

She said it with such earnestness that I had to nod in agreement. Inside, though, I was frankly amused.

Lady, I thought, *if the donor was able to afford a sefer Torah, if he was able to pay for the band and cater this grand-scale affair, then yes, he certainly must have money.* Of all things to pick on, though, the ice lollies.

She however, stood openmouthed at the demonstration of benevolence. She had no idea what a *sefer Torah* cost; she had never tried to shop for one. She didn't know what fees a professional band exacted, or how much an exclusive caterer charged for a portion. She knew that ices, or ice lollies, as she had called them, cost a *shekel* apiece at the local grocery. That much she knew. And a hundred ice lollies at a *shekel* apiece was a small fortune. Let alone a few hundred. I still liked her, though, this unpretentious woman. I like her for her unsophisticated, almost childlike innocence. And I liked her for putting a mirror to my own small-minded perception of things. Sometimes, after all, we need to chuckle at a cartoon before we recognize our own dismaying self featured in the picture. How often, in our encounters with the marvels of life, do we skip over the entirety of our own existence, gloss over the synchrony of creation, and gap at the wonder of ice lollies? How many times do we remark over dramatic one-time phenomena as if they were the most compelling testimony to the Sponsor of the whole affair?

Watch anybody's reaction to a set of triplets, listen to people hoot in utter disbelief at an account of someone's miraculous recovery from illness. Somehow, these disclaimers of nature elicit more awe and astonishment than the ongoing brilliance of nature's design. We are as duly impressed by the ice lollies as that woman, just as taken by the frivolous details of a multimillion-dollar operation.

Not that miracles don't play a very prominent role in the unfolding of our history. Miracles are Hashem's way of blowing the fuse every once in a while, so we inattentive creatures can look up for a moment in startled shock, and say, "Hey, who did that?"

Something about our naïve amazement, though, reflects our shallow appreciation for the fact that gravity never lapses, or that the moon fades in and out of the clouds, or that the leaves turn copper and crimson in autumn.

Like stars overhead, the vast complexity of these wonders twinkles deceivingly small, and if we don't consciously strain to look upward, we can altogether miss them. Miracles are different. They strike like lightning, splitting the skies, and ripping through the darkness below, forcibly diverting our attention.

Which is, after all, what they were meant to do. We are children and we relate to the thrill of ice lollies a lot better than we can appreciate bounty and generosity on a grand and constant scale.

It doesn't end, though, in childish gasps over momentary sensations. It is when we don't get those ice lollies, when we want them and need them and pray for them, that our simplistic amazement does a quick flip into dangerous despair. When nature ruthlessly denies us what we would like, we are suddenly left with the dismal lining of our earlier euphoria, the mistaken perception that the miracles we are pining for are somehow immensely difficult for the donor to provide.

When the medical field puts the odds against us, when we've tried every path out of some predicament, but haven't found a viable way out, when the laws of nature very clearly spell doom, we often forget that miracles are the very same gift and from the same gift

Giver. They are simply the ribbons and wrapping that occasionally replace the staid brown paper of statistics so we can see beyond the label, "sender unknown."

We may need to pray harder, or there may be some reason in the total scheme of things that precludes us from receiving our most fervent desire, but let's not forget; for the One Who orchestrated the entire event, Who donated the Torah and sponsored the band, Who strung the lights and provided the food, and few cartons of the ice lollies are a negligible affair.

In the cold climate of the 21st-century, where facts and figures graph the miracles of everyday existence, we sometimes forget this simple reality. In the frigid temperature of the scientific era, medical and technological advances have built a solid wall, hiding Hashem's Presence safely beyond.

The wall, though, is only a fragile illusion; we don't need a miracle to break it down. It's simply a matter of igniting the *emunah* within us so we can melt the ice.

Our Soul Protection

I must have told the story of *Yosef Mokir Shabbos* dozens of times. I've seen it on filmstrip, I've heard it sung, I've admired arts and crafts depicting the tale. And although I've appreciated different aspects of the narrative at different points in my life,

I've always identified with the hero of the story, the fabled Yosef, who scrimped and saved, and spent his every last penny in order to honor and beautify the *Shabbos*.

As a young child, I mentally spat at the despicable gentile, that cunning scoundrel of a neighbor, who plotted wily schemes to con Yosef out of the reward that was coming to him. As an adult, my reaction was somewhat more restrained. Still, it never occurred to me to sympathize with the conspiring antagonist, or to see the tale, even fleetingly, from his point of view.

I don't know why, but when I picked up the dog-eared paperback last week, and turned to an illustration of the cornered villain awakening from his nightmare, strangely enough, I related to the look of wild panic in his eyes. Momentarily forgetting about Yosef, about the high drama and the happy ending, I suddenly glimpsed something in those darting pupils, that I've seen mirrored in the eyes of those around me as of late. Fear.

I suddenly noticed the trapped expression of a frightened soul, of one whose most cherished possession is in jeopardy. I saw a hunted individual, a prisoner in his very own home, a mind feverishly trying to come up with a way out of its predicament.

Very much like the look one encounters nowadays at the bus stops and the newsstands, very much like the grim expression worn by pedestrians and drivers weaving their way through the thinned traffic, trying to dodge danger.

Perhaps it's not as palpable elsewhere. Almost a year separates September 11 and the bustle of contemporary life; a year that stands like a pane of tinted glass, fostering the illusion that the tragedy lies somewhere behind an opaque wall. Only those who have been behind that partition, whose view of life has been tinted a dark, ominous black, know that it is fragile and transparent.

In Eretz Yisrael, though, ordinary living has become shadowed with peril. Itineraries have become weighty decisions; people anxiously peer out the window when a loved one is a few minutes late in coming. One scrutinizes odd-looking characters in the bank or the post office, and the innocent rumble of thunder can set off a wild stampede of panic-stricken people.

Slowly but surely, the insidious worm of terror is gnawing its way into the hearts of the people, and all the regular motions of everyday living have become encumbered by the heavy burden of fear.

Sometimes we ask ourselves, "What am I doing here, in this country so riddled by bombs and tragedies?" Sometimes others ask it of us. In a mixture of admiration and admonishment, they question our commitment to staying in what appears to be the lion's den. And then, before we've even got a chance to seriously consider the question, some incident somewhere on the globe shakes our equilibrium and offers the answer in our stead.

The heavy clouds of danger aren't static. Like the dark gray harbingers of storm moving rapidly across a winter sky, anti-Semitism traverses the entire globe. Each time we sigh with relief that a certain zone is clear of danger, an explosive event rips the headlines, shredding our sense of security into tiny bits.

Even within the lion's den itself, we desperately attempt to delude ourselves, to somehow make mental demarcations partitioning off areas of safe territory. "Meron is safe. There haven't been any bombs there," or "You don't have to be afraid to travel here; the buses are bullet proof." It doesn't take long for these smug utterances to go up in smoke together with the twisted metal and burning rubber, together with the martyred *kedoshim* who are taken from our midst.

Each time, we awaken from the nightmare in a cold sweat, clutching our lives, shuddering with fear that it could have been us. Like that gentile neighbor haunted by his dream, we desperately tighten our grip on our dearest asset, life itself. We mark yet another place off our map, and we reconsider plans we hadn't given a thought to in the past. We feel the noose closing in on us, and we think, where can we seek a safe haven?

September 11 has proven that anything can happen anywhere. Maybe we've got something to learn from the wealthy neighbor in the classic tale of *Yosef Mokir Shabbos*. Maybe we can pick up a lead from that gentile's effort to protect his fortune.

Looking at the colorful illustration of the man sewing a gem into the lining of his hat, I ponder the plot I've known since kindergarten. Yosef's neighbor didn't attempt to flee or to hide his valuables somewhere far away. He must have had the premonition that his fate would follow him and clamp its iron vise down on his money. Somehow though, he was convinced that his own person was invincible.

So he liquidated all his assets, sold his sprawling estates, converted his furs and silks, gold and silver, and invested his entire fortune in something he could carry on himself. Something he would sleep with and eat with and take along wherever he went. The next picture has him strutting around, unafraid. With the jewel safely stowed beneath his hat, he knew that wherever he would venture, it would be protected.

That Hashem foiled his impermeable plan in the end is irrelevant to us. We've got to imitate the tactic. How does that timeless ad go? *Buy diamonds; diamonds are forever.* It may not be true of jewelry, but it's true of Jewry.

Seeking shelter begins with a deliberate liquidating process; one that varies for each individual. The housewives among us don't share the same task as the yeshivah *bachurim*, those in *chinuch* carry different responsibilities from those in the business world. The medium may differ, but the exchange is the same. We've got to cash in all our interests, channel our strengths and abilities, invest all our physical and mental energies, and the most precious of all, our time in this world, toward the acquisition of one single, inviolable, gem: Torah and the *mitzvos* within it.

For wherever the onslaught may be, one thing's clear; our problem is not geographical, and neither is our escape. There is one single impenetrable shelter, one bit of safe territory that no Arab bomb can infiltrate. And that is under the lining, within each one of us.

Faulty Thinking

Necessity may be the mother of invention, but invention is definitely the necessity of the mother. Whoever said anyone was wasting her creativity sitting home with kids most certainly wasn't a mother. Because as I see it, ingenuity is as directly related to motherhood as math is to accounting.

On the job, I've learned how to turn my bathtub into an ocean, my playroom into a park, and simple wooden blocks into the most delectable dishes. I've learned how to spin tales revolving around a spider crawling up the wall, and how to turn a bunch of uncooperative youngsters into an enthusiastic "cleaning agency."

And I've seen mothers the world over do the same. I'm always amazed at the way parenthood forces even the most uncreative adult to come up with a resourceful solution when push comes to shove, very literally. I've witnessed it in the doctor's office, on the airplane, and during long *Shabbos*-afternoon walks.

Without as much as a candy or a Band-Aid in sight, I've watched many a mother stop her child's tears and put a smile on his or her face. Which is wonderful, magic really. But it can have its downside too. Like Sidewalk Syndrome, for instance.

Sidewalk Syndrome starts innocently enough. It begins with a bang or a bump or a bruise, and a wailing tot squatting squarely in the middle of the sidewalk, refusing to walk another inch. Now, if something like this happens on the home front, Mom has her instruments handy, from Bacitracin and Band-Aids to balloons.

Right there, though, in the middle the street, stripped of her bag of tricks, Mother has only her very own voice to fall back on. So if offering a kiss and a thorough examination of the skinned knee doesn't placate her charge, I've learned that there is another innovative method of appeasing the youngster. It's called, "Smack the sidewalk."

There are numerous variations of the same theme, but the basic idea is the same.

"Look at that awful scrape! It's all the silly sidewalk's fault. There. Smack the sidewalk. Good!"

I've gotten stuck on the sidewalk behind such scenarios more than once, and I've always smirked in amusement at the tactic. Yet, as ludicrous as the solution sounds, I've seen it yield almost instant results time and time again. Which is just what makes it so dangerous.

Watching a 2-year-old vengefully smack the concrete can be comical. How many of us, though, are still smacking the sidewalk at age 20, or 30, or 40? Oh no, we wouldn't raise our hands to strike, and we never as much as stomped the pavement in our lives.

If we really want to know, however, if we're suffering from Sidewalk Syndrome, let's think of the first question we ask when we confront a broken stereo, an open freezer door, or a missing envelope. If the content of the question boils down to "Who did this?" then we're sure victims of the malady. "Who was the last one to use the stereo?" or "Who left this tape within baby's reach?"

Come on, let's be honest. What practical benefit can we possibly derive from knowing exactly which member of the clan left the *siddur* out in the rain, or who exited the house last without remembering to shut the air conditioner? None. Knowing the answer, however, will give us a sidewalk to smack. It'll provide us with an address toward which we can forward a good self-righteous speech about the irresponsibility and inconsideration of whatever was or wasn't done to cause the damage.

Not that it pays the bill, or restores the soggy *siddur.* It doesn't, but for some reason, it makes us feel better. Or at least it makes us *feel* like we're feeling better. So we use it time and time again. We use it to soothe ourselves, and we use it to soothe others. Instead of offering plain old support and empathy, we insist on shading our sympathy with indignant undertones.

"What? You still haven't got water? What kind of contractor are you working with? I've never heard of such irresponsibility. I hope you let him have it!"

Somehow, instead of focusing on solutions, we're concentrating on one destructive, unproductive, almost impossible to prove, word: fault. Like a game of fast catch, fault gets tossed around in a hot volley, with nobody willing to claim ownership. Instead of expending our energy to address more actual and immediate concerns, our minds become primarily occupied with one wholly irrelevant detail. Whom can we blame for the mishap?

In the course of our day, as in the course of our lives, we inevitably absorb some hurtful blows, physical and emotional. The screen door slams shut on our pinky, we bump into an open cabinet door, trip over a briefcase. Before we even manage to register an "Ouch!", our minds are already seething, "If that guy doesn't come down to fix this screen, I don't know what I'm going to do!" Blame just seems to spring up by itself together with the tears and the anger.

And it's not only the little mishaps in life. Some people go around all their lives blaming. Once you're at it, there's an awful lot of things you can fault people for. You can blame your temper and your tardiness, your fat and your failures, your laxity or your laziness.

If you want, you can blame your child's report card and your leaking faucet, your flooded basement and your daughter's stutter. You can even blame the fact that you blame at all (It's my mother's fault! She taught me to smack the sidewalk.).

You can blame the principal, and the bank, you can blame the telephone company and the tax collectors, the neighbors and the *mechutanim*, and of course the favorite victims, the members of your own household. Then, when you finish blaming people, you can start blaming circumstances. There's the hot weather, the cramped apartment, the tight budget. That's shaky territory though, because it's getting awfully close to complaining about the One Above.

So you go back and you look some more, and inevitably you find a person to blame. Because people aren't perfect, and you'll always find *someone* who did *something* that had *some* adverse effect on your life. No matter what you're missing, whether it's a pair of scissors or a sense of serenity, one thing you can always be assured to find is fault.

If you want to, that is. Because pointing a finger is really a cop-out. It's a way of deflecting our own frustration and hurt and disappointment, and turning it into anger to vent on someone else. It's a way of circumventing the issue of accepting Hashem's will, and forgetting that the perpetrators are only His emissaries. Blaming cripples us from taking responsibility and learning to handle our inner selves. After all, it's much easier to put your hands on your hips and fling the bill at somebody else than take care of the payment yourself.

But incriminations keep us stuck in the past. They put us on rewind instead of keeping us in the forward mode. They ensnare us into the tangle of petty arguments and hamper our growth. Because really, if you're stooping down to slap the sidewalk, how can you reach for the stars?

On a Scale of One to Ten

"That's it. You either are, or you aren't!" she pronounced emphatically, her frustration evident in every syllable. "And if you aren't, you'll just never ever know what it means to be."

A pretty universal statement, but she happened to have been talking about being overweight. And I was willing and able to commiserate wholeheartedly.

"Yes," we both sighed indignantly, "those women who sit down to a thick slab of cake without thinking twice, just won't ever begin to realize what kind of battle we fight every waking hour of the day (What about those middle-of-the-night kitchen raids with a baby in one arm?). And it's seven days a week, 52 weeks a year.

"When I see women," she continued, "fitting like models into their *sheva berachos* suits ten years later, I must admit, it takes an earnest effort on my part not to be consumed with envy."

Being a co-sufferer, it wasn't hard for me to understand her utter exasperation, or her sheer envy of those who didn't even know what it meant to count a calorie.

"What 's really getting to me is the fact that this thing is so never ending," she complained miserably. "If I had some tangible, reachable goal, which once achieved, remained stable forever, I could see myself going for it."

Yes, I knew all too well what she was talking about. Each day was either an up or a down; you never just remained status quo. When you were up, you were walking, talking, breathing, thinking, DIET, eating broiled chicken tops and rice cakes with your soup. Your conversations centered upon how to make oven-fried fish, or broccoli quiche and you spent your time waiting on line in the bank feverishly tallying every calorie you ingested up until that time. Unless you were busy brainstorming how to make an all-protein supper; it all depended with which diet you were currently experimenting.

It was either that, or you were hopelessly off the diet. You had some date safely circled on the calendar in the far-enough future, when you were really, but *really,* going to get down to business and start the diet again. Until that time, whenever the guilt feelings came out of the freezer together with the cake, you firmly reminded your conscience that the fateful date hadn't yet arrived. That was your cue to start eating mindlessly, with your conscience safely at bay.

It was sort of a seesaw effect, the numbers on the scale, and the state of your spirits. When one was up, the other was down, and each one gave the other a fair turn before the seesaw went cranking in the opposite direction.

Of course the parties and Bar Mitzvahs and N'shei meetings always arrived on those days when the numbers were riding high, and you were somewhere down below. Then you wearily started the closet-emptying ceremony in a futile attempt to find an outfit that felt fairly comfortable and covered the problem of the bulk, or at least the bulk of the problem.

Your bed soon looked like the dressing room on the night of the 50 percent-off sale, piled high with skirts, vest, blouses, and jackets that just hadn't fit the patrons' criteria, the criterion in this case being none other than you.

Then, inevitably, the phone would ring, and who would it be if not your perpetually size 6 friend, chirping happily that she was coming to pick you up in two minutes, and — hey, what's the matter? Everything all right?

Well, no, not really, not at all in fact, but then why bother explaining? She would never understand anyway.

And you'd probably be right. Chances are, she wouldn't relate to your war-torn bedroom, but then, she very well might relate to your war-torn spirits. Struggles are inherent to the human condition, and diets are only one tiny booth in the carnival of struggles that life is comprised of.

I may be struggling with a diet, *she* may be struggling with an eating disorder. I may be pummeling fists with indolence, while she may be fighting her destructive tendency to run her life like a treadmill on the highest speed. I may be crying in frustration over my inability to say no, and she may be painstakingly trying to pry her fists open and learn to give more freely.

Those are the inner struggles, the battles you take along with you to weddings, on trips, to bed. Those are the wars that take place in your heart, on your conscience, whose enemy tanks rumble mercilessly across your mind whenever you have a free minute, and some quiet, to think.

What about the people who are *really* struggling, those whose lives are enmeshed in trials and tribulations beyond the everyday inner battles? The struggle to make ends meet, to contend with the never-ending pressure of feeding and clothing a family without funds. The test of the childless couple living a life of private pain, or the older single forced to face disappointment after crushing disappointment.

And then there are the soldiers on the front lines, grappling with terminal illness, crippling handicaps, mental disorders.

We dieters, with all due respect, are only tasting a moderate portion (for a change!) of this whole struggling affair. People may not understand the particular variables of our problem, but most of them can most certainly relate to the principle standing behind them. And if they don't, they're bound to at some point or another, because nobody — nobody — is exempt from struggling.

That's what we're here for, to struggle to uproot bad habits, to struggle to balance our imperfections. And just like the diet, you're either on it or you're off it. And just like with the diet, it takes perseverance, determination, and constant awareness. There are no magic formulas, and it doesn't just happen by itself.

So next time you're on the bottom of the seesaw, lying low, and about to be consumed with envy, remember: All this struggling is indeed a weighty matter. And it isn't only about weight.

Naaseh!

My heart lurched when I saw her. Not because of the way she looked, which would have been reason enough. Hunched over a walker as she was, I barely recognized the shadow of my usually robust aunt. Her face was pale and gaunt and it was evident from her deliberate steps, arm linked in her eldest daughter's embrace, that walking was a painful effort.

It wasn't solely the sight of her condition, though, that made something inside me swirl and then sink. It was the sight of her, period. It was her inevitable presence coming toward me that invited wave upon wave of sickening dread.

Only someone who has experienced it, the terrible moment when time slams its merciless door on simmering good intentions, knows the feeling. That tightening knot, that hot flush of shame and guilt, that utterly defenseless sense of remorse.

A million apologies crowded my mind. A million excuses and not one decent reason. It all sounded so ridiculous now, so pathetic, standing here facing her feeble frame. What was I going to say? "Oh Aunt Sarah, I'm so pleased to see you. I think of you all the time"?

"You do? So why didn't you pick up the telephone to tell me?"

"Oh, I've meant to call you so many times. I honestly have. You're on every list in my drawer. But I'll tell you, what I really wanted to do was send you a hot meal, or at least a cake, or at the very least, a pretty card with a heartfelt poem inside it."

"Oh, and that's why you didn't call."

In the two minutes it took for her to painstakingly advance toward the reception area where I was standing, I had the whole miserable dialogue played out in my mind. And I had to admit, it sounded so flimsy, so thoroughly senseless and inadequate, that I preferred the deafening silence as my mind thrashed about for some alternative opening.

"Hi Malky, how are you?" Aunt Sarah broke the uncomfortable lull, and the deep voice coming out of her sagging face felt like a million tiny needles sticking every pore on my burning cheeks.

I saw all the parcels, the gifts and chocolates, the cakes and cards melt in the humiliating heat of the moment, as I gagged on my apologies and tried to articulate my sincere concern for her. Simply, genuinely, the way I could have done two months ago on the telephone, immediately after her surgery. When it would have had the sweetness of forethought and love, not the sour taste of a strained afterthought.

But I had wanted to do it right. I owed Aunt Sarah so much: Wouldn't a tangible piece of my love mean so much more than a trite telephone call? Wouldn't a steaming thermos of vegetable soup, or my warmest wishes in charming rhyme, be appreciated infinitely more than another two-minute call between the hassle of hospital routine?

In a moment of frankness, when I'd been candid enough to admit that vegetable soup and poetry simply weren't materializing, I had considered compromising on my own handiwork and sending flowers or some chocolate arrangement. Granted, so it wouldn't be the very nicest, but it would be.

It wasn't, though. "Aunt Sarah" had begun to represent some sort of a conscience to me.

"Have you spoken to Aunt Sarah lately?" a sister-in-law would innocently ask, and the blood would rush to my head.

"Oh no, I've forgotten to arrange those flowers. I'd better take care of them the minute I hang up!"

" Flowers? Why don't you just call her?"

A simple question. A simple question with a complicated answer. If I had called her immediately, true it wouldn't have been flowers and calligraphy, but it would have sufficed. At this point, a telephone call would be a mockery. A meaningful gesture, I reasoned, would at least somewhat justify the time that had elapsed.

I won't tire you with the details of the arduous journey along guilt-ridden trails, but it swerved crazily between my grand fantasies, and self-condemnation, and the unwillingness to yank the reins on my drive for excellence and settle for a humble destination along the way. It's the journey I've traveled so many times that I know the route in my sleep; it's the trip that goes round and round in ever-widening spirals until it ends in failure.

As I fumbled awkwardly, tripping over my excuses, trying desperately to convey my truest intentions that had somehow turned stale, I saw a glint of understanding in Aunt Sarah's eyes.

She didn't try to smooth my stammering with an all-forgiving "It's O.K.," nor did she discredit my sincerity with a dubious nod.

"Malka," she said knowingly, "you're young and you're going to learn what my mother taught me. If you're going to end up serving plain mashed potatoes, you may as well serve them hot. And if it's between serving them cold or starving your company, then go ahead and serve them cold. But serve them!"

I blessed Aunt Sarah for her keen perception and her forthright advice as I turned her words over in my mind. I ought to put them on a magnet, tack them in some conspicuous spot right above all my lists, I thought.

The problem with me, I concluded ruefully later that night as I jotted her words of wisdom onto a piece of cardboard, is that I've never made peace with the eventuality of mashed potatoes. In an unrealistic pursuit of perfection, I've never really learned to relinquish those dreams of gourmet fare. Oh no, I'm not going to serve mashed potatoes, not me.

"Good, Better, BEST," I've been chanting since third grade, "Never let them rest, until the good becomes better and the better becomes best."

Who said good always became better and better invariably became best? What about the grandiose plans for best that never even became good? Like so many of the finest threads that form the tightrope of life, it's forever that fragile balance between striving for *shleimus* and the realization that in this finite world, perfection is illusory.

Aspirations could indeed be impeccable, unlimited, but that the physical translation of them could be flawless is a myth, a baseless notion, a regretful waste of energy.

Every individual has his own budgeting to do, given the inescapable reality that we each have limited resources at our disposal: our time, our energy, our funds. Sometimes in our blind quest for excellence, we trim our ideals to make our ideas possible. Perfection is about trimming our *ideas* so that our *ideals* will be possible.

It means attending the *simchah* if you can't send the cake, it means calling if you can't attend. It means writing a poem if you can't afford the present, and expressing it in simple words if you can't compose the poem. It means *davening* the *berachos* if you can't finish *Shacharis*, and learning one *blatt* if you can't cover ten.

Perfection is not about feeding our ego in our zeal to do the best, it's not even about never letting them rest; it's about meeting our daily challenges as growing *Yidden* with the spontaneous cry of *"Naaseh!"* reverberating all the way from Har Sinai.

It's the resolution to respond to inspiration with action, and leave the pondering for some other time. Because it's always better underdone than overdue.

Glossary

abba — father

Adar — 12th month of the Jewish year

Ahavas Olam — a section of the *Shacharis* prayer service

ahavas Yisrael — love of one's fellow Jew

Aibeshter — G-d

aliyah — immigrating to Israel

Amalek — nation that wishes to destroy the Jews

Amidah — *Shemoneh Esrei* prayer

aron kodesh - ark

Aseres HaDibros — Ten Commandments

Aseres Yemei Teshuvah — The Ten Days of Repentance, which begin with Rosh Hashanah and end with Yom Kippur.

Asher Yatzar — blessing recited after relieving oneself

askan, pl. *askanim* — community activist(s)

aveilus — mourning

aveirah pl. *aveiros* — transgression

avodah — work; service

avodas Hashem — service of G-d

b'ezrat Hashem — with G-d's help

b'samim — spices

baal chessed — one who does acts of lovingkindness

baal koreh — the person who reads from the Torah in the synagogue

baal middos — a person with commendable character traits

baal tokei'a — the one who blows the *shofar* in the synagogue

baalas simchah — woman who is making a *simchah*

baalas teshuvah — a woman who has returned to being an observant Jew

Babi, Bubby — grandmother

bachur — unmarried young man, especially a yeshivah *bachur*

bachur meyuchad — an exceptional boy

balabusta — housewife

balagan — chaos

balatas — stone floors found in most Israeli buildings

bashert — destined from Above

bechirah — free will

bedikas chametz — the search for *chametz*, usually performed the night before Passover begins

beis din — Rabbinical Court

Beis HaMikdash — Holy Temple

beis medrash — study hall

Beit Hachlamah — convalescent home for new mothers

ben kamah hu? — How old is he??

ben zekunim — child of one's old age

bentch — (1) to give a blessing (2) to recite Grace After Meals

bentchers — booklets containing the Grace After Meals

berachah acharonah — lit. the last blessing. This is recited after eating certain foods.

berachah, pl. *berachos* — blessing(s)

bimah — table in synagogue from which the Torah Scroll is read

birchas Kohanim — blessing of the Jewish people recited by *Kohanim*

birchos haShachar — morning blessings

bitachon — trust

bituach leumi — health insurance

bitul Torah — wasting time that would be better spent in learning Torah

blatt — folio

blech — piece of tin placed over an open flame on the Sabbath

bli neder — lit. without an oath

bubbah maaseh — folk tale

chag — holiday

chalav Yisrael — milk or dairy products that have been under Rabbinical supervision from the time of the milking

challah pl. *challos* — braided loaf of bread; traditional for a Sabbath or Festival meal

chametz — leaven

chamud — dear one

Chanukah — Festival of Lights

chap a minyan — grab a *minyan* — colloquial term

chatzos — midday or midnight

chaval — What a pity!

chavivus hamitzvos — love of *mitzvos*

chavrusa — study partner

Chazal — Sages

chazzan — cantor

cheder — elementary school

cheshbon hanefesh — spiritual accountability; soul searching

chessed — kindness

chiddush — novel thought

chillul Shabbos — desecration of the Sabbath

chinuch — education

chodesh — month

Chol HaMoed — intermediate days of the festivals of *Succos* and *Pesach*

cholent — hot stew served at the Sabbath day meal

chrein — ground horseradish, usually mixed with beets

chupah — (a) wedding ceremony, (b) wedding canopy

churban — destruction, usually referring to the destruction of the Temple or to the Holocaust

Da mah l'hashiv l'apikores — Know what to replay to an unbeliever

daven, davening — praying

dayan, pl. *dayanim* — judge(s)

derech eretz — proper conduct

deveikus — the ecstatic state of cleaving to G-d

dikduk — grammar

dikduk b'mitzvos — meticulousness in mitzvah observance

divrei chizuk — words of encouragement

divrei Torah — words of Torah

dvar mitzvah — a matter involving a mitzvah

eim hamalchus — mother of royalty

eimah — fear

eimas hadin — fear of judgment

Elul — 6th month of the Jewish year

emunah — faith

Erev Pesach — the day prior to the Passover Festival

Erev Rosh Hashanah — the day before *Rosh Hashanah*

erev tov — good evening

erev Yom Tov — the day before a festival

fleishigs — foods containing meat or meat by-products

freilichen — joyful

frum — Orthodox, religious

gabbai — sexton

gadol — outstanding Torah scholar

galus — exile

galus Mitzrayim — the exile in Egypt

galus Yid — Jew in exile; used to describe a certain mind-set *gam zu l'tovah* — this, too, is for the good

gan — kindergarden

Gan Eden — Garden of Eden

gaon pl. *geonim* — brilliant Torah scholar

gelt — money

gemach — free-loan society

geulah — redemption

gevurah — heroism; strength; ability to overcome

gezunt — good health

gezunterheit — in good health

giborah — heroine

Giveret — Madame, Mrs.

gut gebentcht yuhr — "A good, blessed year," a greeting used especially around Rosh Hashanah.

hachna'ah — self-abnegation

hachnassas sefer Torah — ceremony welcoming a newly written *sefer Torah* to a synagogue

HaKadosh Baruch Hu — The Holy One, Blessed is He

halachah pl. *halachos* — Jewish law

halachah shiur — a lecture on Jewish law

Haman — In *Purim* story; evil Persian minister who desired to annihilate the Jews

Hamantashen — three-cornered filled pastry

hashem yinakem damam — May G-d avenge their blood

hashgachah — supervision

Hashgachah Pratis — Divine Providence

Hashgachas Hashem — G-d's personal management of every detail of day-to-day life.

hashkafah — Jewish ideology

Havdalah — prayer recited at the end of Sabbath

hilchos Shabbos — laws of the Sabbath

hishtadlus — effort

histapkus b'muat — being satisfied with the minimum

holipches — stuffed cabbage rolls

Isru Chag — day after *Yom Tov*

Kaddish — prayer recited in memory of a deceased individual

kallah — bride

kaplach — skullcaps

kapparas avonos — atonement for sin

Kashrus — Jewish dietary laws

kavod habriyos — respect for G-d's creatures

kedoshim — martyrs

kedushah — holiness

kesivah v'chasimah tovah — traditional New Year's greeting

Kiddush — (1) blessing over wine (2) festive gathering in *shul*

Kiddush Hashem — sanctifying G-d's Name

kinder — children

kinderlach — little children

Klal Yisrael — the Jewish people

klap — bang

Klei Yakar — commentary on the Chumash

kollel — academy for advanced studies, usually for married men

kollel store — subsidized grocery store for those learning in *kollel*

korban - sacrifice

Kosel HaMaaravi — Western Wall

Krias Shema — three paragraphs from the Torah that we are commanded to recite twice daily

kugel — pudding

lamdan(im) — learned individual(s)

landsleit — people who come from the same town

lebedig - lively

lechem — bread

lehavdil — in contradistinction

leining — reading of the Torah or the *Megillah* portion

levayah — funeral

licht bentching — candle lighting

limud z'chus — (1) benefit of the doubt (2) judge favorably

listig — happy, joyful

Luchos HaBris — The Tablets of the Covenant

Maariv — evening prayer

maasim tovim — good deeds

machsan — Israeli equivalent of American basement

machshavah k'maaseh — good intentions are considered good deeds

machzor — prayer book for the festivals

Mah Nishtanah — lit., what is different. A passage of the Passover Haggadah, usually recited by a child, asking about the differences between that night and other nights.

makolet — grocery store

Malach HaMashchis — Angel of Destruction

Maoz Tzur — poem sung on *Chanukah*

Marror — The bitter herb used at the Passover Seder

Mashiach — the Messiah

masmid pl., *masmidim* — diligent student(s)

mechanchim — teachers, educators

mechilah — absolution

mechitzos — barriers, room dividers separating the genders

mechutanim — the parents-in-law of one's child

Megillas Esther — Scroll of Esther; read on *Purim*

meivin — expert

Melech Malchei Hamelachim — The King of kings

menorah — candelabrum

merov kol — overabundance of everything

mesechta pl. *mesechtos* — tractate of Talmud

mesiras nefesh — selfless dedication

mesorah — Jewish law and tradition transmitted from generation to generation

middos — character traits

miklat — shelter

milchige — dairy

minhag — custom

minyan — quorum of ten men for prayers

misgaber — to overcome

Mishlei — Proverbs

mishmishim — apricots

mispallelim — those who pray

Misrad Hap'nim — Ministry of Interior

Mitzrayim — Egypt

mitzvah, pl. *mitzvos* — commandment, good deed

Modeh Ani — prayer said upon awakening each morning

Morah — teacher

moshav — communal settlement

motek — sweetie

Motza'ei Pesach — the night following Passover

Motza'ei Shabbos — the night following the Sabbath

motzetz — pacifier

mussar — chastisement

Naaseh — "We will do," the Jews' response to whether they would accept the Torah.

nachas — feeling of joy and satisfaction, usually from children

Navi —Prophet

Ne'ilah — closing prayer service on *Yom Kippur*

negel vasser — water used in the ritual washing of one's hands upon awakening

Neshamah, pl. *neshamos* — soul

Niftar — one who is deceased

Ohr HaChaim — section of the Code of Jewish Laws

Olam Haba — The World to Come

omer — see *Sefiras HaOmer*

ozeret — women who helps clean

parashah — weekly portion of the Torah

parnassah — livelihood

paroches — covering over the Ark

pasuk (pl. *pesukim*)— Scriptural verse

pekelach — burdens, bundles

pekele — package of treats, candies, and the like

Pesach — Passover

peyos — ear locks

pirsumei nissa — publicizing a miracle

pitzuyim — reparations

pushka — charity box

rachamim — mercy

rachmanus — compassion

Rashba — commentary on the Talmud

Rashi — commentary on the Bible and the Talmud

Ratzon HaBorei — Will of the Creator

Ribono Shel Olam — G-d

Rosh Chodesh — first day of the Hebrew month

Rosh Hashanah — Jewish New Year

Rosh Yeshivah — dean of a yeshivah

s'chach — covering for a *succah*

sabras — native-born Israelis

safrus — the art of writing Torah scrolls, *mezuzos* or *tefillin*

savta — grandmother

schlep — pull

seder (pl. *sedarim*) — (1) learning sessions (2) meal on first two nights of Passover

Sefardim — Jews whose origins are in Spain, North Africa or Babylon

sefer (*sefarim*) — book(s)

Sefiras HaOmer — counting the *Omer* days between *Pesach* and *Shevuous*

seichel — intellect, good sense

selichah — excuse me

Selichos — special prayers for forgiveness recited prior to *Rosh Hoshanah* and during the Ten Days of Repentance.

seudah — meal

shaatnez — forbidden mixture of wool and linen

shadchan pl. *shadchanim* — matchmaker(s)

shaliach tzibbur — emissary of the congregation

shalom bayis — harmony in the home

Shamayim — Heaven

Shas — Gemara, Talmud

Shechinah — Divine Presence

Shehechiyanu — blessing recited on festivals or certain special occasions

sheitel — wig

shekel — Israeli currency

shemiras halashon — guarding one's speech

Shemonah Esrei — primary prayer of every prayer service

sheva berachos — (1) lit. seven blessings recited at the wedding ceremony (2) festive meals held during the week following a wedding

Shevat — 11th month of the year

shidduch pl. *shidduchim* — match between two people for the purpose of marriage

shiur — lecture

shivah — 7-day mourning period following the loss of a close relative

shleimus — completion

shlugging kapparos — see *kapparos*

shofar — ram's horn

shpiel — play

shtender — lecturn

shtibel — small *shul*

shtuyot — nonsense

shuk — marketplace

shul — synagogue

Shulchan Aruch — Code of Laws

siddur pl. *siddurim* — prayer book(s)

simcha'dig — full of joy, lively

simchah pl. *simchos* —joy, festive occasion

siyata d'Shmaya — help from Above

siyum — conclusion of a portion of Torah or Talmud or the celebration thereof

Siyum HaShas — conclusion of the Six Orders of the Talmud

succah — booth in which one dwells during *Succos*

Succos — Feast of Tabernacles

talmidei chachamim — scholars

Tanach - Scripture

tefillah — prayer

Tehillim — Psalms

terutzim — (a) excuses; (b) responses

teshuvah — repentance

Teves — 10th month of the Jewish year

tikkun — lit. improvement

tinokos shel beis rabban — young schoolchildren

Tishah B'Av — the Ninth of Av; a fast day commemorating the destruction of the First and Second Temples

Tishrei — 7th month of the Jewish year

tzaddik pl. *tzaddikim*) (fem., *tzaddekes*) — righteous individual(s)

tzaros — troubles

tzeddakah — charity

tzeniyus — modesty, in both dress and demeanor

tzitzis — fringes placed on a four-cornered garment

y'mei ratzon — days of favor

y'mei Selichos — lit., the days of forgiveness; the High Holy Day period.

Y'mos haMashiach — Time of Messiah

yahadus — Judaism

Yamim Noraim — High Holy Days

yashrus — integrity

yetzer hara — evil inclination

Yiddishe chein — Jewish charm

yingelach — young boys

yiras Shamayim — fear of Heaven

yirei Shamayim — those who have a fear of Heaven

yom iyun — day of introspection

zemiros — songs of praise sung at Sabbath and Festival meals

Zman Cheiruseinu — season of our liberation/emancipation